AUSTEN CHAMBERLAIN: GENTLEMAN IN POLITICS

Austen Chamberlain: Gentleman in Politics

by
DAVID DUTTON

Transaction Books
New Brunswick (U.S.A.) and Oxford (U.K.)

Published in 1987 by Transaction, Inc.,
New Brunswick, New Jersey 08903
Copyright © 1985 by David Dutton

Library of Congress: 86-30778
ISBN: 0-86360-018-2
Printed in the United States of America

Library of Congress Cataloging-Publication Data

Dutton, David, 1947-
    Austen Chamberlain, gentleman in politics

    Reprint. Originally published: Bolton:
R.   Anderson, 1985.
    Bibliography: p.
    Includes index.
1   Chamberlain, Austen, Sir, 1863-1937.
2.   Statesmen--Great Britain--Bibliography.
3.   Great Britain--Politics and government--1901-1936.
I.   Title. II. Title: Austen Chamberlain.
DA566.9. C43D87 1987   941.082'092'4 [B] 86-30778
ISBN 0-86360-018-2

CONTENTS

ILLUSTRATIONS

ACKNOWLEDGEMENTS

The author acknowledges the gracious permission of Her Majesty The Queen for the republication of material from the Royal Archives which is subject to copyright.

Transcripts of Crown-copyright material in the Public Record Office and elsewhere appear by permission of the Controller of H.M. Stationery Office.

All quotations from letters and other documents by the members of the Chamberlain family are by permission of the University of Birmingham.

For permission to quote from unpublished material in their possession or of which they own the copyright, the author willingly thanks the following: the Rt. Hon. Julian Amery, M.P.; the Earl Baldwin of Bewdley; the Lord Balfour of Burleigh; the Bodleian Library; Mr. Mark Bonham Carter; the Trustees of the Bowood Manuscripts Collection; the British Library; Cambridge University Library; the Rt. Hon. Paul Channon, M.P.; the Viscount Chelmsford; the Master, Fellows and Scholars of Churchill College in the University of Cambridge; Miss Sybil Crowe; the Viscount Davidson; the Earl of Derby; the Viscount Esher; the Viscount Hanworth; the Baron Hardinge of Penshurst; the Lord Harlech; Mr. Tom Hartman; the Clerk of the Records, House of Lords Record Office; India Office Library and Records; Professor Anne Lambton; the Trustees of the Leigh Hall Estate; the Viscount Long of Wraxall; the Hon. Mrs. S. Mason; Mrs. D. M. Maxse; the Lord Melchett; the Countess of Midleton; the Hon. Mrs. John Mildmay-White; the Warden and Fellows of New College, Oxford; Mr. Paul Paget; His Grace the Duke of Portland; the Viscount Runciman of Doxford; the Marquess of Salisbury; the Viscount Scarsdale; the Earl of Selborne; the *Spectator*; Mrs. R. M. Stafford; Mr. A. J. P. Taylor on behalf of the Beaverbrook Foundation; the Hon. H. Williams; the Viscount Younger of Leckie.

For permission to print extracts from published material the author offers his thanks to the following: the Rt. Hon. Julian Amery, M.P. (*Life of Joseph Chamberlain*); Associated Newspapers Group p.l.c. (*Daily Mail*); the Beaverbrook Foundation (Lord Beaverbrook, *Men and Power*); the Birmingham Post and Mail Ltd. (*Birmingham Gazette*); Cambridge University Press (M. D. Pugh, 'Asquith, Bonar Law and the First Coalition' in the *Historical Journal* and M. Cowling, *The Impact of Labour*); Collins, Publishers (Lord Templewood, *Nine Troubled Years* and Lord Beaverbrook, *Decline and Fall of Lloyd George*); Peter Davies

Ltd. (C. Petrie, *The Chamberlain Tradition*); Eyre and Spottiswoode Ltd. (Lord Birkenhead, *F.E.* and R. Blake, *The Unknown Prime Minister*); Lord Hartwell and C. and T. Publications Ltd. (R. S. Churchill and M. Gilbert, *Winston Churchill*); David Higham Associates Ltd. (L. S. Amery, *My Political Life*, published by Hutchinson Publishing Group, and J. Campbell, *F. E. Smith*, published by Jonathan Cape); Hutchinson Publishing Group Ltd. (P. Rowland, *The Last Liberal Governments*, B. Cartland, *Ronald Cartland* and Lord Vansittart, *Mist Procession*); Mr. R. R. James, M.P. (*Memoirs of a Conservative*); the London School of Economics and Political Science (B. Webb, *Our Partnership*); Macmillan Publishers Ltd. (H. Macmillan, *Winds of Change* and *The Past Masters*, V. Massey, *What's Past is Prologue* and Lord Winterton, *Pre-war*); Macmillan Publishing Company (Lord Winterton, *Orders of the Day*, published by Cassell Ltd.); Martin Secker and Warburg Ltd. (P. Brendon, *Eminent Edwardians*); St. Martins Press Inc. (S. Marks, *The Illusion of Peace*); *The Observer* (*The Observer* and A. M. Gollin, *The Observer and J. L. Garvin*); Oxford University Press (T. Jones, *A Diary with Letters* and *Whitehall Diary*); A. D. Peters and Co. Ltd. (Viscount Cecil, *All the Way*); Times Newspapers Ltd. (*The Times*).

If, despite his best efforts, the author has inadvertently infringed the copyright of any individual, he trusts that his apology will be accepted.

PREFACE

I am very pleased to be able to thank some of the many individuals who have helped in the preparation of this book. I am grateful to my publisher, Michael Malone, for taking the project on board with enthusiasm and confidence in my capacity to carry it out. I am delighted to record my thanks to the British Academy and the University of Liverpool Research Committee for financial assistance. I readily acknowledge the help of the staff in the many libraries and archives in which I worked while gathering material for this biography and, in particular, Dr. Benedict S. Beneditz and his colleagues in the Heslop Room of Birmingham University Library where, within earshot of the Chamberlain clock-tower, I came near to establishing squatter's rights within their midst. To the great benefit of his biographer, Chamberlain lived in an era of letter writing and himself contributed substantially to it. He once wrote: 'late recollections are always coloured by subsequent events and nothing but contemporary evidence is of any value as to one's feelings at the moment'. This perhaps is an exaggeration, but this book draws heavily upon the private correspondence of Chamberlain and his contemporaries.

My friends and colleagues, Philip Bell and Patrick Buckland, kindly read through a draft of the book, making a host of valuable suggestions, many of which I have been pleased to incorporate in the final version of the work. His Grace the Duke of Portland, the last surviving member of the British delegation which went to Locarno in 1925, was good enough to read the two chapters relating to Chamberlain's Foreign Secretaryship. His observations and recollections afforded me some valuable insights into British diplomacy in the mid-1920s. I was delighted to have the opportunity to discuss Austen Chamberlain's character and career with his son-in-law and daughter, Colonel and Mrs. A. T. Maxwell. My hieroglyphic scrawl has been transformed into elegant typescript with great professionalism and extreme good humour by Mrs. Betty Plummer and Mrs. Peggy Rider. Dr. Helen Jewell gave freely of her time to check the proofs. Despite all this help, the finished work no doubt contains many errors of fact and judgment. For these the author alone remains responsible.

David Dutton
Liverpool, June 1984

FOR MY MOTHER

INTRODUCTION

'Why aren't there more like you in Politics?'[1]

Writing in 1930, Sir Charles Petrie in his *Life of George Canning* ventured to prophesy that to Austen Chamberlain as to Castlereagh, 'posterity may well be more kind than his contemporaries.'[2] The subsequent half century can scarcely be said to have fulfilled this prediction. Petrie's own two volume *Life and Letters* study, written soon after Chamberlain's death, remains the only significant biography. Petrie toyed with the idea of producing an abridged edition of his work in the early 1960s but never did so.[3] When Chamberlain died in 1937 there were appropriate tributes in the House of Commons to one who had held high office for such a large number of years. Baldwin, Attlee and Sinclair spoke for the three main parties, while the veteran Lloyd George movingly recalled the dead statesman's maiden speech in parliament. Thereafter, however, Chamberlain rapidly faded from the public consciousness. Even on the occasion of his death there was a feeling that the tributes paid were largely a matter of 'good form'. 'Chips' Channon recorded:

I was saddened by how the House of Commons reacted to his death, for after all he has been a Member for forty years. People just shrugged their shoulders, saying 'It's not too good a seat.' 'He only held it by about forty in 1929.' Little more.[4]

The name of Chamberlain continues to figure prominently in modern British historiography, but it is Austen's father Joseph and half-brother Neville who dominate the scene. To an extent this is understandable. Austen Chamberlain was fated at both the beginning and the end of his career to be overshadowed by members of his own family. Moreover, Joseph Chamberlain was patently a very remarkable man and the string of biographies which have appeared in recent years to supplement the magisterial volumes of J. L. Garvin and Julian Amery bear witness to his continuing ability to fascinate the student of political history. Similarly Neville Chamberlain's premiership clearly provides the focal point for anyone wishing to unravel the strands of British policy in the origins of the Second World War. Not surprisingly, therefore, and particularly since the introduction of the so-called Thirty Year Rule governing the availability of state papers for historical inspection, Neville's premiership has received an examination as intense and detailed as that devoted to any comparable

period of British history. By comparison the career of Sir Austen
Chamberlain remains an historical and historiographical backwater. He is
best remembered by a dubious distinction or a convenient catch-phrase.
Austen it was who probably came closer to the premiership without
actually securing it than any statesman since 1900. Austen it is who
remains the only leader of the Conservative party in the twentieth century
who never rose to become Prime Minister. Austen it was who, in a phrase
that has been variously attributed, 'always played the game and always
lost it.'[5]

But what historians have done to Austen Chamberlain only mirrors the
judgment of many of his political contemporaries. To Frances Stevenson,
Lloyd George's secretary and mistress, Chamberlain was but 'a pale
imitation of his famous father ... totally lacking in inspiration ...
conscientious to the point of dullness.'[6] J. L. Garvin, editor of the *Observer*
and biographer of Joseph, variously described him as 'most limited' and
'essentially mediocre',[7] while with little charity 'Chips' Channon summed
up Chamberlain as 'ossified, tedious and hopelessly out of date.'[8] Perhaps
most damning of all was the epithet of Arthur Balfour. Shortly before his
own death, this long-time colleague discussed with Stanley Baldwin
Chamberlain's shortcomings and speculated on the reasons for his failure
to rise to the very top of British political life. 'Balfour looked at S.B. with
his eyes rounded to their widest limit and said, "Don't you think it is
because he is a bore?" '[9]

There is then a basic argument that both Joseph and Neville
Chamberlain were more interesting men than Austen. In other ways,
however, the obsessive historical concentration upon Austen's father and
half-brother is somewhat surprising. Though Joseph held Cabinet office
for a total of thirteen years, the most senior post he occupied was the
Colonial Office. Austen was in the Cabinet for a slightly longer period,
and was Foreign Secretary and twice Chancellor of the Exchequer during
this time. Neville Chamberlain, though only six years younger than his
brother, did not enter parliament until his fiftieth year, by which time
Austen had already held several major offices of state, including the
Exchequer. Not until the late 1920s, when Austen was beginning to
withdraw from the centre of the political stage, did Neville become the
more politically prominent of the two brothers. Being a Chamberlain,
Austen has invariably been judged not in his own right but in comparison
with his father and brother. This fact is central to an understanding of the
combination of mild denigration and studied neglect with which history
has treated him. Yet while the biographer of Austen Chamberlain ignores
the family factor at his peril, its importance has been largely
misunderstood.

That the political career of Neville Chamberlain should come to overshadow that of his elder brother and that history should have judged Neville to be the more significant figure was certainly not the original intention of their father. For it was Austen for whom a glittering political career was carefully planned from the moment when his education began, through his first adoption as a parliamentary candidate in the early 1890s, to his entry into the Unionist government alongside his father. Not since the days of Chatham and the Younger Pitt had there been a father so intent on the political upbringing of his son.[10] For Neville, at least while Joseph was alive, business, commerce and only local politics were always assumed to be the stage upon which his role would be played out. There is, however, some evidence that, before his death in 1914, Joseph Chamberlain had begun to have misgivings about the political capacity of his elder son. Austen's unwillingness to fight to the last ditch, epitomised in his failure to clinch the party leadership in 1911, caused, according to his sister, 'criticism at home',[11] while one observer claimed that in a moment of exasperation Joseph had summed up his son's limitations by saying that 'he was born in a red box, brought up in one and would die in one'.[12] So it was to be Neville and not Austen (or indeed Joseph) who rose to the pinnacle of British political life – something which left him with an uneasy feeling bordering upon guilt. To his sister Hilda Neville wrote of 'this post which ought to have come to the two senior members of the family and only failed to do so because the luck was against them in forcing them to choose between their natural ambition and their principles.'[13]

Yet it is Austen Chamberlain's relationship with his father which is the crux of the matter. Austen was himself largely responsible for the unfavourable comparisons between the two men that have so often been drawn both by contemporaries and by later commentators. His sister Hilda argued that the very anxiety of their father to smooth Austen's path by giving him all the advantages he himself had lacked proved in the end a disservice in not forcing Chamberlain early on in his life to grapple with everyday difficulties.[14] 'He suffered,' writes Mr. Rowland, 'from being the over-groomed offspring of an outstanding personality.'[15] But Chamberlain's own behaviour made it more difficult for himself than perhaps it need have been to stamp out an individual identity. Not only did he strive to be very much his father's son in politics, especially during the eight difficult years between Joseph's sudden removal from active politics and his death, but he even seemed to cultivate a physical appearance down to the inevitable monocle and orchid which only revealed him as a pale image of his more forceful father. 'If only Austen was what he looked how splendid he would be,' remarked the perceptive Arthur Balfour.[16] Leo Maxse, on the other hand, once declared, 'If only Austen would wear

spectacles and grow a beard.'[17] Yet it is worth adding that for the more
astute observer there were physical differences to be discerned, which
accurately reflected differences of character and temperament. By
comparison with his father's aggressive and questing features,
Chamberlain's own were smooth and calm. His relaxed frame lacked the
taut, wiry, almost electric qualities of his father. But the superficial
resemblance was fatal for Chamberlain's image. 'Every public man,'
wrote Leo Amery, 'has to contend with the unreal, conventional picture of
himself drawn by the caricaturist, and, still more, by the lazier journalist
content to copy his own or other journalists' stock epithets from article to
article.' Chamberlain almost invited such caricature and too often
appeared 'as wooden in face and manner, pompously correct, impeccably
virtuous, but frigidly uninteresting.'[18]

Long after Joseph Chamberlain's death, he was never far from
Austen's thoughts. 'Austen had,' wrote Mr. Dangerfield, 'a father-haunted
mind.'[19] Thomas Jones noted in 1922 how 'the talk turned a good deal on
Chamberlain's father as it is apt to do when [Austen] is not talking
shop.'[20] He was ever concerned to defend his father's reputation down to
the smallest detail. It was as if in 1906, with his father's withdrawal from
the political stage, he had been bequeathed a sacred trust which was to be
his enduring commitment in public life. The long delay in the appearance
from Garvin's pen of his father's biography was a constant concern of
Chamberlain's later years. That the image of his father which finally
emerged from it should be accurate and acceptable was an abiding worry.
When Garvin suggested that the elder Chamberlain had been 'a stern
father and something of a martinet', Austen was outraged. 'The
remarkable thing about father', he insisted, 'was how seldom he interfered,
how few orders he gave and how singularly patient he was.'[21] During the
last year of his own life one of Austen Chamberlain's greatest
preoccupations was the centenary celebration of his father's birth. The
emotion of the occasion was almost too much for him. Leo Amery
recorded that, in making the main speech, Chamberlain became 'so
moved that at one moment I feared he might break down.'[22] Neville later
noted that 'from what he told me afterwards it was evident that he had
worked himself into an appalling condition of nerves beforehand and I am
not surprised that when the time came to speak even a strong whisky and
soda was insufficient to restore his control completely.'[23]

Chamberlain constantly referred to the debt which he owed to his
father. With patent sincerity he once wrote:

I think more and more of what I owe to Father and I do not know whether I owe
most to the counsel he has given me when I needed it or to the extraordinary
self-restraint and courage with which he has refused to advise me sometimes

when the temptation must have been very strong.... The result has been that, for better or worse, I have my own career, my own life and influence, and have not been wholly overshadowed by his great personality, though always trying my own actions and decisions by the thought (not exactly of how he would act – that is a different thing) but by what principles and ideals he would be guided. He has *made* me in every sense of the word and, if I accomplish anything in my career, it will be due to his teaching and his example. ... Never did son owe more to his father and never did father more generously or more wisely help his son's career.[24]

Interestingly, though, Chamberlain then continued:

He has been more ambitious for me than ever I have been for myself ... and that is the only point on which I have ever had to resist his counsels.

The fact was there were vast differences between the characters of the two men. Harold Macmillan has written:

Austen was, except in appearance, very unlike his father. He spoke well, but never in the grand style. He was clear, but not incisive. He was loved by all for his courtesy and his sweetness of character, as well as for his high sense of loyalty. There was not really much of Birmingham about him; sometimes he almost seemed a grand seigneur. He was respected, but never feared.[25]

For one thing Chamberlain lacked the basic physical strength which had been central to his father's voracious appetite for politics. In comparatively early middle age he was increasingly disabled by long attacks of sciatica and lumbago, and could never walk long distances or stand for any length of time without pain. He had no taste for prolonged hard work and the anxiety which it brought, for these often left him both physically and mentally drained. Breakdown was only averted by his unusual power of sleep. Reduced to his last reserves of strength, he could always, as he said, 'sleep the clock round' then take up his work again.[26]

In an age when public speaking was an important asset for a leading politician, the contrast between Joseph Chamberlain and his elder son was also marked. While Joseph was remembered for his powerful oratory, Austen, though sometimes quite effective, was never a natural speaker. Though he could be quite convincing when delivering an impromptu address – a facility which Neville envied – his more carefully prepared speeches were often marred by mispronunciations and 'incipient Spoonerisms.'[27] Throughout his long career he probably never rose to his feet in public without a vaguely uncomfortable feeling in the pit of his stomach.

So where the father had been a passionate political fighter, caring intensely for his cause and enjoying and thirsting for battle, Austen was at heart a lover of peace. When disagreement arose he tended by temperament to seek a way out. Yet paradoxically he could, on occasions, be pompous and stubborn over comparatively minor issues, where his father, sensing that political expediency demanded it, was ready to manoeuvre through an apparent impasse.[28] In terms of political philosophy the two men were different again. The father was in all he did a constructive radical, whereas Austen was 'essentially a Conservative, a profound believer in the value of tradition and of existing forms and institutions which embodied it.'[29] This was reflected in differing attitudes towards the forum of the House of Commons from which they both operated. Joseph became a great parliamentarian because he needed to debate effectively and to know how the business of the chamber was conducted in order to achieve his aims. Austen was a great parliamentarian in the sense that he loved the House of Commons with its ways, its ceremonies and its courtesies, all of which embodied a tradition which he held dear in English public life.[30]

Austen Chamberlain was not unaware of these differences. Indeed his most characteristic political trait, his exaggerated sensitiveness to the idea of being thought self-seeking or disloyal, was surely a reaction against what he saw as an unacceptable feature in his father's make-up. 'Pushful Joe' was not an epithet which Austen sought to inherit. So while his devotion to his father's memory was profound and genuine, there lurked at the back of his mind an uneasy, if largely unspoken and perhaps unconscious, anxiety that Joseph Chamberlain had not been entirely a gentleman.

At crucial moments in Austen's career the fact that he was in no sense his father's clone was only too apparent. When he at long last secured the leadership of the Conservative party, he responded with a lack of enthusiasm which would have been unimaginable in his father:

The wheel of fortune turning full circle brings me again what ten years ago I should have liked and what I now accept as an obvious duty but without pleasure or any great expectations except of trouble and hard labour . . . I am inclined to cry Oh cursed spite! but it is useless to lament and I must just make up my mind to face our troubles bravely and do the best I can. But as one after another of one's old colleagues drops out of the ranks I feel sad and lonely and do not experience as of old the joy and fire of battle.[31]

On another occasion he wrote:

My idle year has given me a zest for amusing myself that is far from exhausted – and a hatred of politics. My ambition was never very strong – perhaps I should have been a better man if it had been stronger – and now it is non-existent. I want nothing except to be let alone and left £10,000 a year![32]

Politics, then, were never an all-consuming activity for Austen Chamberlain. Perhaps his father was responsible for this. Joseph once reproached his young son with being too completely absorbed in political work. 'You must have something else to think about or you won't sleep and then you will get ill.' 'Find yourself a hobby' was the paternal advice. Austen took his father at his word and rock-gardening became a passion for the rest of his life. Even as Foreign Secretary in the 1920s he would often escape from League of Nations meetings at Geneva for a couple of hours in pursuit of some alpine plant.[33] In 1936 Neville, reflecting on the characters of the three Chamberlains who had made a name for themselves in national politics, placed Austen at the bottom of the trio in terms of political commitment. 'He has not the eagerness of temperament and the inexhaustible vitality of Father, which kept him ever revolving some constructive idea ... I believe I lie somewhere between the two.'[34] Austen Chamberlain himself cultivated in his own lifetime the image of someone who was probably too decent a man to be entirely successful in politics. When in 1931 he publicly renounced his claim to further government office, Neville noted that his brother's 'latest action has greatly strengthened the "legend" that was already growing up of the "great gentleman" and model of chivalry.'[35]

With such a contrast between the surface similarities and the deeper differences of Joseph and Austen Chamberlain, it was inevitable that critics who recalled the drive, ambition and resolve of the father were harsh on the cardboard cut-out which was, or appeared to be, the son. When Austen seemed likely to return to the Government in 1918 the *Daily Mail* protested:

Mr. Austen Chamberlain, who entered public life with the inestimable advantage of being the son of his father, for which reason he was tolerated long after it became obvious that he had inherited none of his father's genius, has been pushed into one office after another without any serious reference to his qualifications for them. But he has never been more than an assiduous, honourable, ineffective mediocrity. ... To recall him at this junction from his proper obscurity, to set such a man at such a moment in the midst of our supreme council, would be cynical trifling.[36]

But in fact there is no need to think of Chamberlain in terms of the posts he did not attain or in comparison with members of his own family who may have left a more enduring impression upon posterity. Interestingly Neville once expressed the hope that history would measure Austen against a figure such as Edward Grey or Lord Salisbury rather than their father.[37] The fact is that Austen was a major political figure in his own right. As a member of parliament for forty-five years, during more than

thirty of which he was at the very centre of the political stage, he played a
leading role at a time of crucial importance in the development both of his
country and of his party. When Chamberlain first entered politics,
Gladstone was grappling with the second Irish Home Rule Bill; when he
died, still actively involved in national politics, Baldwin's National
Government was sliding irresolutely towards war with Nazi Germany.
The offices Chamberlain held add up to a glittering career in public life.
Civil Lord of the Admiralty when only thirty-two, he was successively
Financial Secretary to the Treasury, Postmaster General, Chancellor of
the Exchequer, Secretary of State for India, Minister without Portfolio in
Lloyd George's War Cabinet, Chancellor of the Exchequer again, Lord
Privy Seal and Leader of the House of Commons, Foreign Secretary and
finally and briefly First Lord of the Admiralty.

Nor indeed in Austen Chamberlain is one simply dealing with an
historical figure 'because he is there', in the way that the mountaineer
looks upon the unconquered peak. Closer study reveals not a cardboard
cut-out but a fascinatingly enigmatic figure, full of paradoxes. One has
been noted already. The born conservative was hampered for most of his
career by his Liberal antecedents and associations, which probably cost
him the premiership.[38] Then again, Chamberlain could not have survived
at the highest level in politics for as long as he did if he had not been more
of a political animal than he was perhaps prepared to admit. The same
man who professed to lack ambition in politics was bitterly disappointed
at his exclusion from the highest councils at the formation of the National
Government in 1931:

But it is just at the F.O. that I think I could render service which no-one else can
give. Elsewhere others can do as well as I – in many cases better – and I do not
care after thirty years of hard work in and out of office during which I have
always been at the very centre of affairs . . . gradually to become a kind of super
or understudy.[39]

Even at the age of seventy-two Chamberlain entertained hopes of
returning to the Foreign Office at the time of the Hoare-Laval crisis in
1935. Similarly, the man who is best remembered for his political loyalty
fumed in private about the shortcomings of the three party leaders under
whom he was successively called upon to serve. Of Balfour he often
despaired, while both Bonar Law and Baldwin he came to despise.

Chamberlain's character provides perhaps the most striking paradox.
The public Chamberlain seemed devoid of a sense of humour, lacking a
lighter touch and punctilious to a fault. When the Conservative Central
Office proposed to make a film showing ministers at work and officials in
shirtsleeves, carrying files and boxes, Chamberlain was shocked. 'Bovril

may do this,' he asserted, 'but should Baldwins?'[40] When Chamberlain took over from Bonar Law as Leader of the Commons in 1921, Sir George Younger, the Party Chairman, came to see him and said how he had been in the habit of visiting Law daily and how happy he would be to help Chamberlain in any way possible. In effect the latter's reply was 'When I feel I need you, I'll send for you.'[41] Tom Jones's favourite story of Chamberlain was that he once succeeded in bringing away from him a set of Cabinet minutes without a single comma having been changed — thereby incurring the jealousy of Maurice Hankey, the Cabinet Secretary, who had never been so fortunate.[42] Would Jones have recognised the private Chamberlain who derived deep but almost childlike joy from the simple pleasures of life, whether it were the beauty of nature, the suspense of an Agatha Christie novel or the happiness of his family?

The man who so often appeared stiff and forbidding in public was, in his private life, 'warm-hearted, considerate and generous.'[43] Leo Amery recalled him as 'the best of good companions [with an] inexhaustible fund of happy anecdotes.'[44] The same man who tended to treat his political peers and subordinates with a coldness and a lack of tact was a devoted father and loving husband who derived the deepest joy from his family life:

Then we played at bears on the floor and crouched in corners and growled at one another and then he took me to the staircase-gate and said Tata! 'Oh, I'm to go am I', said I, but evidently that was not the thing. Miss O'B. interpreted, 'He wants you to take him down to the drawing room' and as soon as my slow wits had seized this fact, he beamed and chuckled with delight and cried Mama! Mama! evidently hoping he would see her.[45]

Scarred by an unhappy love affair, he married late but thereafter turned constantly to his wife, Ivy, for solace and comfort from his political cares. But this was not the man whom the majority of his political associates knew.

The same Chamberlain who could display a remarkable insensitivity to the feelings of others could show deep sensitivity towards the beauties of the world. When asked what in life had given him his greatest aesthetic thrills, Chamberlain named his first view of the sunlit Parthenon, his first view of the Prado's Velasquez and the Rubens in Antwerp Cathedral.[46] His private correspondence turns with great readiness from the cares of a man of state to the beauty of a flower, the condition of his rock-garden and the charms of the landscape.

What follows, then, is an attempt to redress the historiographical balance, to rescue Chamberlain from the near obscurity into which his memory has receded. Austen Chamberlain was certainly not a great man, but then very few individuals genuinely merit this description. His career, however, was certainly both more important and more interesting than it has been usual to suggest. 'Chamberlain', thought Lord Beaverbrook, 'will be a fascinating subject for a biography.' These pages attempt to justify Beaverbrook's words.[47]

Notes

1. F. S. Oliver to A. Chamberlain 4 Dec. 1913, Chamberlain MSS, AC 60/118.
2. Sir C. Petrie, *The Life of George Canning* (London, 1930) p. 254.
3. Lord Beaverbrook to Petrie 2 Jan. 1961, Beaverbook MSS C/270.
4. R. R. James (ed), *Chips: The Diaries of Sir Henry Channon* (London, 1967) p. 117.
5. Churchill is the most likely author of this epithet, although Beaverbrook attributes it to Lord Birkenhead; *Men and Power 1917–18* (London, 1956) p. xiii.
6. F. Stevenson, *The Years that are Past* (London, 1967) p. 184.
7. Garvin to J. Sandars 15 Dec. 1910, Balfour MSS Add. MS. 49795; Garvin to E. Goulding 16 Dec. 1910, Goulding MSS, A/3/2.
8. James, *Chips* p. 73.
9. T. Jones, *A Diary with Letters 1931–1950* (London, 1954), p. 447.
10. Sir C. Petrie, *The Chamberlain Tradition* (London, 1938) p. 130.
11. Memoir by Hilda Chamberlain, Nov. 1956, Chamberlain MSS, BC 5/10/1.
12. T. Jones, *Diary with Letters* p. 318.
13. N. Chamberlain to H. Chamberlain 30 May 1937, Chamberlain MSS, NC 18/1/101.
14. See note 11.
15. P. Rowland, *The Last Liberal Governments: The Promised Land 1905–1910* (London, 1968) p. 50.
16. A. J. P. Taylor, *Beaverbrook* (London, 1972) p. 69.
17. L. S. Amery, *My Political Life* (London, 1953–55) i, 303–4.
18. Article by L. S. Amery, *The Observer*, 21 March 1937.
19. G. Dangerfield, *The Damnable Question* (Quartet edn., London, 1979) p. 73.
20. T. Jones, *Whitehall Diary* ed. K. Middlemas, i, (London, 1969) p. 200.
21. A. Chamberlain to N. Chamberlain 8 Dec. 1932, Chamberlain MSS, NC1/27/108.
22. L. S. Amery, *Life* iii, 201.
23. N. Chamberlain to H. Chamberlain 11 July 1936, Chamberlain MSS, NC 18/1/969.
24. A. Chamberlain to Mary Chamberlain 7 May 1911, Chamberlain MSS, AC4/1/651.
25. H. Macmillan, *The Past Masters* (London, 1975) p. 128.
26. See note 11. 'His stamina is none too good and he can't do the continuous

hard work that Father used to.' N. Chamberlain to H. Chamberlain 22 Oct. 1916, Chamberlain MSS, NC 18/1/85.

27. N. Chamberlain to Ida Chamberlain 21 March 1937, Chamberlain MSS, NC 18/1/999.
28. See note 11; article by L. S. Amery in *The Observer*, 21 March 1937.
29. L. S. Amery, *Life* ii, 303–4.
30. Ibid.
31. A. Chamberlain to H. Chamberlain 20 March 1921, Chamberlain MSS, AC 5/1/194.
32. A. Chamberlain to M. Chamberlain 26 April 1924, ibid, AC 4/1/1243.
33. Lord Avon, *Facing the Dictators* (London, 1962) p. 130.
34. K. Feiling, *The Life of Neville Chamberlain* (London, 1946) p. 287.
35. N. Chamberlain to H. Chamberlain 7 Nov. 1931, Chamberlain MSS, NC 18/1/760.
36. *Daily Mail*, 17 April 1918.
37. See note 27.
38. See note 11; *Sunday Times* 21 March 1937.
39. A. Chamberlain to Ivy Chamberlain 10 Oct. 1931, Chamberlain MSS, AC 6/1/828.
40. G. M. Young, *Stanley Baldwin* (London, 1952) pp. 25–6.
41. T. Jones, *Diary with Letters*, p. 447.
42. Ibid, p. 325.
43. Avon, *Dictators* p. 7.
44. See note 18.
45. A. Chamberlain to M. Chamberlain 1 March 1909, Chamberlain MSS, AC 4/1/386.
46. R. James, *Chips* p. 27.
47. Beaverbrook to Petrie 13 April 1939, Beaverbrook MSS, BBK C/270.

CHAPTER ONE
APPRENTICESHIP

' "You are all I have to live for now", said my Father to us children in his trouble.'[1]
'Certainly it is an unprofitable business sending poor grist to a first-class mill and the care lavished on Mr. Chamberlain's political education doubtless might have been better expended on another subject'.[2]

As is the case with most sorts of men, politicians are more likely to be born than made. If aspects of Austen Chamberlain's later career cast some doubt on whether he really was a born politician, there can be no question that he was at least born into politics. His father Joseph, a prosperous manufacturer of screws, twenty-seven years of age at Austen's birth, was about to set out on a celebrated political career which would take him via municipal politics in Birmingham to the Cabinet table in Whitehall. Austen's childhood and early adult life would be spent in the shadow of his father's political ascendancy. When Austen was ten his father became Mayor of Birmingham, an industrial centre which soon came to enjoy the title 'Second City of the Empire'. Under the guidance of the elder Chamberlain Birmingham took the lead in alleviating some of the worst abuses of the unplanned industrialisation of Victorian Britain. An ambitious three years as Mayor saw Chamberlain transform the life-style of the town's working class with an extensive programme of sanitary improvement and urban redevelopment – perhaps the best example of the 'gas and water socialism' inspired by the nineteenth-century non-conformist conscience. When Austen was almost thirteen his father entered parliament. Four years later he was a Cabinet minister. By the time that Austen was himself nationally prominent his father had become, apart from the Prime Minister, the most powerful man in the land. Politics were thus an inescapable feature of Austen Chamberlain's early life. He soon grew accustomed to the company of the leading men in radical politics at both local and national levels. Not surprisingly, Austen looked forward from boyhood to becoming himself a member of the House of Commons.[3]

If, on the other hand, it really were possible to manufacture politicians, Joseph Chamberlain spared no effort in the endeavour. Almost from his birth Austen's education was engineered with a political career in mind. Chamberlain was determined that his eldest son should follow him in public life and that his progress up that greasy pole should be relieved of the obstacles which the father had had to overcome. Money was not really a problem. In 1874 Chamberlain sold the majority of his business interests and determined to live on the proceeds and devote himself entirely to politics. By the standards of any age an extraordinary man, he could now look forward to the survival of his political dreams and visions into a second generation in the person of his son, Austen. Here though lay a central paradox of the latter's life. The adjective 'extraordinary' may epitomise the character of the father. It has no place in an objective description of the son. 'I do not think,' reflected Lord Birkenhead many years later, 'that, as a young man, Austen Chamberlain saw visions, or that, as an old man, he will dream dreams.'[4] Thus, if Joseph Chamberlain's motivation in politics was an equal combination of genuine commitment to public service and an unbounded and passionate ambition, it was only the first of these qualities which he succeeded in passing on to his son.

Austen Chamberlain was born on 16 October 1863. The joy of the occasion was, however, turned into sadness by the death, a few days after Austen's birth, of his mother, whom Joseph had married only two years before. Harriet Kenrick Chamberlain had been bothered by a premonition of death at the time of the birth of her first child, Beatrice, in 1862, but at first Austen's arrival seemed to pass without complication. Suddenly, however, her condition deteriorated rapidly and the young businessman found his world shattered, with two young children to look after. As a result, Austen's first five years were spent at Berrow Court, the home of his maternal grandparents in the prosperous Birmingham suburb of Edgbaston. Nearly five years after Harriet's death Chamberlain married her cousin Florence and it was the latter whom Austen must later have recalled as his mother. She bore Joseph four more children including Neville, but she too died in childbirth in 1875. As an undergraduate Austen recollected these tragedies of his early life:

I lost my own Mother when I was born and my step-mother who was like a mother to me when I was only 11. Of course it was easier to bear at that age, but yet it was a great trouble. Yet since then I seem to know them both so well and I talk to those who did know them. . . . And it helps me to try to live worthily of them, to try to do what they would have me do were they on earth, to consecrate my life to them and in so doing to strive to help and cheer those who have lost them.[5]

After this second tragedy Austen and the other children were brought up by the father's unmarried sisters, while Joseph, now Mayor of Birmingham, attempted to overcome his sorrow in the intensification of his political work. There is little reference to his children in the elder Chamberlain's correspondence at this time, possibly, as Garvin argues, because the sight of his orphaned children harrowed him,[6] but more probably because he destroyed much of his personal correspondence when he married for a third time in 1888.[7] Small fragments do, however, survive to confirm that Joseph took an intense and caring interest in the up-bringing of his children. To the young Austen he wrote:

You do not spell your words very correctly, and I am afraid that in learning Latin you are forgetting English. . . . You must be more careful and if you do not know the words, look them out in the Dictionary.[8]

The eleven year old Austen was rebuked for a lack of social grace:

I hear that cousin Fanny Martineau invited you to go there and that the only reply you sent was a Post Card just to say you were coming. This was not polite. You ought to have written a letter thanking her for her kind invitation and saying that you would be glad to accept it.[9]

On another occasion his father playfully scolded Austen for a piece of boyhood mischief, uncovered when the latter inadvertently left behind a letter to a friend inviting him to an illicit smoking session:

If you are going to have secrets, I advise you not to leave your letters about open. As to brown-paper cigars, I tried them a long while ago and very nasty they are. If you like them, I don't admire your taste.[10]

Sent to preparatory school in Brighton, the young Chamberlain was unfortunate to encounter an eccentric and intolerant headmaster, named Hanbury. In later life Chamberlain recalled his early education:

in fact his school was run on entirely wrong principles and I cannot say that I look back with any pleasure to the time I spent with [Hanbury]. I believe that later he lost his reason and had to be confined.[11]

Shortly before his fifteenth birthday Austen moved on to Rugby School – a somewhat surprising choice for the son of the rising radical and non-conformist politician, for its atmosphere was dominated by Conservatism and muscular Christianity. Yet he made a success of his time there, rising to be captain of his house and becoming prominent in the school's debating society, where he was a loyal advocate of the advanced causes which his father was now championing on the national stage. Austen formed a close friendship with his housemaster, Henry Lee Warner, and it was with the latter that the father intervened when the headmaster, Dr. Jex-Blake, proposed to beat Austen for a minor infringement of school rules. So strongly did Joseph Chamberlain feel on this matter that he threatened to withdraw his son from the school rather than allow 'this brutal punishment' to proceed. Interestingly, the man who is best remembered as the champion of British imperialism around the turn of the

I Joseph Chamberlain (Birmingham University)

II Austen at Rugby (Birmingham University)

century believed at this stage that 'the ready appeal to physical force is a mental preparation for the rowdy jingoism which is the characteristic of many educated middle-class Englishmen'.[12] Chamberlain's threat proved successful and the penalty was commuted to a detention, but whether Austen welcomed his father's intervention remains open to speculation. Be that as it may, the younger Chamberlain followed his father in a lifelong detestation of corporal punishment, a somewhat untypical attitude for a man who grew up in Victorian England. More than forty years later, when asked to deputise for the Home Secretary, Chamberlain wrote:

My only objection to signing your papers for you is that I have an invincible objection to ordering floggings. But if you are prepared to have every man who is ordered a flogging during your absence let off by a sentimental colleague, I will gladly do this small service for you.[13]

Towards the end of his son's time at Rugby Joseph Chamberlain expressed satisfaction with his progress. He had never, he asserted, been anxious that Austen should excel himself, but had always looked to general character and intelligence as the points of real importance.[14] In reality, however, little was left to chance. The elder Chamberlain came to the conclusion that the best course would be for his son to take up the history tripos at Cambridge,[15] and it is worth comparing the way in which the son's educational career was being planned with the earlier experience of the father. Rugby and Trinity College were deemed to be suitable training for the future statesman, while the father's career had taken him from University College School into industry and commerce, the path of a self-made Victorian businessman. Interestingly Neville, who also went to Rugby, was never destined for a political career, and moved on to Mason College in Birmingham where he studied commerce, metallurgy and engineering design.[16]

Austen Chamberlain went up to Trinity in 1882 and soon became prominent in the Union, making his first speech within a month or so of arrival and moving his first resolution the following May.[17] One of the attractions of Cambridge from the father's point of view was the presence there of the historian, J. R. Seeley, whose influential work *The Expansion of England* was to prove an important text for late Victorian imperialists.[18] At all events, Joseph noted that there was 'no doubt about the interest of the subjects included in the History Tripos and his work will not be thrown away in after life'.[19] As at Rugby the young Chamberlain proved an ardent champion of his father's politics and as in his school he had to argue against the majority opinion of his contemporaries. In May 1883 he proposed the motion that 'the existence of the House of Lords is

injurious to the welfare of the country.' Later he spoke against
proportional representation and in support of the Liberal government.
The young man, who in later years would develop into the archetypal
conservative, asserted that it was by military glory that the Conservatives
'moved and lived and had their being and without which a Tory
administration would be a thing unknown in the future history of this
country.'[20] On one occasion he noted with satisfaction that

I made the Cambridge Tories very angry at the Union last Tuesday by moving
that 'this house regrets the disintegration of the Conservative Party and the
inability of its leaders to control its actions.' They cd. not tell which way to vote
and bitterly complained of the predicament in wh. they were placed.[21]

From Chamberlain's own description it appears that study was not the
most prominent of his concerns during his time at Cambridge. He became
Vice-President of the Union and entertained hopes of the Presidency
itself.[22] 'It's wonderful,' he noted,

how busy one gets here with nothing particular to do – committees, societies,
debates and of course reading, when combined, seem to leave no time for
anything else and hardly enough for each other. I think the Union claims most of
my time.[23]

His three years at Trinity no doubt passed quickly, but thereafter his
father was anxious to continue the wider education of the future
statesman. At Cambridge Austen's historical studies ended with the Peace
of Amiens of 1802. Experience of contemporary Europe would add
significantly to his understanding of the great issues of the day and obviate
any tendency towards parochialism or insularity. Accordingly, in
September 1885 the young Chamberlain left for a nine-month stay in
France as the house guest of the Aumaitre family. In Paris he attended the
distinguished Ecole des Sciences Politiques where he heard lectures from,
among others, Sorel. A few letters of introduction, combined with his
father's name, saw Chamberlain gain access to the political circles of the
day, meeting such figures as Clemenceau, Ribot, Gambetta and Ferry.
His presence was particularly welcome among the leaders of French
radicalism.

Altogether Chamberlain's time in Paris was one of the most enjoyable
and exciting periods of his life. To his sister Beatrice he wrote with
undisguised enthusiasm:

I am very gay and find only one thing to regret: namely that there are but seven
days in the week and you can't dine in two separate places on the same evening.[24]

Even at the end of his life Chamberlain could still recall the pleasures of
Paris in the 1880s – the *belle époque*:

What a varied and interesting society it was among whom I spent these months; how much was taught me; what new horizons it opened out to my eager eyes.... No wonder that ... I prolonged my stay till the middle of May and left at last with real regret that so happy an interlude was over.[25]

By the time that Chamberlain returned to England in May 1886 his father's career had reached a decisive turning point. The General Election of that year, Gladstone's Home Rule Bill and the older Chamberlain's staunch opposition to it set both father and son on a path that would take the two men into partnership with and, in the case of the latter, membership of the Conservative party.[26] Austen vigorously supported his father during the election campaign and had no doubts about the correctness of the older man's course of action. By the autumn the political situation had stabilised sufficiently for the two men, together with Beatrice, to visit the Near-East. This further step in Austen's political education took in Constantinople, Athens and Bulgaria. Early in the New Year he was off again, for the father rightly saw that Austen's experience of France should be balanced by a visit to Germany, which since 1870 had become the dominant force in European politics and diplomacy. There he stayed for a year, but without ever taking the country or the people to his heart as he had done in Paris. It is probably no exaggeration to suggest that many of the basic attitudes and sympathies which Chamberlain revealed as Foreign Secretary in the 1920s were formed as a result of experiences forty years before. Though he again met many of the leading statesmen of the day, including Bismarck, there was something about the German character which repelled him, and, in marked contrast to his Parisian adventure, his time in Germany weighed heavily upon him:

One day succeeds another with great monotony ... and a series of such days carry one through the week and the time to write another letter comes round without my having found anything fresh to say.[27]

Lectures which he attended by von Treitschke on Prussian history filled him with alarm. He feared that if the country's young men were continuously told that they stood on a higher plane of creation than all other nations they would be only too ready to believe it, with possibly disastrous consequences. The prescience of these remarks is too obvious to require comment. Chamberlain no doubt had occasion to reflect upon them in 1914 and, when Petrie first drew attention to them in the late 1930s, they had assumed an even more poignant meaning.[28]

Chamberlain's German gloom was relieved by news from his father in July 1887. Joseph had been approached by the Liberal Unionist association in the Border Burghs to find a candidate for the next election and had put forward the name of his son. It was 'a capital opportunity' and the father advised Austen on his proper course of action:

> You might write a pretty letter . . . saying that you have heard from me – that you feel very much their kindness in thinking of you – that you would be very proud to represent the Border Burghs – and that if selected . . . you would spare no effort to show yourself worthy of their confidence and would be ready on your return from the continent to devote any time that might be necessary to make the acquaintance of the constituency.[29]

Early in 1888 Austen was formally adopted as candidate and made a favourable first impression in the constituency. His first public meeting was to a packed hall of eight hundred people and went off well. 'I do believe', Austen remarked, 'these people would have been pleased with anything from father's son.'[30] At this stage in his career he seems to have created a more attractive image of himself than was always the case in later life. Beatrice Potter noted him as a big fair-haired youth of handsome features, open countenance and sunny, sympathetic temperament,[31] while Joseph Chamberlain himself jokingly remarked that his son was always such a favourite wherever he went that he was beginning to fear that he would cut his father entirely out of the limelight.[32]

Yet the Border seat was by no means a perfect parliamentary niche for the aspiring young politician. Geographically, it was inconvenient and it was not at all certain that even with the Chamberlain name the Liberal Unionists would be able to carry it. In addition, despite rumours that the sitting member might retire, Chamberlain faced the prospect of a long and frustrating delay before the next General Election became due. The eyes of the family were therefore alert to the possibility of a more promising opportunity. In the meantime, however, thought also had to be given to Neville's career and to the family finances which no longer looked as secure as when the father had retired from his business life. Joseph Chamberlain therefore listened with interest to the argument of the Governor of the Bahamas, whom he met in Canada in 1890, that a fortune awaited an enterprising capitalist prepared to invest his money in the growing of sisal, a hemp plant of largely unexplored potential. Before committing himself Chamberlain decided to send out his two sons to investigate on the spot the possibilities of the proposed crop. Austen and Neville arrived in Nassau in November 1890 and rapidly undertook a cost analysis of the large-scale cultivation of sisal. Touring the outer islands in a small cutter, they soon hit upon Andros as the most suitable site for their ambitious venture. Austen's initial conclusions were favourable:

> Neville and I have failed to find the weak point of this business. On the contrary, the more we see of it, the better we are inclined to think of it.[33]

He was concerned, however, at the prospect that, while he would shortly return to the realm of English politics, Neville might be obliged to stay out in the islands for a number of years to supervise the project, in an oppressive climate and with no European society of any kind. He suggested therefore that if Neville only remained for one year and returned for a second year when the machinery was being set up and the process of manufacture had begun, then the project would be acceptable. Thereafter one of the brothers could make an annual visit and, in time, a biennial one.[34] The enterprise has often been highlighted as one of the early failures of Neville Chamberlain's career – by 1896 he had concluded that it could not possibly be made to pay – so it is perhaps instructive to note that in the early and perhaps over-hasty assessment of the project's commercial viability Austen was as responsible as his younger brother.

While Neville Chamberlain busied himself with this ill-fated project, Austen's attention rapidly reverted to the British political scene. By now he was getting impatient to join his father in the House of Commons. 'I do wish I were in Parliament', he wrote to Neville. 'It is weary work waiting on the threshold.'[35] By the end of 1891 his chance seemed to have come. The member for East Worcestershire had embezzled trust funds and fled the country. As soon as he resigned it was likely that Austen would be offered the Liberal Unionist nomination. Geographically speaking, the seat was far more attractive than the Border Burghs, falling only just outside the control of the Chamberlainite caucus. Indeed the constituency included many of what have since become Birmingham's southern suburbs. In the first days of 1892 a joint committee of nine Liberal Unionists and nine Conservatives selected Chamberlain as their candidate. In fact his name was the only one considered. Fortunately for him, the constituency party organisation in the Border Burghs agreed to release him from his commitment there. For the first of many occasions, however, the complications inherent in Austen Chamberlain's position as a Liberal Unionist became apparent. The retiring M.P. had pledged himself to vote against Disestablishment and local Conservatives were anxious that Chamberlain should give a commitment of the same kind. For the son of Radical Joe this was an impossibility and for a while it seemed likely that the Conservatives might run a rival candidate. Arthur Balfour, Conservative leader in the House of Commons, attempted to pour oil on troubled waters with a typically Balfourian compromise, but with Chamberlain standing his ground the Conservatives gave way. In view of the agreement between the two wings of the Unionist coalition that each side should be able to choose the candidate for any seat which its supporters had previously held, they had little alternative.[36] After what had threatened at times to develop into a national issue, it was almost an anti-climax when Chamberlain was elected to parliament unopposed in March 1892.[37]

Chamberlain was introduced into the House of Commons by his father and uncle Richard, then member for Islington, at the end of the month. He later recalled being so moved by the occasion that, with his hand trembling violently, he could hardly sign his name on the roll of members.[38] It was not the most auspicious of moments to enter parliament, for Lord Salisbury's Unionist government was clearly on its way out, and the new member made no recorded contribution to the proceedings of the House before parliament was dissolved in June. Chamberlain, opposed this time by a Liberal, secured a comfortable majority of over two thousand five hundred votes in East Worcestershire. Nationally, however, the election results transformed the tone and temper of politics at Westminster. Towards the end of his long parliamentary career – forty-five years in the House of Commons – Chamberlain recalled this parliament of 1892–5 as 'by far the most exciting.'[39] In part, of course, this reflected youthful enthusiasm. But objectively there can be no doubt of the dramatic situation created by the lottery of electoral politics. Together the Gladstonian Liberals and the Irish Nationalist members had a majority of forty over the Conservatives and Liberal Unionists. Without Irish support, however, the octogenarian Gladstone would have been in a minority. Inevitably, the question of Home Rule for Ireland, without which the support of the Irish members would not have been forthcoming, became the centrepiece of Gladstone's legislative programme.

Before the political battle got under way there was an opportunity for Chamberlain to visit his brother on Andros. By this time Neville was fully engaged in his work on the island and perhaps felt slight resentment towards Austen's advice and suggestions. The younger man kept his brother firmly in his place:

He holds me in poor esteem and does not trust me with much to do. I have served however an apprenticeship in the shop and consider myself rather a good salesman of dress materials; but ... it is very difficult to do up pounds of flour and sugar in flimsy paper without string. ...[40]

Chamberlain clearly missed the political atmosphere of England. He scoured American newspapers for scraps of news of British politics and after a couple of months away complained that he felt as if he had spent a year in Darkest Africa.[41] He arrived home just before Christmas looking fit and well and bringing back optimistic reports of Neville's progress.

When the House of Commons met in January 1893 it was clear that this would be no ordinary session of parliament. The debate on the

Address was only concluded by the unusual expedient of a Saturday sitting, while the debate on the supposedly formal first reading of the Home Rule Bill took up five days. The Unionist opposition clearly intended to make the government's life as difficult as it could and, if possible, deprive it of the time needed to carry out its legislative proposals. Chamberlain found that his new work kept him very busy and that he often did not leave the House until very late. In a theme that was to characterise the whole of his political life, he noted that he looked forward to relaxing at weekends, although by then he often felt 'pretty well played out.'[42] In this situation political passions were roused and for the advocates of Home Rule, Joseph Chamberlain emerged as the most detested man on the opposition benches. While his father led the Unionists' resistance to the government's bill, Austen, who had been appointed a junior whip for the Liberal Unionists, seized the opportunity to make his maiden speech. On the evening of 18 April the young member spoke in the second reading debate on the Home Rule Bill. Though he was 'in a mortal funk beforehand,'[43] it was by all accounts an impressive début. Subsequent events have shown that the argument he put forward was fundamentally sound. There was no guarantee, he pointed out, that Irish politicians would be satisfied with a limited measure of home rule, and complete separation was the most likely long-term consequence of the bill. Whatever the content of Austen's speech, all in the chamber must have been struck by the physical resemblance to his father – even the eyeglass was the same. The Prime Minister, in his customary report of proceedings to the Queen, described the speech as one of the best that had been made against the bill and the speaker as one 'of whom high political anticipations may reasonably be entertained.'[44] Even more remarkably Gladstone took the opportunity some days later of lowering the political temperature in the Commons by congratulating the father on his son's performance. It was a gesture which had the rare effect of visibly moving Joseph Chamberlain.[45]

Despite the vigour of Unionist opposition in the lower house, it was not there but in the House of Lords that the Home Rule Bill came to grief. Somewhat surprisingly Gladstone chose not to make this development the issue for another appeal to the electorate. The Prime Minister was perhaps too old now for another political crusade against the undemocratic powers of the hereditary peerage. When, in fact, in March 1894 Gladstone found his Cabinet opposed to him over the government's naval building programme, he retired finally from office. Under his successor, Lord Rosebery, the inherent disunity in Liberal politics became ever more apparent and the government tottered inevitably towards collapse in the following year. Austen Chamberlain played his part as a Liberal Unionist whip in bringing about the government's defeat on an apparently minor vote on 21 June 1895.

For Joseph Chamberlain, however, this had not been a period of much personal satisfaction. The possibility of Liberal reunion had now vanished, but on the other hand he could never be fully accepted into the Conservative ranks while he still clung tenaciously to his radical credentials. The majority of his new allies seemed unresponsive to the sort of social programme which Chamberlain wanted a future Unionist government to enact. He was separated by a wide gulf even from some of the Whigs among his fellow Liberal Unionists, such as Hartington. As Beatrice Webb noted at this time, 'no one trusts him, no one likes him, no one really believes in him.'[46] Approaching his sixtieth year, Chamberlain enquired of his wife

Should I not be acting rightly if I were to close my political life at this stage and make room for Austen who has a future before him?[47]

The younger man had made a promising beginning in the political arena and had strengthened his financial position by taking on a number of part-time directorships in industry. He had been active in the struggle against the Home Rule Bill, voting in 350 of the 418 divisions in the House of Commons. Was this perhaps the moment for him to take the leading role in the family's political affairs?

What transformed the situation for Joseph Chamberlain was his appointment as Colonial Secretary in the Unionist government of 1895. Offered by Lord Salisbury a free choice of government offices including the Exchequer, his decision to go to the Colonial Office was in many respects surprising. In the past it had been thought of as a stepping stone for young men on the way up, or as a refuge for the second rate and those nearing retirement on the way down the political ladder. During his eight years in this post, however, Chamberlain transformed it into a major office of state, while raising himself to the pinnacle of his career. At the Colonial Office he saw the opportunity to consolidate the unity of the British Empire and redirect its resources into the sort of radical social policies which had always been dear to his heart. For Austen this transformation in his father's fortunes meant that for a further decade he would have to live in the shadow of his illustrious namesake, and see his own political destiny largely determined by the causes which his father espoused. Nevertheless, the formation of Salisbury's government did give Austen his first taste of ministerial office. Though the Colonial Secretary studiously refrained from intervening on his son's behalf, there was great excitement in the family when Austen was offered the position of Civil Lord of the Admiralty. The post delighted him. His sense of the romance of history and of the part played by the navy in England's rise to world power had been intensified by his historical studies at Cambridge. He had read Mahan, Seeley and Froude with enthusiasm. The opportunity to study at first hand the Royal Navy in its modern context greatly appealed to him.[48] Indeed the post fostered in him an ambition that he might one day become First Lord of the Admiralty – a goal that was not to be reached until the very end of his ministerial career, by which time the position had lost most of its attraction for him.

In terms of the duties of his office, however, the five years which Chamberlain spent at the Admiralty were a period of administrative experience rather than political decision making.[49] His immediate superior, George Goschen, the First Lord, was also in the House of Commons, so Chamberlain was not often called upon to play a leading part in debates. Moreover the election of 1895, at which he himself was returned unopposed, saw the combined Unionist forces secure an overall majority of 152 in the lower house. The ensuing parliament therefore lacked the sense of excitement and drama which had characterised its predecessor, when majorities had been small and the outcome of divisions often uncertain. For the most part Chamberlain's work comprised routine duties at a time when the Royal Navy, by far the largest of the world's fleets, was undergoing moderate expansion before the threat posed by Germany's naval construction programme at the turn of the century became apparent. He served on committees dealing with such matters as the training of naval medical officers and drew up reports on the construction of new docks.[50] It was not particularly exciting work, but Chamberlain appears to have found it congenial and he progressively enhanced his reputation as a capable administrator and reliable parliamentarian. The *Birmingham Gazette* was perhaps not the most objective of observers, but its comment is worthy of mention:

Of the younger men whom I have heard suggested for Cabinet rank in the shuffling of the cards, Mr. Austen Chamberlain is one. He has done unprecedentedly well at the Admiralty. ... Mr. Austen Chamberlain has done more as Civil Lord than half a dozen of his immediate predecessors combined. He has raised the post to a dignity and importance never before experienced.[51]

As a bachelor Chamberlain was still close to his family circle and his not too onerous official duties left considerable time for his leisure interests, including his 'darling pastime bicycling.'[52] His sister Ida left a charming account of an outing with her brother to Stratford-upon-Avon:

We found a little inn at a place called Ettington and made an excellent lunch ... after which Austen discovered that he had left all his money at Stratford!! This was humiliating, but fortunately the inn people accepted our rather lame excuses without difficulty and we sent them a postal order for their very modest charge of 3/– for the two of us next day.[53]

Inevitably, however, as the theme of imperialism became ever more prominent in British politics and the fortunes of the Colonial Secretary rose in relation to it, the younger Chamberlain was seen more and more as his father's son, rather than a figure in his own right. He even supported his father's advocacy of ending Britain's 'Splendid Isolation' through alliance with the United States and Germany – a policy which sits uneasily beside the attitude which Austen showed towards Germany during much of the rest of his career.[54] By the turn of the century everyone recognised in Joseph Chamberlain the most dynamic element in the Unionist government. As Winston Churchill later wrote:

At the time when I looked out of my regimental cradle and was thrilled by politics, [Chamberlain] was incomparably the most lively, sparkling, insurgent, compulsive figure in British affairs.[55]

Yet it is now clear that the elder Chamberlain was somewhat fortunate that his reputation escaped without serious blemish from the aftermath of the Jameson Raid of 1895. Over the next four years the problem of relations with the Boer Republics remained at the centre of Chamberlain's concerns. Negotiations failed to provide a satisfactory arrangement for the British citizens living and working inside the Transvaal and increasingly Milner, the new British High Commissioner, drifted towards a solution by force. By 1899 the Colonial Secretary was convinced that the threat posed to the unity of the Empire, upon which he set such store, by the ascendancy of the Boer Republics was sufficiently great to justify recourse to war.[56]

Though Chamberlain had assiduously prepared British public opinion for the possible necessity of a military solution, the Boer War inflamed political passions in a way that had not been seen since the days of the Home Rule Bill. A small but vociferous group emerged among Liberal radicals whose sympathies were fundamentally with the Boers. Austen Chamberlain became an active platform speaker in defence of the British Government's actions in South Africa, which he claimed had been characterised by restraint and infinite patience. In 1900, with the war still raging, the government went to the country in an emotional atmosphere of patriotic fervour in which it could scarcely lose. The Liberal opposition was too divided on the issue of the war to appear as a credible alternative. In fact the election brought little change in the parliamentary position. Austen Chamberlain was again returned unopposed. In his election address he stressed the need to support the government in the present international difficulties, drew attention to the foreign policy achievements of the preceding years and highlighted some of the measures of domestic reform which the government had put through parliament.

By this stage, however, there had appeared the first rumblings of a possible political scandal involving the Chamberlain family – the suggestion that father and son were making money out of the war. The Colonial Secretary had been a particular target for Liberal invective and innuendo during the election campaign, for if by this time he had probably become the most popular politician in the land, he had also become the most hated. Many Liberal speakers had implied that the Chamberlains' business holdings were incompatible with their government offices and that the awarding of War Office and Admiralty contracts had not been unrelated to the financial interests of the two men. The matter came to a head in the debate on the Address on 10 December 1900. It marked the beginning of Austen Chamberlain's long and often changing parliamentary relationship with the young Liberal member for Caernarvon Boroughs, David Lloyd George. The latter, already developing a reputation for his oratorical skills, charged that most of the Chamberlains' munitions interests had been acquired since the Unionists took office in 1895. Government contracts with the Birmingham firm, Kynochs, were the most damning part of his argument, but he also named Austen as a major shareholder in a firm of Admiralty contractors, Hoskins and Sons. There was also the case of Tubes Ltd., in which both Austen and his father were interested as shareholders in an investment trust and of which – like Kynochs – Joseph's brother Arthur was chairman.[57] Accordingly, Lloyd George proposed that no office holder should have an interest in any firm or company competing for government contracts without that interest being declared, so that precautions could be taken to 'effectually prevent any suspicion of influence or favouritism in the allocation of such contracts.'[58] Joseph Chamberlain replied at length to the attack, referring to the 'dreary flow of petty malignity.'[59] In many ways, however, his defence, though commanding majority support in the House, was less than convincing. Austen followed his father with a much briefer but equally uncompelling apologia. Though it would probably be wrong to suggest that the Chamberlains had deliberately feathered their own nests – in the case of Austen, in particular, this would be quite contrary to his undoubted integrity – one study has concluded that there did indeed exist a selective policy exercised by the War Office in this period in favour of a small group of firms including Kynochs.[60]

In November 1900 Austen Chamberlain was promoted to the post of Financial Secretary to the Treasury. Here he was to serve as deputy to Sir Michael Hicks-Beach, Chancellor of the Exchequer since the formation of the Unionist government in 1895. Though outside the Cabinet, the post was an important one and, as Chamberlain was only thirty-seven at the time, his appointment was a clear indication that he was well regarded and destined for Cabinet rank in the not too distant future. It was also good training in the workings of the Treasury for a man who was himself destined on two occasions to become Chancellor. For the time being the whole government remained preoccupied with the South African War and Chamberlain played his part in castigating those Liberal leaders who criticised government policy at a time of national emergency. Campbell-Bannerman's celebrated phrase, 'methods of barbarism', caused him particular offence.[61]

As at the Admiralty, Chamberlain's work at the Exchequer was not overburdening and in the autumn of 1901 he was able to pay another extended visit to the Near East. But his continuing evidence of administrative competence duly secured its reward in the changes that took place after the conclusion of the war in May 1902. A few weeks later Salisbury, now rapidly ageing, resigned from the premiership and was succeeded by his nephew, Arthur Balfour. Joseph Chamberlain may have nurtured faint hopes of the succession, but in all probability he recognised that the control of the Salisbury family, the so-called Hotel Cecil, over the destiny of the Conservative party was still too tight to allow the erstwhile radical and republican to intrude with success. In any case the Colonial Secretary was incapacitated after a cab accident at the time of Salisbury's resignation. Balfour was anxious to bring some new blood into the Cabinet, many of whose members had been in office continuously for seven years. To the Colonial Secretary he wrote:

The first question I ask myself is – What men are there who, if introduced into the Cabinet, would add to its distinction and efficiency? There really are only two – Austen and George Wyndham, both of them in their respective ways quite first-rate – both of them speakers on whom you and I shall largely have to rely ... in general debate.[62]

Accordingly, Austen Chamberlain entered the Cabinet to sit alongside his father as Postmaster General – a junior position, but one which at least made him privy to the decisions of government at the highest level. The promotion was generally well received. Sir Almeric Fitzroy, the Clerk of the Privy Council, noted the entry into the Cabinet of two men, Chamberlain and Wyndham, 'of great promise.'[63]

Chamberlain approached his new post in a mood of cautious enthusiasm:

I think the Postmaster usually gets at least as many kicks as half-pennies, but that there is good work to be done in that office I have no doubt....[64]

His main departmental concerns in his first Cabinet office were with the

V The young statesman (Birmingham University)

VI Joseph Chamberlain at Westminster (Stone Collection, Birmingham Central Library)

position. His call for tariff reform in May 1903 arose at least in part from his determination to regain the initiative in the Unionist alliance. At the same time that his cab accident allowed Balfour to drop the local option clause, Chamberlain was also interrupted in his attendance at the conference of the Prime Ministers of the self-governing colonies, meeting in London. From this conference the Colonial Secretary, who for some time had been groping towards a coherent imperial policy, drew the conclusion that imperial preference represented the only route by which the self-governing colonies might move towards greater integration with the mother country. In a speech in Birmingham in May 1902, which anticipated much of what he would say in his more famous pronouncement a year later, Chamberlain had argued that Britain must bind the colonies together and not stick to old shibboleths, by which he presumably meant free trade.[68] In the Commons on 9 June Austen defended his father's speech. He had not, he stressed, advocated preferential relations, but had refused 'to be deterred from proposing a tax ... merely because it might be used, if the people of this country so willed, to draw closer the ties between the Mother Country and the Colonies.'[69]

The tax to which the Chamberlains referred was a duty on corn. In order to meet some of the expenditure incurred in the Boer War, Hicks-Beach had been forced in April 1902 to revive the Corn Registration Duty, which had been abolished in 1869. In the Chancellor's view this expedient represented nothing but a revenue-raising device, but to Chamberlain it opened up wider horizons and on 21 October he raised in the Cabinet the question of the preferential remission of the corn duty in favour of Canada. In this way the principle of tariff reform might be introduced without an open challenge to the fiscal orthodoxy of the day. Though Ritchie, the new Chancellor of the Exchequer, reserved his position, Chamberlain's proposal secured Cabinet approval and he left England for a much heralded tour of South Africa confident that he had made a substantial first move towards his ultimate goal.

During the months of his father's absence Austen was left to protect his interests inside the Cabinet.[70] Though he was assiduous in reporting the conduct of the government's business to his father, there seems little doubt that Austen failed to appreciate how skilfully Ritchie, his predecessor Hicks-Beach and other Free Traders began to marshal their forces to undermine the Colonial Secretary's objectives. Looking back nearly thirty years later, Austen wrote of a 'period of busy and obscure intrigue' on the part of the Chancellor and claimed that Ritchie had 'fallen entirely under the influence of Sir Francis Mowatt, the Permanent Secretary to the Treasury, a fanatical free trader.'[71] In early February he warned his father, still in South Africa, that they might expect trouble from Ritchie

over the corn duty, but he seemed to underestimate the scale of the
problem:

Ritchie is dead against the remission of the Corn Duties to the Colonies, tho' I
cannot hear of anyone else supporting him unless it be Balfour of Burleigh [the
Secretary of State for Scotland] . . . I don't think Ritchie intends leaving if we
insist, tho' there is said to be danger of it.[72]

Austen perhaps assumed that the undoubted success of his father's South
African tour was such that on his return no opposition to him within the
government would be able to make any impact:

You will, I hope, have seen enough of the English papers to know that your
wonderful success is recognised and appreciated on all hands. There has been no
criticism worth notice in any quarter, but a general testimony borne on all sides
to the spirit in which you have grappled with your gigantic tasks and the results
achieved.[73]

Certainly, without the Colonial Secretary the political world seemed
somewhat empty. 'I never knew a session begin more flatly,' commented
Austen on 24 February.[74] But on that very day Ritchie informed the
Prime Minister that he could not accept the Colonial Secretary's fiscal
proposals. Though it was agreed that no firm decision could be taken in
the latter's absence, on Balfour's advice Austen sent news of this
bombshell to his father, who was by then on his way back from South
Africa. Austen had formed the impression that Balfour was 'by no means
supporting Ritchie's views,' but recognised that the Chancellor's attitude
was a very grave matter.[75] Sensing his junior status within the Cabinet,
Austen had, perhaps unwisely, failed to press for an immediate discussion
of the problem. Certainly Ritchie was able in the intervening period to
consolidate his opposition still further.

When the Cabinet met soon after Joseph Chamberlain's return, Ritchie
secured the victory which he was looking for. Not only was the Canadian
preference dropped, but the corn duty itself was repealed. Recalling the
March meetings of the Cabinet many years later, Austen noted that
opposition to the Corn Tax and its use for preference had strengthened,
but he still believed that Balfour's attitude was sympathetic.[76] When the
Chancellor presented his budget to parliament on 23 April it seemed to be
a triumphant restatement of Cobdenite Free Trade principles. But Balfour
managed to sustain the semblance of party unity by agreeing that there
should be an impartial investigation of the question of imperial preference.
It was in this increasingly strained atmosphere that the Colonial Secretary
delivered his celebrated speech on 15 May from his Birmingham citadel.
Austen was present in the Town Hall when his father declared that the
choice before the British people was whether 'it is better to cultivate the

trade with your own people or to let that go in order that you may keep the trade of those who . . . are your competitors.' 'You have an opportunity,' he concluded, 'you will never have it again'.[77] The son, however, could surely not have known how monumental an event in his own career this speech was to prove. Its message was, argued Leo Amery, 'a challenge to free thought as direct and provocative as the theses which Luther nailed to the church door at Wittenberg.'[78]

As the tariff reform crusade was to be the centrepiece of Austen Chamberlain's political preoccupations at least until 1913, and was to re-emerge periodically into prominence thereafter into the 1930s, it merits consideration at this point. That Britain's industrial and trading position was not as secure as it had been thirty years earlier, there could be no doubt. The country's once acknowledged supremacy was clearly under attack. More recently industrialised nations such as Germany and the United States had come to rival, and in certain crucial respects surpass, the United Kingdom. Britain's traditional trading markets were being successfully contested, while most advanced countries had erected tariff barriers to protect their domestic industries. Whether imperial preference offered a panacea for these problems was, however, a different proposition. Certainly the elder Chamberlain underestimated the extent to which motives of national self-interest were already coming to dominate the thinking of the self-governing colonies, particularly Canada. The future may or may not have belonged to great empires, but whether a consolidated British Empire was ever anything more than the chimerical dream of imperial mystics remains an open question. The economic aspects of the debate, which academics fought out largely removed from the rhetoric of politicians, was a complex one, and the Colonial Secretary himself was more than once caught out by his own lack of understanding in this respect. At one point he had to admit that the further he delved into this matter, 'the more I recognise the difficulty of arguing from figures alone and the more I am inclined to depend upon certain great principles which affect human action and national policy.'[79] If Joseph Chamberlain had to take refuge in such woolly reasoning, the same was true for Austen. Yet the latter probably lacked the sort of character which could ever take up tariff reform in this way with the almost religious enthusiasm which had gripped his father. Even at this early date there is a tantalising indication of the difference in Austen's attitude:

I met Moberly Bell in the train. . . . He told me he had asked Austen whether he was as keen on fiscal reform as his father, to which Austen replied 'No, but then you see I am not so young.'[80]

The task facing the two Chamberlains – a task which after 1906 Joseph

had effectively to bequeath to his son – was a monumental one. Free
Trade was less an economic policy than an article of faith, not only for the
entire Liberal party, but also for large numbers of Unionists. The
economic prosperity of Victorian England had seemed to grow directly
out of the abandonment of protection in the 1840s. For many observers
the two developments were synonymous and to challenge this
fundamental wisdom was economic and political heresy. In addition,
whatever the inherent advantages of tariff reform might be, the apparent
threat to cheap food implicit in the taxation of agricultural produce was,
electorally speaking, potential dynamite. 'Food taxes' or 'stomach taxes'
were to haunt the Chamberlainite campaign throughout.

At this point the character and strategy of the Prime Minister, Arthur
Balfour, assumed critical importance. Balfour's was a complex
personality which Austen Chamberlain never fully fathomed. 'I do not
pretend,' Chamberlain once wrote, 'that I think Balfour's subsequent
handling of the situation wise, but it was certainly not lacking in
courage.'[81] The Prime Minister's intellect certainly operated on a higher
plane than did that of the Postmaster General. Yet over the next three
years in particular, and at times again throughout the remainder of his
career as Unionist leader, Balfour's dialectical subtlety, his definitions,
qualifications and quibbles over fiscal policy, served to exasperate and
bewilder Austen Chamberlain. For all his complexities, however,
Balfour's guiding motivation was simple enough. Chamberlain had had an
insight into it when the two men once discussed the merits of Sir Robert
Peel as a political leader:

My recollection is that A J B's reply was brief and emphatic: He smashed his
party and no man has a right to destroy the property of which he is trustee.[82]

Through all the sometimes Machiavellian developments which now
ensued, Balfour's primary concern was to maintain the viability of his
government and to seek the highest common factor upon which party
unity could be preserved.[83]

During the spring and summer of 1903 the divisions of opinion within
the Unionist party on the fiscal question became more firmly entrenched
with the formation of the Free Food and Tariff Reform Leagues.
Meanwhile, Balfour attempted to evolve his own compromise policy of
retaliation. He asserted that imperial preference was not yet practical
politics, but proposed to use tariffs as a means of reprisal against those
countries which applied them to British exports. The Prime Minister's
attitude clearly represented a significant step in the direction of the
Chamberlainite policy – a move that was confirmed when, prior to the 13
August meeting of the Cabinet, Balfour circulated to his colleagues a

two-part discussion document. The second part of this document, the so-called Blue Paper, made it clear that Balfour was ready to advocate not only retaliation but also preference and food taxes. Though the Cabinet postponed a final decision on the subject until September, it seemed unlikely that on these terms it would be possible to avoid some resignations. Balfour, however, was anxious to retain the services of the Duke of Devonshire as Lord President of the Council. As leader of the Whigs among the Liberal Unionists and a prominent free trader, Devonshire's support might be vital to the Cabinet's survival.

On 9 September Joseph Chamberlain wrote privately to the Prime Minister to offer his resignation in order that he could speak more freely in the campaign that would be necessary up and down the country to convert the electorate to his tariff reform proposals. Prior to the crucial Cabinet meeting Balfour, his brother Gerald and the Colonial Secretary met privately. Here it was agreed that Chamberlain should now resign in order to evangelize the doubting voters, while the Prime Minister, holding on to Devonshire if he could, would only commit the government to retaliation and await the results of the campaign. Despite his Cabinet memorandum Balfour would exclude food taxes for the time being. Yet it seems that Balfour deliberately made no mention at the Cabinet of Chamberlain's offer to resign, in order to ensure the resignation of the three most intransigent free traders from the Cabinet – Ritchie, Balfour of Burleigh and George Hamilton. Austen recalled this crucial Cabinet meeting many years later:

I returned from a short holiday abroad the evening before the critical Cabinet meeting and did not see my father until I met him in Cabinet. I had therefore no knowledge . . . of his intention to resign. I heard him announce that intention at the Cabinet and I drove back with him to Prince's Gardens . . . and reproached him with having taken this decision without a word to me, but added that as he was resigning I should certainly do the same.[84]

But Austen's recollection may be at fault since others, including Devonshire, still had no idea that the elder Chamberlain was about to resign. Balfour only made this clear when he had already received the resignations of the three ardent free traders. The news of Chamberlain's resignation would, he hoped, induce the Duke to remain at his post.

In sum it seems clear that Balfour and Chamberlain, whatever the history of their relationship over the next two years, had at this point reached an agreement involving a substantial consensus on policy. Chamberlain, it seems, would educate the nation from the comparative freedom of the back benches before returning triumphantly into a Unionist Tariff Reform government. The role envisaged for Austen in this bargain is the clearest indication of its existence. In his original offer to resign the Colonial Secretary had stressed that he saw no reason whatever why Austen should follow him and would do his utmost to persuade him to stay.[85] Some members of the government hoped that Austen might go to the War Office in a move to restore public confidence in the administration of the army. When the resignation letter and Balfour's reply were published, it was clear that not only was Austen remaining in the Cabinet, but that he was being promoted to a major office of state.

In the Cabinet changes which followed Joseph Chamberlain's resignation, Austen became Chancellor of the Exchequer. As such he succeeded Ritchie in a post which obviously had crucial importance if the government was one day going to embrace tariff reform wholeheartedly. The promotion, Balfour said, caused him 'gratification, both on personal and public grounds,' giving conclusive evidence that, in his judgment as well as Joseph Chamberlain's, the exclusion of food taxes was the best policy for the time being.[86] Thus Balfour seemed to have engineered the best possible way out of an unpromising impasse. Only the unexpected resignation of the Duke of Devonshire on 2 October appeared to mar his success.

Yet Austen Chamberlain's promotion to the Exchequer at the early age of forty is open to a variety of interpretations. On the whole the move was well received. Even Hicks-Beach, though still a champion of the free trade cause, regarded it as 'the only good appointment' in the reconstruction which Balfour now had to carry out.[87] A much younger free trader, Winston Churchill, was less certain:

Mr. Austen Chamberlain, the echo and exponent of his father, is sent to guard the public purse. Custodes ipsos quis custodiet![88]

But the crucial question is not the reception which greeted the new Chancellor's appointment, but the effect which it had on the cause of tariff reform and the relationship between the Prime Minister and his outgoing Colonial Secretary. To Austen and others, not least among the free trade camp, it seemed that the new arrangement represented a bridge between Balfour and the elder Chamberlain which guaranteed the effective support of the Prime Minister and his government for the broad thrust of the tariff policy. The history of the next two and a half years, on the other hand, suggests that Balfour's intentions may have been altogether more devious. The appointment of the new Chancellor may have been his way of retaining the control of policy firmly in his own hands, while lessening any threat to his government from outside. In many respects Austen's position became that of a hostage. While he remained as Chancellor his father could scarcely attack the government, even if Balfour's adherence to tariff reform began to waver. When Garvin suggested such an interpretation of Austen's promotion to the older Chamberlain, the latter was 'dead silent for a full minute afterwards.'[89] At the same time Balfour may have surmised that Austen, whom everyone would recognise as, in Mr. Amery's phrase, his father's ambassador, would be too junior, despite the status of his office, to exert much influence inside the Cabinet. Balfour could therefore manipulate the son, while still making use of the bridge to the father.

Balfour soon assured the younger Chamberlain that he was 'the most important of my colleagues,'[90] but this reflected no reality within the dynamics of Unionist politics. Balfour always regarded Lord Lansdowne, Unionist leader in the upper house, as his chief lieutenant. He leant heavily also on such senior colleagues as Walter Long, President of the Local Government Board, and Aretas Akers-Douglas, the Home Secretary. Nothing better illustrated Austen's lack of political weight and expertise than a lamentable performance when deputising for Balfour at the opening of parliament in February 1904. Just before he rose to speak he knocked over an ink-pot on his trousers. Mary Chamberlain put the best possible gloss upon his subsequent performance:

He was subjected to the ordeal of interruptions and an uneasy house, a low menacing murmur from the other side and insufficient support as he made his points from our own. . . .[91]

A more objective observer proved less charitable. It was 'one of the most painful incidents in recent parliamentary history.' Only when taking refuge in incoherence did he fulfil his task 'with great courage and adroitness.'[92]

Austen Chamberlain himself clearly envisaged his new role as the custodian of his father's cause. He obviously believed that Balfour and his father were working for substantially the same ends. Now, as Chancellor of the Exchequer and living in 11 Downing Street, he could consolidate the gains that had already been made. His task was to try to close any gap that still existed between the Chamberlainite position and that of the Prime Minister. He nonetheless felt uneasy about staying in a government from which his father had resigned and was glad when he got through a speech on the subject to his electors in Acocks Green. As his step-mother noted, 'the necessity for explaining the situation weighed heavily on his mind.'[93] Over the next two years, however, it became clear that the gap was much wider than Austen had originally imagined. Indeed he probably nourished the illusion of Balfour's fundamental sympathy with the Chamberlainite cause long after such an idea ceased to be tenable. He was unceasing in his efforts to induce Balfour to adopt a more positive and committed attitude on tariff reform, but was largely unsuccessful. The role required of him was a subtle and delicate one and, as his later career often revealed, this was not his forte.

Certainly at this stage of his political life he lacked the finesse to cope with Balfour's adroit use of ambiguity and delay. Whatever Austen threw at him, Balfour, a past master of polished evasion, was able to parry. To Lloyd George Austen was like Casabianca, 'bravely sinking with the ship on his father's orders.'[94] But though he might seethe with indignation that Balfour was letting slip an unprecedented opportunity to redirect the destiny of the British Empire, there was little, short of his own resignation, that he could do about it. From this step he held back, believing presumably, despite all the evidence to the contrary, that his continuing presence in the Cabinet still offered the best guarantee of the ultimate adoption of the whole of his father's policy.

Chamberlain's elevation to the Exchequer brought about a marked change in his personal life. Until this time he had lived at his father's house in Prince's Gardens or at Highbury, the family home in Birmingham. Now he transferred to his official residence in Downing Street. It was a development which clearly moved him:

I cannot close my first evening away from your roof in a house for the time at least my own without writing a line to you. It is so great a change in my life and all about me is so strange, that as yet I hardly realize it. . . . It is at once a great encouragement and a great responsibility to be heir to so fine a tradition of private honour and public duty and I will do my best to be not unworthy of the name.[95]

But in order to ensure that there was no breach of communication between the two men a private telephone line was installed at 11 Downing Street.

Though he clearly saw his role in government primarily in terms of the espousal of tariff reform, Chamberlain could not ignore the fact that he was now head of a major government department. He arrived moreover at the Exchequer at a time when the inability of an essentially eighteenth-century taxation structure to cope with the demands of a modern industrialised economy was becoming only too apparent. As Chancellor, Chamberlain was relatively successful. While in most fields Balfour's government seemed now to drift indecisively towards the electoral catastrophe of 1906, he was one of the few ministers to enhance his reputation. One backbencher commented that his 'modesty, courtesy, knowledge of the House and of the task of his great Department earned him respect and admiration.'[96] He was in office long enough to present two budgets, both of which, though unspectacular, were well received. In the first he increased income tax from 11d to one shilling and put an extra 3d on the duty on tobacco and 2d on tea. In the second budget he took off the extra 2d from tea.[97] Chamberlain thus struck an entirely orthodox balance between direct and indirect taxation.

On coming to the Treasury Chamberlain was concerned at the prospect of a large deficit by 1904 and warned Balfour that it might be necessary to impose new indirect taxes on such commodities as silk and petrol.[98] Predicting deficits for the next two years, he produced a memorandum on the financial situation for his Cabinet colleagues which could easily have been written thirty years later when his brother Neville occupied the same office:

These deficits . . . will have to be met, for the most part, by new taxation; but, in view of the gravity of the situation, I trust that the Cabinet will concur in the necessity for further reductions in our military and naval expenditure. Our defensive strength rests upon our financial not less than our military and naval resources, and I am bound to say that in the present condition of our finances, it would, in my opinion, be impossible to finance a great war, except at an absolutely ruinous cost.[99]

By the beginning of 1904 it seemed that the position was even more serious than he had anticipated.[100] As Budget Day approached Chamberlain was clearly apprehensive. There was, he confessed, 'no credit to be got out of it.' Even though government revenue turned out to be rather higher than had been anticipated, the Chancellor was in very low spirits.[101] In the event Chamberlain's budget speech was among his better parliamentary performances, pleasing his father and earning praise from both sides of the House.

Not surprisingly much of his time was taken up, as Chancellors both before and since have found, in trying to persuade Cabinet colleagues to reduce their departmental expenditure. George Wyndham as Irish Secretary and Arnold-Forster at the War Office posed particular problems.[102] As he prepared for the 1905 Finance Bill, Chamberlain agreed with Lord Selborne, the First Lord of the Admiralty, that it depended on the naval estimates whether the budget was 'vile or passable.' He had to abandon his hope of reducing income tax to the level he had inherited from Ritchie and produced a fairly neutral budget.[103] With Britain's international position increasingly under challenge from the German naval building programme, this was not a time when significant economies could be made.

The state of the national economy was, of course, intimately connected with the progress of the tariff reform campaign. It would be no easy matter to persuade the electorate of the need for a radical departure in fiscal policy if the existing system seemed capable of producing prosperity and full employment. In November 1903 Chamberlain expressed satisfaction with the course of his father's campaign and predicted that the country was approaching a period of acute depression, in which the benefits of fiscal change would be only too apparent.[104] But the improvement in the economy early in 1904 seemed to undermine this argument and by-election losses in January and February confirmed that Joseph Chamberlain had not yet won the argument. In retrospect the fact that the country's major industries, with the exception of iron and steel, continued to prosper under free trade was the most important reason why the Chamberlainite campaign did not achieve more success before 1906. After February 1904 it was clear that, provided he did not go beyond the policy of retaliation, Balfour could rely on sufficient support from Unionist Free Traders – alarmed at what the by-election results implied for a possible General Election – to ensure the continuance of his ministry. This the Prime Minister felt to be essential. It would be a disaster for the Unionist administration to disintegrate at a time when the country faced so many problems in both the domestic and the international spheres.

But if Joe could not yet capture the electorate, he was making strenuous efforts to increase his following within the Unionist party. To Austen he confided that at the next election it would be necessary to get rid of 'the foes in our own household – the Churchills, Seelys, Bowles etc.'[105] On 23 March 1904 Austen was successful in carrying a fiscal resolution at the annual meeting of the Liberal Union Club. By the end of the year the Liberal Unionist wing of the Unionist alliance had been completely captured by the Chamberlains. But while Balfour refused to shift his own position, tariff reform progress was bound to remain circumscribed. Accordingly, Austen went to see Balfour towards the middle of August 1904 and on the 24th of the month sent a long letter to the Prime Minister setting out his views.[106] He argued that the time had come for the government to resign since there was no possibility of hanging on for better times around the corner. The need, however, was for the party which was presently 'timid, undecided, vacillating' to unite on a constructive policy which, Chamberlain hoped, would involve some movement on Balfour's part towards his father's position. If the contending Unionist factions did not come closer together they would inevitably and fatally drift further and further apart. It was very much a long-term strategy. 'We cannot win now but we can lay the foundations of future victory, and even now we may profoundly modify the result of the next elections.' The swing of the electoral pendulum was, after so long a period in government, moving inexorably against the Unionists, but, Chamberlain argued, the party had done no worse in by-elections since his father's Birmingham speech than before it. Chamberlain therefore urged Balfour to commit the party at the next General Election to call a colonial conference to consider the question of imperial trade and to be bound by any constructive proposals resulting from such a conference.

This important letter also revealed Chamberlain's belief that Balfour had not maintained his part of the 'bargain' reached with the outgoing Colonial Secretary in September 1903:

You encouraged my father to go out as a 'pioneer'; you gave your blessing to his efforts for closer union with the Colonies; you assured us who remained that we too thus served the interests of Imperial Union. . . . He undertook this work believing in your sympathy, believing that, when he had proved that the obstacles were not insuperable, you and your Government would be prepared to make some advance.

Yet the tone of the letter remained conciliatory. Chamberlain concluded:

I think we are on the brink of disaster. I know that you can save us, and I cannot rest content without at least trying to convey to you some part of my conviction and of the reasons which inspire it.

Balfour and his close advisers interpreted Chamberlain's initiative as a signal that his father's campaign was in difficulties. The Prime Minister delayed his reply until Austen was on the verge of leaving for the continent and then made it clear that he was not prepared to accept the latter's proposals. The furthest he would go was to suggest a double election plan. If the proposals put forward by a colonial conference were broadly satisfactory, these would then be put before the electorate rather than being enacted immediately. If, as most people now expected, the Unionists lost the next election, this would mean at least three General Elections before imperial preference could become a reality. As Hicks-Beach recognised, 'both [Balfour] and Joe would be undergound before anything could be done.'[107] A masterpiece of subtlety and reassurance, Balfour's reply asked Chamberlain to believe that 'the agreement between your views and mine on the present political situation is so nearly complete that the one difference which seems to divide us obtains perhaps an undue prominence.'[108] Chamberlain, however, was not satisfied. Indeed he was clearly annoyed by Balfour's calculated delay in replying. The difference between the two men was greater, he now told Balfour, than he had thought or than Balfour supposed. If this was the party leader's last word on the subject, Chamberlain did not see how he could possibly come into line with him at the next election. He interpreted Balfour's proposal to mean that the great matter of tariff reform would be put before the British people 'timidly, hesitatingly, amid circumstances of doubt and indecision which obscure the greatness of the issue, which take off the edge of effort

and kill enthusiasm.' The Prime Minister's attitude could only mean a
continuation of the present divisions and disunion inside the Unionist
ranks.[109]

When, therefore, Chamberlain left for his holiday, a crisis in his
relationship with the government seemed to have been reached. But he did
not contemplate resignation:

I think my position this autumn will be made very difficult, but I will do my best
to keep things smooth while this Parliament lasts. But I start today for my
holiday greatly depressed by the conviction to which his letter has brought me,
that when the dissolution comes I shall not be able to see eye to eye with him, or
to conceal our differences of opinion from the public.[110]

Not equal to Balfour's capacity for intellectual gymnastics, Chamberlain
was clearly losing his war of attrition with the Prime Minister. He had not
succeeded in bridging the gap between Balfour and his father, but had
merely watched it grow. Time, moreover, was running out, at least as far
as his father was concerned. Already sixty-eight years of age, Joseph
Chamberlain could not indefinitely maintain the campaign of public
speaking upon which he had embarked a year earlier. On 3 October
Balfour proclaimed in Edinburgh his two-election policy, thereby taking
the sting out of a major speech which Joseph Chamberlain was due to
make in Luton four days later. Since the Prime Minister was giving some
hope of imperial preference, however far off in the future, his speech gave
the Chamberlains no scope to break with him. Then a shift in public
attention to the international arena, when Russian Baltic fleet ships fired
on British trawlers, allowed Balfour to evade the tariff issue completely at
the National Union Conference in October. In vain Austen tried to
persuade Balfour to excommunicate all remaining Unionist free traders
from the party.[111]

By March 1905 the Prime Minister even seemed to succeed in driving a
wedge between father and son. When on 8 March Winston Churchill, who
had now joined the Liberal ranks, moved a resolution condemning
preferential tariffs based on food taxes, the government resorted to the
technical device of 'moving the previous question,' which enabled them to
set the motion aside. Later in the month, however, a similar motion by the
Liberal backbencher Ainsworth, condemning a ten per cent general tariff,
provoked a different response. When Joseph heard that the Chief Whip,
Acland Hood, and Jack Sandars, Balfour's private secretary, were urging
that the party be allowed a free vote on this motion he was horrified. The
two Chamberlains had a long and difficult discussion of the question over
dinner on 20 March, but Joseph refused to give Austen any advice as to
his actions. Yet the impression is clear that he believed that the time had

come for his son to resign. After one of only two sleepless nights caused by political worry during his long career, Austen attended the Cabinet on 21 March and decided to go along with its decision to advise Unionist abstention in the division.

Sandars believed that Austen did not intend to 'mortgage his political future' by standing with his father,[112] but this is too cynical an interpretation of his actions. The episode served to illustrate the inherent difficulties of his position as a political go-between. His loyalty to his father had to be balanced by his sense of collective Cabinet responsibility and his realisation that this was not an ideal moment at which to resign. His heavy heart was evident in the letter he now penned to his father:

This is indeed drinking to the dregs the cup of bitterness, and I have consented to drain it with my colleagues. . . . I might still have announced that I at least was unable to continue to hold office. God knows it was the easiest and simplest course for me to follow and would have saved me personally an infinity of mortification and humiliation.[113]

Chamberlain's family circle appreciated the painful decision which he had been forced to take. Some months later Hilda Chamberlain commented in more general terms on her brother's dilemma:

You have suffered much, I know, and in nothing so much, I think, as in feeling that it has prevented your walking absolutely side by side with Papa, and that by the necessity of the case you were forced to see things at times differently, from inside, from his outside view.[114]

During the second half of May Balfour and Joseph Chamberlain sought to hammer out their differences in personal negotiations. Somewhat surprisingly the Prime Minister now seemed ready to concede that tariff reform, including colonial preference, must be the foremost item in the Unionist programme at the next election. Under pressure from Unionist free traders, he later back-tracked to the extent of refusing to envisage a colonial conference until after the election, but still seemed sound on the central issue. Prevented by illness from making a statement to this effect in parliament at the end of May, Balfour was due to speak on 2 June at the Albert Hall. Austen was given the task of urging the Prime Minister to include in this speech the salient points of the agreement with his father. When, however, the speech was made it was long, vague and ambiguous. The crucial sentences were isolated from one another amidst a mass of complex verbiage and the only comfort the Chamberlains could draw was a weak general commitment to tariff reform. Ruefully Austen commented:

I had told A J B the form was of the utmost importance. He must make it the salient feature – yet he had so spoken that no one understood its importance.[115]

Chamberlain's patience was nearing breaking point, particularly as Balfour had ruled out the possibility of a colonial conference before the General Election. Nothing, therefore, would be gained by further procrastination. By the autumn all Austen could do was to call plaintively for an election as soon as possible. Defeat, he believed, was certain, but the magnitude of the disaster would increase the longer the dissolution was delayed. He had 'never felt so low about our prospects' and watched with a feeling approaching despair the growth of a situation he was powerless to alter.[116] He was particularly annoyed that Balfour had not taken any action against those Unionists who had not even accepted the party leader's minimum tariff proposals.[117] Matters came to a head early in November when, without warning, Lord Londonderry, the President of the Board of Education, declared that the entire programme of tariff reform should be dropped so as to reunite the party. Londonderry's proposal was naïve in the extreme and he and Austen exchanged angry words across the Cabinet table. Yet once again Balfour's ingenuity was 'equal to reconciling the irreconcilable.' 'In the end,' noted Fitzroy, 'Ministers were content to remain bound in the gossamer web of their chief's dexterities and Austen will have to make the best of the situation with his father.'[118]

It was an interesting commentary on the younger Chamberlain's attitude that even now he embraced with some enthusiasm a last-minute compromise proposal from Balfour's brother Gerald, which would have involved dropping the idea of a graduated duty on manufactured imports. Still he nurtured the hope that Balfour and his father could be brought together. 'The real reunion that I want is between you and him.'[119] By contrast Joseph Chamberlain was now thinking in altogether different terms. He had no wish for the sort of reconciliation which would involve his membership of a future shadow cabinet alongside those Unionist free traders who had resisted his proposals for the last three years. He was prepared instead for the election to take place and for a new balance of forces within the Unionist party to emerge, favourable he hoped to his own interests. Joseph was probably relieved that Gerald Balfour's scheme was not pursued.[120] Now he was ready for an open conflict with the party leader. On 14 November the National Union meeting in Newcastle gave overwhelming endorsement to a motion for preference and at the same time criticised party organisation. A week later Joseph Chamberlain made an important speech in Bristol in which he insisted that the Unionist party should fight the next election on the fiscal question. While professing continuing loyalty to Balfour as leader, he pronounced with feeling that 'no army was ever led successfully to battle on the principle that the lamest man should govern the march of the army.'[121] After this attack Balfour could scarcely continue in office. By 30 November Austen was convinced that Balfour would resign and the King call upon Campbell-Bannerman, the Liberal leader, to form a minority government. His relief was evident:

Today, I see, is Thanksgiving Day in America – and here too, is it not?[122]

On 4 December 1905 Balfour finally submitted his resignation to the King, together with a recommendation that the Liberals be invited to form a new administration. Lacking a majority in the House of Commons, Campbell-Bannerman had no alternative but to appeal to the electorate. What all recognised would be a crucial campaign soon got under way. Speaking in Bradford on 14 December Austen Chamberlain argued that the leaders of the Unionist party were united in their central aims and objectives. The electorate, however, having seen the Unionist ranks in increasing disarray over the previous two years, was not likely to agree. In so far as the claim carried conviction it probably worked to the party's disadvantage, since it gave ammunition to Liberal critics who argued that their opponents had indeed embraced whole-hogger tariff reform and that this would mean the rapid imposition of food taxes should the Unionists return to power.[123] For much of the campaign Chamberlain was laid up with sciatica, but it was clear that the tide was running strongly against the Unionists and his father was forced to fight vigorously to maintain his power-base in the Midlands. Polling, which at this date was spread over several days, began on 12 January 1906 and early results indicated a Liberal landslide. Among the first losses was Balfour's own seat in East Manchester and he was rapidly followed by a string of Unionist ex-ministers. Only in Birmingham did the Unionist citadel remain intact. The two Chamberlains were among only 157 Unionist M.P.s in the new parliament.

Whatever interpretation might be placed upon the election result – and it was clear that tariff reform had not been the only issue – the verdict of 1906 was clearly a watershed for the Unionist party and also for Austen Chamberlain. Few could have predicted that the party's return to government would be so long delayed or that two more General Elections would be lost, while the party's internal disputes smouldered on, unresolved, for almost another decade. Defeat, however, clearly gave scope to those who wished to change the course of Unionist politics. 'It would be great fun to be a Tory now,' commented the impish Winston Churchill.[124] As far as Austen Chamberlain was concerned the future looked promising but unpredictable. Partly because of his father's name, partly because of the exceptional circumstances of 1903 and partly on his own merits, he had made rapid advances within the party hierarchy. 'I see,' noted Mary Chamberlain, 'how the training of all those years is now telling.'[125] At only forty-two years of age he stood as a senior ex-minister in the party's much depleted ranks. He had served a long political apprenticeship under the watchful eye of his father. A great deal would now depend on the sort of policies and strategy which the rump of the parliamentary party decided to adopt; more still on the continuing ability of his elderly father to sustain the intensity of effort which had characterised the whole of his political life. The next few months would clarify at least some of these points.

Notes

1. A. Chamberlain to Sayle, 27 October 188?, Chamberlain MSS, AC L. Add. 68.
2. E. T. Raymond, *Uncensored Celebrities* (London, 1918) p. 167.
3. Sir A. Chamberlain, *Down the Years* (London, 1935) p. 69.
4. Earl of Birkenhead, *Contemporary Personalities* (London, 1924) p. 67.
5. As note 1.
6. J. L. Garvin, *The Life of Joseph Chamberlain* (London, 1932) i, 269.
7. Austen Chamberlain later recalled a conversation with his father in which the latter had spoken of another man who had lost his wife in childbirth. 'In a flash I saw for the first time, what he had so carefully concealed from me, that in my earliest years I had been to him the living embodiment of the first tragedy of his life.' Petrie, *Chamberlain Tradition* p. 130.
8. J. Chamberlain to A. Chamberlain n.d., Chamberlain MSS, AC 1/4/4a/1.
9. Ibid, 15 May 1875, ibid, AC 1/4/4a/5.
10. Ibid, n.d., ibid, AC 1/4/4a/3.
11. A. Chamberlain to Canon Melly 3 Dec. 1929, Chamberlain MSS, AC 38/3/107.
12. J. Chamberlain to H. Lee Warner 8 April 1879, D. H. Elletson, *The Chamberlains* (London, 1966) pp. 95–6.
13. A. Chamberlain to Joynson-Hicks 26 Nov. 1926, Chamberlain MSS, AC 53/399.
14. J. Chamberlain to Lee Warner 29 Oct. 1881, Chamberlain MSS, JC 1/9/4. When Austen left Rugby, Lee Warner wrote that he had 'never parted from a boy with greater reluctance.' Elletson, *Chamberlains* p. 96.
15. J. Chamberlain to Lee Warner 16 Jan. 1882, Chamberlain MSS, JC 1/9/5.
16. There is some evidence that Joseph Chamberlain came to revise his opinion of his two sons. In 1902, when Austen was on the verge of Cabinet rank, he is reported to have admitted that of his two sons 'Neville is really the clever one, but he isn't interested in politics; if he was, I would back him to be Prime Minister.' J. Amery, *Life of Joseph Chamberlain* (London, 1951) iv, 275.
17. A. Chamberlain to Mr. Osborne 19 April 1934, Chamberlain MSS, AC L. Add. 49.

18. J. R. Seeley, *The Expansion of England*, ed. J. Gross (Chicago, 1971) p. xi.
19. As note 15.
20. Sir C. Petrie, *The Life and Letters of the Right Hon. Sir Austen Chamberlain* (London, 1939) i, 17. On one occasion Chamberlain even spoke in support of free trade for the Cambridge Union against its Oxford counterpart. Viscount Cecil of Chelwood, *All the Way* (London, 1949) p. 27.
21. A. Chamberlain to Sayle n.d., Chamberlain MSS, AC L. Add. 71.
22. Ibid, 18 Feb. 1885, ibid, AC L. Add. 64.
23. Ibid, 3 May 188?, ibid, AC L. Add. 65.
24. A. Chamberlain to B. Chamberlain 1 Dec. 1885, ibid, AC 1/8/6/13.
25. *Down the Years* p. 28.
26. Those Liberals who opposed Home Rule organised themselves into a separate party, the Liberal Unionists, in which Joseph Chamberlain and Hartington (the Duke of Devonshire) were the most prominent members. They moved increasingly close to the Conservatives and took office under Lord Salisbury in 1895. In 1912 the Conservatives and Liberal Unionists formally merged, despite the misgivings of the by then side-lined Joseph Chamberlain.
27. A. Chamberlain to N. Chamberlain 1 March 1887, Chamberlain MSS, AC 3/2/5.
28. Petrie, *Life* i, 28.
29. J. Chamberlain to A. Chamberlain 16 July 1887, Chamberlain MSS, JC 5/12/1.
30. A. Chamberlain to B. Chamberlain 8 April 1888, ibid, AC 3/2/39.
31. D. Judd, *Radical Joe* (London, 1977) p. 170.
32. J. Chamberlain to Mary Endicott 10 April 1888, Petrie, *Life* i, 31.
33. A. Chamberlain to J. Chamberlain 28 Nov. 1890, Chamberlain MSS, NC 1/6/10/4.
34. Ibid, 22 Dec. 1890, ibid, NC 1/6/10/8.
35. A. Chamberlain to N. Chamberlain 4 Dec. 1891, ibid, AC 5/3/25.
36. C. H. D. Howard (ed.), *Joseph Chamberlain: A Political Memoir 1880–92* (London, 1953) p. 308; Garvin, *Life* ii, 537; H. Pelling, *Social Geography of British Elections 1885–1910* (London, 1967) p. 183; M. Egremont, *Balfour* (London, 1980) p. 125; A. Chamberlain to N. Chamberlain 29 Jan. 1892, Chamberlain MSS, AC5/3/33; Balfour to Wolmer 1 Jan. 1892, Selborne MSS 1.
37. This was not the only occasion on which Chamberlain did not have to contest his seat. In fact in General Elections until 1922 around 110 seats were usually uncontested. H. J. Hanham, *Elections and Party Management* (London, 1959) p. 197. Chamberlain remained member for East Worcestershire until his father's death in 1914 when he transferred to West Birmingham.
38. *Down the Years* p. 69.
39. Ibid, p. 76.
40. A. Chamberlain to B. Chamberlain 9 Nov. 1892, Chamberlain MSS, NC

1/28/5.
41. A. Chamberlain to Ethel Chamberlain 4 Dec. 1892, ibid, NC 1/28/10.
42. A. Chamberlain to N. Chamberlain 16 March 1893, ibid, AC 5/3/57.
43. Ibid, 29 April 1893, ibid, AC 5/3/61.
44. Petrie, *Chamberlain Tradition* p. 135.
45. Garvin, *Life* ii, 563.
46. B. Webb, *Our Partnership* (London, 1948) p. 125.
47. J. Chamberlain to Mary Chamberlain 28 Feb. 1895, Chamberlain MSS, JC 28/A/2/8/27
48. Memoir by Hilda Chamberlain, Nov. 1956, ibid, BC 5/10/1.
49. The years 1895 – 1903 are the least well documented of Chamberlain's career. As a bachelor he continued to live with his family, and the family's political discussions no doubt took place orally rather than in letters as at other times in his career.
50. Petrie, *Life* i, 75.
51. *Birmingham Gazette* ?1900, Chamberlain MSS, BC 4/2/37a.
52. Ida Chamberlain to M. Chamberlain 15 Sept. 1896, ibid, BC 4/2/29.
53. Ibid, 1 Sept 1896, ibid, BC 4/2/30.
54. Petrie, *Life* i, 85–6.
55. C. Cooke and D. Batchelor (eds.), *Winston S. Churchill's Maxims and Reflections* (Boston, 1947) p. 64. R. C. K. Ensor styled the years 1895 – 1902 'the Ascendancy of Chamberlain', *England 1870–1914* (Oxford, 1936) chapter viii.
56. A. N. Porter, *The Origins of the South African War* (Manchester, 1980) passim.
57. D. M. Cregier, *Bounder from Wales* (Missouri, 1976) p. 69; J. Grigg *The Young Lloyd George* (London, 1973) pp. 274–6.
58. House of Commons Debates vol. lxxxviii, col. 375.
59. Ibid, cols. 432–447.
60. R. C. Trebilcock, 'A "Special Relationship" – Government, Re-armament and the Cordite Firms', *Ec. H.R.*, xix, 2 (Aug. 1966).
61. Petrie, *Life* i, 97–8.
62. J. Amery, *Life* v, 75.
63. Sir A. Fitzroy, *Memoirs* (London, n.d.) i, 97.
64. A. Chamberlain to J. St. Loe Strachey 14 Aug. 1902, Strachey MSS S/4/5/1.
65. Petrie, *Life* i, 106–9.
66. J. Amery, *Life* v, 95.
67. Petrie, *Life* i, 111–3.
68. R. Rempel, *Unionists Divided* (Newton Abbot, 1972) p. 20.
69. B. Holland, *The Life of Spencer Compton, Eighth Duke of Devonshire* (London, 1911) ii, 293.
70. J. Amery, *Life* v, 154.
71. A. Chamberlain to Mrs. B. Dugdale 4 March 1931, Chamberlain MSS, JC 18/18/22; J. Amery, *Life* v, 152.
72. A. Chamberlain to J. Chamberlain 5 Feb. 1903, J. Amery, *Life* v, 152.

73. Ibid, v, 141.
74. A. Chamberlain to J. Chamberlain 24 Feb 1903, ibid, v, 140.
75. J. Amery, *Life* v, 154; Ritchie to Hicks-Beach 7 May 1903, Lady V. Hicks-Beach, *Life of Sir Michael Hicks-Beach* (London, 1932) ii, 188.
76. J. Amery, *Life* v, 158; A. Chamberlain to Mrs. Dugdale 21 Nov. 1929, Chamberlain MSS, AC55/148.
77. L. S. Amery, *My Political Life* i, 235.
78. Ibid, p. 236.
79. J. Chamberlain to R. Giffen 4 Dec. 1903, Chamberlain MSS, JC L.Add. 53a.
80. W. Harcourt to L. Harcourt 1 Sept. 1903, J. Amery, *Life* v, 385.
81. *Down the Years* p. 211.
82. A. Chamberlain to Mrs. Dugdale 11 Nov 1929, Chamberlain MSS, AC 55/144.
83. For a detailed analysis of Balfour's reasoning and motivation see A. M. Gollin, *Balfour's Burden* (London, 1965).
84. A. Chamberlain to Lady Desborough 6 Nov. 1930, Chamberlain MSS, AC 39/2/6. When furnishing his recollections for Mrs. Dugdale's biography of Balfour, Chamberlain again insisted that his father had announced his resignation at the Cabinet, A. Chamberlain to Mrs Dugdale 21 Nov. 1929, Chamberlain MSS, AC55/148.
85. J. Chamberlain to Balfour 9 Sept. 1903, J. Amery, *Life* v, 392.
86. Balfour to J. Chamberlain 16 Sept. 1903, ibid, p. 417.
87. Ibid, p. 421.
88. R. S. Churchill, *Winston S. Churchill*, vol. 2, companion part one, (London, 1969) p. 230.
89. J. Barnes and D. Nicholson (eds), *The Leo Amery Diaries* (London, 1980) i, 65.
90. Balfour to A. Chamberlain 1 Jan. 1904, Chamberlain MSS, AC 17/1/29.
91. M. Chamberlain to Mrs Endicott 5 Feb. 1904, ibid, JC 23/2 3.
92. Fitzroy, *Memoirs* i, 184.
93. M. Chamberlain to Mrs Endicott 12 Oct. 1903, Chamberlain MSS, JC 23/2/3.
94. Elletson, *Chamberlains* p. 149.
95. A. Chamberlain to J. Chamberlain 11 Jan. 1904, J. Amery, *Life* vi, 542.
96. Lord Winterton, *Orders of the Day* (London, 1953) p. 8.
97. Elletson, *Chamberlains* pp. 145–6.
98. A. Chamberlain to Balfour 29 Nov. 1903, Chamberlain MSS, AC 17/3/30.
99. 'The Financial Situation', 7 Dec. 1903, ibid, AC 17/2/17.
100. E. A. Hamilton to A. Chamberlain 17 March 1904, ibid, AC 17/2/35; Notes by A. Chamberlain n.d., ibid, AC 17/2/31.
101. A. Chamberlain to M. Chamberlain 11 May and 3 June 1904, ibid, AC 4/1/50, 55; A. Chamberlain to Balfour 7 April 1904, Balfour MSS, Add. MS 49735.

102. A. Chamberlain to Balfour 13 Oct. 1903, Balfour MSS, Add MS 49735; P. Fraser, *Lord Esher* (London, 1973) p. 128.
103. A. Chamberlain to Selborne 12 Nov. 1904, Chamberlain MSS, AC 44/5/5.
104. Fitzroy, *Memoirs* i, 168.
105. J. Chamberlain to A. Chamberlain 11 March 1904, Chamberlain MSS, AC1/4/5/32.
106. This important letter and the ensuing correspondence are reprinted in J. Amery, *Life* vi, 615–25.
107. Rempel, *Unionists Divided* p. 124.
108. Balfour to A. Chamberlain 10 Sept. 1904, J. Amery, *Life* vi, 619–22.
109. A. Chamberlain to Balfour 12 Sept. 1904, ibid, 622–4.
110. A. Chamberlain to Selborne 13 Sept. 1904, Chamberlain MSS, AC 17/3/85.
111. A. Chamberlain to Balfour 9 March 1905, Balfour MSS Add. MS 49735.
112. Fitzroy, *Memoirs* i, 245.
113. A. Chamberlain to J. Chamberlain 21 March 1905, J. Amery, *Life* vi, 682–3. The correspondence relating to this episode is reprinted in Amery vi, 678–83.
114. H. Chamberlain to A. Chamberlain 5 Dec. 1905, Petrie, *Life* i, 166.
115. *Down the Years* pp. 215–6; A. Chamberlain to M. Chamberlain 3 June 1905, Chamberlain MSS, AC 4/1/55.
116. A. Chamberlain to Balfour 25 Oct. 1905, ibid, AC 17/3/10; A. Chamberlain to Lansdowne 29 Oct. 1905, ibid, AC 17/1/73.
117. A. Chamberlain to W. Long 25 Nov. 1905, ibid, AC 17/3/68.
118. Fitzroy, *Memoirs* i, 266.
119. A. Chamberlain to J. Chamberlain 12 Nov. 1905, J. Amery, *Life* vi, 749–51.
120. J. Chamberlain to A. Chamberlain 10 Nov. 1905, ibid, 747–9.
121. J. Chamberlain to Lord Northcote 30 Nov. 1905, Northcote MSS, P.R.O. 30/56.
122. A. Chamberlain to J. Chamberlain 30 Nov. 1905, J. Amery, *Life* vi, 763.
123. A. K. Russell, *Liberal Landslide* (Newton Abbot, 1973) pp. 98–9.
124. Churchill to A. Bonar Law 6 Feb. 1906, Bonar Law MSS 18/8/13.
125. M. Chamberlain to Mrs Endicott 17 Nov. 1903, Chamberlain MSS, JC 23/2/3.

CHAPTER TWO

JOE'S STANDARD BEARER

'As a matter of fact, Austen without Joe is like Shaw Lefevre without Gladstone – a planet without its sun.'[1]

The eight and a half years between the resignation of Balfour's government and the outbreak of the First World War represent a period of transition in the development of the Unionist party from its roots in Victorian paternalism to the successful role it has played in the mass democracy of the twentieth century. Few, however, would have guessed from these years of internecine strife, punctuated by three successive General Election defeats, that political salvation – indeed the role of the country's natural governing party – lay at the end of this metamorphosis. For Austen Chamberlain, too, the period was one of transition in which he gradually emerged as a politician in his own right rather than simply his father's son.

For the Unionist party these years of strife appear as an aberration when set against its general record of pragmatic adaptation to the demands of a changing political society. So too in the career of Austen Chamberlain the period sits somewhat uncomfortably against the rest of his political life. The man who, whatever his failings, seemed always to epitomise political rectitude and personal loyalty found himself in these years the object of scorn and vilification as a result of his own actions. Many contemporaries described Chamberlain in this period in terms which would have caused surprise to the political generation of the 1920s. 'Shocking disloyalty', thundered Jack Sandars; 'very mischievous', thought Acland Hood, the Chief Whip.[2] Such comments do not fit easily with the politician who 'always played the game.' Yet Chamberlain's behaviour was often inconsistent with his membership of the shadow cabinet and, in more recent times, would certainly have merited dismissal from such a body. After one incident the journalist Strachey commented: 'Can one conceive anything worse for the Unionist Party than for it to fall into the hands of Austen Chamberlain and the Birmingham group . . .? The Chamberlain tradition is that you must give no quarter in politics and that the spoils are to the victors.'[3] Similarly, when at a moment of particular exasperation Lord Derby was moved to pronounce 'Damn these Chamberlains. They are the curse of our party and of the country,' it was Austen just as much as Joseph whom he had in mind.[4] Indeed, one historian, basing his assessment of Chamberlain's character upon a study of these years, has concluded that 'Chamberlain *fils* was as great an intriguer as Chamberlain *père*'.[5]

The explanation of this apparent aberration in Chamberlain's career lies in the effective removal of his father from active political life in the summer of 1906. At that time Joseph Chamberlain suffered a severe stroke from which he never fully recovered. Though his brain remained lucid, his body was partially paralysed and his speech permanently impaired. Never again could he address a political meeting. For the remaining eight years of his life, Chamberlain was a backstage observer of the political scene, still desperately trying to affect the course of events and anxious to see the fulfilment of his political dreams. In such a situation Austen was the most obvious instrument through which the stricken statesman could continue to exert an influence upon national politics. Austen therefore found himself in the most difficult of positions. At a time when he was ready to carve out his own and distinctive career in public life, he was called upon to be a sort of surrogate version of his father – indeed to be even more his father's son than he had been before.[6] This meant championing causes to which he personally was not totally committed and, more importantly, adopting methods which were his father's rather than his own. Chamberlain's speeches, for example, tended to express the sentiments which his father would enjoy reading in the following day's newspaper rather than their author's own feelings. The result was that Chamberlain tended to get the worst of both worlds. He did not really have the sort of character which, like his father's, could attract extremes of emotion in both directions. It was unlikely, for instance, that anyone would ever have described Austen, as Keir Hardie did Joseph, as 'this Brummagem upstart, who had no thought beyond his own personal ambition, had neither sense of responsibility nor sense of honour.'[7] Yet, while he failed to sustain the whole-hearted commitment of those Chamberlainites who would have laid down their political lives for Joe, he succeeded in attracting the scorn and contempt of those for whom the elder Chamberlain represented a distasteful, indeed dangerous, tendency in Unionist politics. To no small extent the rest of Austen Chamberlain's career was determined by the experience of these eight difficult years, as he strove to live down the legacy of his father's reputation and establish for himself the sort of unquestionably honourable image to which Joseph had never really aspired.

Not surprisingly, the root of the problem lay in the question of tariff reform. This was not just a single policy but an indication of a radical direction in which Unionist politics might develop. For Joseph Chamberlain the tariff reform crusade was not simply a matter of economic good sense. Rather it represented the means whereby a wide-ranging socio-political vision could be achieved. Certainly imperial preference would serve to unite the British Empire at a time when centrifugal forces were beginning to threaten its coherence, thus ensuring the survival of Great Britain in the twentieth-century world of super-powers, but in addition, Joseph Chamberlain saw in the revenue that would be derived from tariffs the instrument to secure a large number of social reforms. In this way the Unionist party would succeed in breaking from its Tory past and become a vehicle of radical change, taking it some way along the road to collectivism. This, however, was a vision of the political future that struck terror into the hearts of many of the more traditional members of the Unionist alliance and determined them to wage an all-out struggle to save, as they saw it, the soul of their party. It must always be remembered that the so-called Unionist party was in reality nothing more than a coalition of diverse political forces which had come into existence twenty years earlier on the single issue of Ireland, but which had not really succeeded in establishing anything more than a paper-thin consensus over a wide range of other issues. In fact Hatfield and Highbury represented quite different political traditions. 'Chamberlain', one recent historian has written, 'was suspected of planning to convert the Hotel Cecil into a commercial boarding house'.[8]

With the father in eclipse it was inevitable that the son who attempted to fulfil his vision should now attract the wrath hitherto heaped upon the older man. Father and son were tarred with the same brush and often simply referred to by the contemptuous epithet, 'Birmingham'. For an old-style Tory like Lord Salisbury, 'Birmingham' meant 'the caucus and the wire pullers and the programme and the Morning Post and what is called the discipline of party.'[9] A like-minded contemporary argued that the 'Birmingham mind . . . would run an Empire on the principles of Retail Trade', whilst Lord Balfour of Burleigh was convinced that 'the Birmingham influence . . . was pursuing things which by no stretch of the imagination can be described as Conservative.'[10] Many resented the idea that, despite his physical infirmities, Joseph Chamberlain could still effectively pull the strings on the political stage.[11]

Yet by contrast the Chamberlain name was not sufficient to ensure for Austen the smooth assumption of the commitment, devotion and affection of a large number of his father's followers. His role during the period 1903–05 had already convinced many that he would never take any dispute with Balfour to the breaking point should the need arise. Garvin, for example, believed he would 'go on clinging to Balfour indefinitely.'[12] Many Chamberlainites, had they seen Austen's correspondence of the time, would have resented the terms of deep and genuine affection in which he addressed Balfour. So, despite taking on his

father's position in the Liberal Unionist Council and the Tariff Reform
League, no efforts on Chamberlain's part could make him into the
inspiration Joseph had been. It was not long before extreme tariff
reformers, anxious for a show-down with the free traders within the
party, but bereft now of their prophet and messiah, were chafing at
Chamberlain's cautious lead. Deep down, Chamberlain probably
wanted to play the role of mediator between the extremes of opinion
within the party, rather than take the lead on one side of the debate as
his father's illness demanded. But while his essentially moderate
character pulled in one direction, filial loyalty tugged strongly in an
opposite sense. So, as his sister later reflected, Chamberlain was obliged
to subordinate his own ideas to the task of trying to represent his father
in parliament and in the country, 'bound as much by his affections as
by his convictions.'[13] Chamberlain occasionally admitted the difficulties
of his own position. To Walter Long he wrote in 1907:

Through my father's illness I am necessarily forced more into the position of a
protagonist. I cannot be so much the 'link' between the more and the less
advanced as I was while he was active. Hence my appeal to you to play the
part which I am unfit for. . . . I am debited with all the extreme action, though
. . . my influence for what it is worth has consistently been used both with my
father and with others to prevent extremes.[14]

To Lord Beaverbrook he once confessed that tariff reform had been a
millstone round the neck of his political career.[15]

But perhaps of even greater importance for understanding
Chamberlain's failure to enthuse his father's acolytes is the fact that he
was never in any meaningful sense a political radical. His vision,
therefore, of the sort of socio-economic changes which might result
from the introduction of tariff reform was always strictly limited. He
once confessed that he feared the introduction of the referendum into
the machinery of the constitution because it would 'not be a
conservative measure if applied to social questions.'[16] When more
advanced tariff reformers began speculating on the by-products of fiscal
change, Chamberlain was anxious to curb what he saw as their
dangerous flights of fancy. The simple cries of 'cheap food' and 'work
for all' were enough for him.[17] Similarly after 1909 he voiced serious
misgivings about the attempts of advanced tariff reformers such as
Pretyman to commit the party to repeal the Liberal government's land
taxes.[18] The fact was, as his later career displayed, that Chamberlain
had a far greater affinity with the Conservative wing of the Unionist
coalition than he was yet prepared to admit. As his sister Hilda later
reflected, Chamberlain was 'by nature a born Conservative, desirous to

obtain results by patient and understanding negotiation rather than by open fight'.[19]

Such problems, however, seemed a long way off in the immediate aftermath of the electoral disaster of 1906. The results of the poll were open to widely differing interpretations. At one level it appeared that the country had decisively rejected tariff reform and unequivocally repudiated Joseph Chamberlain's efforts of the previous two and a half years. With only 157 M.P.s returned to Westminster, the Unionist party had been all but destroyed as an effective parliamentary opposition. The list of defeated candidates contained the names of many distinguished former ministers, including that of the party leader, Arthur Balfour. Yet when the fortunes of individual Unionist candidates were analysed, a somewhat different picture began to emerge. Interestingly, the Unionists held every seat in Birmingham by increased majorities. In fact contemporary calculations suggested that the overwhelming majority of those Unionists who had been successful tended on the central issue of tariff reform towards the Chamberlainite position rather than Balfour's *via media* or the opposing extreme of the Unionist Free Traders. It could therefore be argued that in so far as the country wanted Unionism at all, it was the Chamberlainite brand rather than any other which had found favour. Even if this analysis reflected no reality as far as the electorate's intentions were concerned, the plain fact was that, in terms of the internal dynamics of the Unionist party, Joseph Chamberlain now found himself in an extremely strong position *vis à vis* the official leadership. In the weeks following the election a trial of strength began to unfold between the contending Unionist factions, which, because of the changed circumstances after the election, was inevitably more direct and decisive than the sparring that had occurred since 1903. The loss of Balfour's own seat meant that not only did Joseph Chamberlain return to the Unionist front bench, but also that he assumed the temporary leadership of the party while Balfour sought to secure his own return to Westminster. Consequently Austen Chamberlain was not called upon to play the crucial intermediary role he had fulfilled during his term as Chancellor of the Exchequer.

Joseph Chamberlain's intentions at this time remain a matter of some debate. Certainly his efforts to commit the party, despite its electoral defeat, to the full-blooded policy of tariff reform, together with his endeavours to capture and restructure the party organisation, suggest that, notwithstanding public denials, his longer term ambition may have been to supplant Balfour from the leadership.[20] At all events it seemed for some time that no compromise could be reached. A meeting between Balfour and the two Chamberlains on 2 February proved abortive and

ended unpleasantly, with even Austen being 'nasty'. Mrs. Chamberlain
recorded that 'they got no nearer each other and at the end of $4\frac{1}{2}$ hours or
more of talk . . . we all (Joe, Austen and I) felt that it was as unsatisfactory
as it could be and it was hard to see any way out of the impasse.'[21] With a
Unionist party meeting arranged for 15 February, an open breach seemed
inevitable. Not until the evening of 14 February, St. Valentine's Day, was
there a breakthrough when, in last minute negotiations between the
Chamberlains, Balfour, Lansdowne, Gerald Balfour, Hood and Douglas,
the seemingly hopeless position was retrieved. The stumbling block had
appeared to be the question of a tariff reform resolution at the party
meeting the following day. For 'two mortal hours' the negotiators fought
over old ground with the Balfourites objecting to a resolution, while the
two Chamberlains professed themselves content with nothing less. It was
Austen, showing in his father's opinion at least 'great tact and skill', who
saw a way out. His suggestion was that an exchange of letters between his
father and Balfour could take the place of a formal resolution. Jack
Sandars added a few qualifying sentences to a draft by Austen, which met
with Balfour's approval. Chamberlain senior also agreed to it and
produced a suitable reply. The exchange of letters was, not surprisingly,
soon given the name of the Valentine Compact.[22] The result was that the
party meeting passed off without serious incident, while majority opinion
held that the Chamberlains had secured a tactical victory over the party
leadership.

Austen Chamberlain was well satisfied with the Valentine agreement.
Balfour's letter did, after all, contain the crucial statement that 'Fiscal
Reform is, and must remain, the first constructive work of the Unionist
Party.' 'Now all will be well,' he commented. The letters did 'not contain
anything which Balfour had not said before but by bringing together in
half a dozen lines what was scattered over ten times that number of
columns in the newspapers, they give to his position that clearness and
precision which was so terribly lacking in his previous utterances.'[23]
Drained, however, by the strain of the past months and not fully recovered
from the sciatica which had troubled him throughout the election
campaign, Chamberlain determined now to leave his father to reap the
political rewards and embarked upon an extended holiday with his friend
Leverton Harris, the member for Tynemouth. The result was that he was
not in the Commons when Asquith presented the first budget of the new
Liberal government. But in Algiers, where he had gone to seek a cure,
Chamberlain met and fell in love with an attractive, fair-haired young
woman in her mid-twenties, Miss Ivy Dundas, daughter of a Colonel
Dundas stationed in Gibraltar. After a whirlwind romance the couple
became engaged. Chamberlain was ecstatically happy and political cares

seemed far away. Characteristically he readily shared his joy within his family circle. To his brother Neville he wrote:

You know how poor I have always felt that life alone was . . . compared to what it might be in the fulness of the great love of man and wife and yet I thought that this crowning happiness was to be denied to me. And now it has come with a strength and glory that fills my heart and soul and will I trust transfigure life for me.[24]

His life was indeed transformed by a partnership that was to last without blemish until broken by Chamberlain's own death three decades later:

Each evening I say nothing can be more beautiful than the day that is past. And each new day is lovelier still. Yes, I am just about as happy and as foolish as a man can be, and you will have to take me as you find me and put up with my folly for a time.[25]

Back in England Joseph Chamberlain was still riding high, even though much remained to be done, particularly in relation to party organisation. To Austen he wrote, 'As far as my information goes, the Central Office is as bad as ever and in all negotiations between it and the country organizations it leans heavily against Tariff Reformers and in favour of the Free Food section'.[26] Balfour had returned to parliament, but appeared to be a shadow of his former self, and with the party apparently committed to fiscal change, the two Chamberlains could look optimistically towards the future, reasonably confident that the Liberal government, following the path of strictly orthodox finance, would run into serious difficulties within a couple of years. Then would be the moment for the advocates of tariff reform to secure their triumph. All such hopes, however, received a stunning setback when on 11 July, only days after scenes of massive popular enthusiasm at the celebration in Birmingham of his seventieth birthday, Joseph Chamberlain suffered a severe and paralysing stroke.

Austen and the rest of the family loyally attempted to conceal the gravity of the illness from the outside world, fearing that the political causes championed by Joe might disintegrate if the truth were known. It was reported that Chamberlain was troubled by a severe attack of gout, but his failure to attend Austen's wedding on 21 July and, as the months passed, his continued absence from the public view inevitably caused comment and speculation. As a result, far from allaying the fears of Chamberlain's followers, particularly within the tariff reform movement, the family's behaviour served only to cause suspicion and irritation. At the beginning of 1907 Leo Maxse of the *National Review* gave vent to his feelings in a long letter to his fellow tariff reformer, Andrew Bonar Law:

I cannot help thinking that in the environment of Highbury there is a feeling that nothing need be done, or should be done, so long as Chamberlain is *hors de combat*. . . . But this won't do. . . . On all accounts it seems to me disastrous to allow the Tariff Reform movement to hibernate.[27]

But as more and more people began to grasp the fact that Joseph Chamberlain would never in fact return to the political stage, the difficulties of Austen's position became apparent. Garvin noted that

Austen Chamberlain has rather misled me in the last few months. He is a good fellow and I for one shall always stand by any of his name unless they openly on tariffs repudiate their father's principles: but his mind is wrapped deep in the cotton wool of platitudes: and in his will or insight I have no longer one particle of faith.[28]

The fact that many prominent tariff reformers now looked outside the Chamberlain family for an alternative leader was a very clear indication that Austen was not regarded as a wholly satisfactory substitute for his stricken father. The most widely mentioned name was that of the imperialist, Lord Milner. The difficulty, however, was to persuade him to descend from his Olympian aloofness to the less congenial realm of party politics. Leo Amery, for example, tried to persuade Milner to undertake the chairmanship of the Tariff Reform League and this he considered. Not surprisingly Austen Chamberlain did not like the idea and in the end Lord Ridley stayed on as chairman. Apart from Milner other tariff reformers canvassed the name of Lord Curzon, who having returned from the Indian viceroyalty was now keen to re-establish a career for himself in domestic politics, while J. L. Garvin even thought of the newspaper proprietor, Lord Northcliffe, as a possible standard-bearer for the cause.[29] But as none of these alternative champions proved willing to throw his hat into the ring, Chamberlain was left as the nominal leader of an increasingly disgruntled and restless section of the Unionist party.

From the point of view of the party leadership the sudden removal of Joseph Chamberlain from the political stage allowed Arthur Balfour to reclaim much of the authority within the party which he had tended to lose since the General Election. More specifically, Balfour found it possible to escape from the constraints imposed by the Valentine Compact and retreat once again, as far as the issue of tariff reform was concerned, into a cloud of ambiguities and imprecision. It was Austen's task to reverse this trend and reassert the primacy of tariff reform as the foremost principle of Unionist policy. This was something which Balfour had no great desire to emphasise. He argued that, with the possible prospect of seven years in opposition before them, Unionists would be better advised to concentrate on the shortcomings of the government rather than attempt to formulate an alternative programme themselves.

Chamberlain's first approach was to try to act through those who were known to have influence over the party leader. To Balfour's brother Gerald he wrote in October 1906: 'For God's sake do all you can to bring the true situation before [Balfour and Lansdowne] . . . I hear from all sides and from all parts of the country of the deplorable feeling of uncertainty created among Conservatives and Unionists.'[30] At this stage Chamberlain was trying to moderate the wrath of some of Balfour's sterner critics, while recognising that there was an element of blind optimism 'when you pin your faith hopefully on Balfour's doing the right thing.'[31] By the end of the year, however, he realised that he would have to take more overt steps to bestir Balfour from his lethargy. Worried by the 'persistent silence of most of our leaders and of Mr. Balfour in particular' on the fiscal question, Chamberlain accepted an invitation to write a New Year's message for the *Outlook* on the position of tariff reform in Unionist thinking.[32] Criticising the conduct of Unionist policy ever since 1903 and calling for an end to 'doubt and hesitation, . . . reticence and reserve', this article was widely seen as a castigation of Balfour's line and a challenge to his leadership. Jack Sandars commented: 'Austen will give trouble before long, I am sure' – an impression confirmed by a 'very mischievous speech' delivered by Chamberlain to the annual meeting of the Liberal Unionist Council.[33]

Before the end of January Balfour had been apprised of this situation:

There is a widespread belief that in the course of next month we shall see a forward move taken by the Tariff Reform party. . . . The result of all this has been a general weakening of your authority throughout the country. To this weakening Austen and Lee, and Bonar Law, Maxse and Amery among others have contributed and are contributing.[34]

Balfour's response was to deliver at Hull on 1 February the sort of speech for which the tariff reformers had waited in vain since the Valentine agreement. If not the statement of a full-blooded whole-hogger, it did at least restate the declaration of the preceding February. To those of his entourage who were complaining about Chamberlain's behaviour, on the other hand, Balfour displayed mild impatience. Though he could see how Chamberlain's speeches had produced irritation, he felt that there was little he could do about the matter. 'In opposition', he confessed, 'I have no authority and can only give good advice.' Charitably, he pointed out that Chamberlain's 'father's one interest now is reading the newspapers. . . . It seems hard to blame Austen too seriously if he too frequently makes speeches which he conceives that his father desires, rather than those which are more in conformity with my taste or my views.'[35] Nonetheless, on 4 February Chamberlain expressed public satisfaction with the Hull speech and in private began to urge Balfour to open the new session of parliament with a motion regretting the absence of fiscal reform from the Liberal government's legislative programme, especially in the light of the forthcoming colonial conference at which representatives from the self-governing dominions would be arriving for discussions in London. Chamberlain hoped that this gathering would afford the opportunity of progress towards commercial union within the Empire on the basis of preference. The discussions and manoeuvres which now ensued merit detailed examination because of the light they shed on Chamberlain's behaviour during these years of his father's illness.

Chamberlain had already toyed with the idea of himself moving a fiscal amendment to the Address. Though he would feel bound to consult Balfour before definitely deciding on such a step, 'nothing could prevent me from supporting a similar amendment if it were moved by anyone else.'[36] He now warned Balfour that he was sure that if an amendment was not moved from the front bench 'some of our men will, and of course in that case I should be bound to both speak and vote with them.'[37] After a few days Balfour replied in terms which epitomised the growing breach between the two men – a breach based less on policy than on the correct tactics for a party in opposition and on the over-riding duties of political leadership:

Everything which induces people overtly to proclaim themselves in different camps, everything which drives them into different lobbies, everything which tends to the formation of sharply defined and antagonistic sub-organisms within the greater organism of the Party must, in my opinion, militate against the ultimate triumph of Fiscal reform, as well as against every other policy to which we wish to give effect.[38]

Such appeals had little impact upon Chamberlain who determined now to take the matter to a meeting of the shadow cabinet. Yet while back-bench Unionists were vociferous in their support of tariff reform, Balfour at this stage retained the loyalty of a large majority of the Unionist leadership. As Chamberlain had already written to Lord Ridley: 'I believe there is no ex-Cabinet Minister on whose assistance I can definitely count in an uphill fight except Arnold-Forster.'[39] To Chamberlain and Forster could be added only three other front-bench spokesmen, Bonar Law, Arthur Lee and Thomas Cochrane. In fact, at a meeting of the shadow cabinet on 12 February, Chamberlain found himself in a minority of one in pressing for a fiscal amendment. His subsequent action reveals both the extent to which he was becoming the prisoner of his own more militant followers and the way in which his personal situation forced him into steps which he might have preferred to avoid. On the day following the meeting of the shadow cabinet Chamberlain took the lead at a specially summoned gathering of over forty committed tariff reform M.P.s. It was significant that Akers-Douglas and Walter Long — two tariff reformers who were nonetheless first and foremost loyal Balfourites — were not invited, and were reduced to a state of 'seething indignation' by this omission.[40] The meeting seems in fact to have been packed. Clearly Chamberlain was not prepared to be bound by the earlier decision of the shadow cabinet. He made little attempt to acquaint his tariff reform followers with Balfour's strong feelings against a fiscal amendment, with the result that when the shadow cabinet met again the same evening it was faced with something like a party rebellion. The Chief Whip heard that, had the meeting known of Balfour's views, the division of opinion would have been much more marked. Balfour and his close advisers had hoped to substitute some general amendment embracing a phrase about closer relations with the colonies but omitting any reference to food taxes, and in this way to take the wind out of the sails of any specifically tariff reform amendment which might subsequently be moved. As it was, after a 'long and wearisome discussion' at the shadow cabinet, Balfour asked his senior colleague, Walter Long, for his opinion. It was that it would be a pity to have any amendment, but that as one would be moved in any event, Balfour would have to speak on it; if he spoke on it, he would have to speak for it and if Balfour spoke for it the whips would have to tell for it. Thus was Chamberlain's strategy secured and a fiscal amendment to the Address forced upon an unwilling party leadership.[41]

Encouraged by this success Chamberlain now began a thinly veiled assault upon the remaining free fooders in the party, effectively inviting such distinguished figures as the Duke of Devonshire to conform or leave its ranks. 'Austen's last speech has fluttered the dovecotes' remarked Jack Sandars at the beginning of April, while the Chief Agent reported that Tariff Reform Leaguers, posing merely as Liberal Unionists, were 'with the encouragement of Austen and Co.' attempting to capture local Conservative Associations.[42] Once more Balfour's response was apparently to make concessions in Chamberlain's direction rather than to take the firm line advocated by his closest advisers. Addressing the Primrose League on 3 May he took up again the theme of tariff reform and imperial preference. Prior to the speech Chamberlain, although recognising that the party leader had been impressed by the attitude displayed by the colonial premiers at the Imperial Conference, had doubted whether Balfour would 'materially advance his position.' After the Primrose League speech, however, Chamberlain was much more optimistic. Though Balfour had still left 'his "i's" undotted and his "t's" uncrossed', he had made a distinct step forward. When Balfour even suggested that the party should arrange for a censure debate on the government's handling of the colonial conference, together with an amendment to the budget calling for a broadening of the basis of taxation, Chamberlain became even more enthusiastic.[43] Never before had Chamberlain felt so confident of the ultimate triumph of his father's crusade.[44] Joseph Chamberlain was able to write confidently of the progress made by the cause and of the discernible advance in Balfour's thinking on the subject.[45] He could also congratulate his son on these developments and assure him that, as a platform speaker, no one on the Unionist side could now hold a candle to him.[46]

Chamberlain now appeared to be making the running within the Unionist ranks. Emboldened by his recent successes he renewed his efforts against surviving free fooders within the party. Lord Hugh Cecil, the talented younger son of the former Prime Minister, Lord Salisbury, and a cousin of Balfour, was an especial object for attack. Such witch-hunts inevitably roused the anger of more traditional Conservatives, and it was Walter Long who began to emerge as the leader of those determined to stem the advance of the Chamberlainite tide, a development that was not to be without significance for the leadership crisis four years later. Towards the end of July he warned Balfour that, unless something were done soon, the party would suffer a gigantic smash. Singling out Chamberlain and Bonar Law for special criticism, Long asked whether it had 'indeed come to this, that the great Unionist Party is to be controlled by men and methods such as these'.[47] In October the Duke of Portland, a local Unionist magnate, took up with Balfour the question of the hostility shown towards Lord Henry Bentinck in the constituency of South Nottingham – an opposition attributed to the notorious Confederacy, a somewhat overblown secret grouping which had been founded expressly to challenge Unionist free traders in their own constituencies. Balfour clearly felt that Chamberlain was not entirely ignorant of the activities of the Confederates for it was with him that he chose to raise the matter.[48]

Chamberlain, however, while expressing regret at 'the trouble in Nottingham', claimed to have no knowledge of the Confederacy, although 'there are so many mischief makers, always ready to impute intrigue etc. to me.' He specifically denied any link between the Confederates and the Tariff Reform League and asserted that he had constantly discouraged anything in the nature of a campaign against sitting free fooders and candidates who had already been adopted.[49] Yet while Chamberlain was careful to avoid direct association with such a body – in fact its organisers had recognised the potential source of embarrassment – the Confederacy could scarcely have existed without his approval and sympathy. It tended, moreover, in later years to fuse with the Tariff Reform League. Mary Chamberlain, indeed, had been one of the first outsiders to be advised of the formation of the group in the autumn of 1906, while there is clear evidence that Chamberlain had money available for use in campaigns against sitting free trade M.P.s.[50] He was quite open in declaring that he did not want non-tariff reform Unionist M.P.s to be in a position to destroy the policy when the next Unionist government came to be formed.[51] Even the speaking engagements of his senior colleagues came under Chamberlain's careful scrutiny. When he made a formal objection to Walter Long addressing an audience on behalf of the free trader, Abel Smith, Long protested again to Balfour and also took advice from Sandars and Douglas on how he should reply to Chamberlain. There were some things that Long would only tolerate from his leader and Chamberlain's 'patronising style and ... ignorance' were 'really extraordinary.'[52] Long was convinced that Chamberlain's methods would only serve to lose the party many seats and was becoming alarmed at Balfour's 'extraordinary weakness' towards him. 'If he [Balfour] allows A.C. to write to him as he does, it is no wonder that his colleagues have to put up with worse treatment.'[53]

Chamberlain, however, was determined to push ahead and in October he presented the party leader with a detailed programme which he hoped would form the basis of a constructive policy for the next Unionist government. Pointing out to Balfour that although the Liberal government was losing ground, the embryonic Labour party was making substantial progress on the strength of an active and positive policy, Chamberlain called for an end to a purely negative approach on the part of the Unionist opposition. What was needed, he said, was a tariff on foreign manufactured goods for the purpose of revenue and retaliation, together with a tax on foreign corn and meat in order to establish a system of imperial preference. The party should commit itself to a contributory old-age pensions scheme and a policy of land purchase and land ownership. Such a programme, Chamberlain argued, would arouse great enthusiasm and support among the electorate.[54] These 'sheets and sheets of admonition and counsel – not so bad on the whole' amounted, as Sandars put it, to a new version of Joseph Chamberlain's 'Unauthorised Programme' of the 1880s.[55] But they ran counter to Balfour's deeply held conviction that the exposition of a detailed policy programme, while the party was still in opposition, was more likely to produce internal dissension than any other result. Nonetheless, when Balfour addressed the National Union Conference in Birmingham at the end of the year, he revealed just how far he had now travelled down the road of fiscal change.

As he told Chamberlain, he was now convinced that 'the impossibility of maintaining our present basis of taxation is becoming so obvious . . . that I do not myself believe that . . . we shall find any important section of the Party difficult to move in the direction of Fiscal Reform.'[56] After Birmingham Chamberlain proclaimed that Balfour had shown himself 'to possess the powers that are needed in a constructive statesman. . . . He has made a pronouncement to his party and the country which will rally us all to his support.'[57] This contrasted markedly with his private statement the previous February that Balfour was 'a bad leader, not because he funks but because he doesn't and can't understand the working of his countrymen's minds.'[58]

The internal struggles within the party continued to rumble on throughout 1908. In January Chamberlain seemed almost ready to support the radical candidate in the Devonshire by-election rather than endorse a free trade Unionist.[59] Long appealed again to Balfour to intervene. Chamberlain's derogatory references to leading free traders such as Lords Cromer and Balfour of Burleigh had given 'widespread offence to our men.' 'Surely a few words from you to Austen would put things straight.'[60] Balfour, however, remained quiescent, while Chamberlain next turned his attention to Joynson Hicks, the Unionist candidate for North-West Manchester, who seemed reluctant to toe the tariff reform line. Later he complained bitterly at Walter Long being seen on a platform in support of Lord Robert Cecil, a convinced and vociferous free trader.[61]

All in all the years 1907 and 1908 represented a period of substantial progress for the cause of fiscal reform. No longer were tariff reformers obliged to preach their gospel against a background of prevailing prosperity. Rising unemployment gave a clear reason to the working man why a change should be introduced in the country's taxation policy. By June 1908 unemployment had reached 7.9% and it continued to deteriorate as the summer progressed. In fact the monthly average for the year as a whole was worse than for any year since the mid-1880s. The down-turn in the economy highlighted the inadequacies of the country's existing taxation system. With some justification Lansdowne told the annual meeting of the Liberal Unionist Council in November that the party would be 'driven to it [tariff reform] by the exigencies of the financial situation.'[62] Against this background tariff reform candidates met with marked success in by-elections throughout 1908 and Chamberlain was widely seen as exercising immense sway in the upper echelons of the party.[63] Even the Central Office seemed now to be adopting a markedly pro-tariff reform stance to the increasing dismay of staunch free traders, while Chamberlain confidently told his father that each passing day gave increasing assurance of the early success of his cause.[64] The reality, however, was somewhat different. Balfour remained far more in control of the Unionist party's destinies than was immediately apparent. His character – 'a locked Chinese box of paradoxes which seemed to defy penetration'[65] – was, as it had been in the years 1903–5, too subtle for Chamberlain's more straightforward mind. J. L. Garvin around this time compared the party leader to 'an eel in a bucket of soft soap.'[66] The fact was that Balfour, rather than being dominated by Chamberlain, was himself making a conscious and considered move in the direction of tariff reform, sensing that this was the way in which majority party opinion was moving. In other words it was less a case of the tariff reform movement capturing Balfour, than of Balfour capturing the tariff reform movement. Still this truth could not prevent Chamberlain feeling great satisfaction when in November 1908 Balfour delivered a speech that was 'all that we could wish.'[67]

* * *

Of course, whatever progress the cause of tariff reform made inside the Unionist party remained of somewhat academic interest while the Liberal government with its huge House of Commons majority was firmly entrenched in power. The year 1909 saw not only a more stark confrontation between protectionist and free trade economics than had yet occurred, but also the beginnings of a constitutional conflict which opened up the possibility of the return of a Unionist government. Chamberlain's own position at the head of the tariff reform movement seemed now far more secure than it had been at the time of his father's eclipse, with erstwhile doubters seemingly reconciled to his leadership. Chamberlain, in the early months of the year, continued to observe with pleasure and some surprise growing evidence of the authenticity of Balfour's tariff reform credentials. A 'very good reference to the subject' in February was followed a few days later by an even more satisfactory statement at a meeting of the shadow cabinet. Chamberlain had gone in 'prepared for a fight and for another of those long uphill collar strains by which our T.R. van has been pulled along. Not a bit of it!' George Wyndham pressed hard for a tariff reform amendment at the opening of the new session and 'hey presto! the thing was done!' despite earlier opposition from Henry Chaplin and Arnold-Forster. This success was confirmed in March when Balfour made a 'capital speech' to the Tariff Reform League Executive, in which he sharply criticised free fooders within the party while omitting any criticism of the excesses of the Confederates.[68] Chamberlain also made strenuous attempts early in 1909 to extend the appeal of Unionism to an agricultural audience, moving towards the position of including occupying ownership in official party policy.[69] Meanwhile a small group consisting of Chamberlain, Bonar Law and the economist, Professor Hewins, began to meet daily to thrash out the details of a tariff reform budget.[70] The whole basis of Chamberlain's strategy, however, received a severe jolt when on 29 April David Lloyd George, the Liberal Chancellor, made his budget statement.

In view of the place which the Finance Bill of 1909 has come to occupy in historical mythology, Chamberlain's initial reaction to the Budget was in no sense dramatic. As the last Unionist incumbent at the Exchequer in an age when the disposition of shadow portfolios was largely determined by the previous experience of ex-ministers, it was Chamberlain's task to give his party's initial response after Lloyd George had delivered what was generally held to be an over-long and less than impressive budget speech. Taking over an hour to do so, Chamberlain 'only skimmed the surface of [the] proposals.' The only immediate objection that he could raise related to the proposed setting up of a new Development Grant at the expense of the Sinking Fund. Certainly there was no suggestion in his speech of resistance *à outrance* in the way that Unionist party policy later developed. The over-all impression created by Chamberlain's speech has been characterised as 'admiration tinged with awe.' In fact he went so far as to say that 'with a good deal of what [Lloyd George] said and with a great number of the objects which he set before the House I, for one, heartily sympathise.'[71] After a little more time for reflection, Chamberlain conceded that it was 'certainly a "great" budget.' Though he did not yet profess to have got its separate provisions or its cumulative effect clearly in his mind, he recognised that it would affect a great many people and make the government many enemies. 'But I should think [it] will be popular with their party gatherings and afford many good texts for their tubthumpers.' Rapidly, however, his opinion changed. The more he looked at it, the worse Chamberlain thought the budget appeared – and the more vulnerable. 'We ought to be able to make them sweat over it, if you will pardon me that very vulgar expression.'[72]

Chamberlain could not at this stage have foreseen the extent to which the Finance Bill of 1909 would dominate both parliamentary and his own time over the next few months. It did not in fact receive its Third Reading in the House of Commons until 25 November. During its passage it expanded from seventy-four clauses to ninety-six and from sixty-two pages to ninety-eight. The budget was debated for seventy-two days and nights, including several all-night sittings when 'we returned home when the milkman was going his early rounds.'[73] The committee stage took up forty-two days and there were five hundred and fifty divisions. Apart from a brief period when he was afflicted with a recurrence of sciatica,

Chamberlain took a leading role in the debate, attending and speaking on nearly every day, generally trying to slow down the bill's parliamentary progress. The daily routine followed a predictable path. In the early hours Chamberlain or Balfour would move to report progress – a device used not to elicit a statement from the government of their intentions but to prolong the debate. When the closure was moved from the government front bench, the opposition would force a division. When this had been carried the government would be forced back into the lobby to defeat a motion to adjourn the debate. This time-wasting procedure might be enacted three times in a single night by Chamberlain, Balfour or one of their lieutenants with the result that a minimum of governmental business could be transacted.[74] Over the period as a whole Chamberlain's speeches filled over five hundred columns of Hansard, a total exceeded only by Balfour and Lloyd George.

At the outset, however, none of this was apparent. In fact Lloyd George's budget was nothing like as revolutionary as subsequent Unionist propaganda maintained. Though it did contain provisions for a super-tax, a land valuation tax and an unearned increment tax, the scale of charges proposed was really very modest. At most 12,000 people would have to pay super-tax and only about 80,000 would be liable to estate duty.[75] Lloyd George genuinely had little alternative but to introduce measures of this kind in order to find the necessary revenue to finance the government's programme of social reform and the increasing demands of national defence. Certainly there is no real evidence that the Chancellor introduced his budget with the primary and devious purpose of provoking the opposition into rejecting the measure in the upper house and thus creating a constitutional crisis of the first magnitude.[76]

What really transformed the situation was the growing realisation of Chamberlain and others that the Finance Bill offered a serious challenge to the intellectual credibility of tariff reform. It reflected the long standing claim of the Liberal party that tariff reform, since it required a tax on the food of the ordinary people, was essentially contrary to their interests. Now Lloyd George seemed to be offering an alternative means of raising revenue, the burden of which would fall largely on the shoulders of the better-off. The respective electoral appeals of the two systems were only too patent. The task therefore for Chamberlain and the tariff reform wing of the Unionist party was to revamp their own policies, while opposing those of the Chancellor, not as a mild measure of income redistribution, but as the first step in an insidious process of confiscatory socialism against which tariff reform would appear as the inevitable alternative. As Lord Lansdowne later put it, 'We opposed the Budget on its own account, and we opposed it because we don't want the country switched off Tariff

Reform and switched on to another policy which we believe to be suicidal.'[77]

The tariff reformers had in fact to show that the budget merely confirmed their long-standing predictions of the inevitable collapse of free-trade economics. Thus, as the summer of 1909 progressed, the leading thrust of Unionist opposition to the budget passed increasingly from the Budget Protest League to the Tariff Reform movement. At the same time, united in its opposition to the government's proposals, the Unionist party began to achieve a coherence and singleness of purpose that had been lacking for several years past. It was, moreover, a unity that was founded on a consensus entirely satisfactory to Chamberlain, since even free trade Unionists seemed ready now to swallow the bitter pill of tariff reform rather than accede to the government's programme. Chamberlain could even express pleasure when a *modus vivendi* was reached with Robert Cecil, allowing extra-parliamentary pressure from tariff reformers in his constituency to be withdrawn.[78]

When Chamberlain and Balfour jointly presided at an enthusiastic rally in Birmingham's Bingley Hall on 24 September, the party leader himself effectively conceded that tariff reform was the only alternative to the government's proposals.[79] The moment for the nation to choose between the two options had arrived. As Chamberlain put it when moving the rejection of the Finance Bill, 'We are told that it is the final triumph of Free Trade and the death blow to the policy of Fiscal Reform. Sir, in the spirit in which it is offered, I accept the challenge and I am ready to go to the country at any moment upon it.'[80]

The obstacle in the way of Chamberlain's ambition was, however, self-evident. With its massive majority in the House of Commons and with possibly three more years before a General Election had to be called, there was no real reason why, with a little patience, the Liberal government should not eventually see its budget safely on to the statute book, whatever delaying tactics the opposition might employ. It was true that the Unionists had with great effect, ever since the electoral disaster of 1906, used their in-built majority among the hereditary peers of the House of Lords to knock deep and wounding holes in the government's legislative programme. But a finance bill was something different. Constitutional precedent, founded in the struggles of Stuart England over two centuries earlier, suggested that this was an area where the veto powers of the upper chamber could not be employed. Gradually, however, the Unionist party moved itself into the position where this constitutionally dangerous action seemed to be its only course. When Chamberlain and Balfour spoke in Birmingham, a message was read out from the former's father, expressing the hope that their Lordships would do their duty and thereby force a General Election. Chamberlain had already told his father that the government now believed that the Lords would reject the budget. As a result the Liberal ministers had altered their tactics in the Commons, where instead of hurrying they were now dawdling in the hope of being able to delay an election until January, when they could appeal on a new register of voters.[81] Gradually Balfour himself was forced towards the policy of rejection. By mid-September he doubted whether he could continue to lead the party if the Lords failed to throw out the Finance Bill.[82] Justifications, which were less than totally convincing, could be offered for the Lords' action. The government, it was claimed, was using the budget to enact a much broader legislative programme than that usually contained in a finance bill. Others argued that the House of Lords was merely recovering its eighteenth-century role as the watchdog of the constitution in ensuring that such wide-ranging proposals were not enacted until the country had been consulted. At all events, on 30 November Lansdowne's motion that the Lords would not be justified in giving their consent to the bill until it had been submitted to the judgment of the country was carried with a massive majority. In such a situation Asquith had no alternative but to ask the King to dissolve parliament. But the Lords' defiance of precedent ensured not only a General Election but also a constitutional crisis of immense proportions.

Chamberlain faced the prospect of a General Election with some optimism. His election manifesto argued belligerently that the Liberal government intended to destroy both the constitution and the Act of Union. He was not dismayed by the new register, which, because it enfranchised more lower-class voters, had generally been seen to favour the Liberal party. Chamberlain believed that 'the class of voter who usually makes a new register unfavourable to us will on this occasion vote for tariff reform and more work.'[83] For Chamberlain, perhaps even more than for the Unionist party, the General Election represented a supreme test, for never before and not again until the 1920s was the cause of tariff reform so central to Unionist strategy. Chamberlain's influence within the party in the whole period before the Great War was now at its height. Against this background the final result of the election must be seen as a considerable disappointment for him. It is true that the massive Liberal majority of 1906 was wiped out. The Liberals won 275 seats against the Unionists' 273. But the government could still rely on a comfortable working majority in the new parliament because of the support of Labour and Irish members. Moreover, the Unionist gain of seats, particularly in the South of England, probably owed more to a natural swing of the pendulum after the wholly exceptional results of 1906 than to any positive endorsement of tariff reform by the electorate. Many, in fact, were ready to blame tariff reform for the Unionist party's second successive electoral defeat, while Jack Sandars soberly concluded that 'the county elector is really more keen on Tariff Reform than his urban brother' largely because 'the dear food cry is more easily dealt with in the country districts.'[84] Yet Chamberlain, almost as an act of faith, seemed determined to draw the most favourable conclusions from the election results:

Tariff Reform was our trump card. Where we won, we won on and by Tariff Reform. Even where we lost it was the only subject in our repertoire about which people really cared. In many cases ... electors said to our canvasser 'Yes we want Tariff Reform but we want the Budget (i.e. the land taxes) too. We'll have the Budget first and we'll have Tariff Reform next time.' The food taxes were of course the great difficulty our men met with. On the whole those who faced this difficulty most boldly came off best. But where the question of food taxation had been shirked or evaded before the contest, it loomed largest in the contest. It requires time and repetition to beat down the cry of dear food, black bread and horseflesh and to make the people look at the question in the proper light as first and foremost, for working men, one of employment. But it can be done if once our candidates see that they must do it.

Where it was palpably clear that tariff reform had not been a winning cry, Chamberlain argued that it was nonetheless popular, but that unfortunately its popularity had been masked in the electors' minds by the unpopularity of the House of Lords. This was disingenuous on Chamberlain's part and perhaps of greater insight in his analysis of the election results was his recognition that the Labour party had come to stay. 'It is much stronger than at first appears from the electoral returns.'[85] In fact, the rise of Labour would be central to Chamberlain's political preoccupations for the next decade and a half.

Chamberlain took advantage of sending these reflections on the election to the party leader to impress upon Balfour his own ideas about party policy for the forthcoming months. Should Asquith, in the light of what had happened to the 1909 Finance Bill, try to persuade the King to create enough Liberal peers to force through a measure to limit the Lords' powers, Balfour ought to be ready to take office in the likelihood of the monarch's refusal. In that event Balfour should dissolve again on the issue of tariff reform. If Asquith did not take this extreme course, then the Unionists must nonetheless be 'aggressive all along the line' and transfer their tariff campaign from the country to the House of Commons. Chamberlain also gave notice of what was to be his attitude in the constitutional crisis that came to a head eighteen months later. The Lords should stand firm and resist any statutory limitation of their powers. 'If they must die, they had better die fighting ... there is nothing to be gained by committing suicide and to consent to limit their veto to a single session would be suicide pure and simple!'[86]

As far as the issue of tariff reform was concerned, Chamberlain was being altogether too sanguine. Though he was loath to admit it, the cause had suffered a severe setback and, as the economic climate brightened in the course of 1910, so its appeal diminished still further. Warned already that the Central Office hoped 'to jettison the Imperial side' of his father's policy,[87] Chamberlain was being forced back into a defensive position as the critics of tariff reform began to demand a reassessment of policy. Lord Salisbury led the way by suggesting to Chamberlain and Bonar Law, as the two leading advocates of tariff reform, that food taxes should be dropped from the party programme. Sensing that another General Election might not be long delayed, Salisbury asked, 'Is it reasonable, is it possible, to ask us to enter into this struggle except upon the best ground we can find?'[88] Chamberlain, on the other hand, argued that the party had no alternative but to go on plugging away at food taxes until the message finally got home.[89] The sanctity of the cause seemed to have blinded him to the realities of practical politics. He even seemed prepared now to see the party make only modest gains at the next General Election before securing a majority at 'a third round.' But, as others such as the former War Minister St. John Brodrick recognised, another electoral defeat might represent a knockout blow. Brodrick therefore 'pressed strongly that the referendum [on tariff reform] should now be trotted out as an alternative ... to be discussed so as to accustom people to it.'[90] In this way the Unionists' tactical consensus established by the 1909 budget began to disintegrate – a process which came to a head during the election campaign of December 1910.

The political situation which unfolded in the months after the January General Election was in many ways confused. Chamberlain summarised it in these terms:

a financial situation of great difficulty and complexity, a parliamentary situation of unstable equilibrium, a Government which might at any moment be upset, an Opposition which is not ready to take office ... and an electoral situation full of doubt and danger for all parties.[91]

To begin with the Unionists believed that it would not be in their interests to secure the government's defeat in the Commons, but by early March Chamberlain had come round to his father's view that the government should be beaten on any 'fair issue'.[92] Much discussion focussed on the eventuality of the Liberals trying to settle the constitutional question through the enforced creation of peers and the possibility of Balfour being called upon to construct a minority administration. Chamberlain

discussed these issues at length with Balfour on 19 April and seemed
ready to contemplate arbitrary government to defy the House of
Commons in such a situation.[93] Attempts to clarify Unionist policy over a
range of issues produced only greater confusion, and in many ways the
party was fortunate to be offered a breathing space following the death of
King Edward VII on 7 May. Both major parties were agreed that, if at all
possible, his inexperienced successor should be spared the fiery baptism of
a major constitutional crisis, and with the cry of a 'Truce of God' echoing
from Garvin's pen in the pages of the *Observer*, the two party leaderships
agreed to the calling of a constitutional conference in the middle of June
1910. Chamberlain was one of a four-man Unionist delegation along with
Balfour, Lansdowne and Lord Cawdor. He felt 'proud and very humble.
Heaven send I may do the work that falls to me.'[94] But the Unionist group
were gravely disadvantaged by going into the conference without having
secured agreement within their own party on the major questions at issue.
The chief figure on the government side was undoubtedly Lloyd George,
who found Chamberlain 'such a slow and commonplace mind that he did
not count.'[95] But whatever his personal role in the discussions
Chamberlain did, through his notes, provide posterity with the fullest
extant account of what went on.[96]

In the early sessions of the conference the crucial point for the Unionist
delegation was to gain acceptance for the concept of a special category of
constitutional legislation, which would be subject to resolution by
referendum in the event of disagreement between the Lords and
Commons. The question of Home Rule for Ireland would have to be
included in such a category. The General Election, by leaving the Irish
members holding the balance in the House of Commons, had made it once
more a live issue. The Liberals on the other hand, pressed the idea of a
joint sitting of the Commons and representatives from the Lords to
resolve disputed legislation. Agreement, though, was lacking on the size of
the Lords' representation at such a gathering and the definition of
constitutional legislation. The Unionists, moreover, were anxious that the
final settlement should include a scheme of reform of the House of Lords,
although they had failed to sort out their own ideas on this question earlier
in the year. Not surprisingly progress in the Conference was slow and at
times Chamberlain sensed that the government wished merely to prolong
the proceedings. 'We did not attempt to hurry them and all of us with great
décorum joined in occupying time without coming to close quarters.'[97] To
the end of his life Chamberlain could never really resolve in his own mind
whether Asquith truly desired a compromise or was merely
prevaricating.[98] A complete breakdown appeared likely at the thirteenth
sitting on 28 July, until Chamberlain secured an assurance from the Prime

Minister that House of Lords reform would not be excluded from the final settlement.[99]

The fact that the Conference was shrouded in such secrecy and lasted so long meant that suspicions were easily and inevitably aroused among rank and file Unionists. For Chamberlain this was potentially very damaging since the ascendancy which he had so recently and with such difficulty established over the tariff reform wing of the party was once again under threat, as radical Unionists began to suspect that compromise and concession were being offered by the party leadership. By the early autumn Chamberlain had become convinced that a public statement was necessary 'to remove the suspicion that the Conference is a "put-up job" between the leaders to silence their followers and damp down all activity.'[100] Nonetheless back-bench misgivings began to coalesce in the formation of the so-called Reveille movement, a back-bench ginger group designed to change party policy from one of negative defence to the elaboration of a definite programme, which in many ways foreshadowed the diehard revolt of the following year. When, moreover, the Conference reconvened in the autumn a point of impasse was soon reached. The sticking point appeared to be whether, as the Unionists insisted, constitutional legislation (including the critical question of Home Rule), upon which there was disagreement between the Lords and Commons should be the subject of a referendum rather than be submitted to a joint sitting of the two houses. By this time, however, the significance of the inter-party discussions had been transformed as a result of a bombshell from the Chancellor of the Exchequer. During the summer recess Lloyd George had drawn up a memorandum, dated 17 August, proposing the formation of a coalition government to deal with many of the major issues which currently caused dissension between the two political parties. Under the plan Chamberlain was to become First Lord of the Admiralty, but if Lloyd George's retention of the Exchequer were to prove a problem he would retire in Chamberlain's favour. Lloyd George's motives in putting forward these proposals have never been explained entirely satisfactorily. But there is some evidence that he presented rather different versions of his scheme to his Cabinet and Unionist colleagues in order in each case to put the plan in the most favourable light. Chamberlain later recalled:

As first put before us, it was more evident what we should get than what we should give. . . . I know that when Balfour first told us of the overtures we were astonished at George's concessions and someone asked, 'But how can he justify such a volte-face?' . . . But . . . later, when he had fully developed his ideas, we said that it would be as impossible for us to justify our acceptance of them to our people as it would be for him to justify his acceptance of them to his people.[101]

At all events, not a word of these secret negotiations was ever spoken at the Conference by any of the eight delegates. 'In the Conference we all acted by common accord as if nothing of the kind were in progress.'[102]

Lloyd George made his overtures to Balfour and it was only in mid-October, after dining with Bonar Law, that Chamberlain got wind of what was afoot. As Chamberlain understood it, Lloyd George was proposing major concessions on the question of tariff reform, and he felt rather indignant towards Balfour for having kept these suggestions from him. It appeared that in addition to giving a preference to the colonies on the existing rates of duty, Lloyd George was ready to set up a commission to report within six months on what further duties it was desirable to impose in the interests of the Empire and that he would accept such recommendations. Additionally, Chamberlain was impressed by the proposals for the introduction of National Service and increased expenditure on the Royal Navy. He was ready 'to give the most attentive and even friendly consideration to these proposals.'[103] These developments were startling enough. 'What a world we live in,' commented Chamberlain, 'and how the public would stare if they could look into our minds and our letter bags.'[104] But from F. E. Smith, whom Lloyd George had apparently taken into his confidence, Chamberlain learnt that there was another vital element in the Chancellor's grand design. Lloyd George put to the forefront of his programme a federal settlement of the Irish question on the basis of devolved government.

Chamberlain's reaction to this proposal is of interest and importance, but his immediate concern was less with its substance than with the impression which Lloyd George had succeeded in creating in Smith's mind. According to the Chancellor the whole Constitutional Conference was in danger of breaking up because of the refusal of the Unionist delegation to consider such a proposition. But, as Chamberlain was quick to point out, this was 'a complete and I think dangerous misunderstanding,' because no such proposal had ever been made inside the Conference, where discussion had been restricted to defining the means by which problems such as Ireland could be resolved, rather than the actual solutions themselves.[105] The point was an important one to establish since so few of the Unionist leaders were actually privy to the secret discussions. If, as seemed likely, the Conference was going to break up, it was important that the responsibility for failure should not be placed exclusively at the Unionists' door. As Chamberlain put it, 'we mustn't let Lloyd George represent that we quarrelled about the exact shade of green suitable for the dining rooms or the respective merits of wallpapers and hangings!'[106]

As regards the proposed Irish settlement itself, Chamberlain showed a somewhat surprising interest – an interest which gave notice that he would never be entirely at one with mainstream thinking within his party on this issue. He did not 'by any means close [his] mind in advance of overtures upon it.' In his opinion the idea of an agreement about devolution must not be dismissed as impossible. There was a great deal to be said in its favour and 'much is possible and safe as a *national* settlement which would be disastrous if passed as a party measure under party conditions.'[107] The situation was very delicate and Chamberlain saw the need to walk warily, but he was prepared to recognise that there had been a real change in the Irish situation. He suspected that separatist feeling in Ireland was dying out under the pressure of new economic and social conditions and that devolution might perhaps be adopted without the dangers of old-style home rule. He recognised that a simple *non possumus* attitude might alienate many of the party's younger men just as there was a danger on the other side of reaction from older figures.[108]

The fact was that the devolution proposals struck a chord in Chamberlain's mind to the extent that they mirrored quite closely the idea of Irish Councils with which his father had toyed back in the 1880s. To Garvin he wrote at this time, 'I ... do not at all close my mind to the suggestion of a great development in Unionist policy towards Ireland, or rather, as I would prefer to say, a reversion to the line of policy which my father was laying before the country before Mr. Gladstone introduced his mischievous and destructive scheme.'[109] Moreover, many of Chamberlain's circle of friends and associates, notably F. S. Oliver, had for some time been putting forward ideas about devolution or 'Home Rule all Round' as a means of rescuing central government in Westminster from its overload of work. Oliver's letters to *The Times* under the pseudonym *Pacificus* had been a topic of interest and debate over several weeks.

The fortunes of Lloyd George's proposals lay, however, far more with Balfour than with Chamberlain, and the former was not the man to risk the unity of the Unionist party in order to experiment with the seductive charms of national government. In the last resort Balfour was unready to accept any significant change in traditional Unionist policy on Ireland, especially as he could not himself see how federalism would ultimately be compatible with maintaining the Union. This insuperable gap became apparent when Balfour and Lloyd George met on 2 November. With the collapse of the coalition proposals it was unlikely that the Constitutional Conference itself would long survive. Chamberlain was anxious that the burden of deciding what to do now should be shared beyond the group of four Unionist delegates. 'I am so much in the thick of it that I feel I have ceased to be quite a good judge of what our public would think if confronted at once with the proposals to which we have come so gradually and by such difficult ways.'[110] When the government made a final concession that a General Election should intervene next time a home rule bill was rejected by the Lords, but on that occasion only, and that future home rule bills should be treated exactly like other legislation, it was evident that the Liberals would advance no further. Equally clearly this was not a basis for settlement that the Unionists could accept. Chamberlain's objection 'to confining the security of Home Rule to a single occasion and to the absence of any general provisions securing that constitutional changes should be specially safeguarded' was unanimously endorsed when the shadow cabinet met on 8 November.[111] Inevitably, therefore, the Conference was formally wound up two days later.

The breakdown of the Constitutional Conference made certain another General Election. When parliament reconvened, the government introduced a Veto Bill into the House of Lords to limit that body's powers. Without waiting for it to be defeated, the government announced the dissolution of parliament. Chamberlain was ready to fight the campaign along traditional lines. To his electors he promised imperial preference, land reform and reform of the House of Lords as an alternative to the Liberal government's plans 'to establish single-chamber rule'.[112] But the advocates of the referendum immediately renewed their efforts to make the party's electoral image more attractive. Their advantage now was that Unionists inside the Conference and without had appeared to concede that the referendum was an acceptable constitutional device. Now it could be seized upon as a means of watering down the party's commitment to tariff reform. It was, as Robert Cecil said, 'not only . . . a protection from the Radicals, but also . . . a safeguard against the wild projects which the extreme Tariff Reformers appear to entertain.'[113] 'But', wrote Jack Sandars, 'Austen will be the difficulty.'[114] On 12 November Balfour sent for Chamberlain to let him know that many Unionists were now advising a 'temporary dropping' of food duties to enable the party to win the election. Chamberlain was aghast to find Garvin among the defectors from his father's cause.[115] He admitted that food taxes might be, indeed were, a handicap, but 'to drop Preference would be destruction.' 'I wouldn't do it if I could and we *can't do it if we would*.' To drop food taxes now would, Chamberlain believed, invite ridicule and contempt. 'Let us win or lose with credit.'[116]

Balfour seemed sympathetic to Chamberlain's protestations, but pressure upon the party leader was mounting all the time and, what was particularly worrying for Chamberlain, much of it was coming from erstwhile whole-hoggers. Garvin seemed to be offering the support of the whole of the Unionist press except the *Morning Post* and the *Birmingham*

Daily Post for the new policy of no food taxes until after yet another reference to the electorate.[117] As Chamberlain told his father, 'we are all flooded with letters from "ardent" but wobbly Tariff Reformers begging us ... to run away from them today that we may live to fight for them again.'[118] Yet Chamberlain was firmly convinced that, should the party duck the issue on this occasion, it would never be able to face it squarely at any time in the future.[119] For Garvin, however, the change in policy was 'simply inevitable' and Chamberlain was doing himself much harm by the 'fossilised rigidity of his attitude.'[120]

What really decided the issue were the demands of electoral politics. The party hierarchy was anxious to build upon the gains made in the January election in Southern England by making progress in the North and particularly in Lancashire, widely held to be 'the very key and centre of the next electoral battlefield.'[121] It was with this in mind that Bonar Law had been persuaded to give up his seat at Camberwell in order to stand for North-West Manchester, where local opinion had already moved in the direction of the referendum policy. Despite his past credentials as a committed tariff reformer, Bonar Law's electioneering experience led him inexorably to the conclusion that the referendum strategy was at least worthy of consideration. Balfour readily seized upon these ideas, exaggerated the extent of Law's conversion and wrote enthusiastically to Chamberlain of 'Bonar Law's idea' and 'Bonar Law's proposal.'[122] As a result, on 29 November and only days before the country went to the polls, Balfour publicly declared in a speech at the Albert Hall that, in the event of a Unionist victory, no food taxes would be introduced until after a referendum had been held on this single issue.

Hearing of Balfour's intention, Chamberlain not surprisingly telegraphed his opposition, but curiously did much to undermine the case upon which he had been standing since the January election by suggesting a compromise formula. He argued that Balfour should make the referendum offer on tariff reform conditional upon the Prime Minister accepting a similar device to settle deadlocks between the Lords and Commons rather than the government's proposed parliament bill.[123] With Balfour's declaration made, Chamberlain was, as he said, 'broken-hearted'. The two men had been four hundred miles apart at the time of the declaration, so direct communication had not been possible. But this fact could not lessen 'the worst disappointment that I have suffered for a long time in politics.'[124] Though he continued to stress that the party remained a tariff reform party,[125] Chamberlain must have recognised that the cause which he had inherited from his father had received a stunning blow. On 1 December he gave the new policy his reluctant support, although expressing doubts as to how effect could be given to it.[126] But he remained determined to show that it had been a mistake. Accordingly, as the election results came in, showing almost no overall change from the position in January, Chamberlain drew up a memorandum on what he considered to be the effects of Balfour's pledge. He derived particular satisfaction from the conclusion that the Unionist Free Traders had no appeal for the electorate. It was 'something to have their influence and strength correctly appraised and its hollowness demonstrated.'[127] Overall Chamberlain felt that the conclusion to be drawn was clear-cut. 'What evidence is there that we have gained any real strength in the constituencies by this new policy [which] encouraged people everywhere to put Tariff Reform in the background and the House of Lords in the forefront and that played straight into the hands of the Government.'[128] His main concern now, therefore, was to ensure that Balfour's pledge did not become a permanent feature of Unionist party policy. Accordingly, Chamberlain took the occasion of a speech in Buxton on 14 December, before the election was over, to stress that the pledge had been for one election only and could not be repeated, having been contingent upon the government agreeing also to submit home rule to a referendum.

Few speeches in Chamberlain's long political life can have caused such annoyance and resentment among his colleagues. 'What the devil is the meaning of Austen's speech?' asked Lord Derby indignantly. Sandars saw it as a 'shocking example of disloyalty in high places [and] wholly indefensible.' It provided great ammunition for the Liberal press and had been 'the staple joke at our expense at election meetings during the last few days.' He felt that the speech could only greatly increase the number of Chamberlain's critics within the party.[129] Garvin denounced the speech as 'a calamity and an outrage ... arrogant as well as stupid', especially as there were signs that F. E. Smith was ready to follow Chamberlain's interpretation. Someone, Garvin felt, should let this 'well-meaning but most limited man' know that he vastly over-rated his importance to the party and that he had made no impression at all on the public mind over the last critical weeks.[130] Garvin foresaw 'nothing but ruin before the party' if, when Joseph Chamberlain's real power was finally extinct, 'the shadow of his historic authority is to give a spurious influence to the essentially mediocre – though very ably mediocre – mind of his son.'[131] Many predicted that Chamberlain's speech would herald renewed conflict within the party between those who agreed with him and those who held that Balfour's declaration had to be binding upon the party for the future, while Maurice Woods wrote of a 'perfect epidemic of internal difference' having broken out.[132]

Not surprisingly the party hierarchy was very wary of Chamberlain's analysis of the impact of the referendum pledge. Both Balfour and

Lansdowne, in fact, rejected its conclusions. Balfour's impression was
that without the pledge 'we should have lost heavily',[133] while Lansdowne
was at pains to impress upon Chamberlain his view that without the
Albert Hall declaration 'we should . . . have lost many of the seats which
we won, or held, by small majorities.'[134] The Unionist peer was not
impressed when Chamberlain wrote to beg him to think very seriously
before tying himself permanently to the referendum proposal.[135] Sandars
was convinced that 'an intelligent examination of the case would . . .
knock to pieces Austen's allegation' and requested evidence on the subject
from the party's Chief Agent.[136] From Lancashire, where the referendum
pledge had been intended to have most impact, Derby urged Balfour to
stick to his guns. If Chamberlain's line was followed, 'we should be swept
out' and many, including himself, would leave politics altogether.
Repeating the charge that Chamberlain was nothing but his father's
voicebox, Derby confessed that he was 'tired of being dictated to by a
paralytic old man.'[137]

For Chamberlain, then, the New Year started on a sour note. His zest
for political battle, never overly marked, seemed to have vanished
altogether. As he himself said 'the bottom has fallen out of the world [and]
the stimulus to work and fight has gone.'[138] 1910 with its two elections had
been a strenuous year, but the problem went deeper than that. Many years
later Chamberlain recollected:

Worse than the physical fatigue and in part its cause was the intense depression
which settled down on me as a result of the Albert Hall Pledge. To have fought so
long and so hard to keep Tariff Reform in the forefront of our programme and to
prevent its being whittled away or postponed, to have come so near, as it seemed
to me, to success and then to see this new obstacle suddenly interposed in haste
and at the last moment . . . left me miserable and exhausted.[139]

Paradoxically 1911 was to end for Chamberlain with the most glittering
political prize open to him – the party leadership and its prospects of the
premiership – dangled temptingly but elusively before his eyes.
Chamberlain's failure to secure this ultimate goal would do much to
determine the future course of his political career.

Notes

1. Unattributed note, Sandars MSS, Eng.hist. c. 763 f.1.
2. Sandars to Short 15 Dec. 1910, Balfour MSS, Add MS 49767; Hood to
   Sandars 1 Feb. 1907, Sandars MSS, c. 753 f.97.
3. Strachey to Curzon 1 Aug. 1911, Curzon MSS, MSS Eur. F112/89.
4. Derby to Sandars 15 Dec. 1910, Balfour MSS, Add. MS 49743.
5. P. Rowland, *The Last Liberal Governments* i, 50.
6. He became also his father's reporter, keeping him in touch with the political

world from which the older man was now removed. The long series of letters which Chamberlain sent to his step-mother to be read to his father were later published as *Politics from Inside, An Epistolary Chronicle 1906–1914* (London, 1936).

7. Speech in Preston 28 Sept. 1900.
8. P. Brendon, *Eminent Edwardians* (Boston, 1980) p. 97. Hatfield House in Hertfordshire is the country home of the Marquesses of Salisbury.
9. Salisbury to Selborne 16 April 1910, Selborne MSS 6 f.53. When Joseph Chamberlain assumed the temporary leadership of the party after Balfour lost his parliamentary seat, Salisbury wrote, 'Altogether I deprecate Joe as deputy unless he is first tamed.' Salisbury to Balfour 24 Jan. 1906, Balfour MSS 49758.
10. Gibson Bowles to Sandars 11 Nov. 1911, Balfour MSS, Add MS 49862; Balfour of Burleigh to Long 5 Dec. 1907, Balfour of Burleigh MSS 30.
11. Strachey to Rosebery 26 April 1910, Strachey MSS S/12/7/21. 'We have had the misfortune of a great party taking its orders from a man who necessarily lives in seclusion and only sees not merely his side but that side under unfavourable conditions. . . . The consequence is orders have been issued by a man living in a fool's paradise.'
12. Garvin to L. Amery 13 June 1907, Amery MSS, C.32.
13. Memoir by H. Chamberlain Nov. 1956, Chamberlain MSS, BC 5/10/1.
14. Petrie, *Chamberlain Tradition* p. 22.
15. Lord Beaverbrook, *Decline and Fall of Lloyd George* (London, 1963) p. 68.
16. A. Chamberlain to Salisbury 22 March 1911, Salisbury MSS 69/129.
17. A. Chamberlain to M. Chamberlain 29 May 1908, Chamberlain MSS, AC 4/1/284.
18. A. Sykes, *Tariff Reform in British Politics 1903–1913* (Oxford, 1979) p. 224.
19. As note 13.
20. D. J. Dutton, 'Unionist Politics and the Aftermath of the General Election of 1906: A Reassessment,' *Historical Journal* 22, 4 (1979), pp. 861–876.
21. Betty Balfour to Alice Balfour 4 Feb. 1906, cited D. Judd, *Balfour and the British Empire* (London, 1968) p. 136; M. Chamberlain to Mrs. Endicott 9 Feb. 1906, cited J. Amery, *Life* vi, 817.
22. G. Balfour to Mrs. Balfour 14 Feb. 1906, Gerald Balfour MSS 118; M. Chamberlain to Mrs. Endicott 17 Feb. 1906, cited P. Fraser, 'Unionism and Tariff Reform: the Crisis of 1906,' *Historical Journal* v, 2 (1962) p. 163; J. Amery, *Life* vi, 846.
23. A. Chamberlain to Mrs. Endicott 20 Feb. 1906, Chamberlain MSS, AC 1/8/6/39.
24. A. Chamberlain to N. Chamberlain 15 May 1906, ibid, NC 1/27/1.
25. A. Chamberlain to his sisters 15 May 1906, ibid, AC 1/8/6/31.
26. J. Chamberlain to A. Chamberlain 4 May 1906, cited Fraser, 'Unionism' p. 164.
27. Maxse to Bonar Law 2 Jan. 1907, Bonar Law MSS 18/3/28.

28. Garvin to Maxse 4 Dec. 1906, cited A. Sykes, 'The Confederacy and the Purge of the Unionist Free Traders, 1906–1910', *Historical Journal* XVIII, 2 (1975) pp. 351–2.

29. A. M. Gollin, *Proconsul in Politics* (London, 1964) pp. 111–114; Gollin, *The Observer and J. L. Garvin* (London, 1960) p. 18; L. S. Amery, *Life*, i, 298–9; V. Chirol to Curzon 27 Sept. 1906, Curzon MSS F 112/13; J. Barnes and D. Nicholson (eds.) *The Leo Amery Diaries* i, 58.

30. A. Chamberlain to G. Balfour 7 Oct. 1906, Gerald Balfour MSS 273.

31. A. Chamberlain to M. Chamberlain 22 Oct. 1906, Chamberlain MSS, AC 4/1/109.

32. Sykes, *Tariff Reform* pp. 122–3.

33. *The Outlook*, 5 Jan. 1907; Sandars to Akers-Douglas 11 Jan. 1907, Douglas MSS c. 601; Hood to Sandars 1 Feb. 1907, Sandars MSS, c. 753 ff. 97–8.

34. Sandars to Balfour 22 Jan. 1907, Balfour MSS, Add MS 49765.

35. Balfour to Sandars 6 April 1907, Sandars MSS, c. 753.

36. A. Chamberlain to Hewins 17 Jan. 1907, Hewins MSS 50/92.

37. A. Chamberlain to Balfour 4 Feb. 1907, Balfour MSS 49736.

38. Balfour to A. Chamberlain 9 Feb. 1907, ibid, 49780.

39. Petrie, *Life* i, 203.

40. Salisbury to Selborne 2 Mar. 1907, Selborne MSS 5/146.

41. Salisbury to Balfour 12 Feb. 1907, Balfour MSS 49758; Note on Chamberlain's meeting with tariff reformers 13 Feb. 1907, ibid, 49780; A. Chamberlain to M. Chamberlain 11, 12, 13, 20 Feb. 1907, Chamberlain MSS, AC 4/1/135, 136, 137, 141; Sykes, *Tariff Reform* pp. 126–8.

42. Sandars to Balfour 2 April 1907, Balfour MSS 49765.

43. *Politics from Inside* pp. 78–9, 82–3, 89.

44. A. Chamberlain to M. Chamberlain 25 May 1907, Chamberlain MSS, AC 4/1/195.

45. J. Chamberlain to Lord Northcote 24 May and 24 Dec. 1907, Northcote MSS, PRO 30/56.

46. J. Chamberlain to A. Chamberlain 29 April 1907, Chamberlain MSS, AC 1/4/5/35.

47. Long to Balfour 29 July 1907, Balfour MSS 49776.

48. Balfour to Chamberlain 23 Oct. 1907, ibid, 49736.

49. Chamberlain to Balfour 24 Oct. 1907, ibid.

50. B. R. Wise to M. Chamberlain 27 Dec. 1906, Chamberlain MSS, AC 4/11/237; J. Chamberlain to Goulding 27 July 1909, Wargrave MSS, A/3/2. '... it rests with Austen chiefly and I think you will find he is quite ready to give a contribution towards Marylebone.'

51. A. Chamberlain to W. Long 20 Nov. 1907, cited C. Petrie, *Walter Long and his Times* (London, 1936) p. 131.

52. Ibid, pp. 129–30; Long to Douglas 10 Nov. 1907, Douglas MSS c. 346/12; Viscount Chilston, *Chief Whip: The Political Life and Times of Aretas Akers-Douglas* (London, 1961) p. 339; Long to Sandars 23 Nov. 1907, Sandars MSS c. 754 ff. 149–51; Long to Selborne 25 Nov. 1907,

Selborne MSS 73/57.
53. Long to Sandars 10 and 23 Nov. 1907, Sandars MSS c. 754/109, 149.
54. A. Chamberlain to Balfour 24 Oct. 1907, Balfour MSS 49736; Sykes, *Tariff Reform* pp. 136–7; B. Dugdale, *Arthur James Balfour* (London, 1936) ii, 47.
55. Sandars to Douglas 7 and 10 Nov. 1907, Douglas MSS c. 478/8, 9.
56. Balfour to A. Chamberlain 23 Oct. 1907, Chamberlain MSS, AC 17/3/19.
57. Speech in Birmingham, 15 Nov. 1907.
58. A. Chamberlain to L. Amery 21 Feb. 1907, Amery MSS C 32.
59. Elliot to Strachey 15 Jan. 1908, Strachey MSS, S/16/2/4.
60. Long to Balfour 19 and 23 Jan. 1908, Balfour MSS 49777.
61. A. Chamberlain to M. Chamberlain 12 March and 23 May 1908, Chamberlain MSS, AC 4/1/225, 280.
62. *The Times*, 21 Nov. 1908.
63. See, for example, St. John Brodrick to Selborne 9 Sept. 1908, Selborne MSS 3/73. 'A.J.B. hears such a lot from Austen, Walter and Acland-Hood that those three men run most things.'
64. Hood to Sandars 16 Dec. 1907, Sandars MSS c. 754/280; *Politics from Inside* p. 129.
65. Brendon, *Eminent Edwardians* p. 70.
66. J. Lawrence to Short 25 Nov. 1907, Sandars MSS c. 754/179.
67. A. Chamberlain to M. Chamberlain 3 Nov. 1908, Chamberlain MSS, AC 4/1/347.
68. *Politics from Inside* pp. 136–57.
69. Sykes, *Tariff Reform* p. 200; J. Collings to J. Chamberlain 26 Feb. 1909, Chamberlain MSS, JC 22/46.
70. L. Amery, Diary 7 May 1909.
71. P. Rowland, *Liberal Governments* i, 221; Petrie, *Chamberlain Tradition* p. 146; J. Grigg, *Lloyd George: The People's Champion* (London, 1978) p. 194; R. Jenkins, *Mr. Balfour's Poodle* (London, 1954) p. 48.
72. A. Chamberlain to M. Chamberlain 30 April and 1 May 1909, Chamberlain MSS, AC 4/1/435, 437.
73. *Politics from Inside* p. 136.
74. A. Chamberlain to M. Chamberlain 4 Sept. 1909, Chamberlain MSS, AC 4/1/447.
75. Grigg, *Lloyd George* p. 179.
76. B. K. Murray, 'The Politics of the People's Budget', *Historical Journal* xvi, 3 (1973) pp. 555–70 and J. Grigg, *Lloyd George* p. 180. C.f. G. Dangerfield, *The Strange Death of Liberal England* (London, 1936) pp. 18ff.
77. *Manchester Guardian* 2 Jan. 1910.
78. A. Chamberlain to M. Chamberlain 4 Sept. 1909, Chamberlain MSS, AC 4/1/447.
79. Rowland, *Liberal Governments* i, 230; A. Chamberlain to M. Chamberlain 20 Sept. 1909, Chamberlain MSS, AC 4/1/449.
80. B. Murray, *The People's Budget 1909–10: Lloyd George and Liberal*

Politics (Oxford, 1980) p. 176.
81. *Politics from Inside* p. 182.
82. A. Chamberlain to M. Chamberlain 20 Sept. 1909, Chamberlain MSS, AC 4/1/449.
83. *Politics from Inside* p. 184.
84. Sandars to Balfour 21 Jan. 1910, Balfour MSS 49766.
85. A. Chamberlain to Balfour 29 Jan. 1910, Chamberlain MSS, AC 8/5/1.
86. Ibid.
87. F. Ware to A. Chamberlain 25 Jan. 1910, ibid, AC 8/3/12.
88. Salisbury to A. Chamberlain 1 Feb. 1910, ibid, AC 8/5/6.
89. A. Chamberlain to M. Chamberlain 20 Feb. 1910, ibid, AC 4/1/472.
90. St. John Brodrick to Selborne 28 April 1910, Selborne MSS 3/114.
91. *Politics from Inside* p. 208.
92. J. Amery, *Life* vi, 949–50.
93. *Politics from Inside* pp. 255–9.
94. A. Chamberlain to M. Chamberlain 15 June 1910, Chamberlain MSS, AC 4/1/583.
95. L. Masterman, *C. F. G. Masterman: a Biography* (London, 1939) p. 163.
96. The account in C. C. Weston, 'The Liberal Leadership and the Lords' Veto, 1907–10,' *Historical Journal* xi, 3 (1968) pp. 523–533 is based on Chamberlain's notes, AC 10/2/35–64.
97. AC 10/2/38.
98. Petrie, *Life* i, 254.
99. AC 10/2/47.
100. A. Chamberlain to Balfour 23 Sept. 1910, Chamberlain MSS, AC 8/6/16.
101. A. Chamberlain to Lansdowne 26 Aug. 1912, ibid, AC 10/2/22.
102. Ibid.
103. *Politics from Inside* pp. 283–4.
104. Petrie, *Life* i, 258.
105. *Politics from Inside* pp. 284–5.
106. A. Chamberlain to Balfour 24 Oct. 1910, Sandars MSS c. 761/255.
107. Ibid, 19 Oct. 1910, c. 761/222–7.
108. Ibid, 25 Oct. 1910, c. 761/259–62.
109. A. Chamberlain to Garvin 21 Oct. 1910, Chamberlain MSS, AC 60/56.
110. A. Chamberlain to Ivy Chamberlain 3 Nov. 1910, ibid, AC 6/1/83.
111. *Politics from Inside* p. 297.
112. Petrie, *Life* i, 265–6.
113. Cecil to Balfour of Burleigh 2 May 1910, Balfour of Burleigh MSS, 37.
114. Sandars to Garvin 11 Nov. 1910, Gollin, *Observer* p. 240.
115. *Politics from Inside* p. 298.
116. A. Chamberlain to Balfour 15 Nov. 1910, Balfour MSS 49736.
117. Gollin, *Observer* p. 247.
118. *Politics from Inside* p. 300.
119. Gollin, *Observer* p. 248.
120. Garvin to Sandars 27 Nov. 1910, ibid, p. 260.
121. Balfour to Derby 6 Oct. 1910, Derby MSS 2/18. Much of Lancashire's

significance derived from the contemporary practice of staggered elections, whereby it was believed that early declarations in the North of England affected voting behaviour in the South.

122. Balfour to A. Chamberlain 28 Nov. 1910, *Politics from Inside* p. 304.
123. A. Chamberlain to Balfour 28 Nov. 1910, Balfour MSS 49736.
124. A. Chamberlain to Lansdowne 18 Dec. 1910, Chamberlain MSS, AC 8/7/6.
125. Petrie, *Life* i, 271.
126. A. Chamberlain to Balfour 1 Dec. 1910, Balfour MSS 49736.
127. A. Chamberlain to R. Jebb 7 Dec. 1910, Petrie, *Life* i, 268–272. After the second General Election of 1910 the Liberals and Unionists each had 272 seats in the House of Commons. The Labour and Irish members again held the balance.
128. Memorandum by A. Chamberlain 5–9 Dec. 1912, *Politics from Inside* pp. 307–11.
129. R. Churchill, *Lord Derby, 'King of Lancashire'* (London, 1959) p. 160; Sandars to Short 15 Dec. 1910, Balfour MSS 49767.
130. Gollin, *Observer* pp. 274–5; Garvin to Sandars 15 Dec. 1910, Balfour MSS 49795.
131. Garvin to Goulding 16 Dec. 1910, Wargrave MSS, A/3/2.
132. Blumenfeld to Sandars 17 Dec. 1910, Blumenfeld MSS SAN 7; Woods to Steel-Maitland 18 Dec. 1910, Steel-Maitland MSS GD 193/149.
133. *Politics from Inside* p. 307.
134. Lansdowne to Long 19 Dec. 1910, Long MSS, WRO 947/445/8; Lansdowne to A. Chamberlain 14 Dec. 1910, Balfour MSS 49730.
135. Lansdowne to Balfour 23 Dec. 1910, Sandars MSS c. 762/204.
136. Sandars to Balfour 21 Dec. 1910, Balfour MSS 49767.
137. Derby to Long 4 Jan. 1911, Long MSS, WRO 947/445/10.
138. A. Chamberlain to M. Chamberlain 23 March 1911, Chamberlain MSS, AC 4/1/626.
139. *Politics from Inside* p. 316.

CHAPTER THREE

TOWARDS THE BRINK

'you have done most things . . . well . . . but you will do better as leader than you have done as a surbordinate.'[1]
'And above all am I thankful that Austen has not been chosen.'[2]

The three and a half years between the General Election of December 1910 and the outbreak of European War in the summer of 1914 were probably the most disappointing and disconcerting of Chamberlain's political life. Even more distressing than the Unionists' failure to return to power at the end of 1910 was the pledge given by his own party leader in the course of the election campaign to submit tariff reform to a referendum, should the party receive the endorsement of the electorate. Conscious of his obligations to his father, Chamberlain felt deeply wounded by Balfour's move, and it was some time before his zest for political activity returned. Even then, his troubles were not over. Thereafter Chamberlain had to face his own failure to secure the party leadership after Balfour's resignation in November 1911; the virtual abandonment by the new leader, Andrew Bonar Law, of the cherished policy of tariff reform in January 1913; and subsequently the party's increasing absorption in a campaign of all-out resistance to Irish Home Rule, a campaign to which Chamberlain never felt totally committed. Saddened by the apparent eclipse of his father's vision, Chamberlain summed up his feelings in March 1913:

The fact is I think our present position illogical and indefensible, our recent history cowardly and disgraceful, our prospects of winning poor, and our prospects, if we do win, alarming; and I say to myself that it would be better that we should be beaten again and learn in that fiery trial to find faith and courage and leadership such as may deserve victory first and be able to use it afterwards.[3]

The continuing divisions throughout 1910 in the ranks of the Unionist party left it in no position to face the important issues which the New Year brought forth. Though 1910 had seen two General Elections, there was a widespread realisation that the climax of political activity still lay in the future. What had happened so far was no more than a curtain-raiser. Ahead lay vital decisions affecting the Constitution and the Union itself. In Sandars' words, 'this Election [of December 1910] is only a prelude – that and nothing else – and a prelude to great things'.[4] Time was therefore short if the Unionist party was going to pull itself together to face these trials. An attempt to hammer out policy at Lansdowne House early in

1911 proved confused and inconclusive with only 'a general canter over policy.'[5] Chamberlain later recorded:

The opening of Parliament found the Unionist leaders ill-prepared and their councils in much confusion. We had declared for the reform of the House of Lords, but there was no agreement as to the extent and character of the change to be made. We had adopted the Referendum, but even among those who welcomed it there was no agreement as to the circumstances in which it was to be applied. The Budget dispute was ended and the Budget which had raised such fears had become law, but we were now to face the battle over the Constitutional issue which the rejection of the Finance Bill by the House of Lords had brought to a head.[6]

When, therefore, in March the shadow cabinet attempted to reach a consensus on Lords' reform and the application of the referendum, further divergences of opinion were apparent. 'What a topsy-turvy world is it not,' commented Chamberlain. 'Even in my present mood I can't help seeing the humour of it.'[7]

What, however, could not be escaped was that the party had now incurred three successive General Election defeats – each one under Balfour's leadership. This fact, combined with the breakdown of the Constitutional Conference and Balfour's failure to give a clear lead during the policy debates of 1910, served to strengthen extremist forces within the Unionist party. Ultimately this would be a factor in forcing Balfour out of the leadership and also, importantly from Chamberlain's point of view, in shaping the style of opposition which would be demanded of his successor. Not surprisingly, the voices of the disaffected began to grow louder in the wake of the December election. Joseph Lawrence was among those who doubted whether 'A.J.B.'s prestige will ever recover from this third defeat. I meet no one who forgives him his bad tactics.'[8]

Chamberlain, however, had already made his own position in relation to the party leadership abundantly clear. Despite the many disappointments which Balfour had caused him over the past seven years, he would not allow himself

to be run against Balfour for the leadership. As long as he likes to keep it, he stands a head and shoulders above the rest of us. I am bound to him by many ties of personal affection, Party allegiance, and political regard, and though I see his faults as a leader I also know his strength, and I will not join any movement, open or secret, directed against him, nor will I allow myself to be used in opposition to him.[9]

If anything, Chamberlain's genuine affection for Balfour had grown over the years. Whether the rest of the party would come to share Chamberlain's attitude depended to a large extent upon the way in which

Balfour marshalled his party's opposition to the Parliament Bill which the government introduced on 21 February. But for those who had already reached the conclusion that the party would never again be successful with Balfour at its head, Chamberlain's attitude at this stage could only reinforce doubts about his suitability for the succession.

The main provisions of the Parliament Bill were that the Lords should not in future be able to amend or reject a Money Bill; that if a bill were rejected by the Lords it would nevertheless become law, provided that not less than two years elapsed between its introduction and its third reading in the Commons; and that the maximum duration of a parliament should be reduced from seven years to five. Through a rigorous use of the guillotine, the government forced the passage of the bill through the lower house, and it passed its third reading on 15 May. For much of this time, Chamberlain was in indifferent health and in April he and his wife took a short motoring holiday in France. He seemed pleased to escape from the internal problems of his own party: 'Well now, thank goodness! I can leave them to their own devices and they must find their own way out of the wood.'[10] On his return he was confronted by Lloyd George's revolutionary scheme for insurance against sickness and unemployment. As Unionist spokesman, Chamberlain, who had already during the last election campaign committed the party to the establishment of a system of state-aided insurance, congratulated the Chancellor for introducing his bill which 'ought not be made the subject of party strife'. Consequently he and his colleagues would accord it their good will and support, although they would have preferred two separate bills.[11]

No such indulgence, however, was to be offered to the Parliament Bill. By the summer, Chamberlain was ready to make his position clear on what had now become the burning political issue of the day: should the Unionist peers allow the bill to pass on to the statute book and thus contribute to their own political emasculation. This question acquired added significance when Lloyd George revealed that the government had extracted from the new King a pledge that the latter would, if necessary, agree to the creation of a sufficient number of Liberal peers to secure the Bill's passage, should their Unionist lordships prove intransigent.

At a preliminary meeting of the shadow cabinet on 7 July, it was already clear that a distinct division of opinion existed among those present, but the majority view, including that of Balfour and Lansdowne, was that it would be unwise to resist the government's thinly-veiled threat of swamping the Lords with Liberal peers. Chamberlain, egged on by his father, found himself among that influential minority of 'ditchers' who wished to fight the government to the bitter end and force them, if need be, into the mass creation of peers. When the shadow cabinet met again on 21

July, eight members including Chamberlain still voted for all-out resistance.[12] Days later a dinner of like-minded Unionists was held at the Hotel Cecil in honour of the aged former Lord Chancellor, Lord Halsbury, who had rather surprisingly emerged as the standard-bearer of the forces of resistance. Here Chamberlain thundered that 'this revolution, nurtured in lies, promoted by fraud, and only to be achieved by violence, is not one to which some of us will submit now or hereafter as long as the Constitution leaves us power to protest or fate leaves us life to work for its repeal'. The government, Chamberlain argued, had been playing and were still playing a gigantic game of bluff. The Prime Minister had 'tricked the Opposition, entrapped the Crown and deceived the people'.[13]

Balfour's own behaviour, however, did little to smooth over what was clearly a potentially serious rift in the party's ranks. Though he had reached his decision on the basis of his assessment of the policy least likely to do long-term damage to the House of Lords, Balfour was rapidly losing control of his party activists. He had singularly failed to convince colleagues such as Chamberlain of the reasoning behind his own evaluation of the crisis. The latter remained convinced that resistance was 'necessary to prevent a repetition of the outrage now being perpetrated by the Government and is an indispensable preliminary to the reversal of that outrage in future'.[14]

In a letter to Lord Newton, designed for publication in *The Times*, Balfour seemed ready to take a strong line in favour of moderation. He announced that he was prepared to stand, or if necessary to fall, with Lansdowne and that his advice to peers, though he did not wish to dictate policy, was that they ought to follow Lansdowne and abstain from voting in the crucial division in the House of Lords. The letter went on to accuse the ditchers of 'abandoning [their] leader'.[15] *The Times* seized upon this phrase and readily branded Balfour's errant colleagues as 'rebels'. Chamberlain was horrified. The letter had caused him 'pain and more than pain', especially as Balfour had earlier implied that this was a matter for the conscience of the individual peer. Writing as bitterly to his leader as he did at any time during their long political association, Chamberlain argued that this about-turn on Balfour's part was less an answer to the die-hard point of view than a denunciation of their conduct, especially as it was delivered to the press. Balfour's 'very unpleasant letter' had made the position of the ditchers extremely difficult.[16] Though Chamberlain claimed to have been 'wounded in the house of our friend',[17] his own letter to Balfour was characteristic of the exaggerated expressions of hurt feeling which periodically punctuated his relations with the party leaders under whom he served.

Yet Chamberlain was adopting a curiously blinkered attitude. He was being little short of naïve in hoping that the Halsbury dinner 'should not be a demonstration against A.J.B. or Lansdowne or even a criticism of them'.[18] The *Evening News*, for example, wrote unambiguously of 'the anti-Balfour dinner'. Moreover, while Chamberlain now protested to Balfour for apparently condemning the ditchers, his own father, Joseph, was busy writing to Lord Halsbury in terms which implied a very clear condemnation of Balfour, Lansdowne, and all who followed their line. 'In this crisis of his country's fate', wrote the elder Chamberlain, Halsbury had 'refused to surrender his principles' – a clear suggestion that Balfour and Lansdowne were ready to surrender theirs.[19] At all events, Balfour was 'incensed' by the letter he received from Austen Chamberlain.[20] In reply he categorically denied that he had accused Chamberlain and his supporters of disloyalty and suggested that Chamberlain had over-reacted to the situation.[21] The episode led to a cooling of relations between the two men. Here was a classic case of Chamberlain being forced in these years into a more extreme position than he would have occupied by choice. As he later told Balfour with patent sincerity, no act of his public life, save a minor breach with his father several years earlier, had 'cost me so much as this difference with you'.[22]

· As the weeks of the long, hot summer of 1911 progressed, many saw in the struggle over the Parliament Bill not only a fight between government and opposition, but also a second contest to determine the future course of the Unionist party. Sensing that the ditcher cause was making ground, moderate opinion, beginning now to despair of Balfour, began to look to Lord Curzon for a lead. Strachey hoped that Curzon would come forward 'to save the Party from destruction' and prevent it from falling 'into the hands of Austen Chamberlain and the Birmingham group'.[23] Chamberlain, though, continued to adhere to the die-hard cause. Besides throwing an interesting side-light on the absence of any contemporary doctrine of collective responsibility within the shadow cabinet, Chamberlain's stance prevented the party leadership from isolating the diehards as a group of extremists on the fringe of the Unionist movement. But his position was an extemely delicate one. For while his stature in the party could not but add a measure of respectability to the Halsbury camp, his actions were placing him increasingly alongside men who were now ready to renounce Balfour's leadership – something which Chamberlain could not contemplate. On 31 July Chamberlain published a letter which commended the diehard stance for saving 'our party from disgrace and our cause from disaster'. Chamberlain did not suppose that the letter 'would exactly please' everyone.[24] Walter Long, in fact, found it 'abominable' and pressed Balfour 'earnestly to màrk his disapproval'.[25]

The outcome of the constitutional drama remained in doubt until the final debate in the House of Lords on 10 August. The question was whether enough Unionist peers would vote with the government to counteract those who were determined to resist the Parliament Bill despite the advice of the leadership. In the middle stood the bulk prepared to follow Lansdowne and abstain. Chamberlain's fellow ditcher, Leo Amery, recorded the last moments of uncertainty:

For a few breathless minutes we were all huddled together in the Lobby. The first we heard was that 111 peers had gone into the No-Surrender lobby and we thought ourselves safe, but a minute or two later came the news that the Government had won. First report by 11, afterwards corrected to 17. Apparently, over 30 peers, not counting a dozen bishops, had voted with the Government for the destruction of the constitution. Went home very angry.[26]

Such an outcome was bound to leave deep wounds and divisions inside the Unionist party. Renewed anger and animosity could not be avoided. Ultimately it was the position of Balfour which suffered most damage from the party's internecine quarrels and heated recrimination, less because of the policy with which he had been associated than because of the way in which he had led or failed to lead his troops. 'Was ever a Party so badly led as ours was on this occasion?' reflected Chamberlain.[27] But for a person like Chamberlain, whose whole parliamentary career had been lived out under Balfour, residual loyalty to the leader could not be shaken off overnight. As he explained, though he sometimes 'despair[ed] of the fortunes of a Party so led', he had worked very closely with Balfour for eight or nine years and was 'too much attached to him ever to join any combination against him or his leadership'.[28]

Chamberlain himself regarded the outcome of the Parliament Bill crisis as serious but not disastrous. His belief was that the Halsbury campaign had averted the calamity which a total surrender would have been.[29] He reacted to political misfortune, as so often in his career, by seeking solace in the company of his family, and in August left with his wife for Switzerland and thence the Italian lakes. It was other members of the Chamberlain clan who advised early in October that the political scene was developing so rapidly that Chamberlain should return to London. On 7 October Neville followed up an earlier telegram by warning that expressions of dissatisfaction with Balfour and Lansdowne were widespread. 'It seems to me serious, and that now is the time for you to come forward and given them a lead'. Neville had no doubt that ' a difference of opinion will arise some time (if A.B. does not resign first) and you will get your way if you have the Diehards solid behind you'.[30] His sister Beatrice also warned that there would be 'the Labours of Hercules at least awaiting you on your return'.[31] In the minds of all members of the

Chamberlain family, however, there must have been doubts as to whether Austen could cope with this epic task. Certainly he seemed reluctant to see Balfour go, telling George Wyndham on 10 October that it was Balfour who had got the party into a great mess and that he should help to extricate it before leaving.[32]

Whether or not Balfour stayed on as leader, those who had dissented from the Balfour-Lansdowne line over the Parliament Bill now had to decide what their future course of action should be. While Chamberlain was on holiday, Selborne and others had taken the first steps towards making the diehard group into a permanent organisation within the party. The result of their activities was the foundation of the Halsbury Club which began to work out a programme of radical, right-wing policies. The motives of each individual member were probably different, but Selborne admitted that he aimed to capture 'the party and Unionist machine lock, stock and barrel'. It was vital for the club to be well represented among the party's leading figures. This would enable their 'views [to] prevail within the Party, which is the same thing as capturing the Party'.[33] Not surprisingly, therefore, when Chamberlain returned from the continent he was greeted by letters from Selborne and others, begging him to attend the next meeting of the diehards.[34]

Chamberlain had already assured Sandars that his chief desire was to see the party close ranks under Balfour's leadership and he only joined the Halsbury Club on the strict understanding that it was not to direct its activities against Balfour. This was somewhat disingenuous on Chamberlain's part. His motive was probably to try to keep the diehards within the framework of the party and 'to prevent the wilder ones running amuck.'[35] Much of the current criticism of Balfour was, he thought, unfounded. There was, for example, no need at this stage for any more detailed policy formulation than existed already.[36] But the club itself contained many Unionists who were now convinced that the party could never again win an election under Balfour's leadership, some of whom were actively campaigning for his replacement. The presence, moreover, of as senior a party figure as Chamberlain as a promoter of an organisation from which Balfour and Lansdowne were excluded – indeed as a member of its executive committee – was anomalous in the extreme.

No matter how honourable Chamberlain's intentions, the very existence of the club meant that there was little chance that the party's internal wounds would be allowed to heal. As Salisbury put it: 'I cannot believe that to keep alive the irritation of last August is wise. . . . We must have conciliation within'.[37] The impossibility of Chamberlain's position became apparent at the club's first Annual General Meeting on 6 November. He had misjudged both his ability to control the wilder

elements and the effect which the foundation of the club had had on
Balfour's will to continue as leader. At the meeting, Chamberlain moved a
resolution of confidence in the party leaders, but met with determined
resistance from many of the younger members who found such a gesture
'preposterous in the highest degree'. As one of them later noted, though
the club was not formed specifically to oppose Balfour's leadership, its
whole *raison d'être* was 'a definite hostility to certain specific acts of that
leadership'.[38] By this stage, however, Chamberlain was aware of the
imminent announcement of Balfour's resignation. On 7 November the
King was informed of the leader's decision to resign and on the following
day this was made public in an announcement to his constituency
association.

No single candidate stood out as the obvious and undisputed successor
to Balfour. Chamberlain, though, had strong claims. He was a senior
ex-minister, and yet young enough to be able to look forward to the time
when the Unionists would return to power. He could probably have
secured the backing of the majority of the shadow cabinet, while Balfour
himself seems to have come to the conclusion that Chamberlain would
succeed him.[39] At a time of earlier rumours about Balfour's possible
resignation, Jesse Collings had found that Chamberlain was widely
regarded as the most likely successor.[40] Leo Amery later reflected that for
general ability, debating power and parliamentary and administrative
experience, Chamberlain was the obvious choice.[41] But at what should
have been the crowning moment of his career to date, the deficiencies of
Chamberlain's character were revealed. In addition, the difficulty of the
position he had occupied since the illness of his father became once more
apparent. To those Unionists who had fought manfully to prevent the
ascendancy of Joseph Chamberlain within their party, Austen was still *a*
Chamberlain. His political ancestry remained suspect. He was not after all
a Conservative. Garvin heard that there was 'a curious lot of old Tory and
Anglican feeling against Birmingham and Unitarianism coming out'.[42]
Though the fact of being a Liberal Unionist was, by 1911, perhaps not
quite the impediment it had been a decade earlier – Austen was even at this
time accepted into that erstwhile Tory preserve, the Carlton Club – the
son of Joseph Chamberlain was still seen as the representative of a
particular grouping within the Unionist coalition. Liberal Unionism was
one thing – after all, Lord Lansdowne himself was a Liberal Unionist –
but 'Birmingham' was another. Chamberlain's recent association with the
Halsbury movement could only confirm these misgivings. He had
recognised at the time of the Parliament Bill crisis that his attitude towards
Balfour might have damaged his chances of the succession. But 'personal
advancement ... should come ... because the Party needs me and

respects me. I am not going to seek it or eat dirt to get it'.[43] During the struggle for the succession, a junior whip noted that there was a strong feeling against Chamberlain 'on the grounds that he had not been loyal to Balfour. The Halsbury Club business went against him too',[44] while in the opinion of Chamberlain's friend, F. S. Oliver, the club's one achievement was to prevent him becoming leader.[45]

Paradoxically, for those Unionists for whom the name of Joseph Chamberlain was still a guiding beacon, the comparison between father and son brought only disappointment. Austen Chamberlain may have carried the family name, but he was not *the* Chamberlain. The two men possessed, after all, differing personalities. In Lord Blake's words, the younger man was 'altogether kinder than his father, more likeable, more honourable, more high-minded – and less effective'.[46] Chamberlain later expressed the difference between himself and his father in these terms:

I will pick primroses and forget politics for a week. I believe that last sentence sums up the difference between Father and me in our outlook on politics. Did he ever *want* to forget politics? I doubt it, but I constantly do.[47]

Thus, as has been seen, Chamberlain had not succeeded automatically or easily to the leadership of the tariff reform movement after his father's withdrawal from active politics. He once noted:

I feel that I stand as Father's son in a very special way for T[ariff] R[eform]; that men look to me to hold that citadel and yet (not unnaturally considering all the concessions I have had to make to Balfour and party unity) that those who are Tariff Reformers before everything do not wholly trust me as they would trust Father.[48]

Though he had by 1910 done much to strengthen his following, the position had begun to change again thereafter. Chamberlain's involvement in the Constitutional Conference of 1910 had reawakened for many radical Unionists questions about his commitment to their cause. His apparent willingness to compromise suggested that he was too much a creature of the *via media* to inspire full confidence. In short, though too much of a Chamberlain for old-style Tories and too closely associated with the Halsbury Club as far as moderate Unionists were concerned, Chamberlain was too much of a compromiser for the genuine diehards. No section of the party was likely to give him unanimous endorsement.

By the end of the year even the ranks of one-time hard-line tariff reformers were in disarray, as some had been persuaded to accept the introduction of the referendum. Policy divisions on other questions saw Chamberlain's former adherents scattering in all directions. By the beginning of 1911 Garvin was drawing away from the idea that

Chamberlain's claims to the succession were irresistible. It reminded him
of 'that occasional medieval custom which enabled heirs apparent to be
crowned in the time of the kings, their fathers'.[49] At the same time, further
divisions became evident among tariff reformers as they disagreed among
themselves as to the real meaning of the Canadian-American Reciprocity
Treaty, which some interpreted as necessitating a radical alteration in the
old Chamberlainite policy, since Canada had now made an important
economic arrangement outside the Imperial orbit. Chamberlain, on the
other hand, refused to accept that the Canadian action invalidated the
basic policy.[50] So while Chamberlain received the support of the majority
of the radical right during the leadership crisis,[51] his backing was by no
means as unanimous or as enthusiastic as he might once have expected.

As Chamberlain could not claim, at this stage of his career, to stand for
traditional Tory values, it was inevitable that another candidate, reflecting
this older strain in the Unionist alliance, should throw his hat into the ring.
Walter Long was a country squire with impeccable credentials to
represent the traditional land-holding influence. He had sat in the
Commons since 1880, was Balfour's most senior colleague on the
opposition front bench and had held a variety of ministerial offices,
including, most recently, the Chief Secretaryship for Ireland. Long could
expect to receive considerable support from the Unionist back benches,
especially from among the ranks of the knights of the shire. Against
Long's candidature, however, was the fact that he was nearly ten years
older than Chamberlain, was not thought of as a good debater and was
recognised by most of his senior colleagues to combine limited intellectual
ability with an unstable temperament. Both Long and Chamberlain were
likely to draw considerable support from different sections of the party.
But neither was likely to receive overwhelming backing, nor were the
supporters of each man likely to acquiesce willingly in the victory of the
other. Neither, therefore, could look forward with much confidence to
reuniting the party after all the divisions of Balfour's leadership.

In these circumstances, the emergence of a third candidate should not
be seen as altogether surprising. Nor for that matter was Andrew Bonar
Law a total outsider as has sometimes been suggested. It is true that Law
had arrived in the Commons much later than Long or Chamberlain and
had never held office of Cabinet rank, but he had made rapid advances
since 1906 and was one of the few men who forced his way into Balfour's
shadow cabinet on the basis of merit rather than because he was an
ex-minister. Some days before Balfour's actual resignation, Chamberlain
had recognised that Law could be a possible candidate for the succession,
and that if he, Chamberlain, proved 'too unpopular with a section of the
Party ... [Law] would like [the leadership] in exactly the same sense as I

should'.[52] As early as August 1911 Law had admitted to Chamberlain that the two men might be 'more or less rivals'.[53] Yet some sort of understanding may have been reached between Chamberlain and Law to the effect that the latter would not challenge for the leadership, since that would endanger the solidarity of the tariff reform vote, as the two men had both been advocates of fiscal change. If such an agreement did exist, Law, possibly under the influence of his wealthy Canadian backer, Max Aitken, seems to have reneged upon it and emerged as a rival candidate.

In the last resort, however, the crucial factor in Chamberlain's bid for the party leadership was less his lack of support in the parliamentary party or the existence of rival candidates than his own attitude and behaviour at the time of Balfour's resignation – in his sister's words, a 'want of vigour, physical and mental'.[54] At the moment of decision he succeeded merely in confirming the doubts and hesitations of those who questioned his capacity for the highest office. Inevitably, the person who was most bitterly disappointed by Chamberlain's lack of drive and determination was his father, still, despite his physical infirmities, an intense observer of the political scene. When at an early stage in the succession crisis Chamberlain made it clear to the Chief Whip that he had no wish to see a vacancy in the leadership, he did so recognising that his father would 'not altogether approve what I said'.[55] When he learnt that Balfour had indeed decided to retire, he responded in terms characteristic of the genuine affection he felt for the out-going leader. Joseph Chamberlain, confronted with such an opportunity for personal advancement, could not have written such words:

There is the great news, sad news to me whatever happens for I love the man and though as you know he has once or twice nearly broken my heart politically, I now can think of nothing but the pleasure of intimate association with him. . . .[56]

Austen's thoughts went not to the challenge before him but to the sacrifices and hardships which the leadership would entail. Could he afford the position? Could he accommodate secretaries in his home? What would be the impact on his family life? He wished that there were 'another Balfour . . . obviously marked out for the post' to whom he would gladly 'play second fiddle'. If someone else were chosen he would utter 'a great sigh of relief'.[57]

It was therefore more with a sense of resigned duty than positive decision that Chamberlain allowed his name to go forward. As no established procedure existed for the election of a new leader in the House of Commons, Lord Balcarres, the Chief Whip, proposed on 7 November to call a party meeting as soon as possible in order to avoid prolonged speculation and uncertainty. The names of four possible contenders were mentioned, Chamberlain, Long, Law and Sir Edward Carson, but the party whips were unanimous in their support for Chamberlain. Long, sensing the beginnings of a Chamberlain bandwagon, intervened to say that it was no business of the Chief Whip to summon a party meeting, but that the decision about the leadership should rest with the Unionist Privy Councillors. When, however, the party's M.P.s were informed of Balfour's resignation, it was they who insisted upon a party meeting as early as possible.[58] The party managers were clearly manoeuvring for a Chamberlain victory. Balcarres believed that if Long were elected he would 'break down and be such a failure that he would be obliged to resign in less than a year'.[59] But Long pressed his own candidature far more determinedly than did Chamberlain his and began to gain ground. His behaviour towards Chamberlain, of whom he had for some years held a low opinion, became abusive and hysterical – an unjustifiable development in view of Chamberlain's continued reluctance to press home his own claims. At one point the two men almost came to blows.[60] But what was working against Chamberlain was his own behaviour towards Balfour, especially over the last twelve months. Loyal party men could neither forget nor forgive his Buxton speech, his independent line over the Parliament Bill or his membership of the Halsbury Club. Few could have known that Long, though toeing the leadership's line over the Veto Bill, had caused Balfour in private far more distress than Chamberlain, when sending the leader what amounted to 'a bold and brutal invitation for [him] to retire'.[61]

It soon became abundantly clear that neither of the two front-runners would be able to secure a clear-cut victory. Balcarres believed that either one might win by a score of votes.[62] Up to this point it had been widely assumed that, in putting forward his own name, Bonar Law was merely drawing the party's attention to his future claims. Now, however, the position began to change. In the first instance, Law could challenge Chamberlain's hold over the tariff reform section of the party. He had, for example, been in the forefront of the efforts in 1907 to tie Balfour firmly to the cause. But the less ideologically committed tariff reformers had noted with satisfaction his readiness in the interests of electoral success to modify the policy by the introduction of the referendum at the end of 1910. At the same time Law seemed a safer option than the volatile and unpredictable Long. In this increasingly complex situation it was ·Chamberlain who took the initiative.

His action at this stage established in the minds of some an unquestionable reputation for personal rectitude. To others, however, it merely confirmed that political incapacity which would always circumscribe his career in public life. He rejected absolutely the advice given by Balcarres and even Law that, if he were to acquiesce now in Long's succession, he would nonetheless himself inherit the leadership in a matter of months, since Long was bound to prove inadequate for the job. Chamberlain could not close his mind to the fact that, though this might enhance his own career, a brief spell of incompetent leadership under Long could prove fatal for a party which might soon have to grapple with the supreme test of a challenge to the Union. 'To choose a leader whom we all thought would be so mauled and mishandled, so utterly unequal to his task, that he couldn't retain the post for six months would be disastrous to the Party and to our cause, and I could have nothing to do with it'.[63] Instead Chamberlain decided to write to Long and stress that serious fissures would emerge in the party's ranks if the choice between the two men were allowed to go to the indignity of a vote. His proposal, therefore, was that both candidates should retire from the contest in favour of Bonar Law.[64] Placed in a position where a refusal would confirm nothing but his own self-interested ambition, Long had no alternative but to follow suit and support the claims of Law. This startling development took the supporters of both Chamberlain and Long by surprise. In the whips' office Bridgeman could not 'understand . . . why the two first choices agreed to give way'.[65]

In such circumstances the election of Andrew Bonar Law proved a mere formality. After the weekend had allowed a chance for the turmoil of the previous days to subside, the party meeting on 13 November passed without incident. Long's opening speech, 'a masterpiece of plain speaking and noble devotion to the best interests of the Party and Country', set the tone.[66] Chamberlain then seconded the proposal that Law be chosen as party leader. Lansdowne agreed to remain as leader in the Lords, thus helping to minimise the impression that Balfour had been ousted by diehard agitation and, by adding an element of continuity, to make the party's reunification more likely.

Chamberlain's attitude towards what had happened was strangely equivocal. He clearly felt resentful towards Law for having pressed his candidature. 'I don't think that if our positions had been reversed I could have acted as he did.'[67] In private he made it plain to Law that he did not necessarily regard the decision as final and that, should the occasion arise, he would have no hesitation in standing again for the party leadership.[68] In fact, Chamberlain never attempted to challenge Law's position, though he did come near to breaking with him over the question of food taxes in the winter of 1912–13. But the episode did serve to colour Chamberlain's attitude towards Law throughout his leadership of the party. The two men were never again as close as they had been when fighting together for the cause of tariff reform. On the other hand, Chamberlain admitted that, save for one thought, the outcome of the crisis was an 'unmixed relief' for him. That one thought was the realisation that his failure would be a source of immense disappointment to his father.[69] Garvin 'seemed to hear great heartstrings snapping at last in Joe and I would have given my life to save him from going down uncomforted to the grave.'[70]

* * *

The motives which determined Chamberlain's course of action during the leadership crisis of 1911 are obviously varied and complex. Certainly, the belief that he was putting the interests of the party before his own political ambition was an important factor which should not be ignored. He was convinced that he could not secure the full support of the party and that this would be damaging to Unionism itself.[71] There was truth in this. His election in 1911 might well have split the party in two a year later at the time of the food tax controversy. Financial considerations – something which Chamberlain had to bear in mind throughout his political life – have also been mentioned. Yet he did express the belief that had he been prepared to pursue his claim he would ultimately have secured victory 'at the second ballot by a small majority'.[72] This was despite his determination to stand aloof from anything which resembled campaigning. Above all else, however, the impression remains that deep down Chamberlain did not have the stomach for the sort of political inheritance which now fell to Bonar Law. The fact was, as all Unionists realised, that the survival of the Liberal government was now dependent less upon its own vitality than upon the support of the Irish members at Westminster – a support which was not freely offered, but bartered in exchange for the pledge of a third Home Rule Bill. This thunder cloud on the legislative horizon threatened the Unionist party to its very core. To the Union with Ireland the party owed not only its name but its primary *raison d'être*. Whoever succeeded Balfour would therefore take on the leadership at a crucial and perhaps decisive moment in the party's history. This was not the sort of role for which Chamberlain clamoured. He would have been prepared to accept the leadership, had it been offered to him on a plate. But he 'lacked that ultimate hardness without which men seldom reach supreme political power'.[73] It was not that he had a low opinion of himself – quite the contrary. But he had a particular fear that anyone should regard him as intent on personal advancement. 'Freud', wrote Leo Amery, 'might see some sort of latent anti-father complex. . . . There was in him none of Churchill's ready assertion of a conscious fitness to lead'.[74]

Lacking total confidence in Bonar Law's abilities, Chamberlain told his father that 'I must do my best to keep (or get) an influence over his mind'.[75] Yet in the months which followed Law's election to the leadership a distinct waning in Chamberlain's influence within the party became apparent. This reflected a loss of will on Chamberlain's part after yet another body blow to his political hopes. It mirrored also a changing focus and emphasis in Unionist politics as the Chamberlainite flame began to flicker less brightly. Additionally, Law, drawing from the experience of his predecessor, soon determined that the shadow cabinet was likely to give more trouble than it was worth and tended to summon it with growing infrequency, thereby denying Chamberlain a forum in which to put his views.[76] By 1912, moreover, the focus of the party's attention was riveted firmly on the question of the Union as the government proceeded to introduce its Home Rule Bill. Over this issue Law turned increasingly to men such as Edward Carson and F. E. Smith whose views coincided more closely with his own than did Chamberlain's. The latter could 'not help but feel that [Law] had withdrawn some part of his confidence from me'.[77] But the factor which really signalled the eclipse of Chamberlainite power was a further internal party wrangle over the question of food taxes.

Chamberlain had been careful during the succession crisis itself to make his own position on tariff reform absolutely clear. Before he or anyone else could be chosen to succeed Balfour, Chamberlain re-emphasised that he personally was no longer bound by Balfour's Albert Hall pledge of a year earlier.[78] He then took pains to bring this fact to Law's attention soon after the latter became leader.[79] But in view of Law's credentials as a committed tariff reformer, Chamberlain had good grounds for believing that, despite Law's hesitation when a candidate in Manchester, the party would now take a more decisive stance in favour of tariff reform than at any time before. As he said to Garvin, 'the things we both care about won't suffer by the choice that has been made'.[80] Indeed, Chamberlain later ruefully reflected that 'it had been my consolation when Long and I withdrew our names and proposed Bonar Law as leader that he had made his reputation by his Tariff Reform speeches and that the cause was safe in his hands'.[81]

Other party figures, however, saw the accession of a new leader as providing the opportunity for relieving the party once and for all of the electoral incubus of food taxes. During the first weeks of 1912, therefore, Law was subjected to a barrage of advice over future policy, with both Long and Lansdowne pressing for the retention of the referendum pledge. Law showed signs of accepting this advice and asked Chamberlain whether he would mind if Law agreed to commit a future Unionist government to submit a tariff reform budget to a referendum, providing Asquith agreed at this late stage on the same course in relation to home rule.[82] This showed not only that Law, conscious that food taxes were a liability, had ceased to be the unquestioning champion of imperial preference that Chamberlain had imagined, but also that the leader agreed with majority opinion in his party that tariff reform could not compare in importance with the imminent threat to the Union. In this shift of party opinion Chamberlain, still pursuing an ideological crusade of filial piety rather than an exercise in practical politics, had been left behind. He made it clear that he could not acquiesce in any such declaration by Law which would 'lead to great trouble'. On this subject Chamberlain had 'burned my boats before you were leader and I cannot unsay what I have publicly stated'.[83] But the most that Chamberlain was able to extract from Law was a promise that he would make no change in the party's tariff policy without first obtaining Chamberlain's assent. Not, however, until the end of February did the matter come before the shadow cabinet for a definite decision.

Chamberlain was confident of success 'though not without some expenditure of time and trouble'.[84] In fact, by the time the shadow cabinet met, Chamberlain's arguments had gained considerable support and the decision to drop the referendum pledge was taken with only Londonderry and Derby dissenting. Law was still reluctant to make any definite statement to this effect, as he wished to avoid doing anything which might resemble a public repudiation of Balfour. But under pressure from Chamberlain he agreed that he would 'find some formula which would make the position perfectly clear.'[85] Yet despite these decisions the debate continued within the party throughout the spring and summer of 1912, and still the explicit statement was not made by the leadership. By the autumn, Lansdowne had become convinced that further delay was impossible and, as he had been privy to Balfour's original declaration, it was agreed that he should make the necessary statement. Accordingly, on 14 November at a meeting of the National Union in the Albert Hall, Lansdowne made public the repudiation of the referendum pledge, as agreed by the shadow cabinet nearly nine months earlier. In the wake of what seemed the definitive pronouncement on the subject, Chamberlain breathed a premature sigh of relief:

Lansdowne spoke admirably at the Albert Hall and disposed of the Referendum most neatly. So that is off my mind, but if you knew how often Law has doubted and hesitated since our decision was taken just after he was made leader, you would know what a weight is off my mind. These declarations were to have been made nearly a year ago and were very nearly *not* made this week.[86]

In other quarters, however, Lansdowne's Albert Hall speech caused nothing but dismay. Law and Lansdowne had apparently judged that in bowing to Chamberlain's point of view they were taking the line least likely to cause internal party dissension. In this they were mistaken. The crisis that now ensued revealed that very few Unionist M.P.s still regarded the whole-hogger programme as a piece of holy writ as Chamberlain did. Majority opinion had reached the conclusion that the party would never win another General Election while the full tariff policy remained unaltered. In the aftermath of Lansdowne's speech, this shift of opinion became only too clear. Chamberlain noted that 'in a few weeks . . . the revolt had become general; the panic had spread to all but a few stalwarts'.[87] What he was observing was not so much a massive desertion from the tariff reform camp but the vociferous expression of fear at the prospect of continued electoral damnation.

Chamberlain seemed oblivious of this fundamental truth. He admitted that 'we have got a bad quarter of an hour to go through', but urged Law to stand firm and suggested a six weeks' campaign to educate the party to the whole-hogger point of view.[88] 'For Heaven's sake', he pleaded, 'don't let us allow a frightened crew to knock the captain on the head and put about! If we do, the party is d——d and deserves it'.[89] Law's nerve, though, was clearly beginning to fail. A major speech by the leader at Ashton, designed to clarify the position, served only to intensify dissatisfaction and uncertainty. By the end of the year Chamberlain was 'very concerned' at 'the most serious stampede there [had] ever been on the question'.[90] Law doubted the possibility of succeeding in the course which Chamberlain wanted him to take. He had become convinced that party policy would have to be modified again but questioned whether this modification would be feasible under his leadership. Law therefore proposed to summon a party meeting and resign. The problem was that if he did so, there was no-one likely to be able to lead the party through the stern parliamentary battles which lay ahead. Chamberlain could scarcely step in as the inheritor of a tariff policy which had forced Law to resign, especially since his parliamentary following had dwindled even since the leadership contest of a year earlier.

The difficulty, therefore, was to arrange for Law a dignified line of retreat. Accordingly, Goulding proposed that a Memorial be drawn up asking Law to postpone food duties until after a further reference to the people, but to retain the leadership. In vain Chamberlain protested. The adoption of this line would 'cover Tariff Reformers with ridicule and destroy every shred of character with which we are yet blessed'.[91] The tide, however, was running strongly against Chamberlain. He refused to sign the Memorial, but in fact no front-benchers were asked to do so and on the backbenches support was overwhelming. Leo Amery believed that had Chamberlain held out and urged his followers to reject the Memorial, he would have secured a large measure of support.[92] This was almost certainly not the case. Notwithstanding a hard-core of irreconcilable zealots, the vast majority of Unionist M.P.s cared infinitely more for saving the Union than for establishing a system of preference. For this primary task, moreover, they had become convinced that Law's continued presence at their head was imperative. Chamberlain's attitude, on the other hand, was much more equivocal. 'If I had to choose between Home Rule and Tariff Reform', he once said, 'I presume that I should try to defeat Home Rule first and to secure T.R. afterwards'. But since he continued to regard tariff reform as the Unionists' only trump card, no such choice really existed in his mind.[93] But Amery's opinion is significant for the light it throws on the decline in Chamberlain's standing among his former supporters. Amery believed that it was his 'fatal oversensitiveness to the idea that he might be thought disloyal, or endanger party unity', which had stood in his way.[94] Certainly in the last stages of the crisis Chamberlain seemed to give up hope and 'would do nothing to dissuade men from signing' the Memorial.[95]

Characteristically, Chamberlain made no attempt to make life more difficult for Law at this awkward moment in his leadership. Indeed he insisted that Law did not have the right to withdraw from the leader's position at this time.[96] Speaking in his Birmingham constituency Chamberlain was at pains to distance himself from the new policy while professing personal loyalty to the leader:

for the first time in my long connection with it, for the first time in the eleven years that I have been permitted to sit in the councils of the Party, I am unable to take any share of responsibility for the decision to which they have come. I cannot turn my back upon myself. . . . But I have been too long engaged in politics . . . to sulk because I cannot now persuade the Party to take . . . the right course and the wise course. . . . I will do my best in the future as I have done my best in the past to support my leaders and to cooperate with my political friends.[97]

Yet in private it was clear that Chamberlain's view of Bonar Law, already damaged by the events of November 1911, had been further clouded. He remained convinced that Law could have saved the day if he had taken the initiative rather than allowing himself to be pressurised by others. His tendency to be generally critical of Law's leadership now became more apparent. In Law, as in Balfour before, Chamberlain sensed what he regarded as the false notion that Unionists could win simply on the faults of their opponents. But his relationship with Law lacked the compensating factor of personal affection which had ever coloured his attitude towards Balfour. In March he wrote:

The fact is that whatever else has happened Law has lost prestige. It has been a great disappointment to me for, though I never thought him strong, I never suspected him of so much weakness and did not think that his weakness, whatever it was, could show itself in this way. He makes very effective speeches up to a point, but it does not seem to me that he thinks any question out or that his judgement is good. . . . I will do my best for him but I am not called upon to shoulder his mistakes to the same extent that I defended Balfour . . . and indeed I do not think that it would be right for me to do it.[98]

There was no escaping that Chamberlain was 'bitterly disappointed and very depressed'.[99] His 'dearest political hopes and personal affections [had] received from fate a cruel blow'.[100] He was very unhappy about the party's prospects, fearing that the new tariff policy combined all the disadvantages and none of the comforts of either extreme. 'It is the half-way house policy which never saved anyone or anything.'[101] In theory the party was still ultimately pledged to the full policy, providing public approval was forthcoming, but in Chamberlain's view, if the Unionists did not face up to food taxes immediately on coming into office, they were scarcely likely to grasp that nettle three or four years later.[102] For this reason Chamberlain could see no alternative to 'going full steam ahead' with food taxes, but that was no longer possible.[103]

For a while he seemed ready to withdraw altogether from public life. He had 'tried for years to get other men to adopt [his] policy . . . but . . . had failed and was now tired of trying'.[104] His position was not strong. For several years he had urged free-fooders to yield to majority opinion in the party. Now it was his turn to find himself in a minority. By April he was wondering 'how long it would be possible for me to remain a Party man. I am weary to death of these constant troubles and should be far happier if I were quit of a Party who seem to me determined to ruin their own fortunes and most of what I hold dear with them!'[105] Though he wanted to kill the Home Rule Bill he had doubts about defeating the government since 'we should be in the most awful mess if we came in'.[106] Thoroughly discouraged by what he saw as the mis-management of the party's affairs, he did his public work without pleasure or satisfaction.[107] Even what was supposed to be a definitive speech by Law in Edinburgh on the theme of tariff reform failed to heal the wounds. But symbolic of the broader failure of Chamberlain's mission in politics was the decision of his father to stand down from parliament at the next election. This conclusion was inevitable and overdue. Though the elder Chamberlain had made some recovery from his stroke, his speech remained largely unintelligible and, more recently, his eyesight had begun to fail. It had been Chamberlain's dearest wish to secure the fulfilment of his father's dream during his lifetime. Now, evidently, this was not to be.

'Do you wonder', wrote Chamberlain in April 1913, 'that politics have lost their charm?'[108] The times were not conducive to such moods of introspection and self-pity. For the first time since 1903 a new issue had begun to replace tariff reform as the focal point in Unionist politics and, if Chamberlain were to take any continuing part in public life, this was a matter which he could not ignore. Yet while the Irish question tended on the whole to bring Unionists closer together as they rallied in defence of the central tenet of their political creed, its effect on Chamberlain was in some ways the reverse. Though himself deeply opposed to the government's proposals, Chamberlain found himself, on this matter, as on tariff reform, increasingly at odds with the party leadership.

The re-emergence of Ireland as a live issue in British public life was almost entirely the function of electoral politics. Less than a year into the life of the Liberal government, Chamberlain had commented that 'just now, for an Englishman at any rate, a speech on Home Rule is like flogging a dead horse'.[109] That, however, was at a time when the Liberal government with its massive majority in the House of Commons had no need for the votes of Irish members of parliament. The General Elections of 1910, though, effectively recreated the parliamentary situation of 1886 and 1892 by leaving the Liberals dependent on Irish support for their continuance in office. That support was only forthcoming once the government had committed itself to the introduction of a third Home Rule Bill. Yet in another aspect the situation after 1910 was markedly different from that of 1886 or 1892. With the passing of the Parliament Act in 1911 it became clear that Asquith's Home Rule Bill would not, indeed could not, meet its demise at the hands of a Unionist-dominated House of Lords, as had Gladstone's second bill. Indeed it was now possible to calculate with an almost eerie precision the bill's path on to the statute book. No matter what action the House of Lords took, it seemed that no constitutional device could prevent Ireland becoming self-governing by the summer of 1914. As a result, Irish politics came to dominate the whole of the political scene from 1912 onwards. One Unionist noted:

In the first place everything except the Irish question became absolutely dull and all other business . . . was quite perfunctory. Our leaders would or could think of nothing but Ireland . . . .[110]

In the face of this seemingly irresistible challenge from the Liberal government, the tendency in Unionist politics was towards extremism. If no constitutional means offered the hope of salvation and if, as was claimed, the government itself was behaving irresponsibly and unconstitutionally, then extra-constitutional action was the only way in which Unionists could save the cause which meant so much to them. At times, the party seemed ready to challenge the accepted conventions of democratic government, to countenance armed insurrection and to defy the expressed will of parliament. Bonar Law's accession to the leadership coincided with a marked ascendancy of die-hard and right-wing elements in the party. Many of the same men who had fought to the last to preserve the ancient powers of the House of Lords were now in the vanguard of the drive to defend the Union. In Bonar Law, moreover, they found a leader who, whatever his private misgivings, was prepared to sally forth and deliver hard, and if need be low, blows at the government. Where Balfour had equivocated, Law struck.

Chamberlain, however, despite his earlier association with the diehard movement, found it difficult to accept this drift towards unconstitutional action. While his father hoped that the party would pull no punches, the son, an inherent conservative, was filled with misgivings. The Irish issue also gave him further scope for his increasingly critical attitude towards Bonar Law's leadership. He found Law's behaviour 'rash' and his language 'dangerous'.[111] Chamberlain had first indicated that he might take an independent line over the Irish question at the time of the Constitutional Conference in 1910. Then he had appeared ready to accept a scheme of devolution as a possible new departure to resolve the Irish impasse, but had failed to carry his leading colleagues along this road.

When the Irish problem became acute following the introduction of the Home Rule Bill in the spring of 1912, Chamberlain seemed for a while ready to follow the line of the party leadership. Like many other Unionists, he saw that Ulster might be the rock upon which the government's proposals would come to grief. In the first instance the Protestant and Loyalist ascendancy in Ulster meant that the government's proposals genuinely seemed most iniquitous when applied to that province. Yet if Ulster with its commercial and industrial potential were removed from a self-governing Ireland, the rump state might prove unviable and Home Rule itself be thereby destroyed. Rejecting the idea that he differed from Law on this question, though 'I should have expressed myself differently', Chamberlain argued that Ulster would be right to resist and that her resistance would be successful if Ulstermen kept cool, resolute and, so far as possible, silent as to their exact intentions. 'The cooler, nay the colder, the resolution of Ulster is, the more impressive it will be and the more terrifying to the Government.'[112] He was concerned that F. E. Smith seemed to regard the Ulster Covenant, by which Unionists took a solemn vow to resist the imposition of Home Rule, as something of a game.[113] But he still had doubts 'about the desirability of indicating that opposition . . . might . . . go beyond the limits of ordinary constitutional action'.[114]

As the months passed, however, Chamberlain became increasingly alarmed at the seemingly inevitable drift towards violence. By the time that the Home Rule Bill had completed its second parliamentary circuit, the emphasis of Unionist opposition was no longer inside parliament. A

large number of Ulster Unionists seemed ready to fight on the streets
rather than give up their birthright, and were preparing themselves for
armed conflict. Chamberlain, on the other hand, was among those ready
to seek a compromise. The alternative, posed by the Home Rule Bill
inexorably working its way on to the statute book only to come up against
the steadfast determination of Ulster Protestants to fight rather than
submit, seemed to him too dreadful to contemplate. Even more than the
prospect of civil war, Chamberlain feared a state of anarchy if the
government attempted to coerce Ulster with an unwilling army and
thereby created a state of opposition between parliament and the armed
forces. 'How will you meet another general strike on the railways or in the
mines?'[115] Even Law recognised that there might be scope for inter-party
discussions on the basis of general devolution or the exclusion of Ulster
from Irish Home Rule.

Chamberlain realised that if the government did propose a solution
involving the exclusion of Ulster, the Unionists' position would be
considerably weakened, since such an offer would largely satisfy British
public opinion and yet involve the sacrifice of Unionists in the South and
West of Ireland. He therefore proposed that Law should try to change the
ground of the debate by resurrecting the idea of Home Rule All Round,
which 'would be infinitely less dangerous than the present bill even with
Ulster excluded'.[116]

Chamberlain received some rather limited backing from Lansdowne
who, with strong personal interests in the South of Ireland, believed that
nothing would be gained while the 'Ulster red herring [was] being trailed
backwards and forwards across the track'.[117] Discussing the question
with Winston Churchill, the First Lord of the Admiralty, in November
1913, Chamberlain again floated the idea of a federal solution to the Irish
question and got the impression that Churchill and several other Liberal
ministers genuinely wanted a settlement, without themselves knowing
how to achieve one.[118] In the meantime, however, Law had opened
personal and secret negotiations with Asquith and seemed more inclined
to seek a solution based on exclusion, since the larger question of general
devolution in the United Kingdom would probably require 'something in
the nature of a coalition' to carry it out.[119] The difficulty, however, was
that Asquith might well propose the exclusion of only the four
overwhelmingly Protestant counties of Ulster and plebiscites in the others
– a solution which Law could never sell even to Ulster Unionists.
Chamberlain and Smith dined with Churchill and Lord Morley,
Gladstone's Irish Secretary, in December 1913, to discuss such issues, but
no agreement was forthcoming.[120]

The Asquith-Law conversations continued to drift, much to

Chamberlain's irritation. 'Law seems to me so afraid of having to take any definite decisions'.[121] It ought, Chamberlain felt, to have been possible to settle the basis of an agreement quickly or find out that agreement was not attainable.[122] Chamberlain feared that Asquith might establish such an ascendancy in the conversations as to do irreparable damage to the Unionist cause and hoped that they would soon be broken off. He also criticized Law for failing to hold the Prime Minister to the commitment, which Asquith gave at their second meeting, to lay before the Cabinet a proposal for exclusion and let Law know the result in a matter of days.[123] But, by the beginning of 1914, it was clear that the government would offer no more than a scheme of home rule for Ulster within Irish Home Rule, a solution which Unionists found totally unacceptable. Not surprisingly, on 15 January Law announced publicly that negotiations for a compromise were at an end.

With the opening of the parliamentary session of 1914 Unionist thought began, in a state of some desperation, to focus on the possibility of amending the Army Annual Bill, a venerable piece of legislation which regulated the army's code of discipline, giving parliament formal authority over it on an annual basis. For the Unionists to tamper with such a measure in the House of Lords was obviously a drastic and dangerous step, but by the end of January Law spoke of Chamberlain as among those ready to take it.[124] At a policy meeting in February Chamberlain 'deprecated too much finesse and advocated as plain a policy as possible, which would leave the party in the country under no delusions and make it clear that we stood for the Union'.[125] Doubts, however, soon began to return. When Selborne pointed out how much advantage the government might gain in terms of propaganda if the Unionists touched the Army Bill, Chamberlain was 'rather shaken'. 'I wish I knew clearly what was the right thing to do, but I do not.'[126] He was 'very perplexed and very troubled' and inclined to urge that Carson should precipitate matters by organising a provisional government in Ulster.[127]

At all events, opposition within the party to the idea of amending the bill became so great that the idea had to be abandoned.[128] In any case, the news of the so-called Mutiny at the Curragh revealed that the army would be an impotent weapon for the coercion of Ulster. When in the wake of this development the Unionist leaders decided to write to Asquith stating the necessity for either excluding Ulster or consulting the electorate by referendum or General Election, Chamberlain once again raised the possibility of offering the government an alternative proposal based on provincial councils and a federal solution.[129] He was concerned that the indiscipline in the army meant that the fabric of society had been loosened and that a tremendous stimulus had been given to syndicalists, socialists and the like.[130] Chamberlain calculated that there were about eighty members on each side of the House espousing a federal solution and many others prepared to swallow it if so advised by their leaders.[131] Yet, while Chamberlain became more and more convinced that devolution offered the only answer, most other leading Unionists including Law, Balfour and Carson disliked the idea. So Chamberlain's dilemma was whether to push the point and risk dividing the Unionist ranks without necessarily achieving any result.[132] If he did nothing, he feared that the party would only drift to the brink of civil war before being forced to accept a solution which involved some scheme of Irish government incompatible with national unity and national strength.[133] The problem was that Chamberlain had singularly failed to convert his senior colleagues to his point of view. Neither in 1910, nor in the autumn of 1913, nor now in 1914 was the Unionist leadership as a whole prepared to embrace Home Rule All Round.[134] Such a solution could not be a last-minute expedient, but would have to be 'worked out on practical lines by a national conference or convention'. For that there was no time, but, as Amery warned, 'to attempt to commit the party [now] to a federal scheme would ... completely wreck it'.[135]

Increasingly the Unionists' room for manoeuvre was being restricted. Little advantage was taken of the Curragh episode for fear of provoking the cry of 'the Army against the People'. When the party did call for a judicial enquiry into what was seen as a government plot to coerce Ulster, its credibility was undermined by the discovery of a massive gun-running exploit by Ulster volunteers. When, therefore, Chamberlain moved his party's motion for an enquiry on 28 April, Churchill was able to brush it aside as 'a most impudent demand' and 'uncommonly like a vote of censure by the criminal classes on the police'.[136] Yet what could not be escaped was that Home Rule would pass indubitably on to the statute book in a matter of weeks. The divided councils of the Unionist opposition were apparent when Law, Carson, Balfour, Lansdowne and Chamberlain met on 5 May. Chamberlain showed that he was still keen on the federal solution and emphasised to his colleagues that he and Lansdowne 'had from the first laid more stress than Carson and Law on the Imperial aspect of the Home Rule Bill and therefore had been anxious to prevent the impression growing that you had only to cut out Ulster in order to make the bill safe'.[137] But when Law and Carson met Asquith later that day, the Prime Minister had a new and unexpected proposal to put before them. He suggested now that the Home Rule Bill should be passed in its existing form under the provisions of the Parliament Act, but that simultaneously an Amending Bill should be introduced into the Lords to tackle the question of Ulster.

In the last stages of the Irish drama, Chamberlain's role was diminished and he took no part in the Buckingham Palace Conference called by the King as a last attempt to work out a compromise between the party leaders. Chamberlain had other matters on his mind. At the beginning of July his father suffered two heart attacks. The whole family hastened to his bedside for the inevitable end. Neville left a vivid account of Joseph Chamberlain's last moments:

There came a slight change and I saw at once from the way Dr. Mathews looked at the nurse that the end was at hand. A. came in again and by the Dr.'s advice went out for Mary. .... At last there came a slight convulsion, the arms were stretched downwards, the colour of the face changed and the breathing ceased altogether. Still the pulse beat faintly, then came one more breath very faint, and all was over.[138]

For Austen, the death of his father was inevitably a momentous event. It meant also much to those who had hitherto viewed him with suspicion as primarily his father's son. Only six months later, Hugh Cecil could write:

No doubt as far as concerns Bonar Law – and I think, now that his father is dead, we may add Austen Chamberlain – there is nothing very serious that divides us from them except the almost decayed barrier of Tariff Reform.[139]

Chamberlain, then, now had the opportunity to stamp out for himself his own individual role in British politics, without having to keep one eye on the wishes of his father. He would do so, however, against a background that was very different from anything he had so far experienced in politics. Just four days before his father's end another more violent death had occurred hundreds of miles away which was destined to change the lives not only of Chamberlain but of millions of others. The heir to the Austrian throne, the Archduke Franz Ferdinand, had fallen at the hands of a Serbian assassin.

Notes

1. F. S. Oliver to A. Chamberlain Nov. 1911, Chamberlain MSS, AC 60/86.
2. Frank Mildmay to Sandars 12 Nov. 1911, Sandars MSS c. 764 ff. 185–6.
3. *Politics from Inside* p. 534.
4. A. Gollin, *Observer* p. 272.
5. St. John Brodrick to Salisbury 18 Jan. 1911, Salisbury MSS 69/12.
6. *Politics from Inside* p. 317.
7. A. Chamberlain to M. Chamberlain 26 March 1911, Chamberlain MSS, AC 4/1/628.
8. J. Lawrence to A. Chamberlain 14 Dec. 1910, ibid, AC 8/7/23.
9. A. Chamberlain to R. Jebb 7 Dec. 1910, cited Petrie, *Life* i, 268–72.
10. As note 7.

11. P. Rowland, *Last Liberal Governments* ii, 34; W. Wilkinson, *Tory Democracy* (New York, 1925) pp. 254–5.
12. B. Dugdale, *Balfour* ii, 68. The 'ditchers' were those who were prepared to die in the last ditch in their efforts to preserve the existing powers of the House of Lords. The 'hedgers' were in favour of compromise.
13. Petrie, *Life* i, 280–81.
14. A. Chamberlain to L. Amery 2 Aug. 1911, Amery MSS D 44.
15. Bridgeman Diary 24–29 July 1911.
16. A. Chamberlain to Balfour 26 July 1911, Chamberlain MSS, AC 9/2/1; A. Chamberlain to Selborne 25 July 1911, Selborne MSS 74/143.
17. A. Chamberlain to Ivy Chamberlain 26 July 1911, Chamberlain MSS, AC 6/1/88.
18. A. Chamberlain to Selborne 25 July 1911, Selborne MSS 74/143.
19. Balfour to A. Chamberlain July 1911, Chamberlain MSS, AC 9/2/2.
20. Sandars, 'Diary of Events in connection with the passage of the Parliament Bill', 12 Aug. 1911, Sandars MSS c 763/162.
21. As note 19.
22. A. Chamberlain to Balfour 5 Nov. 1911, Balfour MSS 49736 f. 188.
23. Strachey to Curzon 1 Aug. 1911, Curzon MSS F 112/89.
24. Sandars, 'Diary of Events'; A. Chamberlain to Ivy Chamberlain 31 July 1911, Chamberlain MSS, AC 6/1/90.
25. Petrie, *Long* p. 160; Long to St. Aldwyn 2 Aug. 1911, Long MSS 448/29.
26. L. Amery, *Diaries* pp. 81–2. See also L. Amery, *Life* i, 381.
27. *Politics from Inside* p. 347.
28. Ibid, p. 352.
29. A. Chamberlain to M. Chamberlain 12 Aug. 1911, Chamberlain MSS, AC 4/1/672.
30. N. Chamberlain to A. Chamberlain 7 Oct. 1911, ibid, AC 9/3/14.
31. B. Chamberlain to A. Chamberlain 5 Oct. 1911, ibid, AC 1/8/8/18.
32. *Politics from Inside* p. 359.
33. Selborne to Willoughby de Broke 18 Aug. 1911, Willoughby de Broke MSS 3/46; Selborne to Wyndham 22 Aug. 1911, ibid, 3/62.
34. *Politics from Inside* p. 358.
35. Sandars to Balfour 17 Sept. 1911, Balfour MSS 49767; *Politics from Inside* pp. 358–60; A. Gollin, *Observer* pp. 354–5. By joining the club Chamberlain took on the role of 'the Honourable Brutus whom the conspirators needed to lend respectability to what was plainly an organized revolt.' J. Campbell, *F. E. Smith, First Earl of Birkenhead* (London, 1983) p. 248.
36. A. Chamberlain to M. Chamberlain 23 Oct. 1911, Chamberlain MSS, AC 4/1/718.
37. Salisbury to Selborne 14 Oct. 1911, Salisbury MSS 71/54.
38. Sykes, *Tariff Reform* p. 252; Lord Winterton, *Pre-War* (London, 1932) p. 230.
39. Dugdale, *Balfour* ii, 87.
40. J. Amery, *Joseph Chamberlain* vi, 951.

41. L. Amery, *Life* i, 385.
42. Gollin, *Observer* p. 358.
43. A. Chamberlain to Ivy Chamberlain 27 July 1911, Chamberlain MSS, AC 6/1/89.
44. Robert Sanders Diary, 12 Nov. 1911.
45. F. S. Oliver to A. Chamberlain 21 Nov. 1911, Chamberlain MSS, AC 60/89.
46. R. Blake, *The Unknown Prime Minister* (London, 1955) p. 72.
47. A. Chamberlain to M. Chamberlain 6 April 1914, Chamberlain MSS, AC 4/1/1113.
48. Ibid, 30 Oct. 1911, AC 4/1/733.
49. Garvin to Sandars 12 Jan. 1911, Balfour MSS 49795.
50. A. Gollin, *Observer* pp. 367–8.
51. G. D. Phillips, 'Lord Willoughby de Broke and the Politics of Radical Toryism, 1909–1914,' *Journal of British Studies*, XX, i (1980) p. 218.
52. A. Chamberlain to M. Chamberlain 27 Oct. 1911, Chamberlain MSS, AC 4/1/721.
53. Law to Beaverbrook 15 Aug. 1911, Beaverbrook MSS, BBK C/201.
54. H. Chamberlain, Memoir, Nov. 1956, Chamberlain MSS, BC 5/10/1.
55. A. Chamberlain to M. Chamberlain 23 Oct. 1911, ibid, AC 4/1/713.
56. *Politics from Inside* p. 378.
57. Ibid, p. 381.
58. Bridgeman Diary 7–8 Nov. 1911.
59. A. Chamberlain to M. Chamberlain 11 Nov. 1911, Chamberlain MSS, AC 9/3/13.
60. Ibid. When Chamberlain explained to Long his arrival at the House of Commons in the company of Henry Chaplin, Long commented: 'Oh you don't think it necessary to explain why you are in a taxi with a man, do you? You haven't come to that yet, have you?'
61. Sandars' note on events leading to Balfour's resignation, 8 Nov. 1911, Sandars MSS c. 764/157; Robert Sanders diary, 5 Aug. 1911.
62. A. Chamberlain to M. Chamberlain 11 Nov. 1911, Chamberlain MSS, AC 4/1/727.
63. Ibid.
64. Sandars to Balfour 10 Nov. 1911, Balfour MSS 49767.
65. Bridgeman Diary 10 Nov. 1911.
66. Ibid, 13 Nov. 1911.
67. A. Chamberlain to M. Chamberlain 11 Nov. 1911, Chamberlain MSS, AC 4/1/728.
68. Sandars to Balfour 10 Nov. 1911, Balfour MSS 49767.
69. A. Chamberlain to M. Chamberlain 10 Nov. 1911, Chamberlain MSS, AC 4/1/724.
70. A. Gollin, *Observer* p. 359.
71. H. Chamberlain, Memoir, Nov. 1956, Chamberlain MSS, BC 5/10/1.
72. As note 67.
73. R. Blake, *Unknown Prime Minister* p. 72.

74. L. Amery, *Life* i, 386.
75. A. Chamberlain to M. Chamberlain 11 Nov. 1911, Chamberlain MSS, AC 9/3/13.
76. R. Punnett, *Front-Bench Opposition* (New York, 1973) p. 48.
77. *Down the Years* pp. 108–9.
78. A. Chamberlain to M. Chamberlain 11 Nov. 1911, Chamberlain MSS, AC 4/1/727.
79. A. Chamberlain to Law 11 Nov. 1911, Bonar Law MSS 24/3/11.
80. A. Gollin, *Observer* p. 362.
81. *Politics from Inside* p. 506.
82. Ibid, pp. 415–6.
83. A. Chamberlain to Law 17 Feb. 1912, Bonar Law MSS 25/2/24.
84. A. Chamberlain to M. Chamberlain 21 Feb. 1912, Chamberlain MSS, AC 4/1/757.
85. Ibid, 1 March 1912, AC 4/1/765.
86. Ibid, 16 Nov. 1912, AC 4/1/889.
87. *Politics from Inside* p. 503.
88. A. Chamberlain to Law 24 Dec. 1912, Bonar Law MSS 28/1/86.
89. A. Chamberlain to H. Gwynne 21 Dec. 1912, Gwynne MSS 17.
90. L. Amery, *Diaries* p. 88.
91. As note 88.
92. L. Amery, *Life* i, 416.
93. A. Chamberlain to Strachey 26 Dec. 1913, Strachey MSS S/4/5/3.
94. As note 92.
95. *Politics from Inside* p. 509.
96. A. Chamberlain to Law 8 Jan. 1913, Bonar Law MSS 31/1/15.
97. J. Amery, *Joseph Chamberlain* vi, 983.
98. A. Chamberlain to M. Chamberlain 16 March 1913, Chamberlain MSS, AC 4/1/952.
99. A. Chamberlain to H. Chaplin 15 Jan. 1913, ibid, AC 9/5/9.
100. A. Chamberlain to Law 8 Jan. 1913, Bonar Law MSS 31/1/15.
101. A. Chamberlain to M. Chamberlain 25 Jan. 1913, Chamberlain MSS, AC 4/1/897.
102. Bridgeman Diary 9 Jan. 1913.
103. Sanders Diary 5 Jan. 1913.
104. A. Chamberlain to M. Chamberlain 8 March 1913, Chamberlain MSS, AC 4/1/942.
105. Ibid, 17 April 1913, AC 4/1/992.
106. Ibid, 22 March 1913, AC 4/1/959.
107. A. Chamberlain to Steel-Maitland 3 July 1913, Steel-Maitland MSS GD 193/152/2.
108. A. Chamberlain to M. Chamberlain 30 April 1913, Chamberlain MSS, AC 4/1/1002.
109. Ibid, 30 Nov. 1906, AC 4/1/122.
110. Bridgeman Diary 10 Aug. 1914.
111. *Down the Years* p. 109.

112. A. Chamberlain to Lansdowne 26 Aug. 1912, Chamberlain MSS, AC 10/2/22.
113. A. Chamberlain to M. Chamberlain 24 Sept. 1912, ibid, AC 4/1/874.
114. L. Amery to M. Chamberlain 27 Feb. 1914, ibid, AC 4/11/11.
115. A. Chamberlain to Willoughby de Broke 23 Nov. 1913, cited J. Ramsden, *The Age of Balfour and Baldwin 1902–1940* (London, 1978) p. 83.
116. A. Chamberlain to Lansdowne 29 Oct. 1913, Chamberlain MSS, AC 11/1/46.
117. Lansdowne to A. Chamberlain 31 Oct. 1913, ibid, AC 11/1/47.
118. Memorandum by A. Chamberlain 27 Nov. 1913, ibid, AC 11/1/21.
119. Law to E. Carson 18 Sept. 1913, cited I. Colvin, *The Life of Lord Carson* (London, 1934) ii, 205.
120. Lord Riddell, *More Pages from My Diary, 1908–1914* (London, 1934) p. 189.
121. A. Chamberlain to M. Chamberlain 11 May 1914, Chamberlain MSS, AC 4/1/1133.
122. A. Chamberlain to Lord Morley 9 Dec. 1913, ibid, AC 11/1/66.
123. A. Chamberlain to M. Chamberlain 11 Feb. 1914, ibid AC 4/1/1069.
124. Law to Lansdowne 30 Jan. 1914, Balfour MSS 49693. P. Jalland, *The Liberals and Ireland* (Brighton, 1980) pp. 215–6.
125. Bridgeman Diary 9 Feb. 1914.
126. A. Chamberlain to M. Chamberlain 15 March 1914, Chamberlain MSS, AC 4/1/1090.
127. Ibid, 16 March 1914, AC 4/1/1091.
128. Ibid, 18 March 1914, AC 4/1/1092.
129. Ibid, 21 March 1914, AC 4/1/1096.
130. Ibid, 24 March 1914, AC 4/1/1100.
131. *Politics from Inside* pp. 636–7.
132. A. Chamberlain to M. Chamberlain 2 April 1914, Chamberlain MSS, AC 4/1/1110.
133. Ibid, 2 May 1914, AC 4/1/1128.
134. P. Jalland, 'United Kingdom devolution, 1910–1914: political panacea or tactical diversion?' *English Historical Review* XCIV, 373 (1979) pp. 781–2.
135. L. Amery to A. Chamberlain 1 May 1914, Chamberlain MSS, AC 11/1/1.
136. L. Amery, *Life* i, 455.
137. A. Chamberlain to M. Chamberlain 5 May 1914, Chamberlain MSS, AC 4/1/1131.
138. N. Chamberlain Diary 2 July 1914, ibid NC 2/20.
139. H. Cecil to R. Cecil 10 Jan. 1915, R. Cecil MSS 51157.

CHAPTER FOUR

FIGHTING THE WAR

'If anyone had told me a few years ago that I should eat my dinner in London three days in one week to the noise of many guns and the whistling of shells overhead, what should I have thought of him?'[1]

When England went to war with Germany on 4 August 1914, Austen Chamberlain had been out of office for the best part of nine years. With his failure to secure the leadership of his party in 1911 and his subsequent partial eclipse from the inner councils of Unionist policy-making, his career appeared to have passed its peak and to be in decline. Battered by successive disappointments his enthusiasm for the political battle seemed to have left him. As he later put it, his ambition had perished for want of sustenance and he could not revive it.[2] By transforming the parameters of British politics, the war enabled Chamberlain not only to return to office, but to begin a new phase in his political career. For Chamberlain as for all others in British public life, the coming of European war was a watershed. Though Chamberlain has not normally been listed among the commanding figures of British politics during the conflict, Lord Beaverbrook once expressed the hope that he would come to occupy 'a leading position amongst the political figures of the first war.'[3] Yet the political world which the war created was markedly different from anything Chamberlain had experienced hitherto. Though the great issues which had concerned him before 1914 did not die overnight – tariff reform and Ireland, for example, were to return to prominence – the structure of politics within which such questions would be discussed was distinctly new. The war, moreover, witnessed a subtle change in many of Chamberlain's own attitudes which enabled him to adjust more easily to the post-war world than might have been expected.

That British politicians were so late in alerting themselves to the gravity of the European scene in the summer of 1914 was only partially due to their understandable preoccupation with the Irish impasse. The fact was that while the delegates at the Buckingham Palace Conference grappled vainly with the possible partition of Fermanagh and Tyrone, politicians and soldiers in Berlin and Vienna, playing for altogether higher stakes, were at pains to conceal from their opposite numbers in Great Britain the true nature of their intentions. Chamberlain was no less deceived than his contemporaries and not until 28 July, when Sir Edward Grey, the Foreign Secretary, told the Commons of the Austrian rejection of Serbia's reply to an ultimatum calling for satisfaction for the Archduke's murder, did the seriousness of the situation become apparent.

Chamberlain was among those who believed that Britain's tacit obligations to France and Russia constituted a commitment of honour which would oblige the government to declare war on Germany in the event that the latter attacked France. On 31 July he joined his family at Westgate confident that the Liberal government would share his understanding of the situation. On 1 August, however, Leo Amery arrived in Westgate and urged Chamberlain to return to London. There they met another Unionist backbencher, George Lloyd, from whom Chamberlain learnt that the decision for war was by no means certain and that opinion inside Asquith's Cabinet was deeply divided. Lloyd also gave the impression that Law and Lansdowne had failed to appreciate the urgency of the situation and that it was Chamberlain's duty to persuade them into action. Chamberlain was shocked by what he had heard and on 2 August went hurriedly to see Lansdowne to urge an immediate démarche. Both Lansdowne and Law argued that they had already sent a message to Asquith and that it would be right to await a reply before taking any further action. Under persistent pressure from Chamberlain, however, Law was eventually persuaded that a further note should be sent to the Prime Minister. The letter was substantially Chamberlain's work. 'It was pretty obvious that Austen had taken the situation in hand,' noted Amery:[4]

Dear Mr. Asquith,
Lord Lansdowne and I [Law] feel it our duty to inform you that, in our opinion, as well as that of all the colleagues whom we have been able to consult, any hesitation now in supporting France and Russia would be fatal to the honour and to the future security of the United Kingdom, and we offer H.M. Government the assurance of the united support of the Opposition in all measures required by England's intervention in the war.[5]

Asquith's reply was, in Chamberlain's opinion, 'most unsatisfactory' and gave him the impression that 'the government were searching for excuses to do nothing.' Asquith was at pains to repeat the assurance he had given some years earlier to the House of Commons that Britain was under no obligation to render military or naval help to France or Russia, though he did concede that it was in Britain's interests to see that France was not crushed. At all events it was decided that Law and Lansdowne should see the Prime Minister on 3 August. From this meeting it appeared that Asquith's will had stiffened and, later in the day, Grey made his memorable statement in the House of Commons about the lights of Europe going out. On the following day Britain and Germany were at war.[6]

Both Chamberlain and some of those within his inner circle seem to
have over-estimated the role he had played in forcing the government to
stand by its quasi-ally France. A few days later Neville wrote:

It makes one fairly gasp to think that we were within a hair's-breadth of eternal
disgrace, and some day the country will be grateful to Amery, G. Lloyd, and you
for having preserved her honour.[7]

Chamberlain did not appreciate the delicacy of the situation existing
inside Asquith's Cabinet, where many of the radical members, ever
suspicious of Grey's foreign policy, did not regard the commitments
entered into with France since 1904 as in any way binding. The skill of
Asquith and Grey, therefore, was in bringing the government round to a
declaration of war on the rather different but less cloudy issue of the
violation of Belgian neutrality. This they did with only a minimum of
resignations – those of Morley and Burns – which were not significant
enough to threaten the administration itself. Such considerations were far
more significant in determining Asquith's course than was pressure from
the Unionist opposition.[8] Chamberlain, though, could take some credit for
stirring the opposition leaders into decided and concerted action. He was
'splendid throughout the crisis'[9] and acted far more decisively than on
many other occasions in his career – probably because he regarded the
issue as a straightforward question of honour about which there was no
room for equivocation. Certainly when, a few months later, Law tried to
take credit himself for an initiative that was primarily Chamberlain's, he
was being less than gracious.[10]

In the first days of the war there was little thought given to anything as
novel as the formation of a coalition government. It would be, as the Prime
Minister said, 'business as usual' in the widely shared optimism that the
whole matter would be settled by Christmas. There were just a few
gestures in the direction of changed conditions. One was the appointment
of Lord Kitchener, the semi-legendary military leader, as Secretary of
State for War. This development may have owed something to a
suggestion from Chamberlain – advice which he and many others had
later cause to regret.[11] A further innovation came with the invitation from
Lloyd George to the two surviving former Unionist Chancellors of the
Exchequer, Chamberlain and the seventy-seven year old Lord St.
Aldwyn, to hold semi-official posts at the Treasury. 'Austen was at all our
meetings and played an honourable part,' Walter Runciman later noted.[12]
On one occasion Chamberlain even took over the chairmanship of a
conference at the Treasury when Lloyd George had to hurry off for a
Cabinet meeting. But Chamberlain was not likely to revolutionise thinking
at the Exchequer about the management of wartime finance as some

would have liked. As Steel-Maitland said, 'Austen's bent is always to take the proper and strict financial view.'[13] Here though were the first tentative steps in Chamberlain's association with Lloyd George – an association which gradually developed from a mood of suspicion and mistrust to the feeling of deep loyalty which cost Chamberlain the leadership of his party in 1922. Even at this early stage he was warm in his praise of the Chancellor's handling of the initial financial crisis of the war:

the Chancellor of the Exchequer has handled a very difficult situation with great tact, great skill and great judgment.[14]

Other aspects, however, of the government's handling of the nation's affairs gave Chamberlain less cause for satisfaction. Though there was now a widespread feeling that so contentious a measure as the Home Rule Bill could not in the circumstances of war go ahead in its present form, negotiations between the two parties failed to produce an acceptable compromise. At a meeting with Lewis Harcourt, the Colonial Secretary, on 11 August, at which Chamberlain put what he regarded as acceptable solutions to the Irish dilemma, he ended by telling the minister,

in a tone which I studied to make inoffensive . . . that I . . . felt so strongly their obligation as men of honour not to proceed with controversial business, that however much I should regret it, their decision to go on under such circumstances would put an end to all friendship and all personal relations.[15]

After an acrimonious debate in the House of Commons on 31 August, Chamberlain still could 'not believe that the Government will commit "an infamy".'[16] Yet though the government's 'house rooted in dishonour stands',[17] the Unionists had now lost their pre-war tactical advantages. As Law recognised, 'We cannot fight the Government now. They have tied our hands by our patriotism.'[18] On 9 September opposition leaders including Chamberlain met at Lansdowne House where they agreed that the proper course for the government to take would be to suspend the Bill in its present position until the end of the war. This Asquith could not accept. He now felt obliged, therefore, to pass the existing Bill, without an Amending Bill to tackle the question of Ulster, but with a provision that its operation be suspended for the duration of hostilities. Chamberlain, with his exaggerated sense of fair play and political rectitude, was horrified. All that he and other Unionist M.P.s could do, however, was to register a theatrical but token protest by walking out of the House of Commons, 'middle-aged gentlemen trying to look like early French revolutionists in the Tennis Court.'[19] But true to his remarks to Harcourt, Chamberlain now refused to speak from the same platform as Churchill at a recruiting rally in Birmingham on 14 September. A barrage of letters was exchanged between Churchill and Chamberlain but failed to produce any reconciliation.[20]

Such an attitude could not be long maintained in time of war. Further Unionist intransigence ran the danger of being equated with treason in the public mind. When opposition leaders met again on 16 September Chamberlain was in a minority in suggesting that even now Home Rule could be held up on a technicality if the Clerk of Parliament were instructed by the House of Lords to detain the official copy of the Bill. Along with most other leading Unionists Chamberlain soon proceeded to give the government steady support in all questions concerning the prosecution of the war effort. As he himself recognised, 'things are so grave abroad that a way of peace at home must be found, and if it must it will.'[21] Chamberlain well expressed his own attitude and that of his senior colleagues in a letter to Francis Acland written in December 1914:

I am deeply impressed by our undeserved good fortune in carrying our people so unanimously with us. There had been nothing beforehand in official speeches or in official publications to make known to them the danger that we ran or to prepare them for the discharge of our responsibilities and the defence of our interests . . . you have a better assurance in our past action than in any words of mine that there is no disposition on the part of any section of the Unionist Party to make capital out of the difficulties of the Government or to say or do anything which can embarrass them in the successful conduct of the war.[22]

Chamberlain had, however, little work with which to occupy himself apart from a number of recruiting speeches. The fact that he took on at this time the chairmanship of the Committee of the Imperial Bureau of Entomology shows that he was largely removed from the centre of political activity. But along with many other Unionists Chamberlain soon began to share growing misgivings about the conduct of the war. He was a regular target for Lord Milner and his supporters who were already proposing the virtual commandeering of the whole nation.[23] Milner seems to have taken note of Chamberlain's decisive action at the time of the war crisis and to have believed that he could again 'help the Government to take decisions which it seems incapable of taking for itself.'[24] What was becoming patently apparent at this stage was less the government's incapacity than its miscalculation. As the first winter of the war passed into the first spring everyone came to realise that the war had developed into something very different from initial expectations. Instead of the short sharp clash of arms anticipated by the so-called military experts of the day, it was clear that the Great War was turning into an increasingly costly war of attrition, a self-perpetuating vicious circle in which vast reserves of manpower seemed to be the chief tool available to the generals in their quest for victory. It was moreover a tool in which the level of wastage and destruction was horrifically high. By the beginning of 1915 even some members of the Liberal government had begun to cast around for alternative means to victory instead of continuing the apparently futile strategy of, as Churchill put it, 'chewing barbed wire' in France and Flanders. Almost no one had foreseen the defensive capabilities of entrenched riflemen and machine-gunners protected by barbed wire. It was in a mood of frustration at the government's apparent inertia that the Unionist Business Committee was formed under Walter Long's chairmanship at the end of January 1915.

This is not the place to enter into the historiographical debate on the origins of the First Coalition. Some years ago one historian wrote that 'unless the papers not so far available to researchers happen to contain an unusually convincing letter in the hand of one of the three men responsible for the decision, this question seems well placed to defy solution indefinitely.'[25] In the present context only Chamberlain's role in the crisis needs to be examined. By May the position was becoming acute. Not only was there continuing stalemate on the Western Front, but Churchill's much vaunted Dardanelles Campaign had failed to fulfil its creator's dreams and was now moving towards defeat, if not fiasco. As Milner put it to Chamberlain:

We are making gigantic sacrifices with very inadequate results. Is there any sign that the Government have a clear idea what they want to be at, or *by what definite procedure* they hope to achieve victory or even to avert disastrous defeat?[26]

On 14 May the shadow cabinet convened at Lansdowne House to consider the suggestion of Lord Robert Cecil that the opposition should demand a committee on the state of the nation to meet in camera in order to hold a frank and open discussion on the government's conduct of the war. This suggestion met with little support, but there was general agreement that some effort would have to be made to spur the government on to greater exertion. In particular Asquith should be pressed to take necessary steps for the eventuality that conscription and the control of industry became imperative. It was agreed that Law and Lansdowne should write to the Prime Minister in these terms, promising Unionist support if compulsion were deemed necessary.

Such developments inside the Unionist party were, however, largely overtaken by a crisis within the government where Lord Fisher's differences with Winston Churchill at the Admiralty over the conduct of the Dardanelles Campaign led to the former's resignation as First Sea Lord. Meeting Law and Lansdowne on 17 May, Chamberlain learnt that

Law had now told Lloyd George that a statement about the resignation would have to be made in the Commons before the Whitsun recess and that criticism of the government could not be avoided. Lloyd George, it appeared, shared the misgivings of the Unionist leadership over the higher direction of the war and, in particular, Kitchener's position at the War Office. Law had taken this as a signal to draft a letter to Asquith suggesting that the time for a coalition had arrived. Law, it seemed, was ready to threaten Asquith with a damaging public debate if the Prime Minister did not indicate that his mind was also moving along these lines. Chamberlain and Lansdowne succeeded in toning down the letter so that it called merely for a reconstruction of the government rather than the formation necessarily of a coalition. Asquith, however, had already taken steps to consult Law over the question of a coalition government. The plans which he had been turning over in his mind involved a far more radical reshaping of the Cabinet than eventually took place. Lloyd George was to replace Kitchener as Secretary for War, Law was to become Chancellor of the Exchequer, Balfour First Lord of the Admiralty and Lansdowne Lord President of the Council, while Chamberlain would be offered the Colonial Office. Law was concerned that Chamberlain might be affronted that he, Law, should get the Exchequer, while Chamberlain had to be content with a relatively minor position. But it would have been difficult for Chamberlain to turn down the post in which his father had achieved so much and, in any case, he was 'content to serve with or without portfolio, in any capacity in which I could be useful.'[27]

Law, however, began to doubt whether he could carry a united party behind him into the Coalition. He suggested a party meeting, but Chamberlain was adamant that Law should take the crucial decision first and only then present it to the meeting as a *fait accompli*. With Chamberlain's assistance Carson, one of the leading doubters, was converted to this line of thought, as was Robert Cecil. For Chamberlain the concept of public duty seemed uppermost:

There are no two ways about it! If our help is asked by the Govt., we *must* give it. God knows each one of us would willingly avoid the fearful responsibility; but the responsibility of refusing is even greater than that of accepting, and in fact we have no choice. If Govt. tapped any of us on the shoulder and said: Go to the trenches, we should go. If they asked us to dig trenches here or work as labourers in the factory we should do it.[28]

Accordingly, when the shadow cabinet met again on 18 May it was unanimously agreed that the Unionists should accept the invitation to join the government. Though misgivings were voiced that Asquith would be staying on as Prime Minister, it was apparent that no one else would be able to take his place at the present time, while it had now become clear that Kitchener's removal could not after all be contemplated because of the demoralising effect it would have on public opinion at home and abroad. Salisbury hoped for a scheme, such as would be proposed at the end of 1916, whereby Asquith would stay on as premier, but place the direction of the war in the hands of a small body of four ministers, including Chamberlain as First Lord of the Admiralty,[29] but at this stage of the war Asquith was far more in control of the situation than has sometimes been suggested.

This was revealed in the disposition of offices when the details of the new government were announced. Had Asquith's original proposals been implemented the Unionist party would have occupied a major, if not commanding, position in the control of the war effort. As it was the leading Unionists were relegated to relatively minor offices. Balfour did receive the Admiralty, but it was Law and not Chamberlain who went to the Colonial Office, while Lansdowne became merely Minister without Portfolio. Chamberlain himself entered the government as Secretary of State for India. Law, it appeared, had been out-manoeuvred. Asquith had succeeded in pulling the teeth of any potential Unionist opposition, while at the same time retaining control over the higher direction of the war firmly in his own hands and those of senior Liberal colleagues.

Chamberlain played little part in the actual formation of the government. In so far as he tried to exert any influence he was largely unsuccessful. When it was clear that Law was not in fact going to the Exchequer — 'second in the Government when in the right hands'[30] — Chamberlain vainly urged that he should press for the newly created Ministry of Munitions.[31] He also failed to get Lord Milner included in the new administration, despite his expressed readiness 'to serve as Under-Secretary to him in any office to which he is appointed . . . or . . . take an office like 1st Comr. of Works or Chancellor of the Duchy' to facilitate Milner's entry.[32] There is, however, some evidence that Chamberlain and Law successfully blocked Haldane's inclusion in the government on account of the Lord Chancellor's supposed Germanophile tendencies.[33]

There can be little doubt that the whole episode served to confirm Chamberlain's misgivings over Law's capacity for leadership. He later reflected that 'we could not have been . . . more inadequately represented by any leader than we were by B.L. in Asquith's Coalition Government.'[34] His first impressions of the new Cabinet, however, were more favourable than might have been expected. There was 'nothing to complain of so far . . . and some things which are decidedly encouraging.'[35] He was particularly pleased that the Cabinet did not seem to divide along strictly

party lines.[36] Upon his new Liberal colleagues, Chamberlain himself made
a less favourable impression. There was general agreement that he would
prove a loyal colleague rather than a dynamic addition to the government.
Margot Asquith, never as discreet as her husband, thought him 'straight
... but ... stupid,' while Runciman, the President of the Board of Trade,
found him 'insignificant and unsuggestive' in Cabinet.[37] Inside the
Cabinet Chamberlain found himself in closest sympathy with Selborne,
now President of the Board of Agriculture, and Curzon, the Lord Privy
Seal, from whom he had been estranged at the time of the Parliament Bill.
Selborne 'could wish for no better company when after tigers.'[38]

The problems of India were not an area of public policy with which
Chamberlain was well acquainted, although in 1913 he had accepted the
invitation of the then Secretary of State, Lord Crewe, to chair a
Commission on Indian Finance. As a passionate believer in the British
Empire, however, Chamberlain soon took a keen interest in his new
department. He was fortunate in being able to strike up a good working
relationship with the Viceroy, the diplomat Lord Hardinge, an advantage
not enjoyed by all previous or subsequent holders of his office. In normal
times the dominating question associated with the India Office would have
been the future of British rule and the slow development of native Indian
institutions. In the context of 1915, however, and against the background
of increasingly heavy casualties on the Western Front, the overriding
concern which greeted the new minister was the nature and extent of
India's contribution to the war effort.

On coming into office Chamberlain inherited from his predecessor a
small military operation in Mesopotamia under the control of the
Government of India, designed in the first instance to protect the oil-fields
at the head of the Persian Gulf. A reluctant Hardinge had been pressed by
London to send troops to the Gulf in October 1914 and the following
month Britain had declared war on Turkey. The town of Basra had been
taken on 23 November and Hardinge gradually became an advocate of a
further advance. In his first letter to the Viceroy on becoming Secretary of
State, Chamberlain emphasised that he would continue his predecessor's
cautious approach and that the generals on the spot would have to be
made to 'take their proper place in the perspective of the whole scheme of
the war.'[39] Some military advances were already under way, but
Chamberlain continued to warn that in the light of the limited manpower
available it was 'very undesirable that we should embark on new and
costly operations ... unless we are absolutely obliged to do so.'[40] The
campaign had been going very well but 'in view of demands elsewhere I
want to keep it within the narrowest limits possible.'[41]

The Viceroy, however, seems to have been convinced by the successes obtained so far that General Nixon, Commander-in-Chief of the Expeditionary Force 'D', should be allowed to push on. Hardinge's own aspirations for post-war British Imperial expansion may have been a contributory factor in clouding his vision. By 20 July Chamberlain had been won over to approve an advance to Kut-al-Amara from which the river valleys of the Tigris and Euphrates could be dominated. This objective had been secured by the end of September. By this stage Hardinge had become positively intoxicated with success and was now assuring Chamberlain that if Baghdad could be captured, the impact of such a prize would be as great in the Middle East as the fall of the Dardanelles would have been in the Near-East.[42] With Nixon expressing confidence that he could indeed secure this goal, Hardinge let it be known that Nixon could take the city with his existing forces, but would need an extra division to remain there.[43]

The fateful decision to advance on Baghdad belonged to the full Cabinet and not to Chamberlain alone. The latter, indeed, was uneasy but the decision has to be set in the context of an increasingly frustrating and depressing war scenario. If such a prize could be obtained for so small an outlay, then surely the risk was worth taking. As even the usually cautious Foreign Secretary reflected, it made more sense to send a division to Mesopotamia 'where we can secure a notable success than merge it in *hopeless failure* elsewhere.'[44] A committee of representatives from the India, War and Foreign Offices and the Admiralty concluded that an early advance upon and occupation of Baghdad was most desirable providing the position could be maintained.[45] This recommendation went forward to the Cabinet and, after its meeting on 8 October, Chamberlain reported that the Cabinet was so impressed with the political and military advantages to be derived from the occupation of Baghdad that the government would make every effort to supply the necessary force, and sought Hardinge's assurance that one extra division would indeed suffice.[46] Several members of the Cabinet, however, including Kitchener and Curzon, remained sceptical.

Yet by this stage at least one member of the government had evidence that the picture reaching London of the situation in Mesopotamia was not entirely accurate. On 4 September Major-General Charles Townshend, Commander of the Sixth Division, wrote to Lord Curzon, himself of course a former Viceroy, in terms which suggested that Chamberlain had been misled about the condition of British forces:

... the heat is appalling, still not cooled down a bit yet and we have not yet done laughing at Mr. Austen Chamberlain's speech about the electric fans, the ice etc., etc. – one or two houses at Basra have got this, we have none of those luxuries here![47]

As the weeks passed it became clear that provision for the sick and wounded was hopelessly inadequate. Yet in August Hardinge had assured the Secretary of State that there was ample money 'for supplying comforts for sick and wounded in Mesopotamia and in India. . . . My Government have arranged for doctors and medicines.'[48]

From October onwards Chamberlain sensed that all was not well and sent Hardinge a stream of increasingly worrying reports of medical conditions in Mesopotamia, urging him to take remedial action. His own memories of the Boer War flooded back as he wrote on the 29th of the month:

. . . you will remember how we received the same assurances from military and medical authorities at the time of the South African War, and yet how much more might, after all, have been done, at any rate in the early days of the campaign . . . I beg that you will take all the steps in your power to stimulate the ingenuity of the medical authorities in making provision for their health and for the comfort of the sick.[49]

On 3 December Chamberlain urged that Hardinge should send someone to the front to make a report on the health of the troops: 'I beg you not to be content with easy assurances.' Rather prophetically he added, 'We shall have no defence if all that is possible is not done.'[50] Yet Hardinge seemed reluctant to believe that there might be any foundation for Chamberlain's fears. Selborne thought it an idea to acquaint the Viceroy with the known level of wastage from sickness in the Dardanelles Campaign since this would 'show him what malaria and dysentery might mean to the Mesopotamian army.'[51] Even when Mark Sykes appeared in person at the War Committee to speak of the extreme unhealthiness of Basra and Nasiriya, Hardinge was ready with a reassuring response:

At the time of Sir Mark Sykes's visit to Mesopotamia troops were still suffering from the effects of the summer campaign. . . . Report dated 30 October, . . . states, however, that British and Indian regiments and units which in June had many cases of malaria were then practically free; the cold weather and rest had had a beneficial effect on health of troops and malaria had not assumed proportions which might reasonably have been expected. In all the occupied areas mosquitoes had been successfully dealt with.[52]

Yet Hardinge's false optimism could not indefinitely conceal what began to emerge as one of the major scandals of the war. In Chamberlain's words, 'the conditions [had] been awful and quite inexcusably awful.'[53] A report on the situation by Surgeon-General MacNeese was misleading, but a second report ordered by Chamberlain at the end of February 1916 from Sir William Vincent and General Bingley exposed the true horrors of the expedition. The Secretary of State began to receive letters from many officers serving in Mesopotamia of which the following was typical:

The worst part of it is the poor wounded. For economy no bandages or comforts have been provided by the Government of India for the thousands who lie unable to look after themselves; there are no hospital boats or accommodation for a quarter of those wounded and many must die from mere rotting away, as no one can dress the wounds. It is heart rending to see the boats packed with men ... with no hope of their being looked after, and no one even to help the worst cases for even purposes of nature; food obtainable with the greatest difficulty and yet one can do nothing.[54]

When Nixon's health broke down in January 1916, he was replaced, *faute de mieux*, by the elderly Sir Percy Lake. The latter confirmed that there was truth in many of the stories of the suffering of the wounded.[55] By the end of February even Hardinge was forced to admit that reports of mismanagement and deficiencies in medical necessities, though not officially confirmed, were true. He argued that the number of prospective casualities had been greatly under-estimated and that the prime reason for the shortage of medical supplies was a lack of river transport. Even his faith in Nixon, who had 'never reported that all was not well' began to falter.[56] Chamberlain regarded the situation as an 'absolute scandal'. Whatever the difficulties over transport there was no excuse for the shortage of bandages, splints and the like, nor for the condition of the barges in which the wounded were transported. As criticism and anger mounted inside the House of Commons, Chamberlain showed his first real irritation with the Viceroy, to whom he had 'both written and telegraphed ... again and again upon the subject', and he was also particularly harsh on the Indian Commander-in-Chief, Sir Beauchamp Duff, who was 'much too easily satisfied and much too ready to assume that all is as well as can be expected.'[57] Finally on 22 March Chamberlain was obliged to admit to the Commons that there had been a lamentable breakdown of hospital arrangements and an inexcusable shortage of basic medical supplies.[58]

The medical deficiencies of the Mesopotamian Campaign might not have attracted such attention had not the whole military expedition turned sour after its initial run of success. The decision to advance on Baghdad turned out to have been a grave mistake. The Turks were far better prepared to meet the advance than had been imagined. Chamberlain could not 'understand why our information was so bad.'[59] Nixon, despite warnings from Townshend, ordered the latter to push on up the Tigris. Townshend seems to have recovered confidence in the feasibility of the operation, but was badly beaten by the Turks at the Battle of Ctesiphon in late November 1915, where he lost a third of his total force of 14,000 men. Retreating to Kut, Townshend's men were placed under siege and unable to withdraw further, despite Hardinge's initial optimism that they could break out at any time and even recommence the advance on Baghdad. Attempts to send out a relief force under General Aylmer proved abortive. Chamberlain noted: 'Townshend gave the impression that he must be relieved quickly. Hence Aylmer moved prematurely. . . . T. has three times varied the date to which he could hold out.'[60] Finally on 29 April Townshend surrendered his 3,000 British and 6,000 Indian troops. A. J. Barker in his study of the campaign commented: 'In the whole history of the British Army there had never been a surrender like this.'[61] Chamberlain even surmised that the fall of Kut might lead to the downfall of the government.[62]

The combination of military disaster and medical scandal ensured that heads would have to roll. In Chamberlain's view the main responsibility lay with General Nixon who 'habitually took too sanguine a view of the situation in front of him and . . . never laid to heart the dictum that an army marches on its belly or co-ordinated his transport and supply arrangements with the military operations he planned.'[63] A longer term factor was that Hardinge's pre-war attempts to strengthen the Indian army had been largely unsuccessful, leaving it in no fit state to face a major enemy outside its own borders. Such problems, Chamberlain believed, were compounded by the nature of the Indian government, where the system established by Kitchener back in 1905 had led to Curzon's resignation as Viceroy. Indeed the Mesopotamian Commission later concluded that the faulty division of responsibility between Britain and India had been at the root of the problem. Under the Kitchener scheme too much authority was concentrated in the hands of the Indian Commander-in-Chief, who had to combine the functions of Secretary for War, Chief of the General Staff and Commander of the forces in the field. Beauchamp Duff was not the man for this position though, 'an Archangel couldn't do the work – even if he were much better supplied with staff.'[64] The very fact that the control of the Mesopotamian Campaign was in the hands of the Government of India was itself an anomaly and on 31 January 1916 Sir William Robertson, the Chief of the Imperial General Staff, drew up a memorandum in which he argued that control should be transferred to himself, thereby combining in the War Office the authority directing operations with that controlling reserves. The proposal met with widespread support, including Chamberlain's, and the change was effected on 16 February.[65] Chamberlain believed that this could only improve relations with Beauchamp Duff who 'will take hints and suggestions from C I G S which he resented from the S of S whom he considered to be merely Barrow [the India Office's leading military adviser] under another name.'[66]

Chamberlain had not found it easy to operate within such a system. Moreover, like all politicians at this time, he found dealing with Kitchener, the War Minister, no easy matter. The latter tried to run the whole of the Great War in the same personal way in which he had successfully managed the tiny Nile Expedition many years earlier, only releasing such information to the despised 'frocks' as was absolutely necessary. Chamberlain complained about the extent to which he was kept in the dark about military operations and was concerned by the way in which individual army commanders communicated directly with Kitchener.[67] That Townshend had expressed misgivings about the advance on Baghdad was, Chamberlain said, 'news to me'.[68] Yet such considerations cannot exonerate Chamberlain of all responsibility for what happened in Mesopotamia. It is true that on occasion he was simply fed false information. In early December 1915, for example, he heard from General Nixon that 'the medical arrangements, under circumstances of considerable difficulty, worked splendidly' and on the strength of this made a statement to the same effect in the House of Commons.[69] Yet the very faith which Chamberlain placed in Hardinge and his reluctance to admit the Viceroy's culpability is open to criticism. At the time of his own appointment to office Chamberlain had stressed to Hardinge that the greatest danger might be that a general on the spot would fail to see the operations in their proper perspective, but he had been confident that this was 'a danger against which no man is better fitted to protect us than [Hardinge].'[70] In fact Hardinge himself allowed his perspective on events to be distorted by his excessive optimism and unfounded confidence in the military leaders, especially General Nixon. The Viceroy certainly failed to probe as deeply into the situation as Chamberlain urged in his private correspondence.

Yet the Secretary of State was also part of a collective failure by the British government to define clearly the limits and objectives of the whole campaign. In some ways Mesopotamia was typical of the amateurishness which characterised so much of the British war effort, as Asquith's government failed to streamline the machinery of war direction. The result was that after each military move was made it proved necessary to attack further on in order to secure the position already reached. Though at one moment Asquith could proclaim to the House of Commons that in the whole course of the war there had never been a series of operations 'more carefully contrived, more brilliantly conducted and with a better prospect of final success,'[71] such piecemeal strategy was always liable to end in disaster. A stronger Secretary of State than Chamberlain might have seen this and grappled more strenuously with the central questions involved. At all events the Asquith government was obliged by the military failures in Mesopotamia and the Dardanelles to set up separate inquiries into the two campaigns. Chamberlain's old colleague, Lord Midleton, Balfour's War Secretary, had urged him at the beginning of April 1916 to set up an enquiry in order to forestall criticism,[72] but Chamberlain objected to forcing government servants to defend themselves in the middle of a war and agreed to the creation of the Mesopotamian Commission only with great reluctance when it appeared that the government's position in the Commons would otherwise be threatened. The Commission was placed under the chairmanship of Lord George Hamilton, India Secretary between 1895 and 1903. To Hardinge Chamberlain expressed some confidence as to the outcome: 'For myself as for you I believe that full enquiry can be only to our advantage.'[73] By the time, however, that the Commission reported, the political situation in Britain was greatly changed.

Mesopotamia was not, of course, Chamberlain's only concern after his entry into Asquith's Cabinet. It was, after all, only a peripheral aspect of the country's war effort. But Chamberlain was not a member of the War or Dardanelles Committee and therefore not immediately involved in the day-to-day conduct of the conflict. He held views on the major strategic issues of the time such as the evacuation of Gallipoli and the beginnings of the campaign in Macedonia, but was not in a position to make these decisive. At times he felt his exclusion, as for example when Grey and Kitchener went to Paris in December 1915 and succeeded in overturning the Cabinet's earlier decision that the British troops based at Salonica should be withdrawn: 'We need to know the why and the wherefore and we are told only the bare result. What is the War Committee doing? Is it meeting?'[74] Chamberlain did, however, serve on several Cabinet committees and from June to August 1915 chaired a sub-committee of the Committee of Imperial Defence, looking at the question of the transfer of enemy vessels in neutral waters. Like all ministers he became conscious of the problem posed by the gap between Kitchener's standing in public opinion and his performance as a Cabinet colleague. From the headquarters of the British Expeditionary Force, Arthur Lee warned him that friction between Kitchener and Sir John French had reached the point where it was a grave national peril.[75] But Chamberlain wanted nothing to do with 'a sordid and cowardly intrigue first to get [Kitchener] out of the country and then, in his absence, to force him out of the Government.'[76] Lord Milner, who wanted to see Kitchener removed to the command in Egypt, called on Chamberlain to resign from the government in December 1915 so as to precipitate the downfall of the Ministry and a drastic reconstruction. Chamberlain would not agree. He believed that such action could only result in the return of the sort of partisan politics which had so hampered the conduct of the Boer War to the sole benefit of the enemy. In Chamberlain's mind, though the present government was far from perfect, there were definite national advantages in preserving it.[77]

The problem of Kitchener was largely resolved when the government took advantage of his temporary absence to elevate Sir William Robertson to the post of Chief of the Imperial General Staff, giving him unprecedented powers which effectively removed the War Minister from day-to-day control over military operations. By keeping the latter in the Cabinet, Asquith avoided a political crisis and continued to draw benefit from Kitchener's enormous prestige among his fellow countrymen. In June 1916, however, Kitchener was drowned while travelling to Russia on board H M S Hampshire. Chamberlain in fact had been invited to travel with him to discuss allied finance but had declined. For a moment it appeared that Chamberlain might become Minister of War in succession. He was the first choice both of Maurice Hankey, Secretary to the War Committee, and of the King, while Robertson 'rather inclined to' him and Asquith thought there was 'much to commend' him.[78] Robertson may well have seen in Chamberlain the sort of quiescent political boss under whom he could continue to develop what was near to becoming a military dictatorship in the country's war directorate. But from sources which 'it is hardly open to doubt', Balfour heard that Bonar Law had objected to Chamberlain's appointment on the ground that it would be a slight upon himself.[79] As a result it was Lloyd George who went to the War Office, while on 29 June, after three or four informal soundings through Law, Asquith sent for Chamberlain and offered him the Ministry of Munitions. The ensuing interview gave an indication of Chamberlain's rare ability to combine righteous indignation with exaggerated humility. Not for the last time in his career Chamberlain gave a display of wounded feelings at being offered such an office. He reminded the Prime Minister that at the formation of the Coalition Government Asquith had been careful to avoid giving the Munitions Ministry to a Unionist. Now that Lloyd George 'had got all the kudos he could out of it and . . . the limelight was . . . elsewhere,' it was no compliment to be offered the post. Chamberlain displayed a second distinctive characteristic in recalling at this time the events of many years before and showing how reluctant he was to forgive those who had crossed him. The whole Liberal party, he reminded Asquith, with the exception of Grey and Morley, had impugned Chamberlain's honour and that of his father at the time of the Boer War on the grounds of family connections with the manufacture of munitions. Yet while he refused absolutely to take on the Ministry of Munitions, Chamberlain offered to leave the India Office and assume a subordinate position if it would aid the Prime Minister in reshaping the government. As it was, Chamberlain stayed in his existing post.[80]

Notwithstanding such political manoeuvres Chamberlain's main concern, apart from Mesopotamia, during the life of the Asquith Coalition was the question of military service. This issue was central to the survival of the government and focussed a growing mood in the country which increasingly recognised that, in the field of manpower as in many others, the Great War would have to be fought on the basis of compulsion. Though he recognised that a most prodigious effort had been made by voluntary means, Chamberlain, who had not joined the National Service movement before the War, believed that universal compulsory service at the start of the conflict would have 'saved us much confusion, much loss and no little danger.'[81] In August and September Chamberlain served on a War Policy Committee under Lord Crewe's chairmanship and signed a minority report in favour of compulsion. In this he was supported by Churchill, Curzon and Selborne. The last two had by this stage become his closest associates in the government. As Selborne later recalled: '[Curzon] hated the P.M.'s ways and Bonar Law's attitude as much as I did and he and I worked in partnership with Austen.'[82] By the middle of October Chamberlain was inclined to leave the Cabinet if conscription were not proposed.[83] But instead of a measure of compulsory service the Coalition Government produced the 'Derby Scheme' by which men between eighteen and forty-one were asked to enrol in groups by age, an unmarried and a married group for each year. While Asquith, 'a convinced voluntaryist',[84] remained at the head of the government, the forces of compulsion made only slow progress. The choice of Derby, an enthusiastic conscriptionist, as Director-General of Recruiting, was a characteristic Asquithian move which left critics such as Chamberlain momentarily off balance.

When the Cabinet met on 1 November Chamberlain was surprised at the lack of support he received on the conscription question from Bonar Law. The Unionist leaders had agreed that Derby's scheme would have to be measured by its ability to produce an army of seventy divisions, but Law put up no fight when Asquith refused to discuss this notion and adjourned any decision.[85] As a result Chamberlain, Curzon and Selborne wrote a joint letter to the Prime Minister calling for an assurance that conscription would indeed be introduced if the Derby scheme failed to work satisfactorily. Faced with a possible Cabinet revolt Asquith gave way, though he still strove to limit the government's pledge.[86] When, however, it was announced at the beginning of January that more than three hundred thousand single men had evaded enrolment, the principle of compulsion was accepted. Asquith in fact had already appointed a Cabinet committee in mid-December to prepare legislation for the compulsory enlistment of single men.

In the first weeks of 1916 Chamberlain served with the Prime Minister and Reginald McKenna, the new Chancellor, on a Committee for the Co-ordination of Military and Financial Effort. The committee laid down as its first objective to secure the largest military force compatible with the discharge of other vital obligations. Chamberlain recognised that the economic strain upon Great Britain and her allies of maintaining the war at its present level might soon become acute and that every effort should therefore be made to bring the war to a decision as soon as possible. If British finance broke down, the country's allies would soon be driven from the field of battle. He saw that the only significant area for extending compulsion was among unattested married men. But even if 'skinned to the bone' this class would only produce 200,000 men. Chamberlain therefore came to the conclusion that the greatest advantage was to be reaped by extending the dilution of labour on private as well as government works and in a severer combing out of badged and starred single men, who had hitherto been deemed exempt from military service.[87] Later in the year Chamberlain tried to put these ideas into practice as chairman of the Manpower Board but came up against violent opposition from the leaders of the Trade Unions and the Labour party. In November a compromise was reached whereby the Trade Unions themselves issued cards of exemption.

By this time, however, the government's attention had been called once again, however reluctantly, to the question of Ireland. The Easter Rebellion had served as a stark reminder that the outbreak of hostilities had postponed rather than solved the country's problems. When the British government, by executing several of the leaders of the rising, added the element of martyrdom to an episode which might otherwise have died a natural death, the situation became acute. Once again Chamberlain was kept largely in the dark as to what was happening, but he felt strongly that Birrell, the minister responsible, had been negligent. The last thing that the government needed at this time was a discontented Ireland on its hands, especially in view of the effect this might have on public opinion in the still neutral United States. Asquith accordingly urged Lloyd George to devise a formula which would at least see them through the War. Lloyd George embarked on conversations with the two sides and, somewhat to his surprise, came up with a scheme that seemed to satisfy both Redmond and Carson. In effect it meant that Ireland minus the six counties would be granted immediate home rule and that the situation would be reviewed at the end of the War. Though Bonar Law seemed ready to go along with this

scheme, Chamberlain was less certain and argued that Lloyd George had
gone beyond the authority given him by the Cabinet.[88] Yet while Long
and Selborne felt obliged to resign from the government on this issue, it
was clear that Chamberlain had moved from the position he had occupied
at the outbreak of war. To Lansdowne he wrote:

I cannot help feeling that while the establishment of any form of Home Rule now
is ... a gamble, the rejection by us, after acceptance by Carson and the
Nationalists, of the proposals made by Lloyd George is not even a gamble but is
certain confusion and most dangerous provocation.[89]

Chamberlain, then, determined to stay in the government while holding
that the Prime Minister had mishandled the situation. 'We are all faced
with *faits accomplis* which earlier consultation might have modified or
avoided.'[90] In fact divisions within the Cabinet ensured by the end of July
that no settlement would be reached. A new Chief Secretary was
appointed and the old system of Dublin Castle administration reimposed.

* * *

By the autumn of 1916 Chamberlain was becoming both tired and
disillusioned. 'The iron of the Mesopotamian miseries,' wrote Selborne,
'entered into his soul.'[91] In October Neville noted that he was 'evidently
very much run down and one of these days he will be having a nervous
breakdown if he doesn't take better care of himself.'[92] A partial collapse
did indeed occur and Chamberlain was ordered to take a fortnight's rest.
A month later, however, Neville's wife, Annie, saw him looking 'very
white and wan and worn.' 'I can only say' added Neville 'that he generally
does nowadays.'[93] In part this was a reminder that Chamberlain never
enjoyed the stamina for continuous hard work. But additionally it
reflected not only disappointment incurred at his own ministry but also
Chamberlain's frustration at the continuing failure of the country's war
effort to produce the hoped-for victory and growing doubts about whether
the present government would ever succeed in this goal. The Battle of the
Somme had consumed massive casualties for but small gain; the failure of
the Royal Navy to secure a decisive victory at Jutland had stunned the
whole British Empire; and the campaign in the Balkans, even with the
intervention of Rumania, had given the lie to those who maintained that a
quick route to victory lay through the soft under-belly of the Central
Powers.

Chamberlain had begun by taking a charitable view of Asquith's
leadership. As the months passed, however, he came to share the
conviction of many others that, despite his many qualities, the Prime
Minister was an inadequate war leader. The Cabinet was 'the worst
managed of any of which I have ever heard' and Asquith 'incurably

haphazard in his ways and ... content to preside without directing.'[94] Chamberlain later described the lack of direction which Asquith gave to Cabinet discussions:

... when he at last intervened with a statement 'Now that that is decided we had better pass on to ...' there would be a general cry, 'But *what* has been decided?' and the discussion would begin all over again.[95]

The fact was that the full Cabinet was too large and cumbrous to act as the executive body for the direction of operations. The War was still, after two years, being fought largely as if it were a typical conflict of the nineteenth century requiring no modification in the machinery of government. The successive setting up of the War Council, Dardanelles Committee and War Committee, consisting of senior political, military and naval figures, was marred by the basic flaw that none exercised plenipotentiary powers. Far from speeding up the decision-making process, therefore, these bodies merely served to duplicate discussion and argument in the Cabinet itself.

The developments which brought down Asquith's government in December 1916 have been exhaustively chronicled, almost hour by hour. Even so discrepancies persist. As Chamberlain wrote to Lord Beaverbrook many years later: 'I suppose that no two accounts of these events will exactly coincide, even though everyone concerned was acting in good faith and tells the truth to the best of his ability.'[96] Here it is not necessary to repeat more than an outline of events which concern primarily the biographers of Asquith, Lloyd George and Bonar Law.[97] Chamberlain played only a supporting role in the dramatic crisis, though one that was not without significance. His actions, though less Machiavellian than portrayed by Lord Beaverbrook, reflect interestingly upon his attitude towards the leading protagonists in the drama.

It was Lloyd George, convinced that a drastic overhaul of the machinery of government was necessary, and Bonar Law, worried that his own position at the head of the Unionist party was under threat from an increasingly disgruntled group surrounding Sir Edward Carson, who took the initiative. Early in November Law told Asquith that some radical change would have to be made at once in the machinery of government. Thereafter Law concerted closely with Lloyd George and Carson in drawing up proposals for the creation of a small War Council with executive powers, but which would have left the premiership in Asquith's hands. After reflection, Asquith, fearing that his own position would soon become vulnerable, rejected the scheme. Only on 30 November were Chamberlain and other Unionist ministers informed of these developments. The reaction to Law's suggestions was almost universally hostile and the Conservative ministers put forward an alternative scheme for two committees of the Cabinet – the existing War Committee and a Home Committee for domestic aspects of the War. Such proposals, however, were rapidly overtaken by the course of events. On 1 December Lloyd George presented Asquith with a new scheme whereby the Prime Minister would not even be a member of the proposed War Council, but would be able to exercise powers of initiative and veto from outside. Asquith, though, insisted that the Prime Minister must be chairman of the War Council and that there had to be a right of appeal from its decisions to the Cabinet.

When the Unionist ministers met again on 3 December they did so in a heated atmosphere created by the premature disclosure in the press that Lloyd George would resign unless Asquith accepted his demands. At this meeting Chamberlain began to assume a prominent role and his actions have been the subject of some debate. According to Lord Beaverbrook, Chamberlain and the other Unionists with the exception of Law were unanimous in their hostility to Lloyd George. Thus, in calling upon Asquith to resign, they did so with the aim of strengthening the Prime Minister's hand by showing his indispensability. This seems unlikely in view of the increasingly critical attitude which Chamberlain had taken towards Asquith's government during the course of 1916. Moreover the Unionists were calling for Asquith's resignation and not simply the reconstruction of the government. After such a development it would be by no means certain that Asquith re-emerged as Prime Minister. According to Chamberlain, on the other hand, the consensus was that Unionist ministers should hold themselves aloof from the quarrel between Lloyd George and Asquith and that it was for Liberals alone to decide whom they wished to see at their head. Chamberlain's aim was to secure a stable government capable of conducting the War successfully. He wanted less to support Asquith against Lloyd George than to resolve one way or the other a situation which had become impossible. At all events a formal resolution was drawn up for transmission to Asquith.[98]

The probability is that Bonar Law himself misinterpreted the attitude of his Unionist colleagues and thus provided Beaverbrook with a misleading basis for his later history. Law's mistake was not to have taken his colleagues more fully into his confidence, thereby creating suspicion, resentment and the grounds for misunderstanding. Certainly Beaverbrook's account was not just the figment of his imagination. Others too were sure that Chamberlain was leading a pro-Asquith rearguard action to save the Prime Minister. Frances Stevenson was convinced of the existence of a 'Conservative clique ... intriguing with Asquith to prevent L.G. from forming a Government,' while Law believed that Chamberlain was intriguing against him and trying to oust him from the

Unionist leadership.[99] Chamberlain's opinion of Law had indeed fallen to its nadir – he had 'little confidence in Bonar Law's judgement and none in his strength of character,'[100] – but it would have been entirely alien to his nature to seek for personal advancement at such a time of national crisis.

At all events Bonar Law continued to add confusion to an already complex situation. Instead of showing Asquith the formal resolution drawn up by the Unionist leaders, he merely conveyed its gist to the Prime Minister. Either he succeeded in giving the premier the impression that the Unionist ministers were about to desert him, or Asquith read more significance into the call for his resignation, rather than the reconstruction of the ministry, than the Unionist ministers themselves had seen. In either case the outcome of this interview was that Asquith decided to compromise with Lloyd George and agree to the creation of a small War Council with the latter as its chairman. The crisis seemed to have passed until the appearance of a leading article in *The Times* on 4 December which implied that under the proposed reorganisation Asquith's powers would be purely nominal. With his will to resist strengthened by loyal Liberals such as McKenna and Grey, Asquith now determined to stand his ground and reject Lloyd George's proposals. He also seems to have heard from certain Unionist ministers who explained, rather more adequately than had Law, the true significance of their formal resolution. According to Beaverbrook, Chamberlain was among this group, though he himself denied it.[101] Certainly it is scarcely credible that at this stage Chamberlain was anxious to save Asquith. Robert Cecil later reflected, in private correspondence and at a time when nothing could have been gained by misrepresentation: 'The suggestion that we went to encourage him to resist Lloyd George is, as far as I can remember, entirely unfounded.'[102]

By now Chamberlain was in despair of Law and had determined to act in conjunction with Curzon, Cecil and Long. He concurred in Cecil's judgement that 'Bonar Law is an amateur and will always remain one'.[103] Frances Stevenson heard that Chamberlain was furious with Law for 'selling his colleagues.'[104] The four men met in Chamberlain's office on 5 December and came to the conclusion that Law had mishandled his interview with Asquith and that the crisis was now too far advanced for the present government to continue any longer. Thus when Chamberlain, Curzon and Cecil saw the Prime Minister later that day they made it clear that they would not be willing to remain in the government themselves if Law and Lloyd George both resigned. In the early evening the dissident Unionists sought clarification from Law as to his handling of the crisis, though the meeting scarcely amounted to the 'court-martial' of which Beaverbrook later wrote. The Unionist ministers agreed that they should all resign from the government and on receipt of this news Asquith tendered the resignation of the whole Cabinet to the King.

On 7 December the three 'Cs', as Beaverbrook dubbed them, and Walter Long accepted office under Lloyd George.[105] Chamberlain, in agreeing to stay on at the India Office without a seat in the Cabinet, was not enamoured of his own position and was still very suspicious of the new Prime Minister. 'I take no pleasure in a change which gives me a chief whom I profoundly distrust. . . . You will see that I am sick of being told how beautiful the new world is and how pleased I must be to live in it.'[106] But he took comfort that in many ways Lloyd George appeared to have been thwarted. Chamberlain's close associate Curzon was to be a member of the new five-man War Cabinet which would have total control of the war effort.[107] Lord Milner was also included, while Balfour, whom Lloyd George had seemed anxious to exclude, now moved up to the Foreign Office. Chamberlain was also pleased to reflect that the War Council and the Cabinet were now one body, which 'I believe I originally stood alone in [urging] when the old War Committee was formed.'[108] Neville on the other hand commented that Chamberlain seemed 'so tired that I can hardly wish that he had a more active post.'[109] If, in fact, events had turned out reasonably satisfactorily, Chamberlain could take little personal credit for this. Throughout the crisis he did not seem to know quite what he wanted and, lacking influence with Asquith, Lloyd George or even Law, never exerted a decisive impact upon the course of events.[110]

Chamberlain determined for a time at least to 'twang my harp in my own little corner.' For many in Britain 1917 was to be the year of doubt when morale weakened and some came to despair of victory ever being secured in any real sense. Chamberlain, however, remained resolute. The War may have been horrific but it was nonetheless necessary. The only thought which gave him qualms was the mortality and suffering among German babies and children.[111] His interpretation of German ambition had been coloured by his experience of that country nearly thirty years before. In March 1917 he told the Imperial War Cabinet that it was of vital importance to frustrate the effort of Germany to secure hegemony in the Middle-East, which threatened British interests in Suez, India and even Australasia.[112] The following month he sat on Curzon's committee to consider Britain's territorial *desiderata* at the end of hostilities. When later in the year Lansdowne wrote his controversial letter to the *Daily Telegraph* calling for a compromise peace, Chamberlain was appalled. His respect and liking for the Unionist peer had grown considerably over the years, but this letter was 'mischievous . . . inopportune . . . unwise,' and would be a great encouragement not only to Germany but to pacifists in Britain.[113]

At a personal level 1917 began with great anxiety for Chamberlain in the premature birth of his son Lawrence on 12 January. Chamberlain did not usually keep a diary, but on this occasion he recorded his feelings:

We have had a fortnight of great and heart-rending anxiety. More than once it seemed that the end had come, but thank God! when the doctors had given him up, he took a turn for the better and has been mending. When first weighed he was only 3 lbs. 12 oz.[114]

Indian affairs, however, could not long be ignored. When Hardinge had returned to London to resume his post as Permanent Under-Secretary at the Foreign Office, Chamberlain had failed to secure either of his preferences, Crawford (Balcarres) or Salisbury, as the new Viceroy. With Lord Chelmsford, however, he soon struck up a good working relationship and the new man proved far less blinkered than his predecessor in relation to the Mesopotamian Campaign. Chelmsford reported that there was 'a lack of grip and drive in the higher command in Mesopotamia' and that the army was 'rotten with disease and exhaustion from the climate.'[115] But with the control of military operations vested now in the War Office, Chamberlain had more time to turn his attention to longer term questions about the future of India. He saw with great clarity the central problem that would face continued British rule:

how is one to meet the legitimate . . . aspirations and ambitions of the small but increasingly united and increasingly influential educated class who look to the institutions of Western democracy for their model . . . when in fact the materials for a democracy do not exist.[116]

With great changes taking place in other parts of the world it could not be assumed that India would stand still:

there is a terrible ferment going on. Things were moving fast before the war, they are moving and will move faster now that all the world is hailing Revolution in Russia, hoping for it in Germany and proclaiming the freedom and independence of peoples.[117]

Slowly Chamberlain was coming round to Chelmsford's point of view that a public declaration would have to be made defining the goal of British rule in India. This could only be the development of free institutions with a view to ultimate self-government. But Chamberlain remained cautious. It should be accompanied by a further very clear declaration that this was a distant aspiration and that anyone who pretended it was realisable in the early future was no friend of Britain or India.[118] By the time of his resignation from the India Office Chamberlain had set himself the problem of how to begin the limited devolution of real responsibility and authority to Indian representatives – a task that was to be hastened under his successor Edwin Montagu.[119] The latter, however, regarded Chamberlain as over-cautious: ' "bold action" . . . is not in my opinion an accurate description of . . . the very inadequate measures which he has under contemplation.'[120]

Chamberlain's resignation was precipitated by the report of the Mesopotamian Commission. Despite his earlier personal optimism, others had foreseen that Chamberlain himself might suffer as a result of the Commission's deliberations. As early as March 1916 Ian Malcolm had admitted that the Government of India rather than the India Office was responsible, but 'I don't quite see how we can censure *them* . . . except indirectly through *you*.'[121] Chamberlain was called to give evidence before the Commission in the first days of Lloyd George's government, but it was not until June 1917 that he got wind of its findings. The Report was 'the saddest and most appalling document' Chamberlain had ever read.[122] He himself was held responsible in two ways. For the decision to advance on Baghdad, which was 'based on political and military miscalculations', the Commission drew up a descending scale of responsibility from Nixon, through Hardinge, Duff, Barrow, Chamberlain and the War Committee. In the question of medical provision it was found that Chamberlain had not brought his anxieties sufficiently into his official, as opposed to his private, correspondence with Hardinge, and had not been quick enough to bring about an enquiry.[123] In addition to these specific criticisms, the Report emphasised that 'so long as the system of responsible departmental administration exists in this country, those who are political heads of departments in time of war, whether they be civilian or military, cannot be entirely immune from the consequences of their own action.'[124] Political colleagues rallied to Chamberlain's defence. F. E. Smith, for example, thought he came out of the Report very well and that it was unfair to have singled him out at all.[125] Chamberlain anticipated 'bad results'. Yet he hoped to prevent injustice being done to individuals and still seemed determined to stand by Hardinge.[126] Curzon, invited by the Cabinet to consider the implications of the Report, argued that if the government did not now take action it would be subject to severe criticism from parliament and the country. The Report was the 'most shocking exposure of official blundering and incompetence . . . since the Crimean War.'[127]

In this increasingly difficult situation the Prime Minister gave Chamberlain the chance of a dignified retreat with the offer of the Paris Embassy. Chamberlain gave the idea careful thought but, warned by Neville that acceptance would mark the end of his career in domestic politics, decided to decline the offer.[128] Another idea with which he toyed was that he might resign his office in order to make a trip to India to see the situation there at first hand.[129] On reflection, however, Chamberlain decided to stay where he was. With useful information from Lord George Hamilton's own period as Secretary of State he was ready to defend his use of private correspondence, while there was plenty of evidence to show that he had drawn repeated attention to the medical deficiencies.[130] Chamberlain believed, moreover, that in some of its criticism the Report had misunderstood the constitutional position of the Secretary of State.[131]

What changed his mind was the decision of the Cabinet to set up a Court of Enquiry which would decide against which individuals action should be taken. This Chamberlain felt was a mistake. The government should have decided upon action in relation to individuals and left the House of Commons to pass its verdict thereafter. The Prime Minister had funked and 'funk is the worst of all policies.'[132] The whole problem could have been avoided, he later told the Viceroy, 'if the Cabinet had been a little more agreed about Hardinge or had had a little more courage to face a 48 hours parliamentary storm.'[133] Feeling that he could not continue to act in the Cabinet or defend his subordinates in this situation, Chamberlain tendered his resignation. To the King he wrote:

When a Minister can no longer protect those who have served or are serving under him, when his own actions are made the subject of review by a Judicial Tribunal ... it is not consonant with the honour of public men or of Your Majesty's Government that that Minister should continue in his employment.[134]

Even an appeal from Lloyd George to reconsider his decision met with no response.[135] 'My resignation is final and cannot be withdrawn.'[136] When the House of Commons debated the report on 12 July, Chamberlain, free from the constraints of office, made an effective defence of his own actions and those of most of his subordinates including Hardinge. His most telling argument was to remind the House that the system set up in India by Kitchener had been expressly designed to give the Viceroy a single channel of military advice. It was therefore somewhat perverse to blame him for having taken it.[137]

Chamberlain's resignation has usually been presented in terms of his high-minded commitment to honour and duty – as an act which no one really thought was necessary. It distressed Leo Amery 'beyond words to think that [Chamberlain] who ... has done all that was humanly possible ... should resign ... just because the Government ... has hit upon this absurd device of a judicial inquiry.'[138] Hardinge argued that Chamberlain's speech had 'knocked the bottom out of the Commission's Report' as far as Chamberlain and the India Office were concerned, and that the Prime Minister should refuse his resignation.[139] The position, however, was more complicated than this. At the beginning of July Edwin

Montagu, soon to be Chamberlain's successor, warned Lloyd George that there was 'very strong criticism of Mr. Chamberlain's retention of office.' The underlying problem was that Chamberlain had done nothing to fit India to play a significant role in a world war, but had then acquiesced in her attempt to play just such a part. It would therefore be inappropriate for Chamberlain to embark now upon a reform of the system of Indian government when he had 'shown that he is intent on mending the lavatory tap when the house is on fire!'[140]

Though sorry to give up the India Office just when he believed he was making progress with that country's problems, Chamberlain was in many ways glad to be relieved of the burdens of office and ready to 'enjoy and profit by the holiday which falls to my lot.'[141] Warned by Lansdowne that his 'official reincarnation will probably take place rather sooner than you would wish,'[142] Chamberlain was at pains to distance himself from the political scene for the time being. Recognising that he could easily become a rallying point for discontented members in the House of Commons, Chamberlain deliberately stayed away from parliament, while admitting that in the future he would have a role to play 'in steadying our friends and rallying some of those who will support the Government in seeing the war through ... to a decently satisfactory conclusion.'[143] Though he kept in close touch with his successor at the India Office and gave freely of his advice and opinions, Montagu insisted that Chamberlain was not the man to be invited to go to India at the head of a proposed delegation to consider postwar development.[144]

His greater leisure allowed Chamberlain to speculate on the future of British politics once the War was over. He believed that Lloyd George saw himself at the head of a post-war Liberal-Labour combination.[145] In such a situation Chamberlain was uncertain what would be the role of men such as himself 'of conservative tendencies.' 'What shall we inscribe on our standard? How and for what seek to rally Unionist and conservative ... forces after the war for the problems which then confront us?'[146] By early 1918 some Conservatives were coming to see Chamberlain as a possible leader against whatever designs Lloyd George and Bonar Law might have for the destruction of the historic Unionist party.[147] The Prime Minister had Law 'absolutely under his thumb and the knowledge that that is so destroys Bonar Law's influence in his own party.'[148] Of the Unionist leader Chamberlain had become almost totally contemptuous: 'He is a curious mixture – at one and the same time over-confident and over-prudent, over-daring and over-timid, ambitious and fearful, satisfied with his own judgment in theory and utterly dependent on his surroundings in practice.'[149] But from Chamberlain's point of view the problem was that Lloyd George, for all his faults, was still the best man to lead the country through a war whose conclusion seemed in the autumn of 1917 as far off as ever. He was the 'personal embodiment of our war policy.' In general, therefore, Chamberlain determined to support the government from outside and did not rule out the possibility of one day rejoining it.[150]

By the end of the year Chamberlain was once again exerting political influence. Through Curzon he let it be known that there might be serious parliamentary trouble if Lloyd George openly criticised the British generals, including Haig. He was not, however, prepared to join with Asquith in open criticism of the Prime Minister.[151] By this stage, in fact, his return to the government was being discussed, though the prospect of the Home Office filled him with no enthusiasm: 'It seems very remote from the war and while the war lasts I should like to be engaged on war work.'[152] In February 1918 Chamberlain's return seemed imminent with Lord Derby on the point of resignation from the War Office after the virtual dismissal of Sir William Robertson as C.I.G.S. Lloyd George consulted Law and between them they agreed to offer the post to Chamberlain. At Law's request the latter, though anxious for a guarantee that the office would carry a seat in the War Cabinet, motored to London only to find on arrival that Derby had changed his mind and withdrawn his resignation.[153]

One further crisis delayed Chamberlain's re-emergence as a government minister. Following the creation of the Ministry of Information under Lord Beaverbrook, Chamberlain raised in the House of Commons on 19 February the question of the presence of newspaper proprietors in the administration. Chamberlain argued that it was wrong of the Prime Minister to seek in this way to secure for himself the support of a powerful group of newspapers. He also knew, although he avoided mentioning this in parliament, that one of Lloyd George's secretaries regularly gave instructions to the press as to what they should say on the events of the day. In Chamberlain's mind the appointment of Beaverbrook and the offer of a post to Lord Northcliffe threatened the line of demarcation which had previously existed between the functions of the press and those of the government. It was probably not beyond his imagination to see that a new and dangerous weapon of propaganda could be employed by an unscrupulous government to sustain political power.[154] Chamberlain clearly felt that this was an example of the way in which the Prime Minister was straining the limits of democratic government and that the 'suspicion and intrigue which now surround the Government are slowly sapping public confidence in it.'[155] His speech on 19 February received widespread support in the House of Commons and many members urged him to table a resolution on the subject which Lloyd

George would have to treat as a vote of confidence. Beaverbrook later recalled: 'His language was strong, his attitude unbending and his support on the benches very considerable indeed.'[156] Chamberlain's attitude towards the government, however, remained ambivalent and he preferred to urge Milner and Curzon to raise the question in the Cabinet and thereby get the matter settled without further debate.[157] When the so-called Unionist War Committee, a ginger group under Lord Salisbury, produced a resolution which went far beyond Chamberlain's strictures, the latter was quick to dissociate himself from it.[158] Chamberlain's problem was that if a parliamentary motion on the subject were carried it would destroy the government; if it failed, the Prime Minister's actions would have been approved. 'And I do not wish to produce either of these results.'[159] Caught in this dilemma Chamberlain preferred to bide his time: 'I don't think if my bluff is called that I hold the winning hand.'[160] As no help was forthcoming from the War Cabinet, he concluded that he would achieve nothing beyond 'having made the P.M. uncomfortable for a week or ten days.'[161]

Nonetheless Chamberlain renewed his attack in the Commons on 11 March and raised the question of recent criticism of Robertson and Admiral Jellicoe in the *Daily Mail*. It was, Chamberlain said, an unfortunate coincidence that soon after this episode Northcliffe had been offered office in the government. Rather to his own dismay Chamberlain received substantial backing from the opposition Liberal benches:

I have tried from the first since this War broke out . . . to support the Government of the day in carrying the War to a successful conclusion. When these hon. Gentlemen can say the same, and not before, shall I desire their cheers or their approval.[162]

Among some of his closer associates, however, Chamberlain's campaign was received with rather less enthusiasm. Milner thought he was 'barking up the wrong tree', while Leo Amery told him that putting great newspaper proprietors into the government was no more heinous an offence than including great landlords for the sake of their local influence. The real question was whether the individuals concerned were fit for the jobs given to them. Amery reflected that the episode displayed all Chamberlain's worst defects: 'his incapacity to realise that we are no longer in the parliamentary world of the '80s and his lack of proportion in dealing with anything that savours of breach of good form, personal loyalty or political etiquette. He is too genteel.'[163]

Despite such misgivings, Lloyd George seems to have concluded that Chamberlain was becoming too dangerous a critic to be ignored and to have resolved to bring him back into the government as soon as possible.

In addition to Chamberlain's campaign over the press, Lloyd George also had in mind his own determination once again to tackle the Irish problem and the possibility that an excluded Chamberlain might provide a rallying point for Unionist malcontents. The Prime Minister confided his intention to Hankey on 24 February and the latter suggested that Chamberlain could be given control of all committees and departments dealing with Supply.[164] Amery later advised Lloyd George that Chamberlain was just the man to help with miscellaneous committee work.[165] Chamberlain, himself, rather liked the idea of a return to office, but was full of 'growing distrust' for the Prime Minister, especially as the latter increasingly turned his attention to the post-war situation. 'I cannot shout myself hoarse over the cry Great is our David or proclaim myself his prophet.'[166] He was still disposed to see Lloyd George as the best Prime Minister for the War if only he would concentrate on the War itself and not allow his attention to be diverted to the problem of founding a new political party.[167]

As the government prepared to introduce an extension to the scheme of compulsory military service, Chamberlain pressed Law to ensure that Ireland was included in any bill brought forward. This was a matter upon which many Unionists felt very strongly and Robert Cecil had already sounded Chamberlain out as to whether he would try to form an alternative administration if the Prime Minister failed to take this course.[168] Using Law as an ineffective intermediary Lloyd George now proceeded to invite Chamberlain to join the War Cabinet. The latter made guarantees on the Irish question the pre-condition of his acceptance. Believing that there was growing cross-party support for his old idea of 'home rule all round', he once more insisted upon a federal solution involving devolution throughout the United Kingdom and a promise that there would be no coercion of Ulster into this general scheme until it had been applied across the British Isles.[169] Chamberlain was now convinced that the old Unionist policy on Ireland had become untenable not because it was wrong, but because the British people would not give it sufficient support. The problem of post-war reconstruction and the strains which this might place upon the Imperial Parliament at Westminster could not but reinforce his case.[170] Influenced also by the way in which so many Irish Nationalists had loyally supported the British cause since the outbreak of the War, Chamberlain was ready 'to regard the Irish problem with new eyes and an open mind.'[171] Lloyd George accepted Chamberlain's insistence upon a federal solution but argued that Home Rule could not be delayed until a complete scheme of devolution had been worked out.[172] Following a talk with Law and after being promised a seat on the committee to frame the Irish bill, Chamberlain agreed to waive his second precondition. 'The situation is so grave', he reflected, 'that one

must help if one can.'[173] In this way Chamberlain returned to the
government as Minister without Portfolio, but to a more important
position than he had occupied hitherto in the War, because of his
membership of the War Cabinet. But he joined the government 'without
any elation and under the gravest sense of the responsibility that I am
undertaking and the difficulties which confront us.'[174] His sense of public
duty was again compelling. 'It isn't a time for balancing between I dare not
and I would, for half-hearted criticism and half-hearted support.'[175]

On entering the administration Chamberlain was immediately
embroiled in the work of the committee to draft a Home Rule Bill. He was
far from sanguine of success and feared that the government's proposals
might well combine Nationalists and Ulstermen in opposition, while
differences of opinion within the Unionist party would be a major
stumbling block. But Chamberlain recognised that as a result of the War
'a new world has come into existence with new problems of profound
gravity.' This made the settlement of old issues such as Ireland more
urgent than ever if government was not going to be overwhelmed with
problems when the War ended.[176] He therefore favoured giving the Irish
Parliament the largest possible powers with which it could safely be
endowed. He believed that the government would have to declare a view
on federalism generally when introducing a bill and indeed that the bill
might be wrecked if it were shown to be inconsistent with federalism.[177] If
a federal scheme could be introduced for the United Kingdom as a whole
it might serve to undermine the opposition of Ulster to Home Rule, but the
time for such a wide-ranging constitutional reorganisation was simply not
available.[178] In fact the federal scheme ran into difficulties as soon as its
financial implications were considered. These particularly impressed
Chamberlain as a former Chancellor of the Exchequer.[179] By June he was
'mightily troubled' about Ireland and could see no way out of the
difficulties.[180] Soon afterwards this latest attempt to deal with the running
sore of Ireland ground to a halt.

Although as a member of the War Cabinet Chamberlain had no
departmental responsibilities, his time was fully occupied. In addition to
the question of Ireland and almost daily meetings on the conduct of the
War, he was made chairman of the Economic Defence and Development
Committee at the beginning of June. During the summer he joined with
Curzon and Montagu in an informal grouping of ministers considering
Indian problems, and did his best to urge patience and restraint upon what
he thought were Montagu's over-hasty judgments.[181] But when Lloyd
George approached him to take over the Admiralty in the temporary
absence of Eric Geddes, Chamberlain drew the line: 'I shall be acting
temporary stop-gap First Lord in spite of all my strong repugnance.'[182]

After four years of unprecedented effort, punctuated by so many false dawns and disappointed expectations, few in Britain anticipated the suddenness with which the end of hostilities finally arrived. Few understood how Germany had been brought to the point of exhaustion by long military effort, coming to a peak in the last desperate push of March 1918, and by the effects of the Allied blockade. Chamberlain was no exception. At the end of September he had his first inkling of what was afoot. 'Does the German edifice begin to crack? I rather think it does, tho' it may yet be long in falling.'[183] He was concerned that the Germans seemed ready to accept the Fourteen Points as a basis for peace. His own inclination was for a 'peace on most onerous conditions for Germany', though he would not fight on for vengeance alone, since this could only lead to a further weakening of British power and the emergence of the United States as the sole arbiter of the peace settlement.[184] As the Armistice approached Chamberlain's thoughts inevitably returned to domestic politics. He regretted that the prevailing mood seemed to favour an early General Election with unforeseeable results. 'It is like dipping in a "lucky bag" which childhood memories tell me was apt to be a disappointment.'[185] His main concern was that the government should remain as broadly based as it had been during the latter half of the War, since it would need a large measure of support from the country to deal with immensely difficult problems of demobilisation and reconstruction.[186]

On the eleventh day of November what had come to seem impossible finally happened and the Armistice came into effect. Upon all the leading statesmen of the time fell an enormous responsibility to ensure that the world which emerged from the ruins of war was a better and safer place for mankind. Chamberlain was to be at the centre of this endeavour in the domestic and international arenas for the next decade. Restored to the ranks of government, he stood now as a prominent member of the War Cabinet which had brought the conflict to a successful conclusion. It was a remarkable reversal in his fortunes considering the apparently declining position he had occupied in 1914 and his enforced resignation from office in 1917. But the Chamberlain who emerged from the war was a subtly different figure from the politician of 1914. It is of course a truism that the Great War transformed the lives of all who lived through it. Yet Chamberlain was more conscious than most that the political environment of Edwardian England could never be recreated. From 1917 onwards he was acutely conscious that the fabric of western society had been profoundly shaken. His correspondence in the last year of the War is full of references to the danger of revolution. One of the reasons why he rekindled the idea of devolution was his fear that, if Westminster were not unburdened of some of its workload, the authority of parliament would be destroyed and 'we should be well on the road which leads to revolution.'[187] Two days before Germany finally laid down her arms, Chamberlain looked forward with apprehension to a future which seemed 'full of difficulty and danger, strikes, discontent and much revolutionary feeling in the air when the strain and patriotic self-repression of the last few years is removed.'[188] His own priorities had thus changed in such a way as to ensure that, with the position he had now carved out for himself in public life, he would play a leading role in redrawing a new party political landscape after 1918.

Notes

1. A. Chamberlain to Lord Chelmsford 1 Oct. 1917, Chamberlain MSS, AC 18/3/3.
2. A. Chamberlain to Ida Chamberlain 4 Nov. 1917, ibid, AC 5/1/45.
3. Beaverbrook to Petrie 2 Jan. 1961, Beaverbrook MSS, BBK C/270.
4. L. Amery, *Diaries* p. 105.
5. Petrie, *Life* i, 373.
6. Chamberlain's own account of these events is to be found in *Down the Years* pp. 92–106.
7. N. Chamberlain to A. Chamberlain 15 Aug. 1914, Chamberlain MSS, AC 14/2/4.
8. D. Lammers, 'Arno Mayer and the British Decision for War: 1914', *Journal of British Studies* xii, 2, (1973) passim.
9. L. Amery, *Life* ii, 19.
10. J. Collings to A. Chamberlain 26 Dec. 1914, Chamberlain MSS, AC 13/3/20.
11. Petrie, *Life* i, 377; see below pp. 126–7.
12. C. Hazlehurst, *Politicians at War* (London, 1971) p. 157. Chamberlain soon became concerned about his own rather anomalous position. To St. Aldwyn he wrote on 27 August, 'I am really in a very difficult position for I am not in constant communication with him [Lloyd George] and very often I am not admitted to the really decisive councils. I have had no really serious discussion with him since I met him with you on the 13th.' A. Chamberlain to St. Aldwyn 27 Aug. 1914, St. Aldwyn MSS D 2455/PCC 87.
13. A. Steel-Maitland to A. Bonar Law 4 Nov. 1914, Bonar Law MSS 35/2/7. See also D. Lloyd George, *War Memoirs* (2 vol. edn., London, 1938) i, 64, 72.
14. C. Hazlehurst, p. 172.
15. Memorandum by A. Chamberlain 12 Aug. 1914, Chamberlain MSS, AC 11/1/38.
16. A. Chamberlain to Lloyd George 1 Sept. 1914, ibid, AC 11/1/61.
17. A. Chamberlain to M. Chamberlain 2 Sept. 1914, ibid, AC 4/1/1139.

18. *Gleanings and Memoranda*, October 1914.
19. H. Asquith, *Memories and Reflections* (London, 1928) ii, 33.
20. Petrie, *Life* ii, 6–14; M. Gilbert, *Churchill* iii, 1, 109–16.
21. As note 17.
22. A. Chamberlain to F. Acland 7 Dec. 1914, Chamberlain MSS, AC 13/1/3.
23. Hazlehurst, *Politicians* p. 271.
24. Milner to A. Chamberlain 17 May 1915, Chamberlain MSS, AC 13/3/71.
25. M. D. Pugh, 'Asquith, Bonar Law and the First Coalition', *Historical Journal* xvii, 4 (1974) p. 813.
26. As note 24.
27. Note by A. Chamberlain 14 May 1915, Chamberlain MSS, AC 2/2/25; see also Petrie, *Life* ii, 20–27.
28. A. Chamberlain to Bonar Law 17 May 1915, Bonar Law MSS, BL 37/2/37.
29. Salisbury to R. Cecil 19 May 1915, Cecil MSS 51085.
30. As note 28.
31. R. Blake, *Unknown Prime Minister* p. 250.
32. A. Chamberlain to Law 21 May 1915, Bonar Law MSS, 50/3/26.
33. Letter from Lady Oxford, published in *The Times* 6 Oct. 1937.
34. A. Chamberlain to Ida Chamberlain 4 Nov. 1917, Chamberlain MSS, AC 5/1/45.
35. A. Chamberlain to Ivy Chamberlain 8 June 1915, ibid, AC 6/1/183.
36. A. Chamberlain to Lord Hardinge May 1915, cited Petrie, *Life* ii, 30.
37. Hazlehurst, *Politicians* p. 285; E. David, *Inside Asquith's Cabinet* (London, 1977) p. 249.
38. Note by Selborne on Cabinet colleagues, 1916, Selborne MSS 80 ff. 285–9.
39. Chamberlain to Hardinge 27 May 1915, cited D. Goold, 'Lord Hardinge and the Mesopotamia Expedition and Inquiry 1914–1917', *Historical Journal* 19, 4 (1976) p. 928.
40. Ibid, 25 June 1915, cited Goold, 'Lord Hardinge' p. 928.
41. A. Chamberlain to Ivy Chamberlain 4 June 1915, Chamberlain MSS, AC 6/1/176.
42. Goold, 'Lord Hardinge' pp. 929–32. Chamberlain's hesitations are evident in a letter to Hardinge of 26 Aug. 1915; 'I am sorry that it should be necessary in the . . . case [of Mesopotamia] to advance to Kut-el-Amarah but your reasons for doing so appear to be incontrovertible'. Chamberlain MSS, AC 62/134.
43. Goold, 'Lord Hardinge' pp. 932–3.
44. Ibid, p. 933.
45. Report by committee, Oct. 1915, Chamberlain MSS, AC 46/7/2.
46. A. Chamberlain to Hardinge 8 Oct. 1915, ibid, AC 46/7/11 and AC 62/142. 'There is, it would seem, an opportunity within our grasp for a great success such as we have not yet achieved in any quarter and it is difficult to overrate the political (and even military) advantages which would follow from it throughout the Far East.' See also B. C. Busch,

Hardinge of Penshurst (Connecticut, 1980) pp. 237–8, and D. Lloyd George, *War Memoirs* i, 482.
47. Townshend to Curzon 4 Sept. 1915, Curzon MSS Eur. F112/163.
48. Hardinge to A. Chamberlain 16 Aug. 1915, Chamberlain MSS, AC 45/2/4.
49. A. Chamberlain to Hardinge 29 Oct. 1915, cited Goold, 'Lord Hardinge' p. 935.
50. Ibid, 3 Dec. 1915, cited Goold, 'Lord Hardinge' p. 940.
51. Selborne to A. Chamberlain 30 Nov. 1915, Chamberlain MSS, AC 13/3/93.
52. Hardinge to A. Chamberlain 24 Dec. 1915, ibid, AC 45/2/8.
53. A. Chamberlain to Balfour 25 Feb. 1916, Balfour MSS 49736.
54. Unsigned letter from serving officer, 16 Jan. 1916, Chamberlain MSS, AC 46/2/58.
55. Hardinge to A. Chamberlain 2 March 1916, ibid, AC 45/2/11.
56. Ibid, 25 Feb. 1916, AC 45/2/10.
57. A. Chamberlain to Hardinge 24 Feb. 1916, ibid, AC 12/31; A. Chamberlain to Willingdon 24 Feb. 1916, AC 12/32.
58. House of Commons Debates, vol. 81, cols 229–34.
59. A. Chamberlain to Curzon 7 Dec. 1915, Curzon MSS Eur. F112/114 a.
60. Ibid, 19 March 1916, Eur. F112/163.
61. A. J. Barker, *The Neglected War* (London, 1967) p. 266.
62. A. Chamberlain to Ivy Chamberlain 28 April 1916, Chamberlain MSS, AC 6/1/204.
63. Memorandum by A. Chamberlain on the Mesopotamian Operations 14 July 1916, Lloyd George MSS E/8/2/5a.
64. A. Chamberlain to Curzon 31 March 1916, Curzon MSS Eur. F112/163.
65. Goold, 'Lord Hardinge' pp. 938–9.
66. As note 60.
67. A. Chamberlain to Hardinge 14 Sept. 1915, Chamberlain MSS, AC 45/2/5.
68. As note 59.
69. Petrie, *Life* ii, 41.
70. A. Chamberlain to Hardinge 27 May 1915, cited Goold, 'Lord Hardinge' p. 928. On 25 June 1915 Chamberlain confessed, 'It is difficult from a distance to say when a forward movement increases our responsibilities and when it is in fact the best means of defence. Provided [Nixon] understands clearly the governing circumstances of the situation and does not embark on new operations in the belief that he can call for more troops whenever he wishes, I shall be satisfied to rely in the main on his judgment.' A. Chamberlain to Hardinge 25 June 1915, Chamberlain MSS, AC 62/123.
71. House of Commons Debates, vol LXXV, col. 509.
72. Midleton to A. Chamberlain 1 April 1916, Chamberlain MSS, AC 46/2/28.
73. A. Chamberlain to Hardinge 21 July 1916, cited Busch, *Hardinge* p. 265.

74. A. Chamberlain to Selborne 10 Dec. 1915, Selborne MSS 80 f.103.
75. A. Lee to A. Chamberlain 24 June 1915, Chamberlain MSS, AC 13/3/45.
76. A. Chamberlain to Law 7 Nov. 1915, Bonar Law MSS 117/1/22. To Hardinge, Chamberlain wrote, '[Kitchener] is not an easy man to deal with, for he talks loosely and changes his mind often.' A. Chamberlain to Hardinge 22 Oct. 1915, Chamberlain MSS, AC 62/146.
77. Milner to A. Chamberlain 6 Dec. 1915, ibid, AC 13/3/75; A. Gollin, *Proconsul in Politics* p. 318.
78. S. Roskill, *Hankey: Man of Secrets* (1970–74) i, 280, 283; A. Chamberlain to M. Hankey 28 Nov. 1916, Chamberlain MSS, AC 12/96.
79. Balfour to Salisbury 17 June 1916, Balfour MSS 49758.
80. A. Chamberlain to Curzon 3 July 1916, Curzon MSS Eur. F 112/116; N. Chamberlain Diary 1 July 1916, Chamberlain MSS, NC 2/20.
81. A. Chamberlain to M. Chamberlain 14 May 1916, Chamberlain MSS, AC 4/1/1175.
82. War Policy Committee Report 7 Sept. 1915, ibid, AC 18/4/8; Selborne's notes on Cabinet colleagues, 1916, Selborne MSS 80 ff. 285–89.
83. E. David, *Asquith's Cabinet* p. 255.
84. Ibid.
85. A. Chamberlain to Law 2 Nov. 1915, Chamberlain MSS, AC 19/1/4.
86. A. Chamberlain, Selborne and Curzon to Asquith 3 Nov. 1915, ibid, AC 19/1/6; A. Chamberlain to Asquith 29 Dec. 1915, ibid, AC 19/1/9.
87. Note by A. Chamberlain on military policy 17 Jan. 1916, ibid, AC 13/3/14; Memorandum by A. Chamberlain for Unionist colleagues 15 April 1916, AC 19/1/40.
88. A. Chamberlain to Asquith 22 June 1916, ibid, AC 15/1/9.
89. A. Chamberlain to Lansdowne 23 July 1916, ibid, AC 14/5/5.
90. A. Chamberlain to Selborne 21 June 1916, Selborne MSS 80 ff. 244–5.
91. Selborne's notes on Cabinet colleagues, 1916, ibid, 80 ff.285–89.
92. N. Chamberlain to H. Chamberlain 22 Oct. 1916, Chamberlain MSS, NC 18/1/85.
93. N. Chamberlain to Ida Chamberlain 12 Nov. 1916, ibid, NC 18/1/88.
94. A. Chamberlain to Ivy Chamberlain 26 April 1916, ibid, AC 6/1/201.
95. *Down the Years* p. 111. To Hardinge Chamberlain wrote: 'Of one thing I am quite certain . . . that the Cabinet, and even the war council as at present constituted, are too big to conduct the war with the promptitude and firmness of decision which are necessary and that we must surrender our corporate power into the hands of a further small Committee who can get to the bottom of questions and can take swift decisions.' A. Chamberlain to Hardinge 22 Oct. 1915, Chamberlain MSS, AC 62/146.
96. A. Chamberlain to Beaverbrook 30 June 1931, cited S. Koss, *Asquith* (London, 1976) p. 221.
97. R. Jenkins, *Asquith* (London, 1964) chapters XXVI–XXVII; S. Koss, *Asquith* chapter 9; P. Rowland, *Lloyd George* (London, 1975) chapter 10; R. Blake, *Unknown Prime Minister* chapters xix–xxi. See also Lord Beaverbrook, *Politicians and the War 1914–1916*, vol. 2 (London, 1932)

passim, and A. Chamberlain, *Down the Years* chapter VII.

98. A. Chamberlain, *Down the Years* pp. 117–8; Beaverbrook, *Politicians and the War* ii, 209–13.

99. F. Stevenson to Beaverbrook 15 Oct. 1928, Lloyd George MSS, G/3/6/21. A. Chamberlain to W. Long 11 Dec. 1923, Chamberlain MSS, AC 15/3/21.

100. A. Chamberlain to Chelmsford 8 Dec. 1916, ibid, AC 15/3/8.

101. A. Chamberlain, *Down the Years* p. 123; Beaverbrook, *Politicians and the War* ii, 239.

102. R. Cecil to A. Chamberlain 30 May 1932, Chamberlain MSS, AC 39/5/39.

103. As note 100.

104. F. Stevenson, *Lloyd George: A Diary*, ed. A. J. P. Taylor (London, 1971) p. 131.

105. Memorandum of conversation between Mr. Lloyd George and certain Unionist ex-Ministers, 7 Dec. 1916, Bonar Law MSS 81/1/36; Curzon MSS, Eur. F 112/130.

106. A. Chamberlain to H. Chamberlain 14 Dec. 1916, Chamberlain MSS, AC 5/1/3.

107. A. Chamberlain to Curzon 8 Dec. 1916, Curzon MSS Eur. F 112/116.

108. A. Chamberlain to N. Chamberlain 11 Dec. 1916, Chamberlain MSS, NC 1/27/6.

109. N. Chamberlain to Ida Chamberlain 9 Dec. 1916, ibid, NC 18/1/92.

110. R. Jenkins, *Asquith* p. 438.

111. A. Chamberlain to H. Chamberlain 14 Dec. 1916, Chamberlain MSS, AC 5/1/3; A. Chamberlain to Ida Chamberlain 8 Oct. 1917, ibid, AC 5/1/39.

112. Minutes of Imperial War Cabinet 22 March 1917, ibid, AC 20/8/3.

113. A. Chamberlain to H. Chamberlain 2 Dec. 1917, ibid, AC 5/1/48.

114. Notes 'copied from an old diary' 28 Jan. 1917, ibid, AC 12/37.

115. Chelmsford to A. Chamberlain 4 Aug. 1916 and 11 Aug. 1916, ibid, AC 61/22, 24.

116. A. Chamberlain to H. Chamberlain 24 March 1917, ibid, AC 5/1/18.

117. A. Chamberlain to Ida Chamberlain 21 April 1917, ibid, AC 5/1/23.

118. A. Chamberlain to Chelmsford 2 May 1917, ibid, AC 21/4/14.

119. A. Chamberlain to Sir Harcourt Butler 17 Dec. 1918, ibid, AC 21/5/3.

120. E. Montagu to Lloyd George 3 July 1917, Lloyd George MSS F/39/3/20.

121. I. Malcolm to A. Chamberlain 22 March 1916, Chamberlain MSS, AC 46/2/68.

122. A. Chamberlain to H. Chamberlain 7 June 1917, ibid, AC 5/1/29.

123. A. Chamberlain to Chelmsford 21 June 1917, ibid, AC 45/2/25. Chamberlain's private letter to Hardinge of 14 Oct. 1915 seems to have been the first occasion upon which he expressed concern about the medical arrangements, AC 62/144. On 8 Dec. 1915 Chamberlain wrote to Hardinge: 'I own that looking back on the past I feel more open to blame for my silence than for the single suggestion which I have made'. AC 62/154.

124. Petrie, *Life* ii, 83.
125. F. E. Smith to A. Chamberlain 28 June 1917, Chamberlain MSS, AC 48/21.
126. A. Chamberlain to Ivy Chamberlain 21 June 1917, ibid, AC 6/1/220 a r.
127. Memorandum by Curzon for War Cabinet, June 1917, ibid, AC 48/77.
128. N. Chamberlain to A. Chamberlain 28 June 1917, ibid, AC 35/1/25.
129. N. Chamberlain to H. Chamberlain 1 July 1917, ibid, NC 18/1/118.
130. N. Chamberlain to Ida Chamberlain 9 July 1917, ibid, NC 18/1/119.
131. A. Chamberlain to Curzon 6 July 1917, Curzon MSS Eur. F 112/164.
132. A. Chamberlain to Lansdowne 19 July 1917, Chamberlain MSS, AC 15/4/76.
133. A. Chamberlain to Chelmsford 1 Oct. 1917, ibid, AC 18/3/3.
134. H. Nicolson, *King George V* (London, 1952) p. 319.
135. A. Chamberlain to Lloyd George 11 July 1917, Lloyd George MSS F/7/2/6.
136. A. Chamberlain to Curzon 15 July 1917, Curzon MSS Eur. F 112/118A.
137. Busch, *Hardinge* p. 271.
138. L. Amery to A. Chamberlain 12 July 1917, Chamberlain MSS, AC 15/4/2.
139. Hardinge to A. Chamberlain 13 July 1917, ibid, AC 12/103.
140. E. Montagu to Lloyd George 5 July 1917, Lloyd George MSS F/39/3/21.
141. A. Chamberlain to Ida Chamberlain 25 July 1917, Chamberlain MSS, AC 5/1/31.
142. Lansdowne to A. Chamberlain 22 July 1917, ibid, AC 12/116.
143. A. Chamberlain to Lansdowne 19 July 1917, ibid, AC 15/4/76; A. Chamberlain to Curzon 30 Aug. 1917, Curzon MSS Eur. F 112/118A; A. Chamberlain to E. Montagu 17 Aug. 1917, Montagu MSS AS IV–9, 1076 (12).
144. E. Montagu to Lloyd George 11 Aug. 1917, Lloyd George MSS F/39/3/29.
145. A. Chamberlain to Lansdowne 25 July 1917, Chamberlain MSS, AC 12/117.
146. A. Chamberlain to N. Chamberlain 24 Sept. 1917, ibid, NC 1/27/12.
147. Selborne to A. Chamberlain 18 March 1918, ibid, AC 15/1/32.
148. A. Chamberlain to Ida Chamberlain 20 March 1918, ibid, AC 5/1/66.
149. Ibid, 4 Nov. 1917, AC 5/1/45.
150. A. Chamberlain to H. Chamberlain 29 Oct. 1917, ibid, AC 5/1/43; A. Chamberlain to Chelmsford 28 Nov. 1917, ibid, AC 18/3/4.
151. Strachey to A. Chamberlain 5 Dec. 1917, ibid, AC 13/3/98; Curzon to Lloyd George 18 Nov. 1917, Lloyd George MSS F/11/8/18; Lord Beaverbrook, *Men and Power* pp. 202–3.
152. As note 149.
153. Note by Chamberlain 18 Feb. 1918, Chamberlain MSS, AC 18/2/1; F. Owen, *Tempestuous Journey* (London, 1954) pp. 462–3; Beaverbrook, *Men and Power* p. 212.
154. D. Dilks (ed.), *Retreat from Power* (London, 1981) i, 52.

155. A. Chamberlain to Carson 22 Feb. 1918, Chamberlain MSS, AC 15/7/5.
156. Beaverbrook, *Men and Power* p. 278.
157. A. Chamberlain to Curzon 21 Feb. 1918, Curzon MSS Eur. F 112/121a.
158. Beaverbrook, *Men and Power* p. 280.
159. A. Chamberlain to Ida Chamberlain 22 Feb. 1918, Chamberlain MSS, AC 5/1/62.
160. A. Chamberlain to H. Chamberlain 2 March 1918, ibid, AC 5/1/63.
161. A. Chamberlain to N. Chamberlain 6 March 1918, ibid, NC 1/27/25.
162. House of Commons Debates, vol. 104, col. 77.
163. L. Amery, *Diaries* pp. 207–8. The Northcliffe Press was particularly hostile, R. Pound and G. Harmsworth, *Northcliffe* (London, 1959) pp. 626–7.
164. S. Roskill, *Hankey* i, 501.
165. L. Amery to Lloyd George 14 April 1918, Lloyd George MSS F/2/1/17; L. Amery, *Life* ii, 150.
166. A. Chamberlain to H. Chamberlain 17 March 1918, Chamberlain MSS, AC 5/1/65.
167. A. Chamberlain to Strachey 19 March 1918, Strachey MSS, S/4/5/8.
168. A. Chamberlain to N. Chamberlain 5 April 1918, Chamberlain MSS, NC 1/27/28. A little earlier Lord Esher had noted that 'Austen . . . seems to be the alternative Prime Minister, if by some mischance Lloyd George were to be killed by a golf-ball.' Esher to H. Wilson 12 March 1918, cited P. Fraser, *Lord Esher* p. 388.
169. A. Chamberlain to N. Chamberlain 12 April 1918, Chamberlain MSS, NC 1/27/33; A. Chamberlain to Lloyd George 10 April 1918, ibid, AC 18/2/6.
170. A. Chamberlain to Lord Hugh Cecil 10 April 1918, ibid, AC 18/2/9.
171. A. Chamberlain to Richard Kelly 24 Jan. 1918, ibid, AC 11/1/44.
172. Lloyd George to A. Chamberlain 13 April 1918, Lloyd George MSS F/7/2/9.
173. A. Chamberlain to Ivy Chamberlain 13 April 1918, Chamberlain MSS, AC 6/1/280.
174. A. Chamberlain to N. Chamberlain 15 April 1918, ibid, NC 1/27/35.
175. A. Chamberlain to Ida Chamberlain 14 April 1918, ibid, AC 5/1/70.
176. A. Chamberlain to Salisbury 22 May 1918, ibid, AC 31/1/12.
177. T. Jones, *Whitehall Diary* iii, 5.
178. A. Chamberlain to Ida Chamberlain 20 April 1918, Chamberlain MSS, AC 5/1/71.
179. T. Jones, *Whitehall Diary* iii, 7.
180. A. Chamberlain to Ida Chamberlain 10 June 1918, Chamberlain MSS, AC 5/1/86.
181. A. Chamberlain to Sir James Meston 5 Oct. 1918, ibid, AC 21/5/28.
182. A. Chamberlain to Ivy Chamberlain 12 June 1918, ibid, AC 6/1/298.
183. A. Chamberlain to Ida Chamberlain 28 Sept. 1918, ibid, AC 5/1/105.
184. Ibid, 13 Oct. 1918 and 26 Oct. 1918, AC 5/1/108, 110.
185. Ibid, 9 Nov. 1918, AC 5/1/116.

186. A. Chamberlain to Law 11 Nov. 1918, ibid, AC 35/1/5.
187. A. Chamberlain to L. Gell 22 May 1918, ibid, AC 31/1/14.
188. As note 185.

CHAPTER FIVE
ASCENDANCY

'No one can foretell what will happen after the war in domestic politics. Parties will be disrupted, new cries and new men very likely will be coming to the front and it is possible that your role might rather be that of the old experienced hand putting a brake on the extravagances of youth. A very useful and necessary but not dazzling function!'[1]

'Chamberlain, [Lloyd George] said, is a Liberal.'[2]

'The Party appears to share the view that I am more of a Conservative than Bonar. And the odd thing is that it is true.'[3]

The politicians whose job it was to win the peace faced as large and formidable a task as those who had won the War. The gravest mistakes were made by those who believed that the pre-war world could be recreated, that England's Edwardian summer could be restored and the impact of the War set to one side. What had happened between 1914 and 1918 had left an indelible impression on the socio-political structure of the country, which post-war politicians would ignore at their peril. Gigantic changes had taken place affecting the relationships between society and government, changes which could not be reversed with the coming of peace. Under the impact of total war the hitherto slow movement towards a more collectivist state, characteristic of the late nineteenth century, had proceeded apace, creating many of the typical features of a twentieth-century society. In terms of the party-political structure the most obvious development was the rise of Labour. A party of protest before 1914, often closely identified with Liberalism, it stood at the end of hostilities, and particularly after the Coupon Election of December 1918, as a potential party of government. On the one hand the Great War had wrought havoc upon the Liberal party, facilitating the task of Labour to replace it. On the other, the handling of the war effort, particularly under Lloyd George, had seemed to vindicate the sort of socio-economic structure of which Labour was the most prominent advocate. In addition the demands of war industry had served to enhance the size and status of Labour's mass following in the Trade Union movement. In an atmosphere coloured not only by recent and continuing events in Russia and on the continent, but also by industrial and social unrest nearer home, the problems posed by this new political force became the single most important concern of many politicians in the two traditional parties. 'The impact of Labour' was the determining factor in the way they analysed and interpreted the political scene. For many the overriding objective was to restructure the political edifice in such a way as to bar Labour's route to power.

By the time the War ended Austen Chamberlain was already something of an elder statesman. His experience of front-bench politics spanned more than two decades and, though in political terms he was still a relatively young man, many of the figures who had been his associates and antagonists in the political arena had already departed or were about to depart from the scene. As the first General Election for eight years, the Coupon Election, fought on a much wider franchise than ever before, created a very different House of Commons from its predecessor. It was the parliament which Stanley Baldwin described as composed of 'hard faced men who look as though they had done well out of the war.' Chamberlain spoke of its members as 'a selfish, swollen lot.'[4] But it was a more democratically based House of Commons than had previously been seen and Chamberlain could not fail to appreciate the significance of its composition. Over sixty Labour M.P.s were present to represent the almost $2\frac{1}{2}$ million votes which the party had secured in the country.

Perhaps because of the length of his parliamentary experience and the perspective which it gave him, Chamberlain was among the more perceptive observers of the political scene which now unfolded, acutely aware that the political dividing lines would have to be redrawn. In 1922 he wrote:

Many questions which divided us before the war have been settled by legislation or by the changed conditions of the world. New problems have arisen, largely in the social order, and such problems are always more delicate and more dangerous than purely political questions.[5]

In the post-war world political divisions were likely to be far more class-based than ever before. Some of the old debates would prove sterile and unprofitable. Labour seemed to offer the voter a completely new range of options:

A new party has come into existence . . . and this party, however moderate be its leaders, is divided from both the old parties on what are likely to be the greatest issues of the next few years, for it challenges the basis of our whole economic and industrial system. . . . We are passing through a time of transition and change comparable to that in which Disraeli began his political career, and surely we who work to fit our party for the new tasks of the new time are acting in the traditions which he left.[6]

Yet, though Chamberlain sincerely believed that his own adaptation to changing circumstances was in the best interests of the party he represented, his actions over the next few years, while bringing him to the very brink of the premiership, strained almost to breaking point his association with the Conservative party. At the same time they did considerable damage to his own image of political rectitude which he valued so highly.

The post-war environment allowed scope for the emergence of Chamberlain's inherent conservatism. Freed now from the influence of parental radicalism, his Liberal past seemed a long way away as Chamberlain developed a reputation as an articulate champion of anti-socialism. Neville Chamberlain, who now joined Austen in the House of Commons, found himself increasingly at odds with his brother, particularly on social issues:

The fact is I always said that if I went into the House we should differ and we are bound to do so because our minds are differently trained. He thinks me wild and I think him unprogressive and prejudiced.[7]

Neville's proposals for government intervention in housing construction horrified Chamberlain. He was 'profoundly alarmed' at the prospect of a new class of tenant voter. In fact, concluded Neville, 'I don't think myself that A. has much sympathy with the working classes; he hasn't been thrown enough into contact with them to know much about them.'[8] In Cabinet discussions on the way to deal with the industrial unrest which became such a feature of the post-war coalition, Austen Chamberlain was invariably on the side of resistance. Of an impending railway strike in September 1919 he wrote:

This is not a quarrel between capital and labour or a question of wages or conditions of employment. It is a revolutionary attempt to subvert government and establish class rule. . . . It is a challenge to the Government and a challenge to the Nation and I believe that both will take it up and fight it through.[9]

His attitude towards Trade Unions was largely determined by his view of the Labour party. He regarded the growth of the latter 'as a serious menace to the nation . . . because of its difference from every other party . . . in being directed and controlled from outside Parliament.'[10] When the question of introducing the referendum into the machinery of the constitution re-emerged into the political debate, Chamberlain expressed decided views:

We are now confronted with an open attack on Parliamentaryism. For parliamentary action it is sought to substitute direct action. The Referendum and the Plebiscite seem to me the direct negation of parliamentary government and the indirect affirmation of the superior claims of direct action.[11]

Even his long-time friend and correspondent, F. S. Oliver, did not recognise in the post-war Chamberlain the political ally of earlier years:

I can only suppose that we have been caught – you by one and I by another – of two divergent gales which stretch out our canvasses and send us sailing in opposite directions.[12]

It was inevitable that the end of the War and the holding of a General Election would occasion some changes in the government. To begin with Lloyd George resisted Bonar Law's argument that Chamberlain should succeed Law at the Exchequer on the grounds of the virulent press attacks which had accompanied his return to the Cabinet the previous April. The Prime Minister seemed more inclined to make Montagu Chancellor and let Chamberlain return to his old post at the India Office.[13] Law, however, continued to press Chamberlain's claims to the Exchequer, while recognising that difficulties might arise if Chamberlain did not receive 11 Downing Street (which Law was anxious to retain for himself) as his official residence, or a seat in the small War Cabinet, which Lloyd George wanted to maintain despite the ending of hostilities.[14] When the offer of the Exchequer was finally made to Chamberlain on 10 January 1919, he reacted in a manner that was to become characteristic of him over the next decade and a half. The pose he struck was that of a senior and dignified colleague who insisted on being treated with the utmost courtesy and respect. In this instance Chamberlain believed that 'things were done as disagreeably as possible.' He was offended that the letter making the offer requested an immediate answer and had been composed by Lloyd George's private secretary rather than by the Prime Minister himself. The letter seemed to Chamberlain unnecessarily curt in the form of its announcement that Law would continue to occupy the house usually allotted to the Chancellor. When Law indicated that the position would not necessarily carry with it a seat in the Cabinet, Chamberlain's attitude hardened against acceptance. The offer was, he told Lloyd George, very much as one might throw a bone to a dog. The Prime Minister felt obliged to point out that at least there was a good deal of meat on the bone.[15]

Chamberlain made it clear to Lloyd George that the office held no particular attraction for him, especially as Law had indicated that the financial situation was more serious than at any time during his own tenure of the post. Chamberlain sought assurances about the support he would receive from the Prime Minister, while the latter outlined what he considered to be the major policy issues confronting the new Chancellor. But the question of Chamberlain's membership of the Cabinet emerged as a major stumbling block. If he were included, argued Lloyd George, the claims of other Secretaries of State would be irresistible and the Cabinet would have to grow to those pre-war proportions which the Prime Minister held to be contrary to the best interests of efficient and business-like government. Finally, it was Law who saw a way out of this apparent impasse. If the personnel of the old War Cabinet continued unaltered, Chamberlain could remain a member in his own right without being appointed to it as Chancellor of the Exchequer. In this way the claims of other ministers could be resisted. On these terms Chamberlain announced that he was prepared to return, albeit without enthusiasm, to the post he had left more than thirteen years earlier.[16]

It was then in a mood of resignation rather than optimism that Chamberlain took on his new and onerous responsibilities. 'I have a heavy heart and not much pleasure in prospect.'[17] The Northcliffe press responded to the news of the appointment with predictable hostility. The task of reconstructing the nation's shattered economy after four years of unprecedented military effort was indeed a daunting one. Difficult decisions would have to be taken and pitfalls awaited the unwary in all directions. How long Chamberlain retained the office depended, he believed, very largely upon the extent to which the Prime Minister gave him his confidence and support – 'a very doubtful factor.'[18] He was discouraged to think that he had no real friend and no one whom he could really trust among the country's present leaders.[19] But the big question was whether Chamberlain, whatever his administrative skills, possessed the imagination and breadth of vision to deal with the enormous problems with which he would be confronted. Though, during his interview with Lloyd George, he had asserted that this was not a time for Gladstonian ideas of financial economy and that there must be large-scale expenditure and a far more liberal outlook than hitherto, many agreed with Waldorf Astor that Chamberlain was 'not the man for new finance.'[20] Even Neville Chamberlain believed that it might have been better to have installed a 'fresher man' and predicted difficulties for his own schemes of municipal housing and banking.[21] Interestingly, when during 1917 Lloyd George had toyed with the idea of promoting Chamberlain to the Exchequer, Edwin Montagu had protested at the thought of having 'so Conservative a Conservative in charge of the Nation's purse,'

a man with so few ideas as Chamberlain possesses. His efficient, humdrum mind will, I think, tend to make him a public danger at the Treasury.[22]

Chamberlain's appointment brought him into political partnership for the first time with Stanley Baldwin, who had been Financial Secretary to the Treasury since June 1917. In view of the long political association which the two men were to experience in the years ahead, Baldwin's initial reaction to Chamberlain's appointment is worthy of notice. The weak point about him, he believed, was his health. Chamberlain was

in that sort of condition that he may crack up, so I shall feel like an understudy at the pantomime (or in a tragedy according to one's mood.)[23]

Within a few weeks, however, Baldwin had come to the conclusion that Chamberlain was very pleasant to work with, slower than Bonar Law but thorough and conscientious, and with plenty of courage.[24]

There was some truth in Baldwin's prediction about Chamberlain's health. The latter found his new duties a great strain and in the post-war years displayed even less stamina for prolonged hard work than hitherto. After only three months in office he confessed to being very tired, anxious about his forthcoming budget and scarcely fit for all the work which it would involve. 'There are times,' he confessed, 'when I wish that I could chuck the whole business.'[25] By June 1920 he was 'as tired as a man could be and could cry for weariness.'[26] Neville was genuinely worried that his brother might be depriving himself of all chance of enjoying life if he went on much longer and had begun to wonder whether he ought not to retire while there was still time to retrieve his health.[27] He seemed to be drifting towards a breakdown which would be crushing and final and leave him a physical wreck.[28] Though this breakdown was avoided, there was little let-up in Chamberlain's work-load. The problems of post-war reconstruction were vast, and, as Chancellor, there was scarcely an issue in which Chamberlain was not involved. Almost every question had a financial angle and Chamberlain complained that he was never able to focus his attention on one problem at a time.[29] At the end of 1920 he described the pressure which he faced:

I reached my home at 6 o'clock on Christmas Eve having sat up the whole of the previous night and attended five Cabinet meetings in two days and a half. But even then the respite was only from Friday evening to Tuesday morning when all the ministers returned to London to try and clear off arrears upon the Cabinet agenda.[30]

A free weekend was something to be valued, but there was little scope for enjoyment:

I sleep and I garden and . . . after I have worked in the garden my hand is so stiff and shaky that I might as well be asleep — which indeed to all intents and purposes I often am.[31]

Chamberlain's task at the Exchequer was no easier than he had anticipated. Indeed the financial situation was even worse than Law had indicated. Additional problems were being created by both the French and the Americans with whom Chamberlain negotiated in Paris in March.[32] Taxation would have to go up even though the majority of the population expected that, with the end of hostilities, a reduction would be possible.[33] One Treasury official later recalled that on taking office Chamberlain summoned his staff to lecture them for an hour on the duty of extracting taxes courteously from the public.[34] A month after taking office the new Chancellor succinctly remarked:

If I survive, it will be a wonder; if I make a success of it, it will be little short of a miracle.[35]

Despite his anxiety, Chamberlain's budget of April 1919 was a source of considerable satisfaction to him, for it contained the first important concession to the principle of imperial preference since his father had begun his campaign in 1903. A preference of $16\frac{2}{3}$% was given to imports of tobacco, tea and sugar and $33\frac{1}{3}$% on cars, cameras and clocks. His speech lasted for two and a half hours, but he was clear and effective throughout, despite occasional slips in confusing thousands with millions. It was well received by the Conservative-dominated House of Commons, though the 40% Excess Profits Tax upset many businessmen and led to protests from Chambers of Commerce and the Federation of British Industries.[36] Yet still Chamberlain regarded the overall financial position as 'desperate' with government expenditure exceeding all estimates.[37] The government seemed to be undertaking obligations in all directions but lacked the means to sustain them.[38] As a result, Chamberlain repeatedly found himself forced into the traditional role of an orthodox Chancellor, trying to curb the spending excesses of his Cabinet colleagues. In June 1920 he told Neville that he was 'fighting his colleagues all the time . . . on expenditure.'[39]

In this position Chamberlain often crossed swords with Winston Churchill, the Secretary of State for War and, especially while Lloyd George was preoccupied with the peace negotiations in Paris, a major force in the formulation of government policy. It was an interesting reversal of the roles the two men would occupy in the Conservative government of 1924–29. Before the end of January 1919 Chamberlain was trying on grounds of economy to impose a cut in the size of the army of occupation proposed by Churchill.[40] In the following month Chamberlain insisted upon his right to scrutinise expenditure in Churchill's department.[41] During April the Chancellor tried to set an upper limit on British military expenditure of £110 million for the first post-war year, a limitation at which Churchill protested.[42] When in July it was apparent that most of the carefully raised Victory Loan would be swallowed up simply in meeting the excess of expenditure over estimates from the current year, Chamberlain appealed to his colleagues to examine most carefully the expenditure of their departments with a view to making reductions.[43] Churchill implied that Chamberlain was exaggerating the scale of the problem and argued that the decline in the purchasing power of money would be directly favourable to the Exchequer as far as

IX A proud father (Birmingham University)

X (*top*) Family group at Twitts Ghyll (Birmingham University)

(*bottom*) With Ivy and **Lawrence** at Twitts Ghyll (Birmingham University)

treated him with great courtesy and was giving him generous support.[61] This was in marked contrast to the way in which Lloyd George handled some of his other colleagues, particularly Curzon. Chamberlain had to admit that he could not envisage himself remaining in the room if he were subjected to the sort of invective that was regularly hurled at Curzon, particularly after the latter became Foreign Secretary in October 1919.[62]

In his second budget speech in April 1920 Chamberlain seemed to view the economic scene with some confidence. But he saw also the paramount need to raise further revenue. The Excess Profits Duty was raised to sixty per cent and a Corporation Tax of one shilling in the pound was imposed on the total profits of companies. In addition, income tax was raised, more people became liable to supertax and there were increases in the duty on beer and spirits. Interestingly, Lloyd George's land taxes of 1909, which had never produced much money, were now repealed. The Chancellor aimed to budget for a large surplus in order to reduce the nation's debt.[63] Once again the budget statement was well received in the House of Commons. Neville noted that Chamberlain had 'still further improved his position in the House which now stands very high. It is very remarkable how he has steadily gone up in general estimation.'[64] With considerable skill Chamberlain piloted the Finance Bill through the House of Commons, earning 'many congratulations from the Prime Minister downwards.'[65] He himself sensed an increasing appreciation of the work which he was doing at the Exchequer:

I think I see a realisation on their part of the problem before them and me, of my honest and determined effort to solve it, of the common interests which they as citizens, taxpayers and businessmen have with me as Chancellor in getting it solved and last but not least of the fact that I am master – for the time at least.[66]

He believed now that the limit of taxation had been reached and that the government's efforts should be concentrated in future on the reduction of expenditure.[67] If this were not achieved, he warned Lloyd George, 'dissatisfaction with our financial administration will be the ruin of your Government.'[68]

Yet while Chamberlain was merely conforming to the economic orthodoxy of the day, espoused by the majority of Treasury officials together with the Bank of England, there is little doubt that his policies contributed greatly to the difficulties which the government now began to encounter. 1919 had been marked by a speculative boom, but the restrictive measures of the Chancellor, particularly in controlling the money supply, tended to aggravate the ensuing slump. By late July 1920 the Cabinet was anticipating serious trouble and soon the unemployment total began to rise alarmingly. The popularity of the government in general started to decline. A junior minister, William Bridgeman, noted that the Cabinet had been living from hand to mouth, never able to look ahead. The Prime Minister was repeatedly absent abroad, playing the role of international statesman. 'As a result we have had ill-considered legislation and considerable dissatisfaction.'[69] By the early summer of 1921 unemployment had reached $2\frac{1}{2}$ millions. Neville sensed the change of mood:

I get unmistakeable evidence of a real setback in industrial prosperity and great nervousness as to what is going to happen in the next 6 months. In fact there is talk of a 'crash' and the panicy feeling finds vent in general abuse of the Budget as the cause of all the trouble. . . .[70]

Chamberlain believed that the scope for social reform was now severely limited by the economic situation. In November 1920 he told the Cabinet that each house built under the scheme of the Minister of Health, Addison, was costing the Exchequer between £50 and £75 *per annum* and would continue to do so for the next sixty years.[71] The defence estimates also came under the Chancellor's scrutiny. A gloomy statement in the House in December on the state of the economy was a prelude to an investigation by the C.I.D. into the country's naval capacity.[72] If Chamberlain had wished to escape from his financial worries the opportunity was opened to him in the autumn of 1920. With the Secretary of State, Montagu, pushing his claims with enthusiasm, Chamberlain was offered the Viceroyalty of India by the Prime Minister. He refused with the wry comment,

I am coming to think that my greatest distinction in life will be the number of high appointments that I have declined.[73]

Despite the gloomy economic outlook Chamberlain looked back on 1920 with a feeling of qualified satisfaction:

We have some things to be grateful for and some that we have not managed too badly.[74]

He could not have imagined that the following year would offer a prize more glittering even than the Viceroyalty – the party leadership itself, ambition for which he had all but given up. On 17 March Bonar Law was forced to resign his position in the government on the grounds of ill-health. This was a major blow for Lloyd George since Law's prosaic qualities had well complemented his own more dashing attributes. The newspapers were very excited, noted Henry Wilson in his diary on 19 March, as to who should succeed Law. 'But they all seem to agree to Austen.'[75] But among leading Conservatives there was little enthusiasm at the prospect of Chamberlain's succession. The names of Birkenhead, Curzon,

Salisbury and Derby were also briefly canvassed.[76] But as all of these were peers the initial question of the leadership of the party in the House of Commons was less in doubt.[77] Chamberlain himself took no steps to foist himself on the party. His attitude was very reminiscent of that which he had adopted ten years earlier. To J. C. C. Davidson he explained:

The truth is that at such a moment and in such matters I have a great horror of anything that savours of intrigue or pushfulness on the part of a possible candidate and felt then as I felt ten years ago . . . that the only right thing to do was to keep quiet and leave members to make up their own minds without either courting their favour or shunning responsibility if their choice fell upon me.[78]

In the event Chamberlain's election passed without incident. 'Austen was excellent,' reported Davidson, 'because he was supremely common-place and as he lacks inspiration said exactly what everyone expected him to and therefore offended no one.'[79]

Chamberlain assumed his new duties as Leader of the House of Commons and Lord Privy Seal without enthusiasm. He took the job 'as a clear duty but I wish that the call of duty had not come.'[80] He recognised the difficulties inherent in a coalition – difficulties that were ultimately to undermine his position – which meant that his leadership would demand opportunistic compromise rather than clear-cut policies.[81] But he was touched and pleased by the expressions of good will which he received and gradually warmed to the idea. 'It is human nature to be gratified by the honours of one's career.'[82] In addition he derived satisfaction from thinking of the joy which this promotion would have brought to his father.[83] At all events he was delighted to hand over responsibility for the Exchequer to Robert Horne after two gruelling years at the post. Thomas Jones noted that he was much less overwrought than when, as Chancellor, he had daily to oppose the demands of his profligate colleagues:

He is now almost gay and debonair with leisure for a joke and a tale.[84]

Yet two major question-marks overshadowed Chamberlain's promotion. One concerned his relations with the Prime Minister. Many believed that the premier would find it difficult to achieve the sort of rapport with Chamberlain that he had rather surprisingly established with Bonar Law. Philip Kerr, the head of Lloyd George's private secretariat, remarked that the Prime Minister 'would never work in harness with Chamberlain', while Derby warned Lloyd George that he would find the position 'somewhat different to what it has been in the past' and stressed the need to work towards the fusion of the two parties.[85] Frances Stevenson noted that Lloyd George had lost in Law an ideal companion with whom he could laugh and joke and enjoy himself, something he could not do with Chamberlain who was 'pompous to the last degree and has become increasingly so since he took Bonar's place.'[86] But by the early summer she had to admit that the Prime Minister was getting on better with Chamberlain than he had expected. 'Austen plays the game and he sees that he can trust the P.M. who conceals nothing from him.'[87] Lloyd George, himself, while telling Law how much he missed him, stressed that nothing could be finer than the way Chamberlain was bearing his share in the partnership. 'He is loyal, straight and sensible.'[88] In all probability the Prime Minister was pleased to see Chamberlain removed from the Exchequer where his unpopularity had become, by the beginning of 1921, a threat to the government.[89]

The explanation for Chamberlain's harmonious partnership with Lloyd George is threefold. His intrinsic loyalty was an important factor. In addition, his close working association with the Prime Minister had given him an increasing respect for the latter's qualities, especially as he came to see in Lloyd George his only reliable ally in Cabinet discussions.[90] To an extent he came, as did many others, under the spell of Lloyd George's masterful personality, a factor which in the latter stages of the Coalition tended to blind him to the growing discontent among his own party and to those other aspects of Lloyd George's character against which the majority of Conservatives revolted. But perhaps most important of all, by 1921 if not earlier, Chamberlain had become a convinced Coalitionist. He hoped to combine in one party men of differing political traditions in order to avoid a peril more dangerous even than the war which had been so narrowly survived. He had no doubt that the Conservative party standing alone would not be able to resist indefinitely the challenge from Labour. Here however lay his major problem. Most Conservatives had taken comfort in the belief that Chamberlain was at heart a party man who would be more attentive to Conservative interests than Law had been. They certainly did not expect him to be more subservient towards the Prime Minister than his predecessor. Yet even when he did exert influence over Lloyd George, he made little attempt to make Conservatives aware of this. Perhaps they should have listened more carefully to the speech with which Chamberlain accepted the leadership:

There are moments when the insistence upon party is as unforgiveable as insistence upon personal things, when the difficulties which the nation has to confront call for a wider outlook and a broader union than can be found even within the limits of a single party and when the traditions of more than one party, the ideas of more than one party need to be put into the common stock.[91]

If Chamberlain had managed to convey to his party his own rationalisation of the political scene and the present need for coalition, the rank and file might have been more prepared to follow him than they were. This, however, he singularly failed to do. He relied too much on stating rather than explaining his views. To one disgruntled backbencher he wrote:

you must allow me to say that in my judgment the principles of Unionism and Conservatism are better served at the present juncture by the union than by the dispersion of the National and Constitutional forces of the country.[92]

Though he was convinced in his own mind that the long term goal should be the fusion of the Liberal and Conservative forces, he believed that this must be a slow process. 'We must glide rather than burst into new conditions.' He therefore rejected absolutely any suggestion that his own accession to the leadership should be the occasion for the official birth of a new party.[93] To many Conservatives, therefore, Chamberlain increasingly resembled Lloyd George's prisoner rather than the leader of the largest party in the House of Commons. Asquith came to liken the Coalition under Lloyd George and Chamberlain to a pair of scissors with only one blade.[94]

The second question-mark concerned Chamberlain's capacity for leadership. As party leader he appeared to have many admirable qualities. He was upright and honourable, and an able and experienced parliamentarian. Neville thought he would make a success of the leadership of the House:

He is certainly no orator ... but for a carefully reasoned statement he has few equals and he convinces by his own sincerity and fairness.[95]

But a vital factor was missing. Chamberlain lacked the common touch. One contemporary noted:

In superficial *bonhomie* he is lacking, wherein he is unfortunate, for that currency is one with which great statesmen can easily finance large political business. A more frequent resort to the smokeroom; a more general revelation of his personal charm would have helped him much.[96]

His elevation to the leadership made him more than ever conscious of his own dignity. He made few efforts to win the affection of Conservative backbenchers, many of whom had only come into the House since the War and knew very little of their new leader. Even the Lord Chancellor, Lord Birkenhead, complained that Chamberlain was 'aloof and reserved. I seldom see him and never seem to get to know him any better.'[97]

It was two months before Chamberlain even addressed Conservative backbenchers and then only as part of a Coalition group which contained numerous Liberals. Even though he was ineffective in conveying his own understanding of the political situation to those beneath him, he very quickly became intolerant of those Conservatives who did not share his views, rather as he had dismissed those who had opposed his line on tariff reform before 1914.[98] He attended only a tiny handful of the major regional gatherings of the party held during his leadership and thus acquired little feel for the mood of the Conservative rank and file. When he did try to lead he was often unimpressive. With Lloyd George continuing to play a major role on the international stage, Chamberlain was frequently left in control of the government at home. In such a situation he seemed to lack conviction. He completely mishandled a parliamentary debate on teachers' pensions in April 1922 while Lloyd George was at the Genoa Conference, while his management of the Irish problem did not inspire confidence. Thomas Jones recorded in August 1921:

At the Cabinet which Mr. Chamberlain summoned ... there were slight indications of apprehension of Mr. Chamberlain's handling of the situation. . . . His own nervous manner conveyed a feeling of mild panic to his colleagues. . . .

Jones concluded that Chamberlain was much too nervous to be left to handle Ireland.[99] To have led the party successfully in these months would have been a daunting task for the most subtle and dexterous of politicians. For Chamberlain it proved almost an impossibility. Much more than his sound administrative skills were needed at this moment in the evolution of the Conservative party.[100]

By the time that Chamberlain became leader there was already developing on the right of the party a diehard opposition, critical of many of the government's policies and anxious to reassert Conservatism's independent existence. The rebels needed to be handled with tact and good humour – qualities with which Chamberlain was not well endowed – if they were not to become a serious threat. Yet in June 1921 the new leader curtly told the diehards that

those men who at the present time would deliberately break up a national combination and a national Government in face of all the difficulties, foreign and domestic, with which we are confronted, would deserve ill of their countrymen, and would meet with condemnation at the hands of their countrymen.[101]

The diehards' first rallying-cry was the demand for government economy and at the beginning of 1921 they had forced Chamberlain to re-establish the House of Commons Estimates Committee, suspended in 1914 and whose restoration Chamberlain had opposed.[102] In the course of the year their attention would focus increasingly on the question of Ireland. In addition, the presence of Bonar Law on the fringe of the political stage gave comfort to those who could never fully reconcile themselves to Chamberlain's leadership. The former leader's health was rapidly restored and the possibility of his return to full political activity could not be ruled out. One M.P. reported to Law at the beginning of June:

your *friends* are not enjoying your absence! Come back again and lead us! Your successor won't do and won't lead many. We want *you* back badly.[103]

Similarly, Edward Goulding, whose defection had been a significant factor in deciding the outcome of the 1911 leadership contest, assured Law that

Things are not going well in the House – the grumble is on all sides – the new man is heavy, with no finesse – while there are many sore heads with the P.M.[104]

* * *

Writing to his wife in 1924 Austen Chamberlain complained that 'Ireland is indeed a fatal influence in British politics.'[105] In terms of the fortunes of the Coalition Government and of Chamberlain's leadership of the Conservative party this statement seems beyond dispute. The end of the Great War and the General Election of December 1918 revealed that the problem of Ireland, which had paralysed domestic politics in the last years of peace, had in no sense been removed. The vast majority of Irish seats were won by Sinn Fein candidates. On 7 January 1919 those Sinn Fein representatives who were not in jail decided to boycott the Westminster Parliament and convene their own Irish Assembly, the Dail Eirann, which proceeded to proclaim Irish independence. The months which followed were marked by an increasing escalation of violence, on the parts of both the Irish Republican Army and of the British authorities, the army and the police, including the notorious Black and Tans. The Government of Ireland Bill under which two Irish parliaments were to be created, one in Dublin and one for the six northeastern counties in Belfast, received the royal assent on 23 December 1920.

As has been noted, Chamberlain's views on the Irish question had never been those of an orthodox Unionist and in the course of the war he had become ever more ready to consider a radical departure in Britain's Irish policy. In the quest for a solution, however, he was as perplexed as anyone else. In July 1920 he wrote:

I don't see my way clear. The old Unionist policy is not possible, for our people won't give it the time necessary to achieve its end. 'Home Rule' seems now equally impossible. Is it to be Dominion Govt?[106]

A month earlier Chamberlain had urged the Cabinet to open negotiations with the Sinn Fein leadership in the hope of reaching agreement with them, but opposition to this policy had proved too strong.[107] By the summer of 1921, however, Lloyd George, too, had reached the conclusion that negotiation was imperative. He perhaps envisaged that the solution to the Irish question, which had defied so many of his predecessors in Downing Street, would be the culminating achievement of his career, after which, with his place in history secured, he would willingly retire in Chamberlain's favour.[108] Chamberlain's support would be crucial to any settlement since the Conservative majority in the Commons was ready to pounce on anything it regarded as a sell-out of Unionist interests. Yet when, after the declaration of a truce, De Valera first arrived for talks with Lloyd George in July 1921, the Prime Minister was not anxious for Chamberlain to play a prominent part in the discussions. The latter, noted Thomas Jones, had a disconcerting way of butting in with speeches during negotiations.[109] His public school formality was not likely to endear him to De Valera and his colleagues.

Chamberlain looked upon the talks with some concern lest, on the one hand, Lloyd George should give away too much or, on the other, the Irish representatives should fail to rise to the occasion – 'What a crowd to have the peace of two nations in their hands', he once remarked.[110] But he was genuinely anxious for some sort of solution, even if it represented a choice of evils, in order to prevent the renewal of civil strife in Ireland.[111] In taking this attitude he increasingly separated himself from a substantial number of right-wing Tories, already concerned at other aspects of government activity, who looked for a simple restatement of those Unionist principles which had once characterised Conservative policy and which, of course, Bonar Law had epitomised in the years 1912–14. By late August Chamberlain was anticipating a backbench revolt of up to forty Conservative M.P.s.[112] In fact it is clear that Chamberlain's desire for a settlement, together with his loyalty to Lloyd George, took him on a path which undermined his standing in his own party and threatened to wreck his career. He faced an almost impossible dilemma between his wish to see Ireland at peace and his knowledge that almost any settlement which might be negotiated would be unacceptable to a section of his own supporters.[113] In October a group of over forty diehards under Colonel Gretton moved what was effectively a vote of censure on the government for even negotiating with the rebels and Chamberlain's defence of Cabinet policy was poorly received.

After a series of meetings with Lloyd George the Irish representatives presented their proposals to the British government on 11 August. These centred upon the proposition of 'external association' – that Ireland rejected Dominion status but was prepared to be associated with the British Commonwealth, though not a member of it. In Lloyd George's absence it was Chamberlain who received the Irish statement. He 'read it and made a remark under his breath about its grave character and he looked more grave than the document itself.' At a hastily summoned Cabinet meeting ministers heard Chamberlain's 'palpitating summary' of the Irish proposals. He succeeded only in spreading panic among his colleagues that the Irish might be about to break the truce, but he insisted that no steps could be taken in Lloyd George's absence.[114] Chamberlain could not believe that De Valera was merely play acting and he regarded the outlook as grave.[115] Eventually the Irish agreed to accept Lloyd George's formula to meet in conference 'with a view to ascertaining how the association of Ireland with the community of nations known as the British Empire can best be reconciled with Irish national aspirations.' The conference opened on 11 October, with Chamberlain one of the seven-strong British delegation.

The course of the negotiations which finally led to the creation of the Irish Free State belongs primarily to the biography of Lloyd George. Its achievement was largely a testimony to the Prime Minister's ingenious skills as a negotiator and his ability to convince the Irish that they had secured more than was in fact the case. Chamberlain's mood fluctuated with the changing fortunes of the conference, while Lloyd George's sometimes Machiavellian manoeuvres gradually wore down the resistance of the Irish delegates. On 24 October Chamberlain sensed the makings of a solution, even though 'it is all contingent, all hypothetical, all liable to be cancelled, withdrawn or upset.' Yet by the following day he could not see a way through the apparent impasse.[116] Even if agreement were reached with the Irish representatives, it remained doubtful whether a settlement could be sold to the Ulster Unionists. Chamberlain was adamant that no part of Ulster's rights could be given away without her consent and he was prepared to resign rather than accept a solution which Ulster rejected.[117] Yet he recognised that if the negotiations broke down over the question of Ulster this would be the worst possible ground from the government's point of view, since 'you could not raise an army in England to fight for *that* as we could for Crown and Empire.'[118] Accordingly he was prepared to put the greatest moral pressure upon Ulster if he believed that any settlement reached was satisfactory, and he was anxious that Lloyd George should not use the opposition of Ulster as an excuse for breaking off the talks.[119]

At an early stage in the negotiations Chamberlain saw that the question of allegiance to the crown might prove an insurmountable obstacle in the path of any settlement.[120] On 25 October he negotiated on his own with two of the Irish delegation and later gave an account of this meeting to the other British representatives. Sinn Fein would not accept allegiance without a concession over the unity of Ireland, yet for Chamberlain the latter might prove fatal in view of the strength of Unionist opinion.[121] A few days earlier he had told the conference that his own position was getting daily more difficult and his authority within the Conservative party less and less, simply as a result of the attempt to reach an Irish settlement.[122] Always in the background stood the vaguely menacing figure of Andrew Bonar Law, to whom dissident Tories increasingly looked for their salvation. As Salisbury wrote:

If Bonar Law comes again into the arena we have at last got a leader in the Commons even if we do not turn the Govt. out at this moment.[123]

It annoyed Chamberlain, no doubt recalling the crises of 1912 and 1915, to think that Law, 'the most yielding of men when Leader or in office,' should emerge now as the champion of resistance.[124] He was convinced that Law, egged on by Carson, was a very ambitious man, whose 'courage is not equal to his ambition,' but who might come forward to lead the opposition against any settlement. Indeed Law's attitude was making it more difficult for Craig, the Ulster Unionist leader, to find a route to peace. He even seemed to assume that he could take back the party leadership from Chamberlain if he so wished. 'In short,' confessed Chamberlain, 'I am fighting for my political life.'[125]

Much depended on Chamberlain's performance at a meeting of the National Union in Liverpool in mid-November. He was clearly worried about the reception he might receive in this stronghold of Ulster Orangemen and sent an urgent appeal to his brother to ensure that Birmingham Unionists were well represented to counteract the 'great whip up' of 'the malcontents':

If there is any difficulty about their expenses . . . will you offer on this occasion to bear them? I will guarantee whatever expenditure you find it necessary to incur but for obvious reasons I should wish it to appear as your personal generosity.[126]

Though himself no avid supporter of the Coalition nor friend of Lloyd George, Neville did his best to oblige. The Birmingham delegates 'greatly enjoyed themselves' and split into three groups to maximise their impact at the meeting. At one point the diehard Leo Maxse felt obliged to retire to the back of the hall where he was followed by three Chamberlainites who proceeded to sit around him.[127] In the event, such precautions were perhaps unnecessary. Lord Derby had taken careful steps to keep the Liverpool party loyal to the leadership, while Chamberlain delivered one of the most effective speeches of his career. He had 'full command both of myself and of the audience and the consequence was that I reached the top hole of what I can do.'[128]

In a speech of unusual power and vigour he implied that a new democratic and constitutional party would ultimately be born out of the

Coalition and then posed with stark clarity the likely consequences of a breakdown in the Irish negotiations. He hinted that success was on the cards, though he could give no details while discussions were still taking place. He even tried to sway diehard opinion by admitting that he himself had been wrong in opposing self-government for the Transvaal and the Orange Free State back in 1906.[129] In the event Chamberlain secured his vote of confidence and thereby postponed a crisis in his leadership at least for the time being. He even managed over lunch with Law on 23 November to allay some of the latter's fears on the question of Ulster.[130]

The basis for Chamberlain's optimism that an Irish settlement could be reached lay in Lloyd George's idea that, if an acceptable treaty could be devised, Ulster should be included in it, but given the right to contract out within a year of its final ratification. If this right were exercised, however, Ulster would have to accept a boundary commission to determine the frontier with the Free State. The key to Lloyd George's plan was the way in which he convinced the Irish delegates that the commission would award such large areas of the six counties to the South as to leave the rump of Ulster without political or economic viability. In such a situation Irish unity under a Dublin parliament would soon become a reality. Chamberlain was evidently excited by the prospect of success:

If we bring it off it will be a triumph and we shall have done the greatest service that any body of men could do at this moment for the British Empire. . . . If we succeed, all men will bless us sooner or later. If we fail, my career will be at an end and many hard things will be said. . . .[131]

In the event, in the early hours of 6 December, the Irish delegates, worn down and out-manoeuvred by Lloyd George, signed the Articles of Agreement, even though they had not achieved their goals in relation either to status or unity. The Free State remained a Dominion under the crown, while the prospect of Irish unity receded rapidly into a distant and elusive future.

Like so many English politicians who have followed him, Chamberlain tackled the Irish problem in a spirit of well-meaning compromise, which could not in the nature of things satisfy the more extreme emotions engendered by this most passionate of political issues. 'If peace is to be secured,' he told one critic, 'all parties to this ancient and bitter controversy must show some measure of good will and be prepared for some concession to the feelings of others.'[132] He believed that he acted in the best traditions of his party's philosophy. Old-style Unionism had failed, so 'surely, under these circumstances, true conservatism dictated that one should seek some new and stable foundation on which to build.'[133] Not everyone, however, could approach the Irish question in such moderate and reasonable terms. By his part in the negotiations Chamberlain had permanently alienated a substantial number of right-wing Conservatives. His actions were to play a significant part in destroying his own leadership and remained to haunt him periodically over the next decade. In the House of Lords Carson proclaimed that Chamberlain's behaviour was very like 'after having shot a man in the back, going over to him and patting him on the shoulder and saying, "Old man, die as quickly as you can and do not make any noise." '[134] Similarly Sir James Craig spoke wildly of having been betrayed and sent Chamberlain an inflammatory letter of complaint.[135] But the most succinct commentary on what Chamberlain had done to his own reputation came six months later, after two Irish fanatics shot dead Sir Henry Wilson, the former Chief of the Imperial General Staff. When Chamberlain visited his widow to offer his condolences, Lady Wilson greeted him with the single word, 'Murderer.'[136]

In the wake of his apparent resolution of the Irish problem Lloyd George's inclination was to call an immediate General Election. But at a meeting of himself, Churchill, Birkenhead and Chamberlain on 20 December no consensus emerged. Chamberlain took the opportunity of the Christmas recess to sound out opinion in the party and wrote to, among others, Salvidge, Sanders, the Principal Agent Malcolm Fraser, the Party Chairman George Younger and his brother Neville. Chamberlain himself was opposed to the idea of a dissolution, partly because he anticipated the need for a great deal of difficult and delicate work before the Irish settlement was absolutely secure.[137] But to Neville he emphasised a more fundamental objection. It was, he said, his hope to have consolidated the Coalition into a single party before the election. In addition he was concerned that an election might change the balance of forces within the Conservative party in favour of the diehards.[138] But Chamberlain respected the prerogative of a Prime Minister to call a General Election whenever he chose to do so, even though in this case the government was a coalition.

The replies provided Chamberlain with the objections he was looking for. Younger responded with indignation to the 'cynical way in which the P.M.'s advisers appear to regard the interests of their chief as paramount to any others.' He told Chamberlain that a procession of M.P.s would support him in opposing an early election.[139] Fraser predicted that although Lloyd George could probably get a majority if he went to the country at the head of a coalition, the result would split the Conservatives from head to toe and result in a substantial increase in the parliamentary strength of the Labour party.[140] Sanders sent an equally gloomy reply, while Neville suggested that the process of fusion would take at least two years and still result in defections from Coalition Liberals and 'hard-shell Unionists.'[141] As a result, when Chamberlain wrote to Lloyd George at the beginning of January he was able to use this weight of opinion in pressing the Prime Minister not to pursue the idea of an election any further.[142]

But what Chamberlain had intended as a private enquiry soon became a matter of public speculation. From 30 December the press carried informed accounts putting forward the arguments for and against an election. Chamberlain denied responsibility for this leak which he privately attributed to Birkenhead.[143] On 4 January Younger wrote to the Prime Minister to warn him that in the event of an early election many Conservatives would break from the Coalition. He enclosed a copy of a letter from Chamberlain which stressed the inevitable dislocation of trade and the fact that the government had not yet fulfilled its election pledge to reform the House of Lords.[144] Thereafter, however, Younger's protest became public in the pages of the *Morning Post*. On 9 January he stated that he and many other Conservatives would refuse to stand as Coalitionists and therefore bring about Lloyd George's downfall, and followed this up with a circular letter to constituency party chairmen arguing that an election would split the party from top to bottom.[145] Though Chamberlain mildly rebuked Younger for issuing his circular letter, he told Lloyd George that the Party Chairman had had no alternative in view of the storm of protest which the premature press disclosures had aroused.[146] But what Chamberlain found most upsetting was that the speculation over an election was

perhaps permanently ruining my effort to join all that is reasonably progressive in the Unionist party with what is sound and not too tied up in old party shibboleths in the Liberal Party.[147]

The net result, Chamberlain believed, would be increased estrangement and jealousy between Conservatives and Coalition Liberals and a growing insistence on the part of the former on standing as Unionists pure and simple.[148] He remained convinced that if the Coalition were to break up the inevitable consequence would be to divide the 'moderate and constitutional forces' into two hostile camps and leave the Labour party to profit from these divisions.[149] But if the diehards continued to organise opposition, it might become necessary to hold an election rather than see the government disintegrate in the way that Chamberlain recalled as the experience of Balfour's ministry after 1903.[150]

So strong was the feeling inside the Conservative party that Lloyd George was forced to abandon his idea of holding an early election. But the episode had done considerable harm to Chamberlain's standing. The

Prime Minister heard that he was 'discredited for lack of leadership.'[151]
The average observer concluded that Younger had had to seize the
initiative because Chamberlain was too weak to oppose Lloyd George.
Speaking in Glasgow on 19 January, Chamberlain tried to rally support
for the Coalition, stressing the government's achievements and paying a
personal tribute to Lloyd George. Neville thought the speech 'excellent,
thoughtful and statesmanlike, with sufficient assertiveness in it to mark his
position as leader.'[152] But whether Chamberlain realised it or not the
election scare had seriously damaged his position. He seemed to many
Conservatives far more tied to Lloyd George than Law had ever allowed
himself to be. Perhaps because he recalled the problems of the Liberal
Unionists as a junior partner in a coalition, he often seemed more sensitive
to the feelings of Coalition Liberals than to members of his own party.
While, moreover, the image of the government and the Prime Minister
continued to tarnish, Chamberlain by associating with them was
undermining his own most valuable asset, his reputation for public honour
and integrity. Many now viewed the leading figures in the government,
particularly Lloyd George, Birkenhead and Churchill, as having been
hopelessly corrupted by power. Some of the uniquely personal qualities
which had stood the Prime Minister in such good stead during the War
had now become the basis of his undoing. Arnold Bennett recorded after a
weekend at Cherkley in the company of Chamberlain, Lloyd George and
Birkenhead that he 'never heard principles or the welfare of the country
mentioned.'[153] Robert Cecil tried to open Chamberlain's eyes to what he
regarded as Lloyd George's real character:

Believe me he is quite incapable of running straight and how you can put up with
him passes my comprehension.[154]

J. C. C. Davidson thought that many of Chamberlain's problems
derived from the fact that he had no one in his personal confidence except
sycophants and yes-men, 'the greatest disaster that can happen to any
politician.'[155] At all events Chamberlain seemed incapable of
understanding the very genuine fears entertained by many Conservatives
that they were in danger of losing their own identity. He repeatedly fell
back on the argument that there was unanimity among the Conservatives
in the Cabinet, as if these men held a monopoly of wisdom, in the face of
which dissident backbenchers should show obedience.[156] 'Is there a single
item in our present policy,' asked Leo Amery, 'which appeals to the
instincts or traditions of Unionists?'

If you say we must enthuse them on the rally against Socialism, I can only
answer that you won't do this as long as your financial policy is ... breaking

down the whole capitalist and individualist economic system under the burden of excessive direct taxation.[157]

Even Neville Chamberlain admitted that the Conservative leaders showed a total lack of constructive policy. Though they were on safe ground in saying that they could not break with Lloyd George unless there was something to break about, if only they had a few ideas of their own there soon would be scope for separation.[158]

A group of thirty-five diehard M.P.s led by Colonel Gretton met Chamberlain and other Conservative ministers on 13 February with a recital of their complaints. They argued that the government should be reconstituted without Lloyd George and asked for an assurance that the party would fight the next election on its own. Chamberlain promised that each partner in the Coalition would go to the country on its own manifesto and repeated the pledge publicly a week later. Yet when he came to address the Oxford Carlton Club on 3 March he seemed to have reverted to the idea that the Coalition would fight the next election as a government.[159] Writing to Gretton on 21 February he warned the diehard leader that the Conservative Cabinet ministers were completely united in their views and that Gretton's behaviour could only do considerable damage to the party in the country.[160]

Not surprisingly many Conservatives were puzzled. The early months of 1922 saw an increasing breakdown in comprehension between Chamberlain and those whom he nominally led. Either Chamberlain was being deliberately ambiguous and contradictory, or more probably an element of confusion existed in his own mind. 'I know what I want', he told his sister Ida,[161] but the average backbench M.P. could be forgiven for not knowing precisely what that was. Though Chamberlain personally saw his goal with adequate clarity, the way in which it would be secured was less evident. He could tell Lloyd George:

My object has been to lead the Unionist party to accept merger in a new Party under the leadership of the present Prime Minister and including the great bulk of the old Unionists and old Liberals so as to secure the widest and closest possible union of all men and women of constitutional and progressive views.[162]

But what this would involve and how and when it could be achieved were less clear. It was inconceivable that all Conservatives and all Coalition Liberals would accept fusion, yet this was a problem Chamberlain seemed unable to grasp. As Beaverbrook recognised, the operation would involve 'an immense wrench and supersession of a separate Conservative leader.'[163] Yet rather than try to explain his own position Chamberlain too readily sought refuge in an appeal to accept his own understanding of what was in the party's best interests. In so doing he was drawing upon a diminishing store of past credit which could not last out indefinitely. To one veteran critic he wrote:

I cannot at this moment find time to enter into a full explanation of my views . . . but I am afraid that I must acknowledge that there is a very considerable divergence of view between us as to what is alike the duty and the interest of the Unionist Party at this time.[164]

To many it was the same fault he had displayed over the Irish question. Then F. S. Oliver had complained:

My main theme is that you are persuading your fellow countrymen to do what they believe to be wrong. (And you are taking no steps whatever to show them that it is right. . . .) And that, in *you* even more than in *them*, is the sin against the Holy Ghost.[165]

Increasingly no one knew whether Chamberlain, in a crisis, would stand up for his party or betray it.[166]

   Attitudes towards the Coalition might have been different if backbench Conservatives, well aware that they were the predominant element in the government, had seen one of their own party as Prime Minister. This could have become a reality at the end of February 1922. In the course of the month Lloyd George told Chamberlain and Law that he was willing to resign the premiership and support either of them in his place, provided they were ready to continue his policy in relation to Ireland and European pacification. Lloyd George made a formal offer to Chamberlain to this effect on 27 February. The Prime Minister's purpose remains obscure and he may simply have wished to reveal his own indispensability. Alternatively the gesture may have been meant to rouse Chamberlain to firmer action in relation to Conservative malcontents. But in all probability Lloyd George was simply exhausted after sixteen continuous years in government.[167] At all events Chamberlain lost no time in declining the offer, begging Lloyd George to remain at his post. His motives seem clearer than those of the Prime Minister. He was too obsessively loyal and perhaps too mesmerised by Lloyd George's talents to think of replacing him. But above all else one senses again, as in 1911, that same self-doubt on Chamberlain's part about his own abilities.[168] When in the middle of March it was rumoured that Lloyd George might have to retire because of ill-health, Chamberlain's correspondence exuded alarm rather than excitement at the prospect of the succession.[169] Conscious of the massive task of political realignment which he saw as the only safeguard against Socialism, Chamberlain had no real confidence in his own capacity to engineer such a revolution in British politics. Nor could he see himself playing the role of international statesman which Lloyd George so relished. As Leslie Scott argued, 'L.G. at the head of the coalition is, for European politics, a far stronger influence than any alternative.'[170] Chamberlain consulted his fellow Conservatives in the Cabinet who all agreed that the Prime Minister should remain in office. The latter, however, was slow to reveal his intentions. Possibly he took seriously Beaverbrook's warning that Churchill was working for a new coalition in which Chamberlain would be Prime Minister but Churchill the dominating influence.[171] On 18 March Chamberlain felt obliged to renew his appeal:

I beg therefore as a friend speaking in your own interests, as a colleague speaking on behalf of your colleagues, and as the leader of one of the Parties whose fortunes are inseparably bound up at the present time with your decision, to take the earliest opportunity of definitely declaring your resolution to continue as Prime Minister the leadership of the Coalition.[172]

Once again the crisis passed. Chamberlain, indeed, seemed to believe that the worst was over. Increasingly in the spring of 1922 he came to resemble a political ostrich, burying its head in the shifting sands from which the Coalition had been fashioned. It seems also impossible to escape the conclusion that Chamberlain was badly advised by those whose task it was to keep him in touch with the mood of the party's rank and file. 'I think the air is clearing and the prospect brighter,' he told Walter Long.[173] 'In spite of the storms that break around our heads,' he assured the Prime Minister, 'we are doing very well.' There was, he believed, 'a considerable reaction in favour of the Coalition.'[174] Even when a meeting of two hundred Conservative M.P.s on 14 March expressed grave misgivings about the policy and conduct of the Coalition and came close to repudiating Chamberlain's leadership, he was confident that it was of 'no real significance' and that any difficulties were merely the result of gross mismanagement of the meeting:

It is a great nuisance that the waters should have been stirred again in this way just when everything was going satisfactorily. But . . . except among the small 'die-hard' section there was no opposition to the Coalition and nothing but the most friendly feeling both to you and me.[175]

Here, though, lay Chamberlain's most serious miscalculation. Misgivings about the Coalition, though as yet barely articulated and largely leaderless, ran much deeper in the ranks of the Conservative party than the small group of right-wingers associated with Gretton. During the spring and summer, though Chamberlain was largely unaware of the development, what he had always assumed to be a minority of dissidents gradually took on the proportions of a majority.[176] Yet he remained confident that, particularly among the industrial districts where the

Labour threat was greatest, feeling in favour of continuing the Coalition
was strong both among M.P.s and party activists:

For some time past I have received many indications of the strength of this
feeling, which was at first slow to express itself, but now comes to me in
numberless Resolutions from Associations in nearly all parts of the country.[177]

Chamberlain's desire to play down the threat from within his own ranks
was very understandable. He had no wish to regard his critics as enemies,
nor did he seek confrontation. He had inherited a united party from Bonar
Law and knew, better than most, what were the sad results of internal
party feuding. It was for this reason that he resisted the idea of a party
meeting which would have brought matters to a head, emphasising
differences rather than healing them. Of the diehards he wrote to Long:

I am most anxious to keep the party together and have very carefully refrained
from saying anything to anger or embitter them. I am disappointed that I see no
sign of their responding in the same spirit. I shall still do my best to keep us
united.[178]

But the effect of Chamberlain's kid-glove approach was further to
undermine his credibility as a leader and to allow the diehards the time to
marshal and augment their forces. Only once did Chamberlain modify his
approach. Just before Easter a backbench M.P., Sir William Joynson-
Hicks, put down a vote of censure. This was too much for even
Chamberlain's long forbearance. In what colleagues and the press were
agreed in describing as his best ever speech, Chamberlain routed the
diehards at Joynson-Hicks's expense:

For the sake of narrow party spirit and old party jealousy they are wrecking the
great causes for which we are working. They have been unable either in the
country or on the floor of this house tonight to state the principles of our party to
which we have been unfaithful.

On this occasion, thought Lloyd George, Chamberlain was more like his
father than ever before. Even Neville had never credited him with such
debating skills.[179] But the singular success of this one occasion was
deceptive. It encouraged Chamberlain to think that the worst was now
over. He looked forward to the next election which, he expected, would see
the Coalition returned with a large though not abnormal majority and 'in
the course of time' to the successful evolution of his vague plans for the
fusion of the anti-Labour parties.[180]

For objective observers, however, there were plenty of indications that
things were not going as well for the government as Chamberlain would
have liked to believe. The attitude of the Dublin government together with
the renewal of violence in Ireland showed that the latest efforts to reach a

definitive settlement of that troubled country's affairs had not met with total success. The scandal over the sale of honours, to the benefit apparently of Lloyd George's private funds, seemed to epitomise the personal corruption which many now believed to characterise the Coalition government as a whole. The behaviour of certain ministers, particularly the Lord Chancellor, only added to the sense of outrage. Discontent was growing over the government's failure to do anything to reform the House of Lords, as had been promised at the time of the Coupon Election. The Geddes Committee had reported on government expenditure in February 1922 and its proposed economies had inevitably created resentment among those affected. Ominously, the unemployment figures showed no signs of improvement. The government as a whole seemed to have lost its sense of direction. With little scope for manoeuvre and with financial stringency still the order of the day, it seemed to have run out of ideas. Neville took the opportunity to ask his brother whether he had thought of any programme if an election did come, and made some suggestions:

I don't know whether they were very helpful but he said they were the first he had had.[181]

But Chamberlain remained concerned that 'a positive policy [was] apt to be associated with the spending of large sums of money.'[182]

Finally, and most damagingly for the Prime Minister, the government's foreign policy seemed in danger of collapse. Lloyd George had attended over twenty major international conferences since the end of the War. That at Genoa in April 1922 was to be the last and most ambitious, and was supposed to settle all outstanding issues. But even before he left England the Prime Minister was running into trouble in the Cabinet. He was anxious to bring the two outcasts of European diplomacy, Germany and Russia, back into the pale of respectability, but both Chamberlain and Birkenhead advised him against granting *de jure* recognition of the Bolsheviks. The former wrote:

Isolated recognition by us would in any case raise great difficulties among our followers in the House of Commons and, if it led to a breach with Churchill, it would be quite fatal to us.

He was concerned also that Russia should offer tangible signs of good faith before diplomatic recognition was accorded.[183] Chamberlain watched Lloyd George's conduct of the conference with some anxiety:

You have seen the few telegrams that I have sent and you will have noticed that they were all directed to pouring as much cold water on his fervid temperament as could be done without causing him to feel that I was meddling intolerably with a situation which I did not understand.[184]

He did not like the thought that Lloyd George might be 'sacrificing French friendship for the beaux yeux of the Bolsheviks.'[185] In the event little was achieved. The French only came to the conference to repeat their claim for full reparations. The Germans and the Russians fulfilled the worst fears of the West by concluding a private arrangment at Rapallo. Lloyd George's foreign policy lay in ruins.

Yet it is too easy for the historian to read history backwards and to see in the events of these months the seeds of the government's inevitable destruction at the Carlton Club in October. Despite all the Coalition's difficulties, Chamberlain's own position in the early summer of 1922 seemed reasonably secure. At the very least, what damage had been done could still be reversed. While the Cabinet itself remained united – and despite all the policy problems which had faced it, the Coalition Cabinet's coherence compared favourably with that of many succeeding administrations – it was difficult to see how any opposition could make significant headway. There was no obvious rival at this date for the Conservative leadership. 'Bonar Law tries on the crown but can't make up his mind to attempt to seize it.'[186] The leading diehards were in no sense charismatic figures. Moreover the personal animosity felt by many towards Lloyd George and Birkenhead was not matched in attitudes towards Chamberlain. The latter had come tantalisingly close to becoming Prime Minister. It was possible to predict that the opportunity might recur. In his own mind Chamberlain must have imagined, even though it was difficult for him to articulate such thoughts, that a General Election, when it finally came, would leave him with an irresistible claim to the premiership. If his parliamentary triumph over the diehards could be repeated, if the policy of fusion could be handled diplomatically enough, if the government could survive until a brighter economic climate prevailed, then his own career might yet blossom after so many disappointments towards a glorious crescendo. In the event, before the year was out, the shortest reign of any Conservative leader in the twentieth century was to end with the most undignified of exits.

Notes

1. N. Chamberlain to A. Chamberlain 28 June 1917, Chamberlain MSS, AC 35/1/25.
2. T. Wilson (ed.), *The Political Diaries of C. P. Scott 1911–1928* (London, 1970) p. 429.

3. A. Chamberlain to Ida Chamberlain 25 March 1921, Chamberlain MSS, AC 5/1/195.
4. R. R. James, *Churchill: A Study in Failure 1900–1939* (London, 1970) p. 99.
5. A. Chamberlain to Earl Fitzwilliam 12 Jan. 1922, Chamberlain MSS, AC 32/2/38.
6. A. Chamberlain to Madge 26 Jan. 1922, ibid, AC 33/1/21.
7. N. Chamberlain to H. Chamberlain 4 Jan. 1919, ibid, NC 18/1/196.
8. N. Chamberlain to Ida Chamberlain 16 Nov. 1918 and 23 Feb. 1919, ibid, NC 18/1/191, 202.
9. A. Chamberlain to Ida Chamberlain 26 Sept. 1919, ibid, AC 5/1/139; see also A. Chamberlain to Ivy Chamberlain 28 Sept. 1919, ibid, AC 6/1/355 and T. Jones, *Whitehall Diary* i, 102.
10. A. Chamberlain to R. Cecil 26 April 1921, Chamberlain MSS, AC 24/3/16.
11. A. Chamberlain to Selborne 18 April 1921, ibid, AC 15/6/16.
12. F. S. Oliver to A. Chamberlain 8 Feb. 1922, ibid, AC 14/6/110.
13. S. Roskill, *Hankey* ii, 35; M. Gilbert, *Churchill* iv, 1, 445.
14. Bonar Law to Lloyd George 3 Jan. 1919, Lloyd George MSS, F/30/3/1.
15. F. Stevenson, *Lloyd George: A Diary* p. 170.
16. Memorandum by A. Chamberlain 13 Jan. 1919, Chamberlain MSS, AC 49/4/2; A. Chamberlain to N. Chamberlain 11 Jan. 1919, ibid, NC 1/27/45; R. Blake, *Unknown Prime Minister* pp. 397–8.
17. A. Chamberlain to Ida Chamberlain 19 Jan. 1919, Chamberlain MSS, AC 5/1/115.
18. A. Chamberlain to M. Chamberlain 21 Jan. 1919, ibid, AC 4/1/1193.
19. A. Chamberlain to Ida Chamberlain 1 Jan. 1919, ibid, AC 5/1/114.
20. K. O. Morgan, *Consensus and Disunity: The Lloyd George Coalition Government 1918–1922* (Oxford, 1979) p. 82.
21. N. Chamberlain to Ida Chamberlain 12 Jan. 1919, Chamberlain MSS, NC 18/1/197.
22. E. Montagu to Lloyd George 1 May 1917, Lloyd George MSS, F/39/3/11.
23. A. W. Baldwin, *My Father: The True Story* (London, 1955) p. 82.
24. K. Middlemas and J. Barnes, *Baldwin* (London, 1969) p. 72. Chamberlain later wrote: 'I find it difficult to express my sense of what I owe to you for the immense burden which you take off my shoulders.' A. Chamberlain to Baldwin 15 April 1920, Baldwin MSS, 175 f.10.
25. A. Chamberlain to Ida Chamberlain 13 April 1919, Chamberlain MSS, AC 5/1/124.
26. N. Chamberlain to Annie Chamberlain 24 June 1920, ibid, NC 1/26/206.
27. N. Chamberlain to H. Chamberlain 13 April 1919, ibid, NC 18/1/208.
28. N. Chamberlain to Ida Chamberlain 20 April 1919, ibid, NC 18/1/209.
29. A. Chamberlain to W. Churchill 19 Jan. 1919, cited M. Gilbert, *Churchill* iv, 1, 468.
30. A. Chamberlain to G. Lloyd 31 Dec. 1920, Chamberlain MSS, AC 18/1/16.

31. Ibid, 18 June 1919, AC 18/1/5.
32. A. Chamberlain to H. Chamberlain 24 March 1919, ibid, AC 5/1/122; A. Chamberlain to Ivy Chamberlain 10 March 1919, AC 6/1/338.
33. A. Chamberlain to H. Chamberlain 9 Feb. 1919, ibid, AC 5/1/118.
34. T. Jones, *A Diary with Letters* p. 18.
35. A. Chamberlain to Ida Chamberlain 16 Feb. 1919, Chamberlain MSS, AC 5/1/119.
36. Lord Edmund Talbot to Bonar Law 1 May 1919, Bonar Law MSS 97/3/1. Baldwin thought Chamberlain's performance in the Commons had done much to restore his position in the House and the Chancellor himself was 'tremendously bucked up by his success.' N. Chamberlain to Ida Chamberlain 4 May 1919, Chamberlain MSS, NC 18/1/211; See also R. R. James (ed.), *Memoirs of a Conservative* (London, 1969) pp. 96–7.
37. A. Chamberlain to Ida Chamberlain 3 Aug. 1919, Chamberlain MSS, AC 5/1/135.
38. War Cabinet minutes 29 July 1919, cited M. Gilbert, *Churchill* iv, 2, 769.
39. N. Chamberlain to Annie Chamberlain 28 June 1920, Chamberlain MSS, NC 1/26/209.
40. M. Gilbert, *Churchill* iv, 192.
41. A. Chamberlain to Churchill 5 Feb. 1919, cited Gilbert, *Churchill* iv, 1, 513.
42. Gilbert, *Churchill* iv, 472.
43. Note by A. Chamberlain for War Cabinet on 'The Financial Situation', 18 July 1919, Chamberlain MSS, AC 34/1/50.
44. Gilbert, *Churchill* iv, 2, 780, 782.
45. T. Jones, *Whitehall Diary* i, 114.
46. A. Chamberlain to Ida Chamberlain 19 July 1919, Chamberlain MSS, AC 5/1/134; Curzon to Lloyd George 1 July 1919, Lloyd George MSS, F/12/20; A. Chamberlain to Curzon 14 July 1919, Curzon MSS Eur. F 112/209.
47. A. Chamberlain to Lloyd George 17 April 1919, Lloyd George MSS, F/7/2/27.
48. A. Chamberlain to Curzon 8 Jan. 1919, Curzon MSS Eur. F 112/209.
49. Gilbert, *Churchill* iv, 240.
50. Ibid, pp. 271–2.
51. Ibid, p. 303.
52. Henry Wilson Diary 25 Oct. 1919, cited ibid, iv, 2, 941.
53. A. Chamberlain to Ida Chamberlain 26 Oct. 1919, Chamberlain MSS, AC 5/1/141.
54. N. Chamberlain to Ida Chamberlain 1 Nov. 1919, ibid, NC 18/1/231.
55. K. Morgan, *Consensus and Disunity* p. 258.
56. A. Chamberlain to N. Chamberlain 20 Oct. 1918, Chamberlain MSS, NC 1/27/43; Note by A. Chamberlain for Curzon 27 June 1918, ibid, AC 12/70.
57. A. Chamberlain to Ida Chamberlain 21 Dec. 1919, ibid, AC 5/1/146.
58. See, for example, A. Chamberlain to Lloyd George 2 Aug. 1920, Lloyd

George MSS F/7/3/16.

59. A. Chamberlain to W. Long 30 Aug. 1919, Chamberlain MSS, AC 25/2/32.
60. A. Chamberlain to N. Chamberlain 1 Sept. 1919, ibid, NC 1/27/50.
61. A. Chamberlain to Law 6 Jan. 1921, Bonar Law MSS 100/1/8. See also A. Chamberlain to Lloyd George 16 July 1920, Lloyd George MSS F/7/3/15.
62. A. Chamberlain to Law 6 Jan. 1921, Bonar Law MSS 100/1/8.
63. K. Morgan, *Consensus and Disunity* p. 255.
64. N. Chamberlain to H. Chamberlain 24 April 1920, Chamberlain MSS, NC 18/1/254.
65. A. Chamberlain to Ida Chamberlain 1 Aug. 1920, ibid, AC 5/1/171.
66. A. Chamberlain to Ivy Chamberlain 5 May 1920, ibid, AC 6/1/370.
67. Memorandum by A. Chamberlain: 'Proposals for New Expenditure', 7 June 1920, ibid, AC 34/1/113; A. Chamberlain to Lloyd George 16 July 1920, Lloyd George MSS F/7/3/15.
68. A. Chamberlain to Lloyd George 2 Aug. 1920, Lloyd George MSS F/7/3/16.
69. Bridgeman diary 17 Aug. 1920.
70. N. Chamberlain to H. Chamberlain 11 July 1920, Chamberlain MSS, NC 18/1/264.
71. K. Morgan, *Consensus and Disunity* p. 97.
72. S. Roskill, *Naval Policy between the Wars*, vol. 1 (London, 1968) p. 221.
73. A. Chamberlain to Ida Chamberlain 22 Oct. 1920, Chamberlain MSS, AC 5/1/176; Montagu to Lloyd George 26 Oct. 1920, Lloyd George MSS F/40/3/27; M. Gilbert, *Churchill* iv, 2, 1223.
74. A. Chamberlain to H. Chamberlain 1 Jan. 1921, Chamberlain MSS, AC 5/1/186.
75. Henry Wilson diary 19 March 1921, cited M. Gilbert, *Churchill* iv, 555.
76. Lord Beaverbrook, *The Decline and Fall of Lloyd George* p. 20.
77. N. Chamberlain to Ida Chamberlain 19 March 1921, Chamberlain MSS, NC 18/1/295.
78. R. R. James (ed.), *Memoirs of a Conservative* pp. 103–4.
79. J. Davidson to Law 24 March 1921, Bonar Law MSS 107/1/4. By May Beaverbrook was writing that 'F. E. Smith means to challenge Chamberlain's leadership of the Tory party.' The latter was 'doing very well', but 'does not control his temper and after 10 p.m. he shows failing powers.' Beaverbrook, *Decline and Fall* pp. 263–4. See also A. Chamberlain to H. Chamberlain 8 May 1921, Chamberlain MSS, AC 5/1/199.
80. A. Chamberlain to M. Chamberlain 19 March 1921, Chamberlain MSS, AC 4/1/1204.
81. A. Chamberlain to H. Chamberlain 20 March 1921, ibid, AC 5/1/194.
82. A. Chamberlain to Law 29 March 1921, Bonar Law MSS 107/1/7.
83. A. Chamberlain to G. Lloyd 11 April 1921, Chamberlain MSS, AC 18/1/20.
84. A. Chamberlain to Ida Chamberlain 23 April 1921, ibid, AC 5/1/198;

T. Jones, *Whitehall Diary* i, 152.

85. S. Roskill, *Hankey* ii, 224; R. Churchill, *Derby* p. 391.
86. F. Stevenson, *Lloyd George: A Diary* pp. 215–6.
87. Ibid, p. 221; see also Beaverbrook to Law 13 May 1921, cited Beaverbrook, *Decline and Fall* p. 262.
88. Lloyd George to Law 7 June 1921, Lloyd George MSS F/31/1/58.
89. 'I suspect that our beloved P.M. has been intriguing away while A. was at sea and making arrangements for the reversion of the Chancellorship.' N. Chamberlain to Ida Chamberlain 23 Jan. 1921, Chamberlain MSS, NC 18/1/287; see also S. Roskill, *Hankey* ii, 216.
90. Even so, Chamberlain sometimes found Lloyd George's way of working irritating. 'To Inverness from Euston 7.30 p.m. with Chamberlain [and other ministers]. Chamberlain's first words were: "This is outrageous, dragging us to Inverness. Why did the P.M. not have the Meeting in Edinburgh?"' T. Jones, *Whitehall Diary* iii, 106.
91. J. Ramsden, *Balfour and Baldwin* pp. 150–1.
92. A. Chamberlain to Col. J. Gretton 20 July 1921, Chamberlain MSS, AC 24/3/47. Edwin Montagu had earlier noted: 'Chamberlain looks anxious and worried, torn between loyalty to his party and loyalty to the Prime Minister.' H. Montgomery Hyde, *Lord Reading* (London, 1967) pp. 370–1.
93. A. Chamberlain to W. Churchill 8 April 1921, cited M. Gilbert, *Churchill* iv, 3, 1431.
94. M. Kinnear, *The Fall of Lloyd George* (London, 1973) p. 8.
95. N. Chamberlain to Ida Chamberlain 19 March 1921, Chamberlain MSS, NC 18/1/295.
96. Earl of Birkenhead, *Contemporary Personalities* pp. 72–3.
97. Birkenhead to Law 5 May 1921, cited R. Blake, *Unknown Prime Minister* p. 428. 'Austen not known enough among the rank and file.' R. Sanders Diary, 2 July 1922.
98. See description of Chamberlain's treatment of Gideon Murray, M.P. in M. Kinnear, *Fall of Lloyd George* p. 58.
99. T. Jones to Lloyd George 11 Aug. 1921, Lloyd George MSS F/25/2/2; T. Jones, *Whitehall Diary* iii, 96–7.
100. M. Kinnear, *Fall of Lloyd George* p. 57.
101. Speech to the Central Council of the National Union of Conservative and Unionist Associations, 21 June 1921.
102. K. Morgan, *Consensus and Disunity* p. 244.
103. J. Remnant to Law 1 June 1921, Bonar Law MSS 107/1/32.
104. E. Goulding to Law 11 June 1921, ibid, 107/1/40.
105. A. Chamberlain to Ivy Chamberlain 31 July 1924, Chamberlain MSS, AC 6/1/546.
106. A. Chamberlain to H. Chamberlain 24 July 1920, ibid, AC 5/1/170.
107. M. Gilbert, *Churchill* iv, 453.
108. F. Stevenson, *Lloyd George: A Diary* p. 230.
109. T. Jones, *Whitehall Diary* iii, 87. See also Stevenson, *Lloyd George: A*

Diary p. 234.

110. A. Chamberlain to Ida Chamberlain 24 July 1921, Chamberlain MSS, AC 5/1/204; A. Chamberlain to Lloyd George 11 Aug. 1921, Lloyd George MSS F/7/4/25.

111. A. Chamberlain to R. McNeill 10 Aug. 1921, Chamberlain MSS, AC 26/3/2.

112. A. Chamberlain to M. Chamberlain 25 Aug. 1921, ibid, AC 4/1/1207.

113. A. Chamberlain to Ida Chamberlain 17 Oct. 1921, ibid, AC 5/1/219.

114. T. Jones to Lloyd George 11 Aug. 1921, Lloyd George MSS F/25/2/2; A. Chamberlain to Lloyd George 11 Aug. 1921, ibid, F/7/4/25; T. Jones, *Whitehall Diary* iii, 96.

115. A. Chamberlain to Ivy Chamberlain 18 Aug. 1921, Chamberlain MSS, AC 6/1/419.

116. Ibid, 24 and 25 Oct. 1921, AC 6/1/430, 432.

117. Ibid, 29 Oct. 1921, AC 6/1/439.

118. Ibid, 31 Oct. 1921, AC 6/1/441.

119. A. Chamberlain to Lloyd George 11 Nov. 1921, Lloyd George MSS, F/7/4/31; T. Jones, *Whitehall Diary* iii, 162.

120. A. Chamberlain to H. Chamberlain 17 Sept. 1921, Chamberlain MSS, AC 5/1/213.

121. M. Gilbert, *Churchill* iv, 672–3. The Party Chairman argued that if Ulster adopted an intractable attitude, 'unquestionably it would create a rift in our own Party which might have serious internal consequences.' Younger to A. Chamberlain 9 Nov. 1921, Curzon MSS Eur. F 112/219A.

122. T. Jones, *Whitehall Diary* iii, 134.

123. Salisbury to Selborne 15 Nov. 1921, Selborne MSS 7 f.114.

124. A. Chamberlain to Ivy Chamberlain 9 Nov. 1921, Chamberlain MSS, AC 6/1/459.

125. A. Chamberlain to H. Chamberlain 13 Nov. 1921, ibid, AC 5/1/220.

126. A. Chamberlain to N. Chamberlain 13 Nov. 1921, ibid, NC 1/27/57.

127. N. Chamberlain to A. Chamberlain 23 Nov. 1921, ibid, AC 26/4/43.

128. A. Chamberlain to N. Chamberlain 22 Nov. 1921, ibid, NC 1/27/58.

129. K. Morgan, *Consensus and Disunity* pp. 248–9; M. Kinnear, *Fall of Lloyd George* p. 99.

130. Note by A. Chamberlain 23 Nov. 1921, Chamberlain MSS, AC 31/2/38.

131. A. Chamberlain to Ivy Chamberlain 13 Nov. 1921, ibid, AC 6/1/463.

132. A. Chamberlain to R. McNeill 14 Nov. 1921, ibid, AC 26/3/6.

133. A. Chamberlain to J. P. Croal 10 Jan. 1922, ibid, AC 32/2/41.

134. H. Montgomery Hyde, *Carson: the life of Sir Edward Carson, Lord Carson of Duncain* (London, 1953) p. 465.

135. T. Jones, *Whitehall Diary* iii, 189–91.

136. R. Blake, *Unknown Prime Minister* p. 441.

137. A. Chamberlain to G. Younger 22 Dec. 1921, Chamberlain MSS, AC 32/2/2.

138. A. Chamberlain to N. Chamberlain 21 Dec. 1921, ibid, AC 32/2/3.

139. G. Younger to A. Chamberlain 24 and 28 Dec. 1921, ibid,

186   *Gentleman in Politics*

AC 32/2/11, 12.
140. M. Fraser to A. Chamberlain 31 Dec. 1921, ibid, AC 32/4/1a.
141. R. Sanders to A. Chamberlain 2 Jan. 1922, Lloyd George MSS F/7/5/1a;
     N. Chamberlain to A. Chamberlain 29 Dec. 1921, Chamberlain MSS, AC
     32/2/13.
142. A. Chamberlain to Lloyd George 4 Jan. 1922, Chamberlain MSS, AC
     32/2/20.
143. K. Morgan, *Consensus and Disunity* p. 274; M. Gilbert, *Churchill* iv, 3,
     1726.
144. Beaverbrook, *Decline and Fall* p. 130.
145. W. Churchill to Lloyd George 12 Jan. 1922, cited M. Gilbert, *Churchill*
     iv, 3, 1726.
146. A. Chamberlain to G. Younger 11 Jan. 1922, Chamberlain MSS, AC
     32/2/30; A. Chamberlain to Lloyd George 12 Jan. 1922, ibid, AC
     32/2/26.
147. A. Chamberlain to Ida Chamberlain 7 Jan. 1922, ibid, AC 5/1/223.
148. A. Chamberlain to Ivy Chamberlain 7 Jan. 1922, ibid, AC 6/1/473.
149. A. Chamberlain to Derby 12 Jan. 1922, ibid, AC 32/2/34.
150. A. Chamberlain to N. Chamberlain 25 Jan. 1922, ibid, NC 1/27/62.
151. F. Guest to Lloyd George 16 Jan. 1922, Lloyd George MSS F/22/3/37.
152. N. Chamberlain to Ida Chamberlain 21 Jan. 1922, Chamberlain MSS, NC
     18/1/335.
153. R. James, *Churchill: A Study in Failure* p. 138.
154. R. Cecil to A. Chamberlain 1 April 1922, Cecil MSS 51078.
155. R. James, *Memoirs of a Conservative* p. 104.
156. A. Chamberlain to A. Steel-Maitland 23 March 1922, Chamberlain MSS,
     AC 33/1/49.
157. L. Amery to A. Chamberlain 26 Jan. 1922, ibid, AC 24/4/1.
158. N. Chamberlain to H. Chamberlain 12 Feb. 1922, ibid, NC 18/1/339.
159. Middlemas and Barnes, *Baldwin* p. 104; Kinnear, *Fall of Lloyd George* p.
     106; Morgan, *Consensus and Disunity* p. 335; M. Cowling, *The Impact of
     Labour* (Cambridge, 1971) p. 141.
160. A. Chamberlain to J. Gretton 21 Feb. 1922, Chamberlain MSS, AC
     33/1/11.
161. A. Chamberlain to Ida Chamberlain 26 Feb. 1922, ibid, AC 5/1/227.
162. Memorandum by A. Chamberlain 6 Jan. 1922, ibid, AC 32/2/27.
163. Beaverbrook to Lloyd George 13 March 1922, Lloyd George MSS
     F/4/6/6.
164. A. Chamberlain to Imbert Terry 1 Feb. 1922, Chamberlain MSS, AC
     32/3/6.
165. F. S. Oliver to A. Chamberlain 9 Aug. 1921, ibid, AC 14/6/108.
166. M. Kinnear, *Fall of Lloyd George* p. 91.
167. M. Cowling, *Labour* p. 156; F. Stevenson, *Lloyd George: A Diary* p. 240;
     Lord Riddell, *Intimate Diary of the Peace Conference and After,
     1918–1923* (London, 1933) p. 355.
168. F. Stevenson, *Lloyd George: A Diary* p. 326. In May 1922 Birkenhead

succeeded in convincing Lloyd George that Chamberlain had been intriguing to replace him. 'Chamberlain was undoubtedly at one time tempted to try his luck.' If this were true, Chamberlain was remarkably successful in keeping his thoughts to himself. F. Stevenson, *The Years that are Past* (London, 1967) p. 203; A. J. P. Taylor (ed.), *My Darling Pussy* (London, 1975) p. 49.

169. A. Chamberlain to H. Chamberlain 18 March 1922, Chamberlain MSS, AC 5/1/230.

170. L. Scott to A. Chamberlain 3 March 1922, ibid, AC 33/1/36.

171. Beaverbrook to Lloyd George 15 March 1922, Lloyd George MSS, F/4/6/8.

172. Memorandum by A. Chamberlain for the Prime Minister 18 March 1922, Chamberlain MSS, AC 33/1/66.

173. A. Chamberlain to W. Long 6 March 1922, ibid, AC 33/1/33.

174. A. Chamberlain to Lloyd George 15 and 23 March 1922, Lloyd George MSS, F/7/5/8, 22.

175. Ibid, 15 March 1922, Lloyd George MSS F/7/5/8.

176. In March Chamberlain wrote: 'The "Morning Post" and the extreme opinion represented by it is certainly only a small, though not an unimportant, section of the Unionist Party ... I shall still do my best to keep us united, but I am sure that this cannot be done by requiring of the great majority a complete surrender to the irreconcilables.' A. Chamberlain to W. Long 29 March 1922, Chamberlain MSS, AC 33/1/54.

177. A. Chamberlain to W. Long 27 April 1922, Chamberlain MSS, AC 33/1/62; Lord Riddell, *Intimate Diary* p. 367.

178. A. Chamberlain to W. Long 29 March 1922, Chamberlain MSS, AC 33/1/54.

179. N. Chamberlain to H. Chamberlain 8 April 1922, ibid, NC 18/1/345; House of Commons Debates 5 April 1922, vol. 152, col. 2373.

180. A. Chamberlain to G. Lloyd 18 May 1922, ibid, AC 18/1/28.

181. N. Chamberlain to Ida Chamberlain 1 April 1922, ibid, NC 18/1/344.

182. M. Cowling, *Labour* p. 181.

183. M. Gilbert, *Churchill* iv, 775; A. J. P. Taylor (ed.), *Darling Pussy* p. 40.

184. A. Chamberlain to Curzon 15 May 1922, Curzon MSS Eur. F 112/223.

185. Ibid, 12 May 1922, MSS Eur. F 112/223.

186. A. Chamberlain to Ida Chamberlain 26 Feb. 1922, Chamberlain MSS, AC 5/1/227.

CHAPTER SIX
DECLINE

'I don't carry loyalty to Austen's extremes. . . .'[1]

'I think therefore that my real political life is ended.'[2]

'I asked Baldwin what I should say about Austen in proposing his health. . . . He said that the only true thing I could say was that he was the stupidest fellow he knew.'[3]

In the early summer of 1922 there were signs that Austen Chamberlain's career might be approaching its peak. As leader of his party he had successfully overcome the crisis of a possible election at the beginning of the year. The Conservatives now seemed somewhat more reconciled to the continued existence of the Coalition government, while at the same time anticipating that when the General Election did take place it would probably leave Chamberlain with an overwhelming claim to take over the premiership. In addition the parliamentary situation seemed relatively stable. Few could have predicted that within a matter of months the Coalition would have ended and Lloyd George would have left office for ever, while Chamberlain would be ousted from the party leadership into a self-imposed exile in which his active political life might easily have come to an end. In the reversal of fortunes of both the Coalition government and Chamberlain himself four developments stand out. One was the assassination of Sir Henry Wilson on 22 June, which reawakened Unionist misgivings about the Irish settlement with which Chamberlain had been intimately associated. A second was the scandal over the government's award of honours which seemed to highlight the uniquely personal nature of Lloyd George's administration which so many Conservatives found unacceptable. A third was the transference of the leadership of the diehard movement into the more capable and effective hands of the former Cabinet minister, Lord Salisbury. And the fourth was the government's inability to keep public opinion in sympathy with its foreign policy.[4]

In his handling of this mounting crisis Chamberlain revealed both the best and the worst features of his character. While his loyalty to Lloyd George never faltered and his conviction remained unshaken that the national interest, irrespective of personal or party considerations, demanded the continuation of the Coalition, his lack of feel for the changing political mood became ever more marked, while his stiffness and arrogance increasingly alienated many who would otherwise have rallied to his support. The criticism of his leadership since March 1921 irritated him and made him more than ever conscious of the dignity and authority of his position. Yet though Chamberlain's course of action was determined by his own deeply held convictions about the political situation, he singularly failed to convince his party that his judgement was correct or even that he really knew what his own ultimate objectives were. Chamberlain may always have played the game, but in 1922 it was by no means clear exactly what his game was.[5] Though he may privately have expected to succeed Lloyd George after an election, he found it difficult to say this in public, thereby giving the impression to many that he was happy to acquiesce indefinitely in a Lloyd George premiership. Throughout the coming months Chamberlain remained largely oblivious of the steady erosion of his power base within the party and apparently incapable of showing the subtlety and compromise which could have secured his position.

The first serious sign of trouble came with evidence that disaffection towards the Coalition had spread to junior ministers within the government. Concerned at the strength of the diehards and the possibility that independent Conservative candidates might be put up against Coalitionists at the next election, and conscious of the strong feeling in the country against the Coalition, they saw it as their duty to warn Chamberlain of the danger he would be in if he did nothing to meet the situation. Led by Sir Robert Sanders, the junior ministers met Chamberlain on 20 July. They emphasised the importance of preserving the solidarity of the Conservative party, and of having a party leader who would be more independent than at present of Lloyd George and who might become Prime Minister himself after the election if Conservative numbers justified it. Lloyd George was so unpopular in areas such as London, the Home Counties, the Midlands and Yorkshire that an understanding to this effect was imperative. Chamberlain seemed sympathetic towards their point of view and said he would talk to Conservative Cabinet ministers about it. It became apparent, though, that the latter, and especially Balfour, did not look upon the proposed understanding at all kindly. This, Chamberlain hoped, would settle the matter for the time being, but the junior ministers were in no mood to accept dictation from the leadership without discussion, and insisted on a meeting with all the Conservative members of the Cabinet. It was the first of the many miscalculations that Chamberlain was to make over the following weeks.[6]

On 3 August the junior ministers were summoned to a meeting in the Lord Chancellor's room in the House of Lords. It was not, Balfour later reflected, 'a very happy occasion, nor one that was very tactfully handled on either side.'[7] Chamberlain set the tone of the meeting with his statement that the proceedings were unprecedented and irregular but that after mature consideration his colleagues had decided that they would condescend to hear their juniors.[8] He pressed for any decision to be delayed until after the reassembly of parliament in the autumn. Balfour delivered a 'silly speech', but the real damage was done by Birkenhead. The Lord Chancellor's contribution to the proceedings was less a speech than a harangue. As Pollock, the Attorney-General, put it:

Lord Birkenhead's attitude was unexpected and both hostile and dictatorial as addressed to inferiors who had no right to express opinions.[9]

It was idle to pretend, continued Pollock, that Birkenhead's attitude and language did not create animosity. He had seldom seen men so stirred. Some of the junior ministers thought of walking out of the meeting. Others merely determined that Birkenhead should never lead the Conservative party or become Prime Minister. From this point he joined Lloyd George as the major focus of Conservative discontent. Significantly Chamberlain's apparent unwillingness to dissociate himself in any way from Birkenhead worked also to the party leader's disadvantage. For 'reasons good or bad, he left the matter in Birkenhead's hands.'[10] In the weeks ahead he became more closely aligned than ever with the Lord Chancellor, a development that was both surprising, in view of the contrasting characters of the two men, and damaging to Chamberlain's position in the party. For at least the next two years Chamberlain was to be damned in the eyes of many Conservatives by his friendship with Birkenhead.

In early September Chamberlain received a further warning shot about the position of the Coalition from the Earl of Derby. Chamberlain had been in politics long enough to know that the Lancashire magnate represented a sensitive barometer of the political climate. Yet the correspondence which now ensued between the two men showed how inadequate was Chamberlain's understanding of the central issues posed by the Coalition's continued existence. When Derby argued that he was becoming more and more convinced of the impossibility of the Coalition, as at present constituted, continuing any longer, and that he himself might be driven to join Salisbury and the diehards, Chamberlain was greatly shocked. Derby suggested that a reformed Coalition with a Conservative at its head might be a different matter, but insisted that the personality of Lloyd George was an insuperable handicap. Chamberlain responded that there was nothing in Salisbury's recent statement of principles with which he could not himself agree – he had manufactured differences where none ought to exist – but in so doing he merely showed his own lack of comprehension. Dissident Conservatives objected less to the policies pursued by the Coalition government than to the permanent loss of their political identity which its continuation seemed to presage. Salisbury, who was in no sense a charismatic figure, at least offered the hope of the independent survival of Conservatism and, as Derby pointed out,

if anybody who would be likely to be a real leader ... came forward at the present moment, in opposition to [Lloyd George], I believe he would secure the majority of the Conservative Party to follow him.[11]

The obvious candidate for the role of 'real leader' was Bonar Law. On 16 September, however, Younger assured Chamberlain that, while Law was not as ready to efface himself as he had once been, his loyalty to Chamberlain remained total.[12] Others, though, were less sure of Law's reliability. Salisbury clearly saw that Law might become the key to the situation and advised him that the demand for a free Conservative party was gathering strength every day and might soon become overwhelming. It was, he stressed, a feeling which now extended far beyond his own diehard followers.[13]

By this stage developments in the international arena had begun to work to the government's disadvantage. Turkey, Germany's wartime ally, was still partly occupied by Allied forces, but the Turkish Revolutionary Army led by Mustafa Kemal was advancing on Constantinople, threatening the Allied fortification of Chanak. From this the French and Italians hurriedly withdrew their forces, leaving the British under General Harington to face Kemal's army alone. When Lloyd George seemed ready to take the country to the brink of war in support of Greece against Turkey, independently-minded Conservatives were provided with a policy issue through which they could readily distance themselves from the Coalition. At a meeting of the Cabinet on 15 September, Chamberlain sounded a note of caution, but the majority of ministers followed Lloyd George in seeing in the Turkish national movement of Mustafa Kemal a threat to British honour and prestige in the Middle East.[14] By 27 September Chamberlain himself was arguing that a withdrawal now would constitute a humiliation for the British Empire.[15] The government seemed to be heading for a major military confrontation, while the timing of its appeal for help from the Dominions served only to upset the latter. Large sections of Conservative opinion were amazed to find the country almost at war. Though Chamberlain tried to reassure waverers such as Griffith-Boscawen, the Agriculture Minister, that the government would not 'risk the bones of a British soldier for Asia Minor or for Thrace or to prevent Constantinople passing again to the Turks', many were alarmed by their leader's stance:

A matter which disappointed all of us very much was the fact that the Lord Privy Seal appeared to side with [the "war party"].[16]

Although the crisis fizzled out early in October, for many the Chanak episode was the turning-point in their decision to break from Lloyd George and the Coalition. It also gave further scope for the re-emergence of Bonar Law as a potential alternative leader of the Conservative party. His letter to *The Times* of 7 October in which, while offering the government general support, he warned that Britain could not act alone 'as policeman of the world', was not endowed by contemporaries with the same significance as that attributed by some later historians. But it did serve to remind the party that its former leader was still a force to be reckoned with.

On 17 September the leaders of the Coalition met at Chequers to assess the political situation. Chamberlain informed them that the Coalition ought to be able to secure a majority at the polls, but that this majority might be in danger if the Conservatives were not allowed to choose a Prime Minister from their own number. Younger, in fact, had just advised him to make Lloyd George hand over the premiership at once.[17] But Chamberlain was anxious to play down the personal resentment felt towards Lloyd George, stressing rather the natural desire of a party to have its own leader. In so doing he was consciously distorting the true picture. In the event, it was decided that an election should be held as soon as the foreign situation allowed, with the government going to the country as a coalition. Chamberlain acquiesced without enthusiasm in this decision, but must have known that the National Union, which was due to meet in mid-November, was likely to declare against continued partnership with Lloyd George.[18] The problem was that Chamberlain's speeches to the National Union in February and the Oxford Carlton Club in March had been widely interpreted as giving permission for Conservatives to stand as Conservatives pure and simple. Some M.P.s later came to the conclusion that Chamberlain had deliberately misled them. Not surprisingly, therefore, the party managers were horrified by this latest decision. Younger was 'frankly appalled' at the results which it would entail. If the Coalition Conservatives went to the country with Lloyd George at their head, they would split the party in two.[19] The Chief Whip, Leslie Wilson, warned that the situation was grave:

My great fear is that you, personally, may not realise the actual position and when a General Election comes you may find the majority of your followers not following but, under the influence of their Associations, finding themselves forced into a position which will leave you, as Leader of the Party, in a position in which none of your friends and none of your colleagues would wish or intend you to be.[20]

He urged Chamberlain not to announce the decision before consulting the junior ministers and the party as a whole and informed him that 184 constituencies had so far declared their intention to run independent Conservative candidates.[21] A crisis in Chamberlain's leadership was clearly approaching as an increasing number of Conservatives saw him to be failing in his central duty. As Younger argued:

it is his first duty to try to preserve Party unity, and to adopt a policy which he knows perfectly well will rend us in twain without . . . taking steps to ascertain that the great majority of the Party is behind him would be, in my opinion, an outrage.[22]

Chamberlain's understanding of the situation was fundamentally different. In his opinion the rise of the Labour party and the possibility that it might secure a parliamentary majority remained the crucial and determining consideration. 'Those who think,' he assured one correspondent, 'that the Conservative . . . Party, standing as such and disavowing its Liberal allies, could return with a working majority are living in a fool's paradise':

Confronted with such a danger [from the Labour party] I conceive that it is our business to try to rally all the conservative elements of the country, for we shall need all the strength that we can muster.[23]

His calculation was that at the next election only a coalition could prevent an anti-Conservative majority and that no arrangement with the Coalition Liberals would be possible except under a Lloyd George premiership. He therefore believed that the only option for all Conservatives in positions of responsibility was to stand together and urge this strategy upon the party in the hope that the majority would fall into line.[24] Not even an appeal from Walter Long, now very much one of the party's elder statesmen, that unity could only be preserved if Lloyd George ceased at once to be Prime Minister, shook him from his conviction.[25] Chamberlain looked to the forthcoming by-election at Newport, where an independent Conservative was standing against the Liberal candidate, for the proof of his thesis. If, as he confidently expected, the seat was lost to Labour, his case would be greatly strengthened.[26]

Chamberlain reiterated these arguments at a meeting of senior Conservatives on 10 October, where it was again agreed that the government should continue as a coalition under Lloyd George and call an election as soon as possible. The only minister who took a definite line against the Coalition as such was Baldwin,[27] but others including Curzon

objected to the transparent attempt to pre-empt any decision which the
National Union Conference might reach in November by holding an
election beforehand. Griffith-Boscawen thought it a 'typical F. E. Smith-
Winston trick', and one to which, unfortunately, Chamberlain had
assented.[28] On the following day both Younger and Wilson declared that
they would publicly repudiate Chamberlain's leadership if the Cabinet
persisted in its decision and gave the party no chance to express its views.
Wilson argued that the party would be broken into fragments and 'it will
take many a long year before the fragments can be united again.'[29] Such
an attitude, claimed Chamberlain, placed him in an 'absolutely
impossible' position. If his opinion and that of his senior Conservative
colleagues carried so little weight, 'my usefulness is gone and I cannot
continue to occupy the nominal position of leader.' In such a situation the
party would have to look for its leaders elsewhere than among its present
representatives in the Cabinet.[30] Speaking in Birmingham on 13 October
Chamberlain reiterated his theme that the Coalition should be maintained
in the face of the 'common foe.' If those who sought to preserve the
existing social order were divided, only the Labour party would gain.[31]

Chamberlain was apparently becoming intoxicated with the illusion of
his own indispensability. Rather like Asquith in 1916 he seemed out of
touch with mainstream thought in his own party and to be seriously over-
rating his own strength. No one seemed able to divert him from the course
upon which he was now set. Derby argued that an election now might
prove disastrous. 'There would be a break away of the Party which I think
even you can hardly realise.'[32] But still Chamberlain held his ground. He
now informed Birkenhead that he proposed to seize the initiative by
calling a meeting of all Conservative M.P.s 'to tell them bluntly that they
must either follow our advice or do without us.' In the latter case,

they must find their own Chief and form a Government *at once*. They would be in
a d—d fix![33]

In fact many senior Conservatives were already preparing for just such an
eventuality. Long and Salisbury were agreed that Lloyd George would
have to resign, but that Chamberlain would not be a suitable successor.
The choice would lie between Balfour, Curzon and Bonar Law, of whom
the last was the best. Salisbury was willing to serve under any of these,
providing Chamberlain and Birkenhead were not included in the
government.[34]

Liberal and Conservative members of the Cabinet dined at Churchill's
home on 15 October and agreed that Chamberlain would put the
Coalition case to the meeting of Conservative M.P.s four days later. A
further meeting between the junior ministers and Chamberlain and his

colleagues took place on 16 October. The meeting listened to a statement from Chamberlain to the effect that support for the Coalition was indispensable. Chamberlain was 'needlessly stiff and uncompromising' both in his opening remarks and in his replies.[35] Amery intervened frequently and was conscious that he had upset Chamberlain.[36] Nonetheless some of those present felt that if only Chamberlain could unbend a little and become more coaxing in manner the rift might yet be healed. Accordingly, Pollock, Edward Wood and Jock Gilmour called on Chamberlain again, but still found the party leader unbending. As Pollock noted:

he seemed to feel that it was not consonant with his position to seek to induce the recalcitrant group to join him. Rather it was for them to offer loyal obedience.[37]

Amery, too, sought a private interview and found him 'as usual altogether on the question of personal obligation and loyalty.'[38] Amery's object was to find a compromise which would establish the Conservative party's claim to independence while preserving Chamberlain's position as leader. By 18 October he believed that he had succeeded. Wilson informed him that Chamberlain was ready to accept a further party meeting after the election by which time the pressure for a Conservative Prime Minister might be irresistible.[39]

The Conservative junior ministers were not the only group to flex their muscles at this point. Following a meeting of over seventy back-bench M.P.s, a three-man delegation consisting of Samuel Hoare, Ernest Pretyman and George Lane-Fox called to see Chamberlain on 18 October. The latter was visibly shaken by some of the names he found on the list of those who had attended the back-benchers' meeting. He regarded the deputation as a direct personal attack and made it clear that he would fight back at the Carlton Club. Hoare recorded his impressions:

I told him the position in as friendly a way as possible, gave him ample opportunity to agree to all that was really demanded, namely that the Conservative Party should fight the election as a party and on no account should it be fused into some new organisation of the centre. I further told him that the meeting from which we had come seemed very representative of the party in the House of Commons and I hinted that unless he could meet us I felt sure that there would be very strong opposition to the Government at the Carlton Club meeting next morning.

Chamberlain, however, remained 'completely wooden', and made no attempt to discuss the position or suggest a compromise. He ended by implying that he knew more about the party than the three M.P.s did and that the great majority of Members were with him. Pretyman and Lane-Fox, both senior and respected figures – Pretyman had even proposed Chamberlain for the leadership the previous year – felt that they had been very roughly treated. 'We therefore left him in as polite and friendly an atmosphere as we could maintain.'[40]

If Chamberlain really believed that his line would be endorsed by the Carlton Club meeting, it was the gravest miscalculation of his career. Perhaps sensing that the task of reconciling his loyalty towards Lloyd George, his determination to maintain the Coalition, his concern for his own dignity and his desire to hold the party together was creating an impossible situation, he was ready to stake everything on a massive gamble. Finesse was never his strong point and he was not going to try it now. He presumably thought that he could drive his critics into a corner and demand their obedience. The meeting had been carefully timed so that the result of the Newport by-election would be available to support Chamberlain's case if, as he confidently hoped and expected, the Labour candidate was victorious. He had given his opponents little time in which to organise their forces, and the meeting was confined to Conservative M.P.s who, it was believed, were more in sympathy with the Coalition than were peers and parliamentary candidates.[41] There is also some evidence that Chamberlain calculated on several known diehards being out of the country and unable to attend the meeting.[42] But at the same time he did little to ensure the support of those whom he expected to back him. Moreover, even if he had secured a victory at the Carlton Club, there remained no guarantee that the Coalition's long-term future was secure. With over a million and a half unemployed and with a host of unresolved foreign policy problems, its survival would have remained precarious. The summoning of the meeting was thus above all a gesture of defiance on Chamberlain's part.

The Carlton Club meeting has secured for itself a place in historical mythology. Yet, as Chamberlain later conceded, 'it is of course nonsense to describe it as a Belgravia intrigue or a revolt in the kitchen.'[43] Few of those attending were out for Chamberlain's blood. 'Everyone was very restrained and very sad at having to ventilate our differences with our leader.'[44] The meeting began on a note of farce. Beaverbrook records that one M.P. arranged for glasses of brandy to be placed in front of Chamberlain and Birkenhead. 'Chamberlain eyed the liquid through his hastily-adjusted monocle, gave a start and with a gesture he hid the tumbler behind a chair.' Birkenhead displayed no such restraint.[45] It was Chamberlain who opened the meeting. His thirty minute speech, 'domineering in tone, but weak in substance', was an unbending restatement of his oft-repeated argument that it was imperative to maintain the Coalition in order to fend off the challenge of Socialism. He cited a recent speech by Arthur Henderson, outlining Labour's policies for a capital levy, nationalisation of the great industries and the right to work or of maintenance for every citizen. These, argued Chamberlain, were irresponsible objectives at a time when the economy was still struggling in the aftermath of a great war. The speech was ill-judged and received without enthusiasm. It was, thought one M.P., a 'lecture'. To another it appeared 'dictatorial in tone.'[46] It sounded 'like the last of a series of tedious encores to a song of which they had long sickened.'[47] Leo Amery soon realised that Chamberlain had gone back on the compromise which he thought he had secured. He later learnt that Birkenhead and Balfour had talked Chamberlain out of it.[48]

Chamberlain's speech seemed to imply that the only man who could really lead the country was the man whom practically the whole of the Conservative party now regarded as an evil genius, David Lloyd George. His statement that there were no significant differences of policy to divide the two wings of the Coalition evoked cries of dissent. He seemed in general most concerned not to alienate the Coalition Liberals, without realising that in doing so he was alienating Conservatives. He left it unclear whether the Coalition would be restructured after the election, but his praise of Lloyd George as the man who had led the government through all its trials and tribulations gave no expectation to Conservative M.P.s that they could look forward to serving under a Prime Minister of their own party. Nor did he explain how far the Conservatives' obligations to the Coalition Liberals would extend or whether the parties would fuse in the next parliament. But what Chamberlain had expected to be his trump card turned out to be the joker. Before he spoke it was already known that the independent Conservative candidate had won the Newport by-election. At a stroke Chamberlain's theory that the Coalition must be preserved, because the Conservatives standing alone would enable Labour to profit from a split vote, fell to the ground.

A speech by Balfour in support of Chamberlain failed to capture the mood of the meeting. By contrast Baldwin aptly summed up Conservative misgivings about the Prime Minister, whom he described as 'a dynamic force . . . a very terrible thing.' But the crucial intervention was that of Bonar Law.[49] As Law took his place at the meeting, Pollock noticed Chamberlain's reaction. 'His face blanched with surprise and anticipation of what it meant, and well it might.'[50] Law had given Chamberlain no hint of his intention to attend the meeting, but his conscious decision to do so must have been taken in the knowledge that it might be fatal to Chamberlain's leadership. As Pollock recorded:

I have never been able to understand or indeed to excuse this silence [over Law's intentions]. Bonar Law thereby placed Austen in a compromising and ambiguous position.[51]

In fact, with his speech Law emerged as the alternative party leader whom many M.P.s had been looking for. He later argued that the only other course of action open to him was to retire altogether from public life. It was not an explanation with which all could agree. Churchill was particularly vehement in his scorn:

He made a speech deliberately calculated to destroy Mr Chamberlain and deliberately intended to intimate his readiness to take his place. It is not easy to regard this as a transaction free from personal ambition. It seems rather to be a transaction directly inspired by personal ambition and by personal ambition not hampered by chivalry and only partially hampered by scruple.[52]

Leslie Wilson also spoke against his leader, a conversion which Birkenhead later described as 'swifter than any known in secular or sacred history since Saul of Tarsus changed his name.'[53]

Even so Chamberlain seemed bent on his own destruction. His manner was that of an extremist and its effect was to cast his opponents into the mould of moderates.[54] One M.P. proposed adjourning the meeting to give the leadership time to frame a compromise, but Chamberlain pressed for an immediate and decisive conclusion. To Derby Chamberlain later explained that his unbending attitude was largely determined by Law's presence at the meeting. He believed that if the former leader came to the Carlton Club it would be to oppose him.[55] Ernest Pretyman put forward a motion for independent Conservative action. Though this was a moderate request and did not rule out the possibility of cooperation with the Liberals in the immediate future, Chamberlain insisted on treating it as a personal vote of censure. Samuel Hoare believed this was sufficient to turn against him a number of M.P.s who had come to the meeting undecided.[56] Many others, noted Tom Jones, voted for the resolution without knowing what it involved in Chamberlain's mind.[57] Yet Chamberlain had no alternative resolution or amendment ready. Altogether it was an unimpressive performance by him and one that highlighted his deficiencies as party leader. He failed to assess the strength of feeling among some Cabinet ministers, including Baldwin; he underestimated the will of the junior ministers; and he miscalculated the mood of the mass of back-bench M.P.s, the majority of whom had no connection with the diehard movement.[58] Jones thought his whole handling of the meeting 'clumsy, unsympathetic and inept.'[59] On the day after the meeting George Younger noted:

I have never been so disappointed with anyone in politics as I have been with Austen. He is as obstinate as a mule and seems to have no outlook at all, and I should certainly never again trust him with any responsible political position.... He thoroughly deserves the defeat he has sustained.[60]

It was as if Chamberlain were trying to cast himself into the role of tragic hero without the substance and capacity which such a role would have demanded. Chamberlain had forced the M.P.s into a position where they had to choose between loyalty to the leadership and, as they saw it, loyalty to the party, and they chose the latter.

Pretyman's motion was passed by a majority of nearly one hundred and the Coalition was at an end. The size of the majority showed that the revolt extended far beyond the ranks of the diehards and that Chamberlain had succeeded in alienating nearly all the Conservative back benchers who had no specific reason for supporting the Coalition. Meanwhile Lloyd George was seated in the Cabinet room awaiting the outcome of the meeting. A telephone message arrived to the effect that the vote had gone against the government. Almost immediately Chamberlain burst into the room and, more agitated than Frances Stevenson had ever seen him, exclaimed, 'Well, we must resign. We are beaten.'[61] Chamberlain inevitably felt bitter at what he regarded as a breach of loyalty. For Leslie Wilson he felt particular scorn, since the latter had seemed to accept Chamberlain's proposed line of action at the Churchill dinner:

It is, I suppose, the first occasion on which the Chief Whip has thought it necessary ... that he should work and speak against his Leader at such a gathering. I hope you will find yourself in sufficient agreement with Bonar Law to make it unnecessary for you to repeat so unfortunate a precedent.[62]

Following the resignation of the government the King invited Law, now elected Conservative leader in Chamberlain's stead, to form a new administration. It was the first purely Conservative government for nearly seventeen years. Law at once called an election. As leader of a one-party government he did not have the problem over its timing and implications which had beset the Coalition for the past year.

* * *

Chamberlain's loss of office after four and a half years in government gave him time to reflect upon what had happened to him and upon his prospects for the future. He recognised that, although events had moved with great rapidity in the last days before the Carlton Club meeting, the storm had been rumbling for a long time. No government could have remained in office through the traumatic years since the end of the War and not accumulate upon its shoulders a mass of discontent and disappointment. When the government happened also to be a coalition which could not command the unquestioning support which a party often gives to an adminstration formed exclusively from its own ranks, then its problems were likely to be intensified. 'What did you was the Coalition!!' commented the veteran Henry Chaplin with concise and simple accuracy.[63] About his own past actions Chamberlain had few regrets. He could not, he argued, have done anything to remove Lloyd George from the premiership, bearing in mind the latter's contribution to the success of the Coalition in its early years and the fact that there were no major policy disagreements between the leading figures in the Cabinet. As regards the future he could not see how he would be able to join Bonar Law's government. Despite rumours that Law wanted him back as Lord Privy Seal, he was insistent that he would decline any such offer,

because . . . to enter the Govt. now would mean for me a loss of self-respect and public credit, secondly because I could not be comfortable with him after the way he has behaved to me and thirdly . . . because 'Love me, love my dog!' I won't go back without my friends.[64]

Indeed Chamberlain felt considerable personal resentment at the way in which Law had behaved:

And I must add that I think Bonar Law behaved badly to a man who, after all, had made him leader, had been very loyal to him throughout his leadership and had succeeded only when Bonar's health broke up, and when, as Bonar himself said, difficulties were thickening around the Coalition.[65]

Though there was always the possibility that Law's health would break down again and the leadership become vacant, Chamberlain was far from sure that he could take over once more unless the party was 'in a wholly different temper from that which dictated the Carlton Club decision.'[66]

Chamberlain doubted Law's capacity to succeed in his new position. The latter had never before 'gone into action without a stronger man beside him'.[67] He probably hoped that Law would fail to secure an absolute majority at the election. The new Prime Minister's success in doing so did nothing, however, to reconcile Chamberlain to him. Nor did it alter his fundamental understanding of the political situation:

Unless I am mistaken in my forecast three or four years hence this Government will be sinking under a load of unpopularity and Labour will be more formidable than ever. Whether it will then be possible to re-knit the conservative forces of the country in the broadest sense of that term into a united and co-operating whole, I do not know. But unless it be possible I expect that Labour will then secure its triumph.[68]

The election result was not as clear-cut as it first seemed. Though Bonar Law had secured a massive parliamentary majority, this was largely the distorted creation of the voting system. What was striking was that Labour had 'polled over four million on a bad programme, against a new

Government, a united press and a general reaction towards Conservatism. Ca donne à penser.'[69] Chamberlain absolutely rejected the view that the two non-socialist parties would forever alternate gracefully in their claims to government. The present Conservative majority gave no guarantee that the four million and more Socialist voters would be beaten at the next election unless special efforts were made to bring Liberals and Conservatives together.[70] In the circumstances, though the future held many imponderables, Chamberlain had no doubt of the course which he and those who agreed with him should pursue:

The object of myself and my friends now is, without creating an opposition to Bonar Law and whilst maintaining our position as members of the Unionist Party, to keep in touch with Lloyd George, to encourage him in his determination to exercise a similar restraint and to keep the way open for the reunion which we believe will be necessary.[71]

Speaking to a Birmingham audience in March 1923 he renewed his message. Faced with an attack upon the whole social order it would be madness for the forces of conservatism to lay themselves and the country open through their divisions to the Socialistic and subversive doctrines of the Labour party.[72]

But Chamberlain's personality was not one which easily bounced back into the political fray after personal disappointment. The early weeks of the Law government saw him at a low ebb. He could see little future for himself in politics. The pressure in the constituencies for Liberal reunion was already making it difficult for him to maintain his links with Lloyd George. Some Liberals had long believed that Chamberlain simply meant to 'lassoo [them] as a little Liberal wing of the Tory party.'[73] Feeling against him inside the Conservative party remained strong, particularly among the diehards, while the men who had risen so rapidly within the party hierarchy were scarcely likely to give up their places to facilitate the return of ex-Coalitionists. Only an electoral disaster might heal the party breach and 'by the time that the disaster comes I shall be too old to care to take up the burden of leadership again.'[74] He felt betrayed and disillusioned and wished, he said, that he could give up the House of Commons altogether.[75] The fact that he was now separated, at least in political terms, from his brother caused him the sort of anguish that minor differences with his father had occasioned in the past. When Law offered Neville the position of Postmaster General, the latter naturally consulted his brother. Austen implied that this might mean the end of personal relations between them, at which Neville decided that he could not possibly accept the post. Urged, however, by Amery that if he declined office at his age the opportunity was not likely to occur again, Neville went back to his brother and tried to argue that his membership of the government would be seen as a link between Law and Chamberlain, perhaps facilitating the latter's acceptance as leader in the event of Law's health giving way. Chamberlain remained unmoved and only when Neville said that he would decline the position and at the same time terminate his political career did Chamberlain relent. Even so, Neville's decision 'hurt awfully.'[76]

The new government's comparative success in its first parliamentary session only added to Chamberlain's bitterness. So too did a series of diehard promotions, including that of Reginald Hall as Chief Agent, a particularly 'serious offence.'[77] Chamberlain would not respond to any gestures of reconciliation from the government and declined the chairmanship of a Royal Commission on the Indian Civil Service.[78] Curzon, who had stayed on as Foreign Secretary under Law, had the idea that Chamberlain might go as British representative to the League Council in Geneva, but Law doubted whether he would accept and the offer was not made.[79] By April 1923 Chamberlain had reached the conclusion that the government was not so much 'second rate' as 'fourth rate', but he preferred to snipe from the sidelines rather than work actively against it. While Birkenhead intrigued with Rothermere, confident that the government would 'presently founder under the weight of their own conceit and incompetence', Chamberlain preferred to stay away from parliament rather than become a focal point for discontent in the House of Commons.[80] Ex-ministers from the Coalition should 'go away and play' and let the new government 'stew in its own juice.'[81]

As regards Chamberlain's political future, therefore, there was nothing to do but wait and see.[82] The imponderable factor in the situation remained Bonar Law's health. On the day following the Carlton Club meeting Chamberlain had written with uncanny accuracy to his long-time colleague, Walter Long:

... at heart I feel sorry for Bonar, for I think he has undertaken a task which will be his death warrant.[83]

By the spring of 1923 it was clear that the Prime Minister was indeed a sick man. At the end of April he was sent on a sea voyage by his doctor to recover his strength. Tests, however, revealed that he was suffering from an inoperable cancer of the throat. Law had clearly been concerned at the lack of ministerial experience at his disposal when forming his government. Critics had rapidly dubbed his administration the Cabinet of the 'second eleven' and Law had told Sir Archibald Salvidge on the eve of the Carlton Club meeting that he would have to have Chamberlain and Birkenhead back as soon as possible.[84] In the middle of April

Chamberlain was approached by Rothermere, acting for Beaverbrook, ostensibly on the Prime Minister's behalf, with the offer of the post of Lord Privy Seal, on the clear understanding that Law would resign through ill-health in the late summer and recommend Chamberlain as his successor with a free hand to reconstruct the government. Horne was also to be offered immediate office. If this was indeed a genuine initiative on the Prime Minister's part it represents another moment at which Chamberlain came tantalisingly close to the premiership. Law's condition was much worse than anyone realised and long before the autumn he resigned and in October he died. In such a situation Chamberlain might have become Prime Minister, with his brother Neville his likely ultimate successor, while Stanley Baldwin faded into relative obscurity.

Yet there are reasons to doubt whether Beaverbrook was really acting with the Prime Minister's authority. When Law did resign in May his preference for the succession seems to have been Baldwin. Chamberlain, he argued, could make a good speech but lacked first-rate political ability.[85] Neville Chamberlain certainly doubted the authenticity of the offer. The idea that Law would send such a message through a third or fourth party seemed 'so grotesque as to be incredible.' It is doubtful, indeed, whether Law could have pledged the party to accept Chamberlain on the latter's terms – which would presumably have involved the return of Birkenhead. Neville surmised that the initiative must have emanated from Beaverbrook's own brain and it seems probable that the newspaper magnate was trying to please his sick friend by securing a reunification of the party, although on terms which Law himself might have resented.[86] At all events Chamberlain showed no interest in Beaverbrook's offer. His response was entirely in character. If Law had anything to say to him he would have to say it himself. Chamberlain would not take messages from him through third parties. In any case he would have nothing to do with a plan so certain to discredit everyone concerned with it.[87] When Neville suggested that a meeting between Chamberlain and Law might help clear the air, the former showed that he had not forgiven the premier for his behaviour the previous October:

His ideas and mine on the obligations of friendship and colleagueship differ. . . . He can't undo what he has done and would do it over again if it were still to do. All he could say is that he was sorry that I should 'feel like that about it.'[88]

As a result, when Law did resign a few weeks later, Chamberlain was still outside the government and had little chance of being considered for the succession.

The suddenness of Bonar Law's removal from the political scene caught Chamberlain by surprise. On his return from his cruise on 11 May the Prime Minister was very weak and hardly able to speak. When the news of his resignation was announced, Chamberlain was on holiday with his wife in the Pyrenees. In London, however, the Chamberlainite faction gathered for urgent consultations.[89] At a succession of meetings Horne, Locker-Lampson, Worthington-Evans and Birkenhead discussed their likely course of action in a series of eventualities. The possibility of Derby, Curzon or Baldwin succeeding to the premiership was examined. If the King's choice fell upon Curzon, then it was agreed that Chamberlain should join the government and become Leader of the House of Commons. Steps were taken to alert Curzon to this possibility. In such a situation it might not be politic for Birkenhead to come in immediately, but the ground could be prepared for his future rehabilitation. If, however, it was Baldwin who was sent for, it was not expected that Chamberlain would feel able to serve. In the event Baldwin was asked to form a government on 22 May and almost immediately the Chamberlainite ranks began to waver. Worthington-Evans wrote to their leader about the dilemma they now felt:

It is now or never. I don't want to see the Baldwin Government fail, if it fails the Tory Party fails . . . I cannot see, if we want to support the Government, why we should refuse to join if asked to do so . . . I suppose you can't serve under Baldwin. I wish you could.[90]

Despite the crisis in London, Chamberlain was in no hurry to return from abroad. He did, however, move to Paris where he was able to consult with Birkenhead. Supremely conscious of his own dignity, he did not wish to appear either as 'an eager solicitor for office or as a self-satisfied fool who thought himself indispensable and believed that everyone would throw themselves at his feet.' He was conscious also of his continuing unpopularity with the diehards, even if the party leaders might wish to have him back 'humbled and subservient' to make use of his debating skills. While freeing his colleagues from any constraints about accepting office themselves, Chamberlain was therefore at pains to stress that no one should make any suggestion that he sought or might be prepared to accept a position under Baldwin.[91]

Speculation, however, was rife that Chamberlain's name might be among those included in the new government. From the Cabinet Office Tom Jones heard that great efforts would be made to appoint Chamberlain to the Foreign Office if Curzon, as seemed probable in view of his mortification at being passed over for the premiership, refused to stay on.[92] Baldwin told Horne that he was ready to offer Chamberlain the Colonial Office in the hope that filial sentiment might influence him to accept, but he warned Neville Chamberlain that he would not press for

Austen's inclusion if it meant the resignation of some of those who had 'stuck by the ship in difficult times.'[93] In the event opposition to Chamberlain's inclusion was too powerful for Baldwin to resist. Amery, Salisbury and others let it be known that they would not serve alongside him. To the King's secretary Salisbury wrote that Chamberlain was

identified in the public mind, not unreasonably, with the abandonment of principle and the disintegration of Conservatism which was the reason or one of the main reasons for the fall of the late Government.[94]

In addition, a deputation headed by Sir Frederick Banbury called upon the new Prime Minister to insist that Conservative opinion was strongly against Chamberlain joining the government. Neville, surprised at the degree of opposition to his brother's return, tried to rationalise the situation:

Austen has kept aloof and on the few occasions when he has intervened there has been a somewhat acid note about his remarks. Moreover he is believed to have been very closely associated with Birkenhead who is positively hated and despised.[95]

When, therefore, Chamberlain returned to London on 25 May, most of the important government offices had already been filled and it was clear that he was still excluded from them. Meeting with his colleagues on the following day, he emphasised that no communication of any kind had been made to him by Baldwin. He had hoped that the Prime Minister, if genuinely anxious for party reunion, might ask to speak to him as head of his group, but he felt that he had been treated with discourtesy and that he was evidently still 'a proscribed man.' Chamberlain heard that he was now likely to be offered the Washington embassy which he regarded as an insult.[96] The Chamberlainites agreed that they should make a public statement before the party meeting at which Baldwin would be elected leader and it was decided that this should take the form of a letter from Chamberlain to the chairman of his constituency association in West Birmingham.[97] In this letter Chamberlain argued that although he had been anxious to assist the reunification of the party he had not been invited to help.

In the meantime, however, Baldwin had asked Chamberlain to visit him at Chequers. For Chamberlain the invitation came a week too late. The interview, which lasted an hour and a half, got off to a bad start from which it never fully recovered. Though there was no loss of temper on either side, it was a good illustration of the difficulty Baldwin had in handling Chamberlain throughout their long political association. Chamberlain always expected to be treated by Baldwin with a degree of courtesy and consideration which reflected his status as an ex-party

leader, a status which differentiated him from other leading
Conservatives. At the same time he failed to see how the events of October
1922 had irreversibly changed the balance of forces within the party.
While over-sensitive about his own position, Chamberlain showed little
understanding of the difficulties confronting Baldwin in the construction
of his first ministry.

   Granted that Chamberlain had deliberately remained aloof throughout
Bonar Law's premiership, making no gesture of reconciliation, Baldwin
had behaved impeccably. He would not approach Chamberlain about
taking office until he was sure that such a step would be acceptable to the
party as a whole. As it was not acceptable, no communication had been
made. Now he hesitantly asked Chamberlain to consider the possibility of
taking office in a few months' time in the event of the situation changing.
He also suggested that Chamberlain might like to consider a job outside
politics. The Washington embassy would soon become vacant and was
Chamberlain's for the asking. Chamberlain, though, was almost
determined to take offence. As regards the contingent possibility of future
government office, he was 'not prepared to be treated as a boy on
probation who was told that if he behaved well he might get a remove next
term or to have a bundle of carrots dangled before my nose to induce me
to gallop.' He further told Baldwin that at earlier stages in his career he
had already turned down not only the Washington embassy but also that
in Paris and the Indian Viceroyalty. The offer now being made was even
less acceptable:

You would have the appearance of trying to buy off possible opposition and I of
accepting a fat salary as compensation for the discourtesy shown to me.

When Baldwin made the very reasonable comment that, as he was
younger than Chamberlain and therefore likely to block the latter's
possible return to the leadership, he had thought that a non-political
position might be attractive to him, Chamberlain only managed with
difficulty to control his temper. He announced that he would stay in
parliament and, as under Bonar Law, take his place as an independent
member of the party. He used the free hand he had given to
Worthington-Evans to accept office under Baldwin as evidence that he
had not been trying to insist that all the Coalitionists must be taken back
en bloc. Yet he could not conceal that he felt hurt by Baldwin's failure to
consult him earlier. 'Why, my dear Stanley,' he kept repeating, 'why didn't
you send for me?'

The Prime Minister twice repeated slowly and, as I thought, sadly, 'I am very
sorry. I never thought of it.'[98]

Chamberlain's pride had been badly damaged. In public he tried to put a brave face on the affair. He and his wife made a point of being seen everywhere in society and of looking happy, well and even gay.[99] But he pointedly absented himself from the meeting at which Baldwin was elected leader and his hurt feelings were only just beneath the surface. Reporting his interview with Baldwin to his brother a week later, he became 'very emotional, shouting loudly and banging the table with the greatest violence ... evidently writhing under the humiliation he had undergone.'[100] The offer of the Washington embassy still rankled: 'I will accept nothing from men of my own Party who do not think me fit to sit at Council with them.'[101] Neville tried to offer comfort but was clearly becoming irritated by Chamberlain's determination to stand on his dignity:

I am convinced that Baldwin never intended to show you discourtesy. He may have blundered ... but I am sure he did it unintentionally ... he is evidently made of a coarser clay than you and doesn't enter into your feelings as you would have done with anyone else.

Chamberlain had even taken exception to the way in which Baldwin had finally asked to see him:

Surely you don't think he intended that it should be given to you like that. I have no doubt that he told his secretary that he wanted to see you and that he was to get in touch and fix up an appointment with you. The thing was mismanaged and perhaps Baldwin should have written a personal letter.[102]

When Neville had the opportunity to discuss the matter with Baldwin, he suggested that any future approach to his brother might be directed through himself to avoid further wounded feelings.[103]

The problem was, as Neville recognised, that Chamberlain did not really know what he did want.[104] One half of him dreaded the humiliation that office under Baldwin would entail. Politics, he said, had become 'hateful' to him and he thought it not unlikely that he would not stand for re-election to parliament.[105] But the other half clearly wished to be back in government. His dilemma was evident in a long letter sent to Birkenhead at the end of May. Chamberlain expected that within a few months Baldwin would invite him to join the Cabinet. In that situation he did not see how he would be able to refuse. Yet even so, 'it would be distasteful to me to enter the Cabinet, no matter how honourable the position which was offered to me or how conciliatory his method of making the offer.'[106] If Chamberlain was expecting comfort, he was disappointed. Birkenhead, while stressing that his friendship with Chamberlain had become the closest political association he had ever formed, argued that if Chamberlain joined the government he would find himself surrounded by men younger than and inferior to himself, many of them his avowed and bitter enemies. The mere fact of joining would be an admission that the decision of the Carlton Club meeting had been right and the Coalitionists wrong. The ex-Lord Chancellor placed his faith in the result of the next General Election when, if as he expected, the Conservatives suffered a reverse, the Chamberlainites would be left in a strong bargaining position.[107] Rothermere, he later assured Chamberlain, foresaw a future reconstruction of which Chamberlain would be the head.[108]

Yet no General Election seemed imminent and, whether or not Baldwin later offered Chamberlain a post in the present government, the fact was that the latter's position was far from strong. He had little with which to bargain. As Neville pointed out:

A's personality is not sufficiently dominating to force itself on people's attention and the fact is that he does not . . . stand for much with the H of C which hardly knows him nor with the country at large to whom he has never made a popular appeal. This is not in the least discreditable to him but it is a fact.[109]

In the circumstances Chamberlain's attitude towards the Baldwin government was bound to remain equivocal. He would, he said, be a back-bench supporter, permitting himself perhaps a somewhat greater independence than the ordinary run of party man.[110] He proved to be particularly critical of the government's foreign policy in relation to France and Turkey. Britain was in danger of becoming the 'scold of Europe', running about 'shaking our fists in peoples' faces, screaming that this must be altered or that must stop.'[111] Only, he claimed, his brother's position in the government and the fact that the two men were both members of parliament for Birmingham kept him from criticising the government more vigorously.[112] On occasions he seemed to go out of his way to alienate himself from the government. His scathing attack on McKenna, to whom Baldwin had offered the Exchequer, during the Report Stage of the Finance Bill on 3 July was, he admitted, calculated to show 'that he was not hankering for office.'[113] Neville regretted this speech since it played 'directly into the hands of his enemies':

though he doesn't recognise it, he has a lot of friends who earnestly desire to see the breach healed and it puzzles and pains them when he kicks over like that.[114]

Chamberlain seemed determined to repel the hand of friendship which those who sought a united party were prepared to offer: '*That's* why they are pained and puzzled and it's no use fighting against human psychology.'[115]

When Neville was elevated to the Exchequer in August, Chamberlain sent his congratulations but it was still easy to sense 'some bitterness in his soul'. He seemed to imply that he was deliberately sacrificing his own career in order not to interfere with his brother's. Yet it was extraordinarily difficult to see how he could come back into the government. The only possible position for him seemed to be the Foreign Office where Curzon remained firmly entrenched.[116] In fact Chamberlain insisted that only if the government were to take up with vigour the old question of Imperial Preference would he come back to the fold and separate himself from some of his present associates.[117]

Such an eventuality seemed improbable in the summer of 1923. The burnt fingers of a previous generation of Conservative leaders offered a sober warning. Baldwin moreover had a comfortable majority in the House of Commons and possibly another four years in office before a General Election had to be called. In addition Bonar Law had given a pledge that there would be no change in the fiscal system during the lifetime of the current parliament. But, faced with a worsening economic situation, Baldwin became convinced that some new departure was needed to tackle the mounting problem of unemployment. At the same time the policy of preference would further the cause of party unity – he had already told Amery that he still wanted to bring Chamberlain back into the Government[118] – differentiate Conservatism from Liberalism and thus end renewed talk of another coalition, and possibly pre-empt Lloyd George whose fertile brain was suspected of moving in the same direction.

When Neville advised his brother that a tariff initiative might be imminent, Chamberlain declared that he would be 'pledged by all my traditions to throw myself wholeheartedly into the fight and give them any support that I can.' But, haunted by his past disappointments, his response was permeated with doubt as to whether the idea was feasible and with fear as to the consequences of another failure.[119] By the time that the matter came before the Cabinet on 23 October, it was clear that it would not be 'the *whole* hog but . . . the major part of the animal.' In other words ministers were agreed that it would not be possible to carry food taxes for the time being since the danger of losing seats and wrecking the party was too strong.[120] This news caused Chamberlain to hesitate. His experiences of 1912–13 had convinced him that if the party was again allowed to renounce food taxes, he would not live to see full imperial preference:

This is Father's policy with all that part left out for which he cared most and which was his incentive to the vast exertions that he made. Oh dear! Your talk had excited me greatly. Your letter has depressed me.[121]

When Baldwin publicly announced the policy at Plymouth on 25 October, Chamberlain's doubts were confirmed. The Prime Minister's speech was vague and he seemed to be making a personal statement rather than declaring party policy. Speaking at the Birmingham Constitutional Club four days later, Chamberlain said he would support Baldwin if the Prime Minister was indeed proclaiming a great policy, but that at this stage he was unclear what his exact meaning was. Other government ministers seemed to be speaking with different voices. As a result,

The impression left on everyone's mind is one of doubt and perplexity.... You can't hunt hounds that way. Unless [Baldwin] takes control quickly all the hounds will be scattered after different foxes – unless indeed the bulk of them hunt a rabbit.[122]

Chamberlain clearly wanted the government to fight on the issue of old-style tariff reform, exactly as his father had preached it. It was not, thought Neville, a particularly helpful attitude. He believed that if only his brother would declare himself delighted with the steps taken so far, he would greatly strengthen his position. Imperial Preference on food was bound to follow its introduction for manufactured goods. 'We must', he stressed, 'be content to go one step at a time and demonstrate by actual experience that protection helps the working man.'[123] But Chamberlain continued to predict that indecision was bound to lead to disaster.

In view of the pledge given by Bonar Law, Baldwin's tariff initiative made an election inevitable. The need for the Conservatives to present a united front to the electorate raised again the question of Chamberlain's return to the government. Briefly there seemed to be a move afoot to remove Curzon from the Foreign Office in order to facilitate Chamberlain's return, but the latter made it clear that he would not be party to any intrigue to oust the Foreign Secretary.[124] Nonetheless on 10 November Chamberlain and Birkenhead met to consider their attitude in the event of being offered office either immediately or after the election. Chamberlain's initial inclination was to decline to assume direct personal responsibility for a policy on which they had not been consulted, but, after listening to Birkenhead, he agreed that if a suitable offer were made to them they would be compelled to join.[125]

Chamberlain and Birkenhead met the Prime Minister on 12 November and, after some preliminary sparring, Baldwin expressed the hope that, if they could all fight the election together, it would be possible for the two ex-ministers to rejoin the Cabinet afterwards. To Chamberlain this smacked too strongly of the sort of contingent offer, dependent as he saw it on good behaviour, which he had unhesitatingly and indignantly rejected the previous May. He insisted therefore that if they were to join at all they must do so immediately. They were ready, however, to take posts without portfolio or salary in order not to force displacements from

Baldwin's present Cabinet. After the election, however, Chamberlain stressed that they would insist upon offices commensurate with those they had previously held. For Chamberlain this would mean something like the Privy Seal, but for Birkenhead nothing less than the Lord Chancellorship would be adequate. In addition, posts would have to be found for Gilmour, Scott, Crawford and Locker-Lampson. These were tough conditions and Baldwin made no commitments.[126] But at a second meeting on the same day Baldwin, after securing the King's consent to a General Election, seemed to have been convinced. He introduced the two men to Lord Derby as 'colleagues' and Derby was led to believe that they would both be present at the meeting of the Cabinet on the following day. Chamberlain himself firmly expected to join the Cabinet providing Baldwin accepted a suggestion of preference on wheat and meat based on a subsidy to freight.[127] Baldwin's motive, however, may have been to head off Derby's resignation from the government, with the important electoral implications this would have in Lancashire. Derby, who favoured postponing the election, had already told the Prime Minister that he 'could not hope to keep Lancashire solid' unless Birkenhead and he were on the same platform.[128]

Baldwin's true intentions are far from clear at this point. Whether he sincerely desired to see Chamberlain and Birkenhead rejoin the Cabinet or whether he was simply manipulating both them and Derby for his electoral purposes remains open to conjecture. Yet when the Cabinet met on 13 November Derby was surprised to find that Chamberlain and Birkenhead were not present and Baldwin made no mention to the rest of the Cabinet of having asked them to join the government. Derby was perplexed:

I said something to Mr. Baldwin afterwards, 'why were they not there' and his answer was that there were some difficulties. I never went further into the question as I went straight away from the Cabinet to Lancashire ... but my impression is that their absence from the Cabinet meeting was due to the influence of Lord Salisbury and one or two others.[129]

In fact several ministers had raised serious objections. Amery argued that the election was going to be a 'soldier's battle' and that the impression Baldwin created upon the country might be 'blurred' by the inclusion of Birkenhead. Cecil too argued that Birkenhead's return would 'ruin' the government.[130] The party managers insisted that feeling against Birkenhead in the country was so strong that it would be hopeless to try to rehabilitate him.[131] It seems, therefore, that while most of the party would have been prepared to swallow Chamberlain's return, that of Birkenhead was a different matter, but 'as he and Austen stood together, the result has applied to them both.'[132] Neville Chamberlain summed up the resentment felt towards the former Lord Chancellor:

It is his reputation as a drunkard and loose liver, on which his rectorial address has set the climax, that has roused intense feelings of abhorrence and contempt and which has made it impossible to take him in now without splitting the party again.[133]

When in May Baldwin had avoided approaching Chamberlain until he had determined whether or not the latter's return would be acceptable to his colleagues, the Prime Minister had caused Chamberlain great offence. Now he had reversed the procedure, but had still failed to secure acceptance of the other's inclusion in the Cabinet. Baldwin seemed not to know what to do and it was Chamberlain who broke the silence:

The time which has elapsed . . . clearly indicates that the proposal to include us in the Government has met with unexpected difficulties. . . . We are now obliged to infer that . . . our inclusion is unwelcome to some of those on whose support you are obliged to rely. As far therefore as we are concerned, the matter is at an end and our assistance must be confined to the platform support which . . . we should give. . . .[134]

Baldwin replied rather lamely, giving no hint of the opposition which the possible inclusion of Birkenhead had aroused. To have made 'supernumerary appointments' to the Cabinet on the eve of the election would, he said, have been open to obvious objections and extremely difficult to justify.[135] He also made it appear that the approach had come from Chamberlain and Birkenhead rather than himself, a gloss upon the episode which Chamberlain rightly regarded as unfair.[136] The latter was left to conclude that the Prime Minister was 'a thoroughly "rattled" man.'[137]

Not surprisingly Chamberlain reacted badly to this latest rebuff. He had a 'good deal to forgive or at least forget before I can regard Baldwin with any cordiality.'[138] Neville found him 'froissé and stiff' and the whole episode did nothing to help relations between the two brothers:

Do you wonder that I am sore? He has wounded me in every spot but most of all in making you an unconscious party to the proscription of your brother.[139]

In the circumstances Chamberlain found it difficult to throw himself with enthusiasm into the election campaign, even though he had promised to give independent support on the platform. His speeches were 'not very helpful' and he took the opportunity to expose the shortcomings of Baldwin's tariff programme. 'With no tax on corn, it was a policy of currants and tinned salmon.' Bridgeman, who perhaps did not know the details of the recent negotiations, concluded that Chamberlain was 'quite unable to resume his old generous personality.'[140] In the event Chamberlain's worst fears were confirmed. The Conservatives lost badly in terms of seats. Though they were still the largest party in the Commons with 258 M.P.s, they were in a minority against the combined Liberal and Labour parties. Looked at as a verdict on Baldwin's tariff policy the result was a disaster. Just before the election Balfour had summed up the situation with characteristic wit:

Obviously Baldwin is an idiot – the only question is whether he is an inspired idiot![141]

The electorate's verdict did not indicate much inspiration.

* * *

The Conservatives' defeat in the General Election of 1923 raised two immediate problems for the party. One was the position of Stanley Baldwin as party leader. Only the electorate's overwhelming endorsement could have justified his decision to go to the country at a time when he already had a perfectly adequate parliamentary majority. Yet, however else the electorate's verdict might be interpreted, it was certainly a clear rejection of Baldwin's tariff initiative. The second problem concerned the action which the government, which still had more seats in the House of Commons than either of the other parties, should now take. Its options were to resign immediately, to face the new parliament and invite defeat in the House of Commons, or to attempt to forge some new association with the Liberal party to prevent the impending disaster of a Labour administration. Baldwin's position seemed for a while to be in danger and there were rumours of a plot concerted by ex-Coalitionists to replace him. The chief conspirators, thought Bridgeman, were Rothermere and Beaverbrook, who had done their best during the election campaign to discredit the Prime Minister. Chamberlain, Birkenhead, Derby, Worthington-Evans and Balfour were 'said to be assisting.'[142] One idea was that Balfour should use his authority as elder statesman to urge the King to send not for MacDonald or Asquith but for another Conservative, Derby or Chamberlain. The latter confirmed that under no circumstances would Asquith join forces with Baldwin, but that he might give benevolent support to himself and Balfour to prevent MacDonald from forming a government.[143]

Confusion, in fact, was the order of the day. To the extent that a plot did exist (and Chamberlain's primary concern seems to have been to block MacDonald rather than to supersede Baldwin), the participants could not agree on a suitable replacement for Baldwin. At the same time they greatly underestimated the degree of support which the Prime Minister still had in the parliamentary party, much of it a spontaneous reaction to the press campaign against him. Birkenhead heard that Baldwin intended to resign and that the King would take advice from Balfour, who would recommend that the monarch should send for Chamberlain. But Birkenhead's information bore little relation to reality.[144] Balfour had no doubt that in terms of political experience and debating power Chamberlain was 'incomparably . . . superior' to Baldwin. But he was not convinced that the party wanted a change at this moment. It had already been damaged by the folly of the recent election and was still torn by personal divisions. Anything in the nature of an intrigue against Baldwin could only exacerbate matters still further.[145] On the other hand Derby and Samuel Hoare were agreed that Robert Horne was the only possible alternative to Baldwin. Chamberlain 'was quite impossible.'[146] The party would not 'kill Baldwin to make Austen king.'[147] Neville Chamberlain learnt with some surprise that the feeling in the party against his brother was still very strong, largely because of the way in which he continued to make favourable references to Lloyd George in his parliamentary speeches.[148] One back-bencher complained of Chamberlain's 'perverted sense of loyalty to the two men in British public life – Lloyd George and Birkenhead – whom I dislike and distrust most.'[149] In the circumstances, talk of a change in the party leadership came to nothing.

As regards the line which Baldwin should now adopt there was more scope for discussion. Chamberlain argued that the King should be advised to send for MacDonald and Asquith together or in turn, and ask whether either could form a combination that promised a stable majority. But in view of the attitude Chamberlain had consistently maintained on the Labour party since the end of the War, it was not surprising that he believed that irreparable harm would be done if MacDonald was allowed to form a Labour government.[150] He clearly hoped that an anti-Labour coalition was still possible, probably with Asquith at its head. Inevitably, therefore, he blamed Baldwin for failing to approach Asquith as soon as the election result was known and thereby allowing the initiative to pass from his hands.[151] Speaking in Birmingham on 7 December, Chamberlain argued that it was 'in harmony with the tradition of the great Constitutional Party that we should offer no vexatious opposition to any moderate government which [could] be formed . . . to resist fundamental changes . . . ruinous to the industrial, social and economic constitution of the country.'[152] Yet others such as Amery regarded the possibility of Conservative support for a Liberal government as dangerous in the extreme. It would mean 'the final break-up of our Party.' Chamberlain's call for 'a moderate government' was the cry of a 'born idiot', 'a damn faint-hearted ass if ever there was one.' Amery's object rather was to convince Baldwin that the Conservatives' immediate task was the destruction of the Liberal party and the absorption of as much of its carcass as possible.[153]

In the end Asquith's conviction that Labour, as the larger of the two free trade parties, should be given its chance to form a government, together with MacDonald's readiness to accept this responsibility, proved decisive. A minority Labour government took office on 22 January 1924. For Chamberlain this event and the circumstances which had brought it about were of critical importance for the way in which he regarded the party political scene. It meant in effect the abandonment of his idea of a broad anti-Labour alignment of Conservatives and Liberals for which he had striven since the Coupon Election. The change in his attitude was clearly evident in the no-confidence debate in the House of Commons on 21 January, which finally brought down Baldwin's government. In a speech in which 'he mingled sarcasm, wit and bitter irony', Chamberlain launched a stinging attack on the Liberal party.[154] With considerable prescience he pointed to the implications of what had taken place:

[Asquith] has taken his choice and he has by that choice constituted his own immortality. He will go down to history as the last Prime Minister of a Liberal Administration. He has sung the swan song of the Liberal Party. When next the country is called upon for a decision, if it wants a Socialist Government it will vote for a Socialist; if it does not want a Socialist Government it will vote for a Unionist. It will not vote again for those who denatured its mandate and betrayed its trust.[155]

A week later he was writing to Samuel Hoare in very much the sense of Amery's outlook on the situation. The Conservatives' business now was 'to smash the Liberal party'. Two thirds of it, Chamberlain claimed, was already Labour in all but name and the task of Conservatism was to draw over and eventually absorb the other third – rather as the Liberal Unionists had been absorbed into the Unionist party. Baldwin's blunders and Asquith's folly in allowing Labour to take office had given the Conservatives one further chance. The question was whether they would have 'the wit to take it.'[156]

The party's return to opposition raised again the possibility that steps might be taken to reunite its ranks and remove once and for all the divisions which had existed since October 1922. Baldwin had recently made a gesture towards Chamberlain by inviting him to join a committee on reparations, but the latter had declined in view of the Conservative government's uncertain future. Chamberlain's damning indictment of Asquith on 21 January earned Baldwin's praise. It was, the out-going Prime Minister said, 'one of the best bits of work as a speech that I have ever heard you make. And that is saying much.'[157] He anticipated that it would do much to restore Chamberlain's standing with the Conservative party, particularly as he seemed now to have renounced the idea of a Conservative-Liberal coalition.[158] But at this stage Chamberlain insisted that he had no intention of rejoining the Conservative front bench. He would, he said, be rather relieved if he could remain on the back benches and not take responsibility for Baldwin's stupidity.[159] At the very least he was determined that if he did return it would be on his own conditions. When Neville discussed the matter with him he made it clear that the inclusion also of Birkenhead and Horne would be the *sine qua non* of his reconsidering his position.[160] Neville promised to work 'like a beaver to that end' and was hopeful of success.

The younger brother raised the question at a meeting of House of Commons ex-ministers on 24 January. It was the position of Birkenhead rather than Austen Chamberlain which created most difficulty. The former Lord Chancellor's reputation for immorality – 'the fact that he publicly and shamelessly exhibits his weaknesses to the world' – together with his recent Rectorial Address at Glasgow University, in which he had poured scorn on the idea that anything other than self-interest could or should govern the actions of states in the international arena, meant that many leading Conservatives regarded him not only as an unacceptable colleague on personal grounds but also as an electoral liability. But there was a general feeling that, if necessary, it was better to have 'F.E. in than Austen and Horne out,' especially as there was 'all the difference in the world' between treating Birkenhead as if he had been a member of the last Cabinet and appointing him to a public office in which 'his conduct might bring discredit on the administration of the country.'[161] Neville also believed that once his brother and Birkenhead had returned to the fold, Chamberlain would regard his obligation of loyalty to Birkenhead as discharged and the link between the two men would disappear.[162]

In an attempt to forestall opposition among Conservative peers, Baldwin wrote to Salisbury to point out that the Commons ex-ministers were unanimous that 'if it is Austen and F.E., or no Austen, we feel it must be Austen and F.E.'[163] Salisbury was ready to kill the fatted calf for Chamberlain's return. Though he still held him responsible for the Coalition government's Irish treaty and Indian policy, he conceded that Chamberlain was a 'great anti-Socialist' and an able man of the highest character with great parliamentary and administrative experience. The return of Birkenhead, however, still filled him with alarm.[164] Salisbury's brother, Robert Cecil, agreed that Chamberlain's return was entirely desirable. Cecil, though, believed that Baldwin should resist any attempt to make Chamberlain's reinstatement conditional on that of Birkenhead, whose general attitude towards political questions was 'repugnant to the deepest convictions of the vast majority of his fellow countrymen.' If, argued Cecil, Baldwin was not prepared to accept this advice, then his best course might be to resign in Chamberlain's favour. 'Then he would have the responsibility for his own actions and we should know where we really were standing.'[165] Baldwin, however, remained determined to win back Chamberlain even on the latter's terms, and even if it meant that Cecil and Salisbury would refuse to attend the shadow cabinet. He presumably expected that the return of Chamberlain would make it easier for him to abandon Protection after the electoral *débâcle*, lessen his dependence on Salisbury and the Conservative right wing and reduce the possibility of the Chamberlainites forming another coalition in the event of MacDonald's government falling.[166]

Concerned that Baldwin seemed to have an almost unlimited capacity for offending his brother, Neville took it upon himself to act as intermediary in bringing the two men together. The important points were that Baldwin should act quickly to avoid press speculation, show no hesitation and not indicate that there was any problem over the inclusion of Birkenhead.[167] With Neville as host, a dinner was arranged for 5 February and a reconciliation effected. By the end of the evening the two antagonists were addressing one another in terms of personal endearment. Baldwin said that it was time 'for all of us to get together.' He had arranged a meeting of ex-ministers to consider party policy and wanted to know whether Chamberlain would attend and sit on the opposition front bench. If he accepted, Baldwin was ready to invite all the other ex-ministers who had left office in October 1922. After a moment's hesitation Chamberlain accepted this offer and added that he was in a position to accept also on Birkenhead's behalf. Thereafter the after-dinner discussion turned to questions of policy, with apparent agreement that the party should revert to its pre-election attitude on tariffs. Chamberlain also made it plain that Baldwin should not feel obliged to submit himself for re-election as leader 'like a company auditor.' Instead, he should come to the next party meeting as leader and give his followers a clear statement of policy which, Chamberlain believed, would receive overwhelming backing from the party.[168]

When, therefore, the shadow cabinet met on 7 February its numbers had been augmented by the inclusion of Chamberlain, Birkenhead, Balfour and Crawford. Rather surprisingly Baldwin made no allusion whatever to their presence, but allowed Chamberlain to take the lead in urging that the policy of protection should be put on ice for the time being.[169] As the electorate's verdict had been decisive, the party should revert to the *status quo ante*. Those present 'tumbled over themselves' to emphasise their agreement with Chamberlain's point of view, with only Bridgeman and Amery uttering words of dissent. The contrast with the attitude Chamberlain had adopted at meetings of the shadow cabinet after the electoral defeat of 1906 was stark. It must have been particularly striking to Leo Amery who, far more than Austen, had remained faithful throughout to Joseph Chamberlain's original vision.[170] Later in the year Amery reflected:

His father's policy has always been to him a hereditary incubus about which he has felt dutifully zealous or dutifully bored, but which has never been to him a great object in itself.[171]

Though his relationship with Baldwin was always likely to be uneasy, Chamberlain seemed superficially to have recovered most of his old authority within the party hierarchy. At the shadow cabinet's crucial policy meeting on 7 February he was 'splendid' and had taken 'complete charge' of the discussion. If any outsider had been in the room, noted Derby, he would have thought that Chamberlain and not Baldwin was party leader. The latter had taken practically no part in the discussion.[172] In fact Chamberlain now became deputy leader in his brother's place and took charge of overseas policy in the distribution of shadow portfolios in the House of Commons. Neville willingly acquiesced in this arrangement – 'nothing else was conceivable' – and increasingly saw the possibility of Chamberlain rather than Baldwin being the next Conservative Prime Minister.[173] The respective performances of the two leaders in a debate on preference on 18 June 'at once set men gossiping and discussing the leadership afresh.' Even Amery conceded that Chamberlain's was 'about the best speech I have heard him make, an admirable parliamentary performance.'[174] Yet though many of the younger M.P.s admired Chamberlain's parliamentary skills and recognised that he could 'make rings round S.B. in the matter of debate, resourcefulness and knowledge of procedure', older colleagues still regarded him as a coalitionist in mind if not in practice. Even in the debate on 18 June he had gone out of his way to pay a compliment to Lloyd George, a gesture which struck many Conservatives as not only unnecessary but undeserved. When in July Baldwin spoke at Lowestoft, Chamberlain took exception to his leader's apparent unwillingness to hold out a hand of friendship to those Liberals who were regularly supporting the Conservatives in the division lobbies in the Commons. A fortnight earlier he believed he had secured Baldwin's acquiescence in such a policy:

Why again did you not tell me that you had changed your mind? . . . Why, oh why? I am off to the country with a sad heart.[175]

Yet in his hankering after 'co-operation' Chamberlain was out of touch with the general sentiment in the party. So while Neville doubted whether Baldwin would be the next Conservative Prime Minister, he recognised that if his brother's name were put forward, 'there would be a bitter controversy.'[176]

In private Chamberlain made it clear that his reconciliation with his leader was less complete than it might have seemed to outsiders. He did not feel towards Baldwin 'as I like to feel towards my "leader".'[177] Yet, at least in respect of Chamberlain, it is difficult to accept Mr. Cowling's conclusion that Chamberlain and Birkenhead offered to support Baldwin 'because they felt they had a better chance to manage, and replace, him by burrowing from within.'[178] Chamberlain still regarded Baldwin as 'unequal to the post', but argued that until he discovered his own inadequacy and retired of his own accord, he would retain enough backing within the party to make the position of any alternative leader untenable.[179] It would be 'worse than useless' to try to displace him.[180] Therefore, he told Beaverbrook, 'you will probably see F.E. and me on his platform.'[181]

Baldwin's qualities seldom showed to advantage when in opposition and the brief period of Labour government did nothing to enhance Chamberlain's opinion of him. In April he wrote to his sister:

Stanley himself never fires more than a popgun or a peashooter at critical moments and hasn't a ghost of an idea how to *fight*.[182]

Two months later he castigated the party leader as 'stupid and uncommunicative'. His habit of 'bursting out with some inconceivable folly' was 'both disconcerting and exasperating.'[183] In July, after some confusion over who should speak in a House of Commons debate on foreign affairs, Chamberlain complained of being kept in a constant state of discomfort by not knowing how much of what Baldwin arranged with him was imparted to other colleagues. It was, said Chamberlain, a curious position. 'No one seems to have much confidence in Baldwin except himself.'[184] Nor was Chamberlain impressed with the opposition front bench as a whole. It was, he asserted, inferior to anything he had known. 'It has no "punch", no grip.'[185] Individual episodes exacerbated the relationship between Chamberlain and Baldwin. One was the candidature of Winston Churchill as an Independent Constitutionalist at the Abbey, Westminster by-election in March 1924. Chamberlain clearly welcomed the idea of the eventual reinstatement of his fellow Coalitionist in the Conservative ranks and, at a meeting of ex-ministers on 6 March, got 'angry and excited' when it appeared that some of his colleagues were ready to speak on behalf of the official Conservative candidate.[186] But

Chamberlain seems to have changed his mind and become convinced that it was both too early for Churchill to come out as a Conservative with credit to himself and unwise to rush his fences by a rash attempt at the Abbey division.[187] Beaverbrook reported that, to Baldwin's surprise, Chamberlain now maintained that Churchill should not be supported 'until he repented in sackcloth and ashes for his Liberal past and joined the Tories openly as a penitent convert.'[188] In May Chamberlain understandably took offence at an article in *The People* based upon an interview with Baldwin. The piece contained many unflattering references to the Conservative leader's senior colleagues and gave the impression that he was obsessed with the idea of conspiracies and plots to unseat him. Though recognising that Baldwin had been grossly misrepresented by an irresponsible journalist, Chamberlain thought that he had clearly been indiscreet in listening to wild gossip and had also said one or two foolish things to the reporter. He therefore took the occasion to speak and write 'very bluntly' to Baldwin, stressing that he would never be a rival to him as long as Baldwin cared to remain leader, though 'if he gave it up and it were offered to me, I should probably accept it.'[189]

Yet Chamberlain still set his face against any attempt to dislodge Baldwin from the leadership. To one disaffected back-bencher he set out his position:

I have no obligation to Stanley Baldwin except the ordinary obligation of an honourable man not to work against Baldwin behind his back whilst associated with him as I now am in council. . . . He may gradually develop in power and decision, or he may fail and himself become convinced that he is unequal to the task. But while he is in the field any movement against him would only strengthen his hold upon his own followers and confirm him in his position.[190]

Chamberlain remained, therefore, in the role of a disgruntled and touchy colleague, looking down somewhat disdainfully from the eminence of his long parliamentary and ministerial career upon the inadequate efforts of the far less experienced man whom the irony of fate had placed as his leader.

Britain's first experience of Labour administration proved not to be the unmitigated national disaster which Chamberlain and others had anticipated. For a variety of reasons, not least its lack of a parliamentary majority, the government did not take many excursions along the road to a Socialist Utopia. Instead Labour gained a useful, if brief, experience of the mechanics of government, while establishing in the public mind its credentials as a responsible and patriotic party of government. Chamberlain gave public expression to his views on the political situation in an article in the *Evening News* on 20 July. Though Labour was gaining a steady stream of recruits from the left wing of the Liberal party, he sensed no comparable movement towards the Conservatives from moderate Liberalism. It was clear that he felt that the Conservatives were still suffering from the mistakes of the previous year. Though the party had made 'good progress', it would be 'folly to pretend that there is such a marked reaction in our favour as would restore us to the position won by Mr. Bonar Law in 1922.'[191] By the early autumn Chamberlain was becoming increasingly exasperated with the failure of the Liberal party to side with the Conservatives and defeat the government in the House of Commons.[192]

In the event it was the government which sealed its own fate. A prosecution was begun against the Communist, J. R. Campbell, for publishing a seditious article in *The Workers Weekly*. Under pressure from Labour back-benchers the politically inexperienced Attorney-General, Sir Patrick Hastings, dropped the case. This was enough to unite Conservatives and Liberals in the allegation of improper interference in the judicial process and a vote of censure led to the government's defeat in the Commons. Parliament was therefore dissolved and an election held in late October, with the issues focused increasingly upon that point where, in the atmosphere of the 1920s, Labour was most vulnerable. The Campbell Case seemed to imply that there might be sinister forces at work behind the acceptably moderate façade of the Labour government. It also raised important question marks over the government's proposed treaties with the Soviet Union. When shortly before polling day a letter was made public from the Soviet leader, Zinoviev, giving instructions to British Communists, substance seemed to be added to the allegations of Labour's political opponents. The matter was mishandled by MacDonald, allowing the Conservatives to imply that he was implicated in some wide-ranging Bolshevik conspiracy. In such circumstances it was not surprising that the Conservatives, freed now from the commitment to protection, made substantial gains. With 419 Conservative members returned to the House of Commons, the electoral situation could not have been clearer. Baldwin, his leadership triumphantly confirmed, was in a position to construct a government that would last for its full term.

For Austen Chamberlain the General Election of 1924 represented a landmark in his political career, closing one chapter and opening up another. For six years he had been one of the more thoughtful and perceptive observers of the domestic political scene. With greater clarity than many of his contemporaries he had recognised that the Great War marked a watershed in the nature of the party political debate in this country. The fundamental dividing lines of the nineteenth century, which had remained the focal point of conflict throughout the Edwardian era and about which Chamberlain himself had felt as passionately as most men, no longer had the same relevance after 1918. The issues that had separated Unionists and Liberals could no longer engender the same controversy or the same emotion:

The questions which are coming up for a settlement are not those which divided the parties in pre-war days but are economic and social questions challenging the very basis of our national life and industry upon which the older parties have always been agreed.[193]

In his efforts to adapt to these changed circumstances, Chamberlain had all but destroyed his own career. Though his understanding of the fundamental issues was good, his tactical handling of them was often inept. Nothing epitomised this better than his personal commitment to Lloyd George and Birkenhead. Yet the election of 1924 did much to confirm Chamberlain's prognosis. Now there clearly was a new alignment in British politics. It was not Labour who suffered disastrously at the polls. They were still ten seats better off than they had been in 1922 and had increased their total vote by about one million. The real losers were the Liberal party. Only a shattered remnant of forty M.P.s returned to Westminster. Symbolically, Asquith himself was among the ranks of the defeated. Yet paradoxically 1924 marked also the end of Chamberlain's obsession with the domestic political scene. For the rest of his life foreign affairs became his abiding concern. Despite the personal and political disappointments of the past years and the hints that he was ready to withdraw from public life, he stood now on the threshold of his most celebrated ministerial appointment and that which ultimately gave him his most intense satisfaction.

Notes

1. N. Chamberlain to Annie Chamberlain 18 Aug. 1923, Chamberlain MSS, NC 1/26/326.
2. A. Chamberlain to Ida Chamberlain 10 March 1923, ibid, AC 5/1/268.
3. L. Amery, *Diaries* p. 330.
4. M. Cowling, *Labour* p. 184 ff.
5. M. Kinnear, *Fall of Lloyd George* p. 126.
6. Bridgeman diary, July 1922; L. Amery, *Diaries* p. 288; Middlemas and Barnes, *Baldwin* p. 108; M. Cowling, *Labour* p. 187; J. Ramsden (ed.), *Real Old Tory Politics: The Political Diaries of Robert Sanders, 1910–1935* (London, 1984) p. 179.
7. Lord Winterton, *Orders of the Day* p. 116.
8. Bridgeman diary, Aug. 1922.
9. Memorandum by Pollock on the Fall of the Coalition Government,

Pollock MSS, d 432. Much of the memorandum is cited in R. F. V. Heuston, *The Lives of the Lord Chancellors 1885–1940* (Oxford, 1964).

10. Ibid. Yet Chamberlain apparently disapproved of Birkenhead's performance on 3 August, J. Ramsden, *Sanders* p. 180.
11. Derby to Chamberlain 1 and 9 Sept. 1922 and Chamberlain to Derby 7 Sept. 1922, Derby MSS 33.
12. Younger to A. Chamberlain 16 Sept. 1922, Chamberlain MSS, AC 33/2/20.
13. Salisbury to Law 23 Sept. 1922, Bonar Law MSS 107/2/61.
14. M. Gilbert, *Churchill* iv, 3, 1992; D. Walder, *The Chanak Affair* (London, 1969) p. 212.
15. Gilbert, *Churchill* iv, 3, 2037.
16. Notes on the Eastern Crisis, 6 Oct. 1922, Griffith-Boscawen MSS Eng. hist. c 396 ff 98–105.
17. Petrie, *Life* ii, 195–6.
18. Ibid, pp. 197–8; M. Kinnear, *Fall of Lloyd George* p. 117.
19. Younger to A. Chamberlain 22 Sept. 1922, Chamberlain MSS, AC 33/2/21.
20. L. Wilson to A. Chamberlain, Sept. 1922, ibid, AC 33/2/26.
21. R. Blake, *Unknown Prime Minister* p. 450.
22. Younger to R. Sanders 25 Sept. 1922, cited M. Cowling, *Labour* p. 181.
23. A. Chamberlain to Parker Smith 11 Oct. 1922, Chamberlain MSS, AC 33/2/38.
24. A. Chamberlain to Ida Chamberlain 24 Sept. 1922, ibid, AC 5/1/249; 'I do not think', wrote Leo Amery, 'Austen yet realises the position in the Party or the fact that in the present temper of the country the half is a great deal more than the whole, i.e. that the Unionist Party is likely to get more seats standing on its own than the whole Coalition are likely to get standing together.' *Diaries* p. 293.
25. M. Cowling, *Labour* p. 196.
26. A. Chamberlain to Fraser 6 Oct. 1922, Chamberlain MSS, AC 33/2/32.
27. T. Jones, *Diary with Letters* p. 61.
28. 'The Break-up of the Coalition,' memorandum by Griffith-Boscawen, Oct. 1922, Griffith-Boscawen MSS, c. 396 ff. 119–123.
29. L. Wilson to A. Chamberlain 11 Oct. 1922, Chamberlain MSS, AC 33/2/43.
30. A. Chamberlain to L. Wilson 12 Oct. 1922, ibid.
31. M. Kinnear, *Fall of Lloyd George* pp. 120–1.
32. Derby to A. Chamberlain 13 Oct. 1922, Chamberlain MSS, AC 33/2/36.
33. A. Chamberlain to Birkenhead 12 Oct. 1922, ibid, AC 33/2/52.
34. Salisbury to Selborne 12 Oct. 1922, Selborne MSS 7 ff. 135–6.
35. Notes by Curzon on events leading to the break-up of the Government, Oct. 1922, Curzon MSS Eur. F 112/319.
36. L. Amery, *Diaries* pp. 296–7.
37. Pollock memorandum, cited R. Heuston, *Lord Chancellors* p. 389.
38. L. Amery, *Diaries* p. 298; L. Amery, *Life* ii, 237.

39. L. Amery, *Diaries* p. 299; L. Amery to A. Chamberlain 18 Oct. 1922, Chamberlain MSS, AC 33/2/70.
40. "The Fall of the Coalition", Templewood MSS XX/5; Lord Templewood, *The Empire of the Air* (London, 1957) p. 27; J. A. Cross, *Sir Samuel Hoare* (London, 1977) pp. 76–7.
41. R. James, *Memoirs of a Conservative* p. 121.
42. M. Kinnear, *Fall of Lloyd George* p. 125. After the Carlton Club meeting Walter Long wrote: 'I made certain there would be a sufficient majority for you and I can't help feeling that there must have been some dreadful mistake.' Long to A. Chamberlain 19 Oct. 1922, Chamberlain MSS, AC 33/2/103.
43. A. Chamberlain to Ida Chamberlain 21 Nov. 1922, Chamberlain MSS, AC 5/1/252.
44. Bridgeman diary, citing letter to his son of 22 Oct. 1922.
45. Beaverbrook, *Decline and Fall* p. 200.
46. R. James, *Memoirs of a Conservative* p. 127; L. Amery, *Life* ii, 238–9; his 'uncompromising and somewhat aggressive attitude' surprised many M.P.s and, even before Bonar Law's speech, persuaded many waverers to support the break up of the Coalition. Lord Hemingford, *Backbencher and Chairman* (London, 1946) p. 42.
47. Lord Birkenhead, *F.E.: the Life of F. E. Smith, First Earl of Birkenhead* (London, 1959) p. 451.
48. L. Amery, *Diaries* p. 299; L. Amery, *Life* ii, 238–9.
49. As note 44; T. Jones, *Whitehall Diary* i, 210–11.
50. Pollock memorandum.
51. Pollock memorandum, cited R. Heuston p. 390; M. Cowling, *Labour* p. 208.
52. M. Gilbert, *Churchill* iv, 3, 2103–4.
53. M. Cowling, *Labour* p. 253.
54. M. Kinnear, *Fall of Lloyd George* p. 130.
55. R. Churchill, *Derby* pp. 487–8.
56. J. Cross, *Hoare* p. 80.
57. T. Jones, *Whitehall Diary* i, 210–11.
58. K. Morgan, *Consensus and Disunity* p. 351.
59. As note 57. Curzon later noted, 'My own impression ... was that the meeting had been handled with the minimum of skill and dexterity by Chamberlain and that, had he adopted a less unbending attitude, he might have escaped the hostile vote and built a bridge till the General Election.' Notes by Curzon, Oct. 1922, Curzon MSS Eur. F 112/319.
60. G. Younger to J. Strachey 20 Nov. 1922, Strachey MSS S/19/4/26b.
61. F. Stevenson, *Lloyd George: A Diary* p. 311.
62. A. Chamberlain to L. Wilson 22 Nov. 1922, Chamberlain MSS, AC 33/2/95; J. C. C. Davidson later noted that Wilson 'played rather a double game with Austen, not keeping him properly informed about the movements inside the Party.' R. James, *Memoirs of a Conservative* p. 117.
63. Lord Chaplin to A. Chamberlain 24 Oct. 1922, Chamberlain MSS,

AC 33/2/98.
64. A. Chamberlain to Ida Chamberlain 18 Nov. 1922, ibid, AC 5/1/250.
65. A. Chamberlain to G. Lloyd 7 Dec. 1922, ibid, AC 18/1/35.
66. Ibid.
67. A. Chamberlain to Ida Chamberlain 21 Nov. 1922, ibid, AC 5/1/252.
68. As note 65. With 345 seats in the new parliament, the Conservatives had a majority of 75 over all other parties combined.
69. As note 67.
70. M. Cowling, *Labour* p. 255.
71. As note 65.
72. M. Cowling, *Labour* p. 258.
73. A. Mond to Lloyd George 29 Oct. 1922, Lloyd George MSS G/14/5/1.
74. A. Chamberlain to Ida Chamberlain 10 March 1923, Chamberlain MSS, AC 5/1/268.
75. Ibid, Dec. 1922, AC 5/1/256.
76. N. Chamberlain to H. Chamberlain 31 Oct. 1922, ibid, NC 18/1/370; A. Chamberlain to Ida Chamberlain 18 Nov. 1922, ibid, AC 5/1/250; K. Feiling, *Neville Chamberlain* p. 101; I. MacLeod, *Neville Chamberlain* p. 87; L. Amery, *Life* ii, 242.
77. M. Cowling, *Labour* pp. 253–4.
78. A. Clark (ed.), *A Good Innings: The Private Papers of Lord Lee of Fareham* (London, 1974) p. 237.
79. Curzon to Law 28 Nov. 1922 and Law to Curzon 5 Dec. 1922, Bonar Law MSS 111/12/35, 38.
80. Birkenhead, *F.E.* p. 485; c.f. M. Cowling, *Labour* p. 254.
81. A. Clark, *Innings* p. 236.
82. N. Chamberlain to H. Chamberlain 24 March 1923, Chamberlain MSS, NC 18/1/389.
83. A. Chamberlain to W. Long 20 Oct. 1922, ibid, AC 33/2/104.
84. S. Salvidge, *Salvidge of Liverpool* (London, 1934) p. 238.
85. T. Jones, *Whitehall Diary* i, 236.
86. N. Chamberlain to A. Chamberlain 23 April 1923, Chamberlain MSS, AC 35/1/35; Middlemas and Barnes, *Baldwin* p. 159; M. Kinnear, *Fall of Lloyd George* p. 207; R. Blake, *Unknown Prime Minister* pp. 508–9; J. Ramsden, *Balfour and Baldwin* p. 174; N. Fisher, *The Tory Leaders: their Struggle for Power* (London, 1977) pp. 27–8. Kinnear, Blake and Ramsden regard the offer as genuine, Middlemas and Barnes do not.
87. A. Chamberlain to H. Chamberlain 14 April 1923, Chamberlain MSS, AC 5/1/270; A. Chamberlain to N. Chamberlain 22 April 1923, ibid, NC 1/27/69.
88. A. Chamberlain to N. Chamberlain 25 April 1923, ibid, NC 1/27/71.
89. Memorandum by Worthington-Evans on the events of May and June, 1923, Worthington-Evans MSS c. 894 ff. 32–42; note by Chamberlain on the formation of Baldwin's government, 27 May 1923, Chamberlain MSS, AC 35/2/11.
90. Worthington-Evans to A. Chamberlain 22 May 1923, Worthington-Evans

MSS c. 894 ff 9–14; R. James, *Memoirs of a Conservative* p. 160.

91. A. Chamberlain to Worthington-Evans 24 May 1923, Worthington-Evans MSS, c 894 ff. 17–21.
92. T. Jones, *Whitehall Diary* i, 237.
93. Worthington-Evans Memorandum; N. Chamberlain diary 23 May 1923, Chamberlain MSS, NC 2/21; R. James, *Memoirs of a Conservative* p. 167. To Neville Chamberlain Baldwin implied that the post to be offered was that of Lord Privy Seal.
94. Salisbury to Stamfordham 23 May 1923, cited Middlemas and Barnes, *Baldwin* pp. 173–4.
95. N. Chamberlain to Ida Chamberlain 26 May 1923, Chamberlain MSS, NC 18/1/396. Mr Cowling even doubts whether Baldwin seriously hoped to include Chamberlain in the Government. M. Cowling, *Labour* p. 269.
96. Worthington-Evans Memorandum.
97. Memorandum by A. Chamberlain 27 May 1923, Chamberlain MSS, AC 35/2/11a.
98. Ibid, AC 35/2/11b; A. Chamberlain to Ivy Chamberlain 27 May 1923, AC 6/1/503; K. Young, *Stanley Baldwin* (London, 1976) p. 46; Middlemas and Barnes, *Baldwin* pp. 175–6; R. James, *Memoirs of a Conservative* p. 169.
99. A. Clark, *Innings* p. 239.
100. N. Chamberlain diary 1 June 1923, Chamberlain MSS, NC 2/21.
101. A. Chamberlain to N. Chamberlain 1 June 1923, ibid, NC 1/27/72.
102. N. Chamberlain to A. Chamberlain 5 June 1923, ibid, AC 35/1/36.
103. N. Chamberlain diary 8 June 1923, ibid, NC 2/21.
104. N. Chamberlain to Ida Chamberlain 8 July 1923, ibid, NC 18/1/401.
105. A. Chamberlain to N. Chamberlain 30 Aug. 1923, ibid, NC 1/27/74.
106. A. Chamberlain to Birkenhead 31 May 1923, ibid, AC 35/2/18.
107. Birkenhead, *F.E.* p. 482.
108. Ibid, p. 486; Middlemas and Barnes, *Baldwin* p. 214.
109. As note 100.
110. A. Chamberlain to G. Lloyd 8 June 1923, Chamberlain MSS, AC 18/1/36.
111. A. Chamberlain to Ida Chamberlain 22 Sept. 1923, ibid, AC 5/1/290.
112. A. Chamberlain to N. Chamberlain 30 Aug. 1923, ibid, NC 1/27/74; L. Amery, *Diaries* p. 333.
113. A. Chamberlain to Birkenhead 6 July 1923, Chamberlain MSS, AC 35/2/22; Chamberlain told Leo Amery that 'only Birmingham and Neville' kept him from criticising the government more vigorously over its foreign policy. L. Amery, *Diaries* p. 333.
114. N. Chamberlain to Ida Chamberlain 8 July 1923, Chamberlain MSS, NC 18/1/401.
115. N. Chamberlain to H. Chamberlain 15 July 1923, ibid, NC 18/1/402.
116. N. Chamberlain to Ida Chamberlain 2 Sept. 1923, ibid, NC 18/1/407; N. Chamberlain to H. Chamberlain 9 Sept. 1923, ibid, NC 18/1/408.
117. L. Amery, *Diaries* p. 333.

118. Ibid, p. 330.
119. A. Chamberlain to N. Chamberlain 15 Oct. 1923, Chamberlain MSS, NC 1/27/78; A. Chamberlain to M. Chamberlain 21 Oct. 1923, ibid, AC 4/1/1233.
120. N. Chamberlain to A. Chamberlain 23 Oct. 1923, ibid, AC 35/3/10.
121. A. Chamberlain to N. Chamberlain 24 Oct. 1923, ibid, NC 1/27/80.
122. Middlemas and Barnes, *Baldwin* p. 231; A. Chamberlain to L. Amery 31 Oct. 1923, Chamberlain MSS, AC 35/3/1; A. Chamberlain to N. Chamberlain 29 Oct. 1923, ibid, NC 1/27/81.
123. N. Chamberlain to Ida Chamberlain 26 Oct. and 11 Nov. 1923, Chamberlain MSS, NC 18/1/414, 415.
124. P. Hannon to A. Chamberlain 31 Oct. 1923, ibid, AC 35/3/16; A. Chamberlain to P. Hannon 31 Oct. 1923, ibid, AC 35/3/17.
125. Note by A. Chamberlain on events of 10 Nov. 1923, ibid, AC 35/3/21a. According to Beaverbrook, Chamberlain, Birkenhead, Lloyd George and himself met at Cherkley on 12 November and discussed the unlikely idea that Birkenhead and Chamberlain should join the government and work from within it in favour of free trade! This was presumably in anticipation of reforming the Coalition on a free trade ticket. The idea seems so implausible as to defy belief. A. J. P. Taylor, *Beaverbrook* p. 216; J. Campbell, *Lloyd George: The Goat in the Wilderness 1922–1931* (London, 1977) p. 50. Yet in 1935 Beaverbrook claimed that he had put to Chamberlain a plan for imposing food taxes on the Prime Minister – a plan which Chamberlain rejected as disloyal to the party and damaging to the leadership. Draft review of *Down the Years*, 11 Sept. 1935, Beaverbrook MSS, BBK C/79.
126. Memorandum by A. Chamberlain on the events of 11 and 12 Nov. 1923, Chamberlain MSS, AC 35/3/21b; N. Chamberlain diary 12 Nov. 1923, ibid, NC 2/21; R. James, *Memoirs of a Conservative* p. 185; M. Cowling, *Labour* pp. 320–1.
127. A. Chamberlain to H. Chamberlain 14 Nov. 1923, Chamberlain MSS, AC 5/1/297.
128. Derby to Baldwin 13 Nov. 1923, Baldwin MSS 42 f. 132; Memorandum by A. Chamberlain on the events of 14 Nov. 1923, Chamberlain MSS, AC 35/3/21d; R. Churchill, *Derby* pp. 531, 534–5; H. Montgomery Hyde, *Baldwin: the Unexpected Prime Minister* (London, 1973) p. 185.
129. R. Churchill, *Derby* pp. 534–5.
130. L. Amery to Baldwin 14 Nov. 1923, Baldwin MSS 42 f. 125; R. Cecil to Baldwin 14 Nov. 1923, ibid, f. 126.
131. N. Chamberlain diary 18 Nov. 1923, Chamberlain MSS, NC 2/21.
132. H. Montgomery Hyde, *Baldwin* p. 189.
133. N. Chamberlain to H. Chamberlain 17 Nov. 1923, Chamberlain MSS, NC 18/1/416.
134. A. Chamberlain to Baldwin 14 Nov. 1923, Baldwin MSS 35 f. 95.
135. Baldwin to A. Chamberlain 15 Nov. 1923, Chamberlain MSS, AC 35/3/4.
136. Memorandum by Worthington-Evans on events of Oct–Nov. 1923,

Worthington-Evans MSS c 894 ff. 57–78.
137. A. Chamberlain to Ida Chamberlain 17 Nov. 1923, Chamberlain MSS, AC 5/1/298.
138. A. Chamberlain to N. Chamberlain 18 Nov. 1923, ibid, NC 1/27/82.
139. Ibid; N. Chamberlain diary 18 Nov. 1923, NC 2/21.
140. Bridgeman diary Dec. 1923.
141. A. Chamberlain to Lord Lee of Fareham 14 Dec. 1923, Chamberlain MSS, AC 35/3/18.
142. Bridgeman diary Dec. 1923; Ormsby Gore to Baldwin 29 Jan. 1924, Baldwin MSS 42 ff. 182–7.
143. R. Churchill, *Derby* p. 544.
144. Derby to Birkenhead 11 Dec. 1923, cited Churchill, *Derby* p. 556.
145. Balfour to Birkenhead 11 Dec. 1923, cited Churchill, *Derby* p. 554.
146. Churchill, *Derby* pp. 558–9.
147. N. Chamberlain diary 19 Dec. 1923, Chamberlain MSS, NC 2/21.
148. Ibid, 18 Dec. 1923, NC 2/21.
149. Ormsby Gore to Baldwin 29 Jan. 1924, Baldwin MSS 42 ff. 182–7.
150. A. Chamberlain to N. Chamberlain 8 Dec. 1923, Chamberlain MSS, NC 1/27/83.
151. A. Chamberlain to H. Chamberlain 29 Dec. 1923, ibid, AC 5/1/300.
152. M. Cowling, *Labour* p. 332.
153. L. Amery, *Diaries* p. 361; L. Amery to Baldwin 8 Dec. 1923, Baldwin MSS 35 ff. 169–72.
154. H. Montgomery Hyde, *Baldwin* p. 199.
155. Cited I. MacLeod, *Neville Chamberlain* p. 100.
156. A. Chamberlain to Hoare 28 Jan. 1924, Chamberlain MSS, AC 35/4/19.
157. As note 154.
158. Baldwin to George V 22 Jan. 1924, cited H. Montgomery Hyde, *Baldwin* p. 199. Leo Amery was less impressed by the speech with 'its exaggeration of the danger of Socialism'. *Diaries* p. 364.
159. A. Chamberlain to M. Chamberlain 27 Jan. 1924, Chamberlain MSS, AC 4/1/1239.
160. N. Chamberlain to H. Chamberlain 24 Jan. 1924, ibid, NC 18/1/423.
161. Ibid; N. Chamberlain diary 24 Jan. 1924, NC 2/21; L. Amery, *Diaries* p. 365.
162. L. Amery, *Diaries* p. 367.
163. Middlemas and Barnes, *Baldwin* p. 261.
164. Salisbury to Baldwin 26 Jan. 1924, Baldwin MSS 159 f. 259; Salisbury to R. Cecil 28 Jan. 1924, Cecil MSS 51085 f. 117.
165. R. Cecil to Baldwin 1 Feb. 1924, Baldwin MSS 35 ff. 203–06.
166. M. Cowling, *Labour* p. 392.
167. N. Chamberlain diary 4 Feb. 1924, Chamberlain MSS, NC 2/21.
168. Ibid, 6 Feb. 1924, NC 2/21; N. Chamberlain to H. Chamberlain 9 Feb. 1924, NC 18/1/425; Note by A. Chamberlain 7 Feb. 1924, AC 35/4/5.
169. Amery had earlier urged Baldwin to give 'a definite lead, expressing his views pretty fully.' L. Amery, *Diaries* p. 367.

170. N. Chamberlain diary 7 Feb. 1924, Chamberlain MSS, NC 2/21; Bridgeman diary 1924; R. Churchill, *Derby* p. 565; L. Amery, *Diaries* p. 367.

171. L. Amery, *Diaries* p. 377.

172. R. Churchill, *Derby* p. 565.

173. N. Chamberlain to Ida Chamberlain 16 Feb. 1924, Chamberlain MSS, NC 18/1/426; M. Cowling, *Labour* p. 396.

174. L. Amery, *Diaries* p. 377; N. Chamberlain to Ida Chamberlain 22 June 1924, Chamberlain MSS, NC 18/1/441.

175. A. Chamberlain to Baldwin 18 July 1924, Baldwin MSS 159 f. 195.

176. N. Chamberlain to Ida Chamberlain 22 June and 3 Aug. 1924, Chamberlain MSS, NC 18/1/441, 446; N. Chamberlain to H. Chamberlain 17 Aug. 1924, ibid, NC 18/1/447.

177. A. Chamberlain to Ida Chamberlain 9 Feb. 1924, ibid, AC 5/1/307.

178. M. Cowling, *Labour* p. 392.

179. A. Chamberlain to N. Chamberlain 30 Jan. 1924, Chamberlain MSS, NC 1/27/66.

180. As note 177.

181. A. Chamberlain to Beaverbrook 8 Feb. 1924, Beaverbrook MSS, BBK C/79.

182. A. Chamberlain to Ida Chamberlain 18 April 1924, Chamberlain MSS, AC 5/1/315.

183. Ibid, 29 June 1924, AC 5/1/322.

184. Ibid, 14 July 1924, AC 5/1/324.

185. As note 182.

186. L. Amery, *Diaries* p. 372.

187. H. Montgomery Hyde, *Baldwin* p. 205.

188. K. Young, *Churchill and Beaverbrook* (London, 1966) pp. 69–70.

189. Memorandum by A. Chamberlain on Baldwin's interview with *The People* reporter, Chamberlain MSS, AC 21/5/24; H. Montgomery Hyde, *Baldwin* p. 215.

190. A. Chamberlain to W. Chilcott 1 April 1924, Chamberlain MSS, AC 35/4/14.

191. J. Ramsden, *Balfour and Baldwin* pp. 198–9.

192. A. Chamberlain to Ivy Chamberlain 7 Oct. 1924, Chamberlain MSS, AC 6/1/561.

193. A. Chamberlain to Earl Fitzwilliam 12 Jan. 1922, ibid, AC 32/2/38.

CHAPTER SEVEN

THE FOREIGN OFFICE – LOCARNO

'I am Secretary of State for Foreign Affairs. My garden will go to ruins and you need not expect to get a letter from me for the next four years if I survive so long.'[1]

'Last night he talked almost without stopping from 8 till 11.00 on Locarno, very naturally perhaps. The rest of the world does not exist for him.'[2]

If one single event stands out in the long career of Austen Chamberlain it is the conclusion of the Treaties of Locarno in 1925. Though the central provisions of Locarno were violated with impunity by Hitler when he invaded the Rhineland in 1936, and the treaties had ceased to carry any weight long before the outbreak of war in 1939, many have continued to look back on Locarno as the most constructive diplomatic achievement of the inter-war years – the most promising basis upon which a lasting peace might have been created to spare Europe from a further recourse to war. Many contemporaries seemed to lose a sense of proportion in the 'orgiastic gush'[3] with which they greeted the five agreements which collectively made up the Locarno accord. 'This morning the Locarno Pact was signed at the Foreign Office,' noted George V in the privacy of his diary. 'I pray this may mean peace for many years. Why not for ever?'[4] Observers were perhaps carried away in the almost fairy-tale atmosphere of Locarno itself, a small Swiss lakeside resort, where the treaties were initialled on 16 October 1925. Chamberlain himself wrote to a government colleague:

I rub my eyes and wonder whether I am dreaming when the French Foreign Minister invites the German Foreign Minister and me to celebrate my wife's birthday, and incidentally talk business, by a cruise on the Lake in a launch called *Orange Blossom*, habitually used by wedding parties.[5]

Certainly no other single achievement of Chamberlain's political life earned him so much praise and admiration. The Garter and the Nobel Prize for Peace were the most tangible of the accolades heaped upon him. A peerage could certainly have been his had he so wished it.[6] Though coming within the first year of his tenure of the Foreign Office, Locarno remained the principal motif of British foreign policy throughout Baldwin's second government. It was for Chamberlain 'the crowning point of his career to which he looked back with justifiable satisfaction for the rest of his days.'[7] It would be, he hoped, the event by which he would be judged at the bar of history. At the end of Chamberlain's ministerial career, Stanley Baldwin wrote to him in terms which he would have found gratifying:

But when the history of these years comes to be written with the fuller knowledge time brings, justice will be done and a place will be secured for you which your father would deem not unworthy of his son.[8]

An analysis of Locarno must therefore constitute a central feature in Chamberlain's biography. That he should have had the opportunity to guide British foreign policy was, however, no foregone conclusion in the autumn of 1924. Though Chamberlain's reconciliation with the party leadership meant that he was bound to receive government office whenever Labour fell and Baldwin returned to power, the Foreign Office was in no sense marked out for him. With the Conservative party reunited Baldwin faced a host of claims to high office, only complicated by the size of the party's election victory. As the magnitude of the Labour rout became apparent, Chamberlain sent Baldwin a note of congratulation, tinged with caution:

I am a little dazed, as you will be already thinking of the great responsibilities that face you. So large a majority creates dangers of its own. I have one clear conviction which you will share. Reaction would be fatal.[9]

Chamberlain's first thought had been that he might take on a non-departmental office – Lord President or Lord Privy Seal – possibly combined with the leadership of the Commons. In other words he envisaged returning to the sort of position he had occupied under Lloyd George after Bonar Law's first retirement. Baldwin, however, made it clear that these posts were required for Birkenhead and Curzon. The Prime Minister was adamant that the latter's return to the Foreign Office would be disastrous for Anglo-French relations. The choice before Chamberlain was therefore between the Foreign Office and the India Office, and his first inclinations were towards the latter because it was a field of government in which he already had experience, and was both less exacting and less expensive than the Foreign Office.[10] When Chamberlain finally decided to opt for the more senior post he did so with the diffidence and misgivings which accompanied most of the changes and initiatives in his career. Rapidly, however, he found his feet and took especial satisfaction in the belief that his father had thought the Foreign Office a suitable position to which to aspire. After a year in the job he was certain that he was both more useful and happier as Foreign Secretary than he could ever have been as Prime Minister.[11] The appointment was generally well received, with *The Times* sensing that Chamberlain's qualities were perhaps well suited to the dignity of the office:

The shortcomings in leadership which have been attributed to him in his long political career – that he is aloof from his younger colleagues, rather wooden in his outlook on domestic problems, punctilious to the point of rigidity where there is any question of fulfilling even a supposed obligation – are none of them serious faults, may some of them be positive virtues in a Foreign Secretary.[12]

In one respect Baldwin seemed anxious to emphasise that the divisions of 1922 were now a thing of the past. Chamberlain was touched by the gesture of being offered in addition to the Foreign Office the post of Deputy Leader of the House, which he interpreted as a symbolic recognition of his senior status within the party.[13] In other ways, however, Baldwin was determined to underline his own leadership of the party and Chamberlain was able to exercise little influence in the distribution of the other major offices of state. A little harshly Lord Lee of Fareham reflected that 'Austen never did have much punch or drive about getting things done for his colleagues or followers.'[14] Chamberlain was particularly upset that Sir Robert Horne, who he hoped would return to the Treasury, was by-passed. 'I am afraid that my opinion carries no weight with you,' he lamented somewhat petulantly. Had the Exchequer gone, as Baldwin first implied, to his brother Neville, Chamberlain's indignation might have been less pronounced. Instead Baldwin made the bold decision to appoint the maverick Winston Churchill. The latter's return to the Conservative fold, after two decades in the ranks of the Liberal party, was too recent an event for many Conservatives including Chamberlain to regard his rapid promotion as showing other than indecent haste.[15] Chamberlain was also less than enthusiastic about Amery's nomination to the Colonial Office and he thought Steel-Maitland at the Ministry of Labour 'a shocking appointment.' Baldwin was evidently 'stiffened' by his electoral triumph and 'not inclined to accept advice or suggestions unless they chimed with his own ideas.' When he learnt more details of the way in which the offices and particularly the Exchequer had been filled, Chamberlain could only conclude that 'S.B. is mad.'[16]

An appointment of more immediate concern to Chamberlain was that of Lord Robert Cecil to be Chancellor of the Duchy of Lancaster. In the last Conservative government Cecil as Lord Privy Seal had had special responsibility for League of Nations affairs and had established an important and often independent voice for himself in the direction of British foreign policy. Chamberlain was determined that while he was Foreign Secretary British diplomacy would only have one spokesman and Cecil's request that he should be a minister within the Foreign Office was firmly resisted.[17] One of the first impressions Chamberlain gained in his new office was that in recent years Britain appeared to have spoken with two voices – one at Geneva and the other in London – 'and our reputation for good faith has suffered in consequence.' Unity of control and representation in foreign policy had to be restored.[18] Chamberlain gave an early indication of his attitude towards the control of foreign policy when he opposed Cecil's request that, as Chancellor of the Duchy, he should receive all Foreign Office papers as of right. As the experienced permanent head of the Foreign Office warned:

Were he to be given them, it is quite conceivable that he would use the fact, sooner or later, as a basis for claiming a special right to take a more strenuous part in the conduct of foreign affairs in general and League of Nations affairs in particular, than may perhaps be agreeable to you.[19]

Chamberlain recognised that, in relation to the League of Nations in particular, he and Cecil held rather different views. Cecil, of course, had been one of the early advocates of an international organisation during the Great War, and the League became for him a body of almost spiritual significance. Chamberlain's vision of the League was altogether more circumscribed. Cecil later expressed the difference in these terms:

He thought of it as just one cog in the diplomatic machine, to be used or not at the discretion of the Cabinet. I regarded it as the essential international organ for the maintenance of peace.[20]

Not surprisingly it was not long before Cecil began to chafe under the restrictions placed upon his ministerial powers. By March 1925 he was already 'beset with doubts' as to whether he was doing any good at all as a member of the Government. The idea that he would be specially consulted by Chamberlain on League matters had proved to be 'a pure illusion.'[21] In the event his resignation was delayed until 1927.

Cecil was not the only Cabinet minister in a position to challenge Chamberlain's monopoly of the direction of foreign policy. The role of the Empire, and especially the self-governing colonies, could not be ignored, particularly after the enhancement of their international status occasioned by the Great War and Peace Conferences. In Leo Amery, the Colonial Secretary (and from June 1925 also Dominions Secretary), Chamberlain faced a sometimes formidable Cabinet critic and one with whom he was no longer as closely aligned on personal grounds as at the time of his father's campaign for tariff reform. In his first speech as Foreign Secretary Chamberlain spoke as if the imperial alliance of the war years was still in being:

The first thoughts of an Englishman on appointment to the office of Foreign

Secretary must be that he speaks in the name, not of Great Britain only, but of the British Dominions beyond the seas, and that it is his imperative duty to preserve in word and act the diplomatic unity of the British Empire. Our interests are one.[22]

The experience of his Foreign Secretaryship, however, would show that Joseph Chamberlain's imperial vision had gone forever and that the Dominions were anxious now to pursue their own foreign policies rather than a single imperial policy, even if the mother country were prepared to concede to them a voice in its creation.

   Winston Churchill, Chancellor of the Exchequer throughout Baldwin's second government, was an even more formidable Cabinet colleague than Leo Amery. His long experience of government, his forceful personality, his clear-cut views on the major questions affecting Britain's world role and the seniority of his office combined to make him a significant voice in Cabinet discussions on foreign policy. Chamberlain soon came up against Churchill's fixed convictions on the question of relations with the Soviet Union. As a leading architect of Britain's Soviet policy at the end of the Great War, Churchill was unlikely now to take a passive line. 'The more I reflect on the matter,' he told the Foreign Secretary, 'the more sure I am that we should revoke the recognition of the Soviet Government which was decided on by MacDonald.'[23]

   Like most Chancellors, Churchill was anxious to curtail expenditure and the heavy cost of foreign and defence policy was an early focus of his incisive mind. In marked contrast to the role for which he is best remembered in the 1930s, the Chancellor set out to persuade his Cabinet colleagues to trim the defence budget. Within six weeks of coming to office he warned that to accept proposed increases in armaments, 'is to sterilize and paralyse the whole policy of the Government. There will be nothing for the taxpayer and nothing for social reform.'[24] Churchill believed that defence planning should be based upon the assumption that Britain would not have to fight a first-class naval power for the next twenty years. His determination to scale down the country's commitment in the Far East created problems not only for Chamberlain but for all who conducted British foreign policy in the 1930s. The understandable priority which Churchill gave to economy naturally led to a different emphasis in his attitude to international questions from that given by Chamberlain. The Chancellor urged Chamberlain to place war debt reclamation from France and Italy among the leading objectives of his foreign policy.[25] But when Churchill went to Paris to negotiate on the question of war debts, the Foreign Secretary was not a little uneasy:

I had far sooner that he sacrificed some hundreds of thousands and smoothed our political path than that he collected a little more money at the expense of our good relations with America and the Allies.[26]

As with every Foreign Secretary before and since, Chamberlain's most important Cabinet colleague was the Prime Minister himself. Chamberlain's long political association with Stanley Baldwin is among the most complex and important of his career. Graduates of the same Cambridge College, the two men missed each other there by a term, but their later careers are repeatedly intertwined. This is not the place to enter the wider debate on Baldwin, a man whose political reputation has undergone more violent fluctuation than that of most public figures. But certainly Chamberlain never fully understood Baldwin or appreciated his very real qualities. By the 1930s he regarded him with almost total contempt. In 1931 he wrote:

The truth is that he has no House of Commons gifts, can't debate or think or act quickly . . . and with it all he is so terribly complacent and talks more than ever of what I, I, I will do till he makes me sick.[27]

Yet Baldwin's ascendancy in British politics could not have been sustained for so long had his abilities been as insubstantial as Chamberlain sometimes maintained. Though the years 1924–29 were among the more cordial of their association, Bridgeman was probably right when he noted at the end of this period that Chamberlain 'never seemed quite at home in Baldwin's Cabinet'.[28] Chamberlain found it difficult to accept as leader a man whom he regarded in all ways as his junior. It was the same slightly condescending attitude he felt towards Bonar Law, only deeper and more obvious. Having held high office before Baldwin even entered parliament, having had Baldwin as his junior at the Exchequer after the War, and being convinced that Baldwin's rapid rise within the party had been occasioned solely by the exceptional circumstances of 1922–3, Chamberlain's relations with the man who was now Prime Minister were always likely to be strained and tinged with resentment. Nor, more specifically, could he easily forget the events of October 1922 or forgive Baldwin's part in them. Chamberlain's petulant response to Baldwin's decision over Sir Robert Horne at the formation of the government has already been noted. Yet Chamberlain's advice to Lloyd George in 1921 that Horne should remain at the Board of Trade had also been ignored, without the same sort of reaction. To his sister he wrote revealingly shortly before the Conservatives took office:

I have accepted Baldwin's leadership and cannot jump his claim to first place in the House. I am often sorely tempted to spring in, half rise from my seat and then remember that it's his job, fall back and wait for him till it is too late.[29]

In the light of this unpromising basis for a political partnership, the

Chamberlain-Baldwin relationship between 1924 and 1929 was less fractious than might have been expected. This reflected less a personal rapport between the two men than Baldwin's general attitude towards the premiership and his own lack of interest in foreign affairs. He clearly regarded his most important task as Prime Minister to be the choosing of his subordinate colleagues, but having selected the best available men he had no intention of interfering in the day-to-day running of their departmental affairs. This was particularly the case in relation to foreign policy, where even in the 1930s Baldwin found it difficult to interest himself. When challenged on this point, he is reputed to have said 'I can't do everything. What is the use of having a Foreign Secretary? It is his job.'[30] The result was that Chamberlain, unlike many of his successors, was rarely inconvenienced by prime ministerial interference. After nearly a year in office he commented:

[Baldwin] leaves me to go my own way, pursue my own policy and face my own difficulties. I presume that he has some confidence in my handling of my own job and I suspect that he feels that he knows less than nothing about foreign affairs and has no opinion to offer. On the whole it works well tho' sometimes I wish that he showed a little more interest and gave a more active support.[31]

After leaving office Chamberlain claimed he had never been able to get a decision out of the Prime Minister.[32]

In fact Baldwin, though very conscious of Chamberlain's weaknesses, had a reasonably good opinion of him, dating back to his time as Financial Secretary when Chamberlain had been Chancellor. He was initially nervous about appointing him to the Foreign Office on the ground of the rigidity of his mind,[33] but was clearly impressed by Chamberlain's early successes in his new post. At the end of 1926 Baldwin wrote:

It has been a great comfort throughout this year to feel that I never need worry about foreign affairs and to feel perfect confidence in the judgement and wisdom of the Foreign Secretary and for all this I am grateful.[34]

The result was that Chamberlain could usually rely on at least passive support from the Prime Minister in Cabinet and, in fact, after the main lines of his policy had been determined in March 1925, had little difficulty in carrying the Cabinet with him. When on occasions thereafter the Cabinet did try to reassert itself, Chamberlain, always rather intolerant of criticism, tended to react indignantly:

The Cabinets have been very tiring and contentious and I have been disappointed at receiving so little support from some of my colleagues and having my informed and considered opinions swept aside so lightly by them under pressure from the Daily Mail and the backbenches who don't know what I know of the state of Europe. ...[35]

A final factor in the generally harmonious relationship between Prime Minister and Foreign Secretary between 1924 and 1929 was that in this period Chamberlain's opinion of his leader, based largely on his handling of domestic politics, also began to improve. As early as January 1925 Chamberlain was greatly impressed by Baldwin's performance in Cabinet on the question of the political levy.[36] The Prime Minister's position, which had been 'steadily growing ever since he formed ... his second Administration', was 'enormously strengthened by his handling of the [General] strike' in 1926.[37] He had, Chamberlain felt, become 'a great figure in the country' by virtue of the personal confidence which he inspired in all men irrespective of their political creed.[38] When the government turned its mind to the question of Trade Union legislation, Chamberlain placed full confidence in the Prime Minister's judgment:

I will back your experience and judgement in these matters whether they coincide with my own views or not, for I know that your objects are mine, and as to means I shall trust confidently your more intimate knowledge of this subject.[39]

Inside the Foreign Office Chamberlain rapidly established a marked ascendancy. He made all the major appointments himself, unchallenged even by the Treasury and consulting only the Permanent Under-Secretary.[40] This was perhaps only natural in a figure of his seniority. Having first entered the Cabinet over two decades earlier, he had ministerial experience which only Balfour and Churchill could match. His personal relations with his staff, including the Permanent Under-Secretaries, Crowe and then Tyrrell, were generally good. Some even saw the lighter side of Chamberlain's character which was so rarely apparent in his public life:

Is it essential to Your Lordship's well-being or to the enjoyment of Your Lordship's proper rest on Sundays that such formal signatures as are required from the Secretary of State ... should be habitually required of Your Lordship's poor slave after midnight or on Sundays? ... But if this is merely a practical joke ... why damn it, sir, it has gone on long enough, and I beg you henceforth to send them to my Private Secretary with instructions to choose a convenient moment to put them before me or, by heavens! there will be a deuce of a row. ...[41]

When Chamberlain took office decisions were required on a number of important issues. The Foreign Secretary was given the chair of a powerful Cabinet committee inquiring into the Zinoviev letter, which had played such a large part in the outcome of the recent election. The committee· reported on 19 November that the letter was indeed authentic. This finding was announced in parliament on.10 December and five days later Chamberlain added weight to his committee's conclusion by saying that the government's knowledge was derived from four separate sources.[42]

The Foreign Secretary was also involved in another major decision for which the Baldwin government is well remembered, the return to the Gold Standard. While Labour was still in office, Chamberlain had chaired a committee to consider financial questions including the restoration of the Gold Standard. Despite hearing several adverse views, the committee reported unanimously in favour of this move and Chamberlain urged Churchill to act promptly:

I feel sure that, if you make your announcement with *decisive confidence* on your own part, the operation will now be found, all things considered, an easy one. . . . If we do not do it, we shall not stay where we were, but inevitably *start a retrograde movement.*[43]

But the most important of the outstanding foreign policy issues confronting the new Secretary of State was the future of the Geneva Protocol, a visionary and idealistic agreement negotiated between Ramsay MacDonald and his French opposite number, Edouard Herriot, to supplement and strengthen the Covenant of the League of Nations. Until this question was settled British policy would, Chamberlain recognised, remain 'hand to mouth.'[44] The Protocol was designed to close all loopholes which allowed for the waging of private war without penalty. Under its provisions aggression was clearly defined and arbitration would become compulsory in all disputes. All signatories capable of doing so would be obliged to enforce sanctions on the aggressor. The clear implication was that Britain, on signing the Protocol, might become the world's policeman with unlimited obligations to fulfil. Chamberlain's reaction to the Protocol must be seen in the context of his attitude to the central foreign policy problems which, since the end of the war, had defied the ingenuity of British statesmen to resolve them.

The major failing of the Treaty of Versailles was its inability to settle the question of Franco-German relations on other than a temporary basis. The war left Germany still potentially the strongest nation in Europe but embittered beneath the more punitive clauses of the peace settlement. By contrast France sought desperately to perpetuate the essentially artificial verdict of 1919, seeking the guarantees of her future security which only a major ally could ensure. Chamberlain understood better than many who had gone before him the dominant sentiment in French diplomacy. As early as January 1920 he had noted that the French 'live in nightmare horror of Germany', while five years later he heard Herriot say 'I tell you I look forward with terror to her [Germany] making war upon us again in ten years.'[45] But, again unlike many of his predecessors, Chamberlain was 'as true and warm a friend of France as any Englishman can be.'[46] In July 1924 he had informed the House of Commons that 'we should make the maintenance of the Entente with France the cardinal object of our policy.'[47] By easing French fears of Germany, Chamberlain hoped to exercise a restraining influence on French policy and promote a general relaxation of European tension in which the causes of legitimate German grievance could be safely removed. If moreover Germany could be conciliated it would obviate the danger that she might one day throw herself into the arms of Russia in an anti-western bloc.[48] But the Germany to which concessions might be made would have to be one which accepted its legitimate obligations under the Treaty of Versailles.[49] Chamberlain's thoughts were not confined to the present. He looked to a date perhaps forty years on when German strength would have returned and when the prospect of war would again cloud the horizon unless its risks were too great to be incurred and the actual conditions 'too tolerable to be jeopardised on a gambler's throw.'[50] 'Appeasement' in the mind of the elder of the Chamberlain brothers was an entirely noble concept. But he was convinced that there could be no effective agreement between France and Germany to which Britain was not prepared to be a party.[51] Baldwin must have been aware of the general thrust of Chamberlain's thinking and there was clearly a determination on the Prime Minister's part that Conservative foreign policy should be sensibly modified from that associated in earlier years with Lord Curzon.[52]

The central question for British policy makers was the extent to which Britain, with her aims and ambitions largely satisfied by the outcome of the War, could now divorce herself from the affairs of the continent, reassured and safe within her island fortress. Advice on this fundamental issue was not lacking for the new Foreign Secretary. To his right stood committed isolationists such as Churchill, Amery and Birkenhead, supported by the Beaverbrook press. These men thought of Britain as an Imperial rather than a European power. Chamberlain clearly understood the strength of the opinion which they represented. Interestingly he told Stresemann in 1927 that if he were obliged at that date to bring the Locarno treaties before Parliament again, he would not be able to get them accepted.[53] To his left were internationalists who, with the exception of Cecil, were not well represented in government, but who had important extra-parliamentary backing in the League of Nations Union.[54]

On this basic issue Chamberlain had decided views. 'If we withdraw from Europe I say without hesitation that the chance of permanent peace is gone.'[55] He clearly believed that Britain occupied a unique position to 'do what no other nation on the face of the earth can do' and decide the great question of war and peace.[56] He was, he said, 'much more of an "European" than most of my countrymen, for I have a clearer perception than they of the inextricable way in which our interests are bound up with

every possibility of the European situation.'[57] Situated so near to the
shores of the continent, Britain could not, in Chamberlain's mind, be
indifferent to what went on there. The important question though was to
define the extent and limits of British commitment and involvement.[58] In
1926 he told the Imperial Conference that owing to scientific development
the true defence of the country was no longer the Channel, but the
Rhine.[59] It was on this point that the universality implied by the Protocol,
and indeed by the League itself, posed problems for the Foreign Secretary.

Chamberlain certainly did not consider himself an opponent of the
League, but neither did he share the grandiose vision of its potentialities
entertained by members of the League of Nations Union. The instinct of
the practical politician in Chamberlain prevented him from being carried
away in extravagant flights of fancy about what the League could achieve.
He recognised it as a fact of contemporary diplomacy which could not be
ignored in the current state of British public opinion. It was serving a
useful purpose and, providing not too much was expected of it or
attempted by it, it might steadily grow in strength and influence.[60] But
Chamberlain's firm conviction was that the League's true line of progress
was to proceed from the particular to the general and not the other way
around.[61] The chief value of the League lay not in the sanctions which it
might impose once war broke out, but in its capacity to prevent war in the
first place. 'Its friends should work in the spirit of the missionary rather
than the hangman.'[62] Certainly Chamberlain's regular attendance at the
League did much to enhance its prestige and convince Europe that Britain
took it seriously. Even so his original decision to go in person to Geneva
may have had no other motive than to prevent Cecil going in his stead and
putting forward his own League-based ideas as British policy.[63]

Chamberlain's general thinking on foreign policy inevitably
conditioned his approach to the Geneva Protocol. His gut reaction was to
resist anything which served to extend the obligations into which Britain
had already entered. So while he was anxious to stress that he undertook
his new duties without *idées fixes*, it was never likely that a Conservative
government with Chamberlain at the Foreign Office would ratify the
Protocol. Indeed there is no clear indication that even MacDonald's
Labour government would have been able to do so. An early exchange of
letters with Robert Cecil showed the direction in which Chamberlain's
thoughts were moving. In answer to Cecil's essentially enthusiastic
response, Chamberlain pointed out that while in theory the Protocol
imposed no new obligations beyond those already inherent in the
Covenant, 'all our old obligations are very much tightened up and
rendered more precise and specific.'[64]

On 25 November 1924 the Foreign Secretary urged Baldwin to set up a sub-committee of the Committee of Imperial Defence to examine the implications of the Protocol. He was clearly anxious that whatever conclusion was reached should be national rather than party political in nature, and called for the inclusion of Haldane and Grey to represent the other two parties.[65] A few weeks later Chamberlain set his own staff in the Foreign Office to work on a comprehensive review of the state of Europe. The Protocol was unlikely to be acceptable to the self-governing colonies, while America also felt serious misgivings. The C.I.D. showed itself totally opposed to the Protocol and on 16 December assigned to a sub-committee under Maurice Hankey, the Cabinet Secretary, the task of seeing whether it could be amended in such a way as to make it acceptable to Britain. This body did not report until 13 February. By the end of January, however, Chamberlain could confidently assert that there was 'not the slightest chance of our ratifying the Protocol as it stands, or indeed, without such large changes as would make it very different from what it is.'[66] The conclusion of the Foreign Office staff was that the best hope for European peace lay in a firm British commitment to France. It was a conclusion which Chamberlain accepted. At the back of his mind was the idea that eventually, 'but I must admit only eventually',[67] a pact with France might be extended into a reciprocal agreement with Germany. He was now ready, moreover, to define the extent to which Britain should rightly be involved in the affairs of Europe:

I would say broadly that in Western Europe we are a partner; that comparatively speaking in Eastern Europe our role should be that of a disinterested *amicus curiae*. Our safety in certain circumstances is bound up with that of France or Belgium or Holland. If this be secured I do not believe that it is bound up with Roumania for example.[68]

Hankey's thoughts too were moving in the same direction, though without great enthusiasm. Assuming that either a pact with France or the Protocol was unavoidable, since to offer neither would seriously damage Anglo-French relations, Hankey believed the former was 'by far the less objectionable' as a choice of evils. The commitments of a pact were definite, limited geographically and their application was within Britain's own control.[69] But Chamberlain's warm feelings towards France were not shared by many important members of the Cabinet, only too mindful of her wayward policy since the end of the War, especially at the time of the Ruhr invasion. The Foreign Secretary was, in his own words, 'the most pro-French member of the Government.'[70] Churchill, in particular, opposed the idea of giving France the sort of guarantee she sought and argued that only by standing aloof could Britain ascertain the degree of importance which France attached to her support.[71] He spoke out forcefully at the C.I.D. on 13 February and again six days later, when he claimed that a bi-lateral pact with France would be 'a tremendous risk'.[72] In addition, both the Liberal and Labour parties were ready to start on the war path at the first suggestion that the Foreign Secretary was contemplating a regional pact.[73]

Matters came to a head at two meetings of the Cabinet in the first week of March. Chamberlain was due to leave for Geneva to announce Britain's rejection of the Protocol, but he was determined to offer an alternative policy. With such trenchant opposition to the idea of an Anglo-French pact the Foreign Secretary was obliged to fall back upon a proposal which had come from a very different source some weeks before. On 20 January the German government had put forward proposals for a mutual security pact relating to the Rhineland. They were moved by concern that France was unlikely to evacuate Cologne by the date fixed at Versailles,[74] and by a mistaken belief that an Anglo-French military alliance was imminent. In the inception of this move the British ambassador in Berlin, Lord D'Abernon, played an important role. He believed that a British commitment to France, by reviving the war-time alliance, would cause great offence in Germany, make European pacification more difficult and drive Germany into the embrace of Russia. It would also be contrary to Britain's traditional role of seeking to maintain the European balance of power.[75]

Chamberlain's initial response to the German proposal was at best equivocal. Even if he had at the back of his mind a long-term arrangement with Germany, there was no doubt that he wished to settle matters with France first. Indeed at the Guildhall in November he had spoken of Britain's desire to secure a 'more intimate friendship' with her former Allies than with other countries.[76] At the time the German proposals arrived in London, moreover, the Foreign Secretary was still hopeful that he could carry the Cabinet along with him in the quest for an Anglo-French pact. Accordingly, while assuring the German ambassador that he welcomed evidence that Germany appreciated the reality behind French fears, he argued that the new proposals could not be discussed until Britain's attitude towards the Protocol and the question of French security had been defined.[77] Chamberlain suspected that Stresemann, the German Foreign Minister, intended to make his proposed pact dependent on total Allied evacuation of the Rhineland and saw in it also an attempt to drive a wedge between Britain and France. The German request that the proposals should not yet be disclosed in Paris merely confirmed this impression. The German démarche was, Chamberlain concluded, premature and inopportune and he even declined to give the proposals his backing in principle.[78] When Germany next sent a similar memorandum

The British delegation at Locarno (Birmingham University)

LOCARNO.

Telegram to Sir W. Tyrrell, October 15, 1925.
D. 12.25 p.m. October 15 1925.

Private.

Following from Secretary of State for Sir W.
Tyrrell.
Cock-a-doodle-do!!

XIII   Success in the negotiations! (Birmingham University)

XIV Signed menu card from Locarno (Birmingham University)

Crowe gave Chamberlain a worrying picture of the extent of Cabinet hostility to the Foreign Secretary's policies. He had never heard even Ramsay MacDonald in his most woolly-headed pronouncements talk 'such utter rubbish as Mr Amery poured forth.' The attitude of Churchill and Birkenhead left Crowe with the clear impression that their aim was not that of dealing with the problem on its merits, but to make Chamberlain's position untenable.[90]

The Foreign Secretary was understandably concerned that the Cabinet, in his absence, was going back on its previous decisions, and took particular exception when, from Crowe's account, it appeared that Baldwin had done little to support him. He was also shocked that Birkenhead, 'the friend who owes most to me', seemed to be working hard against him. Not surprisingly he made it clear that, if Crowe's report was an accurate representation of the situation in London, he would have to resign. To his wife Chamberlain set out the situation in a thinly disguised code:

If the servants get out of hand, it is Mrs. Watson's [Baldwin's] business (I do not mean in her capacity as plain cook where she is admirable, but as head of the household) to keep them in order. And I yesterday sent her a wire to say that either my apartment must be run as I wished and the meals served as I ordered them or I should leave her lodgings . . . I can't do my work if the other tenants are always making a racket and sticking their brooms and buckets just where I am bound to fall over them.[91]

Baldwin did his best to calm the situation. The informal meeting of ministers must not, he stressed, be taken as in any sense constituting a Cabinet decision. Though the attitude of Birkenhead and Churchill indicated that there might be difficulties ahead, Baldwin implied that he would be ready to support the Foreign Secretary when it was clear what line Herriot was taking towards the German proposals.[92] After a meeting with the Prime Minister on his return from Europe, Chamberlain felt reassured:

Mrs. Watson says that she will insist upon my having my own way about my own apartment and that the interference of the other lodgers with my comfort shall be stopped.[93]

Baldwin's backing, together with the death of Curzon, proved decisive and on 20 March the Cabinet authorised Chamberlain to tell parliament that the German government's proposals represented the most promising basis for European security, that they could not be put into effect without British co-operation, and that this co-operation would be limited to Germany's western frontiers.

With hindsight it appears that the Cabinet's decision of 20 March was the turning point in the diplomatic process which culminated at Locarno in October. Though minor alarms and difficulties lay ahead, Chamberlain had in fact now overcome the most serious obstacles in his path. A major parliamentary debate in late June left the Foreign Secretary well satisfied. Even Churchill told him that he ought to be pleased 'for your fence is behind you'. As far as British public opinion was concerned, Chamberlain concluded that 'we really have the pact in our pocket.'[94] There were still problems posed by Leo Amery about whether the Dominions would be able to associate themselves with any pact, but by the time the Powers met at Locarno there was no doubt that Chamberlain had the reins of British diplomacy firmly in his own hands. Baldwin even ruled out the idea that any other Cabinet minister should accompany him to the conference.

Throughout the spring and summer of 1925 Chamberlain worked assiduously to bring about the Pact of Mutual Guarantee, which, though not his in its inception, he now adopted with the devotion of a natural parent. The process was one for which the Foreign Secretary was well equipped. Working with patience and tact in close co-operation with his ambassadors in Paris and Berlin, he calmly set about a difficult set of negotiations, clearing away misunderstandings, narrowing the issues of disagreement through the exchange of written notes and only holding the crucial meetings when a firm basis for agreement had been secured.[95] When the Canadian Vincent Massey met Chamberlain for the first time at the Imperial Conference in 1926 he produced a telling assessment of the Foreign Secretary's qualities:

Austen Chamberlain did not seem to me to be a man of first-rate mind, but he obviously possessed high character and the sort of disinterested goodness and amateur methods that now and then have enabled British statesmen to play notable roles in negotiations with foreign diplomats, even when the latter have been armed with subtler minds and the traditional techniques.[96]

The achievement of Locarno was, thought Leo Amery, a tribute to Chamberlain's 'plain good intent', which Edmund Burke rated above all other qualities in public life.[97]

The months of negotiation which now ensued confirmed Chamberlain's basic attitudes towards France and Germany, formed nearly forty years earlier. In doing so, however, it became difficult for Chamberlain or Britain to maintain the even-handed approach in the years ahead which was supposedly central to the Pact proposals. This was particularly the case once Aristide Briand became French Foreign Minister in April. The co-operation and growing affection between Chamberlain and Briand was a striking characteristic of the months ahead. Chamberlain found his French opposite number 'amazingly reasonable'. Briand almost took his 'breath away by his liberality, his conciliatoriness, his strong and manifest desire for peace'.[98] Germany, however, was a different matter. Even before the negotiations proper got under way, Chamberlain wrote:

Successive German governments appear to me seldom to do the right thing and even more seldom to do the right thing at the right time or in the right way. They seem much more anxious to have a grievance than to promote a settlement.

He was at a loss to know how to promote better relations with a people who would not allow themselves to be helped and who continually played into the hands of those elements most hostile to them.[99] A typical example of German tactlessness was to publish a White Book on the Separatist Movement in the Rhineland which revived all the bitterest memories of the French occupation of the Ruhr in 1923.[100] At one moment of exasperation Chamberlain noted that 'if the French showed a tenth part of their [the Germans'] unreason, there would be no pact and no peace.'[101] When France replied positively to the German proposals it seemed for a while as if Berlin wanted to draw back from its own scheme. The Germans were like a woman who 'having had a liaison is mortified to find herself giving birth to a baby and still more so when the baby loudly proclaims its maternity.'[102] But if the Germans did draw back, 'all the world will see that Germany does not mean peace and will have to frame its policy in consequence.'[103] As the long process of negotiation neared its conclusion, Chamberlain still argued that the German attitude was 'niggling, provocative, crooked.' The problem, he surmised, derived less from Stresemann than from nationalist elements in the German Cabinet. From first to last every obstacle to the success of the negotiations had come from Berlin.[104]

Only very early on in the proceedings did Chamberlain have serious misgivings about the French attitude. In mid May he was 'getting a little uneasy' about Paris's commitment to the success of the negotiations.[105] When the French draft reply to the German proposals was received a few days later, it appeared that France, because of her alliances with the states of Eastern Europe, was looking for the same sort of commitment from Britain for Germany's eastern frontiers as for the Franco-German border. To resist such a tendency was central to Chamberlain's objectives. If Britain's obligations in the two areas were to be the same then, in Chamberlain's words:

I should be placed in the dilemma of either exalting our obligations to the eastern neighbours to the level of those which I thought we ought to undertake in regard to the western frontiers, or of whittling down our obligations on the west to those which public opinion might be ready to accept in regard to the east.[106]

It was the British conception which prevailed. Briand and Chamberlain agreed that Britain could not offer additional guarantees beyond her obligations under the Covenant to the *status quo* in Eastern Europe, but that France would be free to aid her Eastern allies without British interference. To Chamberlain's mind, the final French note in response to the German proposals was 'a great act of peace.'[107] By the time that the Powers met at Locarno in October, there was little left to divide the British and French delegations.[108]

It was a *sine qua non* of Chamberlain's scheme that Germany should join the League of Nations unconditionally. By doing so she would tacitly accept the provisions of the Treaty of Versailles, though gaining also the right to work for the modification of the treaty from within the League system. If, however, Germany tried to make her membership conditional, 'it would destroy our whole policy and thrust us all back into Poincaréism.' Though Chamberlain believed that it had been a mistake to include the 'War Guilt' clause in the Treaty of Versailles, that was an established fact which could not now be undone.[109] On the very eve of the Locarno meeting, however, the Germans insisted that the War Guilt question must be settled before any further progress on the Pact was attempted. 'The Germans continue stupid to the last', cried Chamberlain despairingly.[110] But the Foreign Secretary stood his ground and the Germans gave way. Yet the effect on Chamberlain's mind was important and lasting:

At every stage the Germans sow distrust in my mind. At every stage Briand disproves the common assertion that the difficulty is now with France.[111]

Finally it was agreed that a Five Power Conference should be held in the Palace of Justice in Locarno near the Swiss-Italian border, a location designed to suit the convenience of the Italian dictator, Mussolini. The conference itself passed without serious difficulty. Chamberlain was in his element. His old-fashioned courtesy and consideration for small details contributed to the warm atmosphere in which the conference proceeded. The British delegation managed to arrange that the closing ceremonies at which the Pact was initialled[112] took place on 16 October, Chamberlain's sixty-second birthday. The scene was an emotional one, as was perhaps inevitable for statesmen of a generation which had so recently seen Europe ravaged by war. Chamberlain and Briand both wept with joy. Briand embraced Luther. Mussolini kissed Mrs Chamberlain's hands. Crowds danced on the village square while church bells rang out across the lake and fireworks illuminated the night sky.

Congratulations soon flooded in to the Foreign Secretary. Baldwin telegraphed his appreciation of Chamberlain's 'personal creation' and his success in a matter which had defied the efforts of every statesman since the War.[113] Balfour was even more fulsome in his praise. November 1918 might mark the end of the Great War, but October 1925 would mark the beginning of the Great Peace. The verdict of history would ensure a pre-eminent place for Chamberlain in an event which might well prove a turning point in the history of civilisation.[114] Even Leo Amery, despite his earlier misgivings, offered 'a thousand congratulations'.[115] Neville Chamberlain was gratified to think that after so many disappointments in his political life his brother had now secured a real triumph. His international standing would help convince the House of Commons that he was 'a bigger statesman than they thought.'[116] Chamberlain, himself, was tired, but happy. 'Our prestige,' he told the Prime Minister, 'is a thing to be proud of at this moment – and to cherish.'[117] After much searching of his non-conformist conscience, Chamberlain accepted the Garter in recognition of his achievement. Neville suggested that he might as well take a peerage. If one was going to have a title one might as well go the whole hog and take a good one.[118]

What though had been achieved? Whatever it was, Chamberlain was ready to take the credit. With delight he repeated Briand's remark, 'Ah, sans lui, je ne l'aurais jamais tenté.'[119] To his sister Ida he stressed that the British government's policy was 'found by me, imposed upon the Cabinet by me . . . reimposed by my telegram . . . to the P.M. . . . It depended for its success on my personal handling of each situation as it arose and on the confidence which French and Germans felt . . . because I was . . . foreign secretary.'[120] Under the Locarno agreements Britain, France, Germany, Belgium and Italy agreed to observe the demilitarisation of the Rhineland, to defend the existing borders between Germany and France and Germany and Belgium, and to render military assistance to any signatory who fell victim to a flagrant violation of these promises. In addition the Pact included arbitration conventions between Germany and her neighbours, France, Belgium, Poland and Czechoslovakia. Chamberlain clearly believed that the agreements were of fundamental importance and marked the real dividing line between the years of war and the peace that would follow.[121] But at the same time he fully understood that Locarno was a beginning and not an end, and he was somewhat alarmed at the extent and generosity of the public recognition accorded him. This, he thought, would rapidly fade once it was realised that 'there are still difficulties to be faced and still a long road to travel.'[122] A year later he was still reminding Briand that 'our work is as yet far from accomplished.'[123]

Yet any objective assessment of Chamberlain's achievement at Locarno must start from the fundamental truth that in its origins the Pact was not the brainchild of Chamberlain but of Stresemann and the German government, men who were first and foremost German nationalists. The extent to which Germany's policy and Chamberlain's policy really coincided is not easy to assess. Chamberlain gave different impressions of the strength of his wish to involve Germany in an Anglo-French Pact. At times he made it appear that the German proposals had only hastened his own plans. At others it seemed that they had been sensibly modified.[124] But this cannot alter the fact that in a very real sense Locarno should be viewed as an achievement of German foreign policy.

The fundamental criticism that has been levelled against Locarno is that, in adding a specific guarantee to the Franco-German frontier, it had the effect of dividing up Europe into areas of first and second-class importance, thereby implying that there were frontiers in Europe – creations of the Versailles settlement – for whose defence Britain would not be ready to fight. From a British point of view Locarno was all about limiting commitments. 'I do not think,' Chamberlain told the House of Commons in the debate on the ratification of the Pact, 'that the obligations of this country could be more narrowly circumscribed to the vital national interest than they are in the Treaty of Locarno.'[125] As late as April 1935 Baldwin and Chamberlain both brushed aside criticism of Britain's non-intervention in Manchuria on the grounds that the country's settled policy excluded general intervention beyond the framework of Locarno.[126] Chamberlain believed that the Franco-German border was the most sensitive frontier in Europe, that Britain was vitally involved in this area and that no progress towards general pacification could be made while this question remained unsettled. There can be no doubt, moreover, that Locarno did serve to lessen tension in this troubled region. Additionally, a Pact involving Germany was a distinct improvement on a bilateral Anglo-French alliance, since the latter could only have served to perpetuate the era of victor and vanquished, begun in 1918–19 and inherent in the structure of the League as then created. The Foreign Secretary held that a wide and general guarantee could carry no conviction whatever and give no sense of security to those whom Britain in theory guaranteed. The important point, then, was to define the extent of British commitment and as Chamberlain said, in perhaps his most famous remark, the Polish Corridor was something 'for which no British Government ever will or ever can risk the bones of a British grenadier.'[127]

Chamberlain recognised the difficulty which this created. Soon after he came to power, the Polish minister in London pointed out that a guarantee to France and Belgium would be almost an indication to Germany that she could attack Poland with impunity. It would point to an attack on Poland as the easiest way for Germany to reopen the questions settled by Versailles without bringing Britain into the struggle.[128] Chamberlain tried to argue that in endeavouring to make peace more secure in the west,

Britain was in no sense trying to license or legitimise changes in the treaty position in the east, but his reasoning was unconvincing and too much based upon hope rather than expectation:

I did not believe that any sensible man in Germany wished for a new partition of Poland or contemplated an attack upon her, and it was so much in the interest of Poland to be on good terms with Germany that, if we could once get away from the bitterness and hatred left by past history, I believed that Poland and Germany would find their common interest in coming to terms.[129]

Security in the east was a problem for the future, but not one in whose resolution Britain would be intimately involved.[130] Chamberlain argued that Germany's entry into the League and her full acceptance of the obligations which this imposed, together with the arbitration treaties contained in the Locarno Pact, would remove the fears of Germany's eastern neighbours.[131] The premise behind this argument was clearly the sort of gentlemanly good conduct in diplomacy which Chamberlain epitomised and which he expected others to emulate. Yet nothing could alter the fact that after Locarno certain parts of the Versailles settlement were endowed with a greater degree of sanctity than others. In fact the Foreign Secretary may well have envisaged a long-term modification of the German-Polish border:

But if she comes into the League and plays her part there in a friendly and conciliatory spirit I myself believe that within a reasonable number of years she will find herself in a position where her economic and commercial support is so necessary and her political friendship so desirable to Poland that, without having recourse to the League machinery, she will be able to make a friendly arrangement on her own account directly with the Poles. ... If the German public and press could be restrained from talking so much about the eastern frontiers, they might get more quickly to a solution.[132]

Even within its own limits Locarno did not give a blanket British guarantee to the Franco-German frontier. Chamberlain had no wish to be dragged into recurrent Franco-German quarrels, irrespective of the nature or cause of the dispute. The violation therefore had to be a 'flagrant' one and to constitute 'unprovoked aggression', with Britain left to judge whether both conditions applied. Interestingly, Leo Amery, during the course of the negotiations which led to the Pact, surmised that 'in the end what we shall commit ourselves ... to is something so remote and contingent that we are not likely in fact ever to be called on to intervene.'[133] It was in the hope of limiting the chances of Britain being obliged to come in that Chamberlain sought to place the Pact in the context of the League so that no party would have to resort to war until the methods of arbitration and conciliation by the Council had been exhausted.[134] Though it is difficult to see a man of Chamberlain's integrity attempting to renege on Britain's obligations, his inclination was to view Locarno more as a guarantee of permanent peace than as a statement of commitments which might one day have to be honoured. It was meant as a deterrent which would remove the sort of uncertainty which had existed in 1914 about whether Britain would intervene in the event of an attack on France. The Pact was, of course, mutual, yet it is difficult to envisage Chamberlain recommending war against France in the event of a French attack upon Germany.[135] Hankey was rather alarmed at Chamberlain's reluctance to have the military implications of the Pact considered by the service chiefs and the C.I.D. 'Some day', the Cabinet Secretary warned, 'the cheque might be presented and we should have to honour it.'[136]

Locarno should also be considered in the context of the League of Nations, the body which had been set up to guarantee the peace settlement. On the very day that the Pact was initialled Chamberlain wrote to assure the League's Secretary-General that 'we have done nothing to injure League or Covenant'.[137] He had also told Briand that the pivotal idea of the Locarno Treaties was that there would be recourse to the League whenever trouble arose. Yet it is noticeable that this period saw a marked deterioration in the Foreign Secretary's relations with the League of Nations Union where support for the Geneva Protocol remained strong.[138] Chamberlain argued that Locarno should be seen as a supplement to the League in that it added specific obligations to the general ones imposed by the Covenant.[139] But it is possible to interpret the Pact in another sense. After six years of trying to secure peace through the machinery of the League, culminating with the Geneva Protocol, the Powers were now negotiating an agreement outside its framework, thus advertising to the world the League's failure to fulfil its self-imposed task. Certainly there were aspects of the League which Chamberlain found distasteful. When defending the government's decision to abandon the Geneva Protocol, Chamberlain told a Birmingham audience that

It seemed that there were questions so vital to the honour or the necessities or even the life of the nation that they would not consent to refer them to arbitration.[140]

Locarno may thus be viewed as a first step in the abandonment of the sort of principles which underlay the Covenant, with its belief that peace is indivisible, and a reversion to old-style foreign policy and the priority of national self-interest.

Hindsight makes it easy to point to the flaws in the Locarno settlement. Scope now clearly existed for Germany to work towards the revision of the Versailles settlement in Eastern Europe, free from the threat of British interference. This is precisely what happened in the 1930s. In a very real sense, however, Locarno represents Chamberlain's honest attempt to resolve an impossible dilemma which confronted all British policy makers after 1919. In the memorandum which Balfour drew up for the Cabinet and which formed the basis of Chamberlain's speech to the League in March 1925 rejecting the Geneva Protocol, the central point was made that the creation of the League and the United States' simultaneous renunciation of her projected membership had left Britain with an intolerable burden of responsibility. Even in the greatest days of the *Pax Britannica* Britain had not had the means effectively to intervene in the affairs of Central and Eastern Europe. To expect her now to assume such obligations with her resources diminished after the punishing experience of the Great War was totally unrealistic. The failure at Locarno to conclude a final settlement of the security of Eastern Europe was not of immediate significance in 1925. For the time being France, even without British support, had the means and the will to aid her Eastern Allies. Chamberlain could perhaps foresee the time when the European balance of power would have changed and this would no longer be the case. What, however, he could not foresee was the rise of a new generation of German politicians for whom the traditional norms of diplomatic behaviour had no meaning. It was an ironic coincidence that a few weeks after Chamberlain took office as Foreign Secretary Adolf Hitler left Landsberg Gaol to begin his quest for supreme power in Germany.

Notes

1. Elletson, *Chamberlains* p. 243.
2. N. Chamberlain Diary 22 Oct. 1925, Chamberlain MSS, NC 2/21.
3. Nicolson, *George V* p. 409.
4. Ibid.
5. L. Amery, *Life* ii, 303.
6. Tyrrell to A. Chamberlain 31 Oct. 1925, Chamberlain MSS, AC 52/772. Chamberlain was too fond of the House of Commons and too wary of imposing additional financial burdens upon himself and his successors to accept the offer.
7. L. Amery, *Life* ii, 303.
8. S. Baldwin to A. Chamberlain 31 Oct. 1931, Baldwin MSS 45 ff. 189–90.
9. A. Chamberlain to S. Baldwin 31 Oct. 1924, Chamberlain MSS, AC 35/5/3; c.f. A. Chamberlain to Ivy Chamberlain 31 Oct. 1924, ibid, AC 6/1/587.
10. A. Chamberlain to Ivy Chamberlain 10 Oct. 1924, ibid, AC 6/1/563.
11. A. Chamberlain to L. Amery 21 Nov. 1925, ibid, AC 37/13.
12. *The Times* 7 Nov. 1924.

13. A. Chamberlain to S. Baldwin 9 Nov. 1924, Baldwin MSS 42 ff. 270–1.
14. Clark, *Innings* p. 257.
15. N. Chamberlain Diary 6 Nov. 1924, Chamberlain MSS, NC 2/21; A. Chamberlain to S. Baldwin 6 Nov. 1924, ibid, AC 35/5/4.
16. A. Chamberlain to Ivy Chamberlain 5 Nov. 1924, ibid, AC 6/1/592–3. The Duke of Portland recalls an occasion when, arranging the transport of the British delegation to Geneva, he put Chamberlain and Amery in the same compartment, thinking they would be happy gossiping together. He received a sharp message that Amery was to be placed elsewhere. Duke of Portland to the author, 27 April 1984.
17. D. S. Birn, *The League of Nations Union 1918–1945* (Oxford, 1981) p. 59; Viscount Cecil, *A Great Experiment* (London, 1941) p. 163. On an earlier occasion Chamberlain had described Cecil as 'the worst type – the sentimentalist with some of the wisdom of the serpent.' T. Jones, *Whitehall Diary* i, 148.
18. A. Chamberlain to Salisbury 2 Jan. 1925, Chamberlain MSS, AC 52/704; A. Chamberlain to S. Baldwin 9 Nov. 1924, Baldwin MSS 42 ff. 270–1.
19. Crowe to A. Chamberlain 20 Nov. 1924, F.O. 800/256/114.
20. Cecil, *All the Way* p. 190.
21. Cecil to Salisbury 30 March 1925, Cecil MSS Add MS 51085.
22. C. Barnett, *The Collapse of British Power* (New York, 1972), p. 196.
23. W. Churchill to A. Chamberlain 14 Nov. 1924, Chamberlain MSS, AC 51/56. See below p. 275.
24. Ibid, 15 Dec. 1924, FO 800/256/372. 'I expect to be rather a heavy burden to you in your diplomacy.' Churchill to A. Chamberlain 1 Dec. 1924, M. Gilbert, *Churchill* v, i, 279.
25. Ibid, 1 Dec. 1924, Chamberlain MSS, AC 51/64.
26. A. Chamberlain to Crewe 15 Jan. 1925, ibid, AC 52/180.
27. A. Chamberlain to H. Chamberlain 21 March 1931, ibid, AC 5/1/535.
28. Bridgeman Diary, Nov. 1929.
29. A. Chamberlain to H. Chamberlain 27 Sept. 1924, Chamberlain MSS, AC 5/1/333.
30. R. James (ed.), *Memoirs of a Conservative* pp. 174–5. 'I believe', recalled the Duke of Portland, 'that the only foreigner whom Baldwin liked was the Porter at the hotel at Aix-les-Bains which he visited every August.' Duke of Portland to the author, 27 April 1984.
31. A. Chamberlain to M. Chamberlain 20 Sept. 1925, Chamberlain MSS, AC 4/1/1264.
32. H. Nicolson *Diary and Letters 1930–39* (London, 1966) p. 268.
33. T. Jones, *Whitehall Diary* i, 303.
34. S. Baldwin to A. Chamberlain 21 Dec. 1926, Chamberlain MSS, AC 53/54.
35. A. Chamberlain to Ida Chamberlain 20 Feb. 1927, ibid, AC 5/1/410. Bridgeman noted that Chamberlain was 'always sensitive and rather intolerant of criticism,' Diary, Nov. 1929.
36. Middlemas and Barnes, *Baldwin* p. 294.

37. A. Chamberlain to R. Cecil 20 May 1926, Cecil MSS, Add. MS 51078.
38. A. Chamberlain to [?] 15 June 1926, Chamberlain MSS, AC 53/122; A. Chamberlain to H. Chamberlain 25 April 1926, ibid, AC 5/1/380.
39. A. Chamberlain to Baldwin 17 May 1926, Baldwin MSS 11 f. 26.
40. Walford Selby to Davidson 12 Nov. 1952, James, *Memoirs of a Conservative* p. 176; Middlemas and Barnes, *Baldwin* p. 342.
41. A. Chamberlain to Bland n.d., Chamberlain MSS, AC 53/77. See also Lord Vansittart, *The Mist Procession* (London, 1958) p. 344. Cecil regarded Chamberlain as 'a mere phonograph of Crowe', Gilbert, *Churchill* v, i, 348.
42. Middlemas and Barnes, *Baldwin* p. 362.
43. A. Chamberlain to Churchill 8 Feb. 1925, Chamberlain MSS, AC 52/153.
44. Middlemas and Barnes, *Baldwin* p. 348.
45. Petrie, *Life* ii, 155, 263.
46. A. Chamberlain to Tyrrell 19 Sept. 1927, F.O. 800/261.
47. House of Commons Debates, vol. CLXXXVI, cols. 109–10.
48. A. Chamberlain to Sir G. Grahame 26 Feb. 1925, Chamberlain MSS, AC 50/50.
49. A. Chamberlain to Lord Lugard 1 Dec. 1924, ibid, AC 51/185.
50. A. Chamberlain to Stamfordham 9 Feb. 1925, F.O. 800/257/260–1.
51. A. Chamberlain to L. Amery 19 June 1925, Chamberlain MSS, AC 52/38.
52. D. Johnson, 'The Locarno Treaties', in N. Waites (ed.), *Troubled Neighbours* (London, 1971) p. 102. Under Curzon Anglo-French relations had reached a post-war nadir at the time of the occupation of the Ruhr.
53. E. Sutton (ed), *Stresemann: His Diaries, Letters and Papers* (London, 1940), iii, 230.
54. D. Carlton, *Anthony Eden* (London, 1981) p. 19.
55. As note 51.
56. F. S. Northedge, *Troubled Giant* (London, 1966) p. 258.
57. As note 46.
58. Northedge, *Troubled Giant* p. 249. As early as 1920 Chamberlain had sought to identify two fundamental principles of British foreign policy: 1. that the independence of the Low Countries was of the first importance. 2. that Britain could not afford to see France overwhelmed. T. Jones, *Whitehall Diary* i, 116.
59. C. Barnett, *The Collapse of British Power* p. 332.
60. A. Chamberlain to Howard 4 June 1925, Chamberlain MSS, AC 52/498; Memoir by Hilda Chamberlain, ibid, BC 5/10/1.
61. A. Chamberlain to Crewe 16 Feb. 1925, ibid, AC 52/189.
62. *The Times*, 27 Feb. 1930; D. Carlton, *MacDonald versus Henderson* (London, 1970) p. 89.
63. Cecil, *All the Way* p. 166.
64. Cecil to A. Chamberlain 17 Nov. 1924, F.O. 800/256/87; A. Chamberlain to Cecil 19 Nov. 1924, Chamberlain MSS, AC 51/42.
65. A. Chamberlain to Baldwin 25 Nov. 1924, Baldwin MSS 114 ff. 260–1.
66. Howard to A. Chamberlain 9 Jan. 1925, Chamberlain MSS, AC 52/476;

A. Chamberlain to Howard 28 Jan. 1925, ibid, AC 52/479.
67. A. Chamberlain to D'Abernon 11 Sept. 1930, ibid, AC 39/2/35.
68. Johnson, 'Locarno' pp. 111–2.
69. Memorandum by Hankey 23 Jan. 1925, F.O. 800/257/198.
70. A. Chamberlain to Crewe 20 Feb. 1925, Chamberlain MSS, AC 52/191.
71. Notes by W. Churchill 23 Feb. 1925, ibid, AC 52/156. At an earlier date Churchill had favoured a defensive alliance with France and Belgium. Roskill, *Hankey* ii, 209.
72. M. Gilbert, *Churchill* v, 122–3.
73. A. Chamberlain to Crewe 16 Feb. 1925, Chamberlain MSS, AC 52/189.
74. Under the terms of the Treaty of Versailles, Allied troops were due to leave Cologne and the surrounding area in January 1925.
75. F. G. Stambrook, ' "Das Kind" – Lord D'Abernon and the Origins of the Locarno Pact,' *Central European History* 1, 3 (Sept. 1968) p. 245. See also *An Ambassador of Peace: Lord D'Abernon's Diary* vol. 3, (London, 1930), passim. The Duke of Portland believes that D'Abernon succeeded in manipulating his talks with Stresemann so that the latter put forward the proposals as his own. Duke of Portland to the author, 27 April 1984.
76. M. Gilbert, *The Roots of Appeasement* (London, 1966) p. 111.
77. A. Chamberlain to D'Abernon 30 Jan. 1925, Chamberlain MSS, AC 50/31; ibid, 3 Feb. 1925, AC 52/256.
78. Ibid, 1 Oct. 1930, AC 39/2/38.
79. A. Chamberlain to Crewe 16 Feb. 1925, AC 52/189.
80. Ibid, 20 Feb. 1925, AC 52/191.
81. A. Chamberlain to Ida Chamberlain 1 March 1925, AC 5/1/347.
82. Roskill, *Hankey* ii, 396.
83. N. Chamberlain to H. Chamberlain 7 March 1925, Chamberlain MSS, NC 18/1/475.
84. Middlemas and Barnes, *Baldwin* pp. 350–1; Hyde, *Baldwin* p. 244; Johnson, 'Locarno' p. 114.
85. A. Chamberlain to Ivy Chamberlain 10 March 1925, Chamberlain MSS, AC 6/1/602.
86. A. Chamberlain to Crowe 8 March 1925, ibid, AC 52/238; A. Chamberlain to Ivy Chamberlain 8 March 1925, ibid, AC 6/1/601.
87. Birn, *League of Nations Union* pp. 59–60; W. N. Medlicott, *British Foreign Policy Since Versailles, 1919–1963* (London, 1968) p. 334.
88. Bridgeman Diary, 11 March 1925.
89. Crowe to Baldwin 14 March 1925, Baldwin MSS 115 ff. 63–5. The confusion may have arisen because the meeting of ministers continued for some time after Crowe had withdrawn.
90. Crowe to A. Chamberlain 12 March 1925, Chamberlain MSS, AC 52/240.
91. A. Chamberlain to Ivy Chamberlain 15 March 1925, ibid, AC 6/1/603; A. Chamberlain to Crowe n.d., ibid, AC 52/241.
92. Crowe to A. Chamberlain 15 March 1925, ibid, AC 52/244.
93. A. Chamberlain to Ivy Chamberlain 19 March 1925, ibid, AC 6/1/605.

94. A. Chamberlain to Crewe 27 June 1925, ibid, AC 52/221.
95. G. A. Craig and F. Gilbert (eds.), *The Diplomats 1919–1939* (Princeton, 1953) p. 42.
96. V. Massey, *What's Past is Prologue* (Toronto, 1963) p. 113.
97. L. Amery, *Life* ii, 303.
98. J. Jacobson, *Locarno Diplomacy* (Princeton, 1972) p. 59.
99. A. Chamberlain to Baroness Scherr Thoss 9 Feb. 1925, Chamberlain MSS, AC 52/715.
100. A. Chamberlain to Baldwin 27 Aug. 1925, Baldwin MSS 115 ff. 90–1.
101. A. Chamberlain to Cecil 28 Sept. 1925, Chamberlain MSS, AC 52/142; c.f. A. Chamberlain to H. F. Spender 19 Sept. 1925. 'If France raised as many difficulties as the Germans . . . you would be the first to say what an impossible nation they were or at least how desperately blundering was their diplomacy.' F.O. 800/258/519.
102. N. Chamberlain Diary 22 Oct. 1925, Chamberlain MSS, NC 2/21.
103. A. Chamberlain to D'Abernon 10 July 1925, F.O. 800/258/301–2.
104. Ibid, 30 Sept. 1925, Chamberlain MSS, AC 52/297.
105. A. Chamberlain to Crewe 12 May 1925, ibid, AC 52/211.
106. Ibid, 14 May 1925, AC 50/70.
107. A. Chamberlain to D'Abernon 10 July 1925, F.O. 800/258/301–2.
108. Jacobson, *Locarno* p. 58.
109. A. Chamberlain to Cecil 28 Sept. 1925, Cecil MSS 51078 f. 86.
110. A. Chamberlain to Baldwin 26 Sept. 1925, Baldwin MSS 115 f. 97.
111. A. Chamberlain to D'Abernon 30 Sept. 1925, Chamberlain MSS, AC 52/297.
112. It was formally signed in London on 1 Dec. 1925.
113. Baldwin to A. Chamberlain 15 Oct. 1925, Chamberlain MSS, AC 37/1.
114. Balfour to A. Chamberlain 16 Oct. 1925, ibid, AC 37/24.
115. Amery to A. Chamberlain 20 Oct. 1925, F.O. 800/258/587. With an eerie anticipation of the praise that Chamberlain's brother would receive in 1938, Amery asserted that the Foreign Secretary had brought back 'Peace with Honour all round'.
116. N. Chamberlain to H. Chamberlain 17 Oct. 1925, Chamberlain MSS, NC 18/1/505.
117. A. Chamberlain to Baldwin 31 Oct. 1925, Baldwin MSS 160 f. 18.
118. Macleod, *Neville Chamberlain* p. 117. Chamberlain later wrote, 'It is some swank to wear the Garter being a Commoner. . . . Frankly it gives me almost childish pleasure and I am surprised and just a little bit ashamed of myself.' A. Chamberlain to Ivy Chamberlain 13 Feb. 1926, Chamberlain MSS, AC 6/1/643.
119. A. Chamberlain to Tyrrell 18 Oct. 1925, ibid, AC 4/1/1265.
120. A. Chamberlain to Ida Chamberlain 28 Nov. 1925, ibid, AC 5/1/370; see also ibid, 27 June 1925, AC 5/1/357.
121. A. Chamberlain to D'Abernon 4 Nov. 1925, ibid, AC 37/98; A. Chamberlain to Drummond 16 Oct. 1925, F.O. 800/258/575.
122. A. Chamberlain to F. S. Oliver 3 Nov. 1925, Chamberlain MSS,

AC 37/323.
123. A. Chamberlain to Briand 29 July 1926, ibid, AC 53/81.
124. Compare A. Chamberlain to H. F. Spender 19 Sept. 1925, ibid, AC 52/731 and A. Chamberlain to D'Abernon 11 Sept. 1930, ibid, AC 39/2/35.
125. House of Commons Debates vol. 188, col. 429. Even so Locarno did not commend itself to the Dominions who declined to take part in it. Smuts to A. Chamberlain 21 Oct. 1925, F.O. 800/258/589.
126. L. Amery, *Life* ii, 304–5.
127. A. Chamberlain to Crewe 16 Feb. 1925, Chamberlain MSS, AC 52/189.
128. A. Chamberlain to Sir Max Muller 1 Dec. 1924, ibid, AC 50/21.
129. A. Chamberlain to Crewe 31 March 1925, ibid, AC 50/56.
130. A. Chamberlain to L. Amery 6 Aug. 1925, ibid, AC 52/51.
131. A. Chamberlain to D'Abernon 18 March 1925, ibid, AC 52/264.
132. Ibid.
133. L. Amery to A. Chamberlain 15 June 1925, ibid, AC 52/37.
134. A. Chamberlain to Crewe 27 June 1925, ibid, AC 52/221.
135. Jacobson, *Locarno* pp. 24, 37.
136. Roskill, *Hankey* ii, 396.
137. A. Chamberlain to Drummond 16 Oct. 1925, Chamberlain MSS, AC 52/333.
138. Birn, *League of Nations Union* p. 61.
139. A. Chamberlain to Grahame 14 July 1925, Chamberlain MSS, AC 50/107.
140. *The Times* 7 April 1925.

CHAPTER EIGHT

THE FOREIGN OFFICE AFTER LOCARNO

'in this last year I have done a big thing which not only would not but *could* not have been done without me'.[1]

'I hope Locarno will not give Austen swelled head.'[2]

The summit of Locarno towers so high in the career of Austen Chamberlain that it is easy to forget that he remained on as Foreign Secretary for nearly four more years after its signature. Chamberlain himself fully recognised that much still remained to be done, that there were other peaks to conquer. The Treaty, he said, should be seen as the beginning of the work of appeasement and reconciliation in Europe and not its end.[3] There were, he told D'Abernon, 'still difficulties to be faced and still a long road to travel'.[4] But the verdict of history has been that in the remaining years of the Conservative government the promise of Locarno was not fulfilled. By the time Chamberlain left office, many saw the Treaty as a false dawn, while by the early 1930s its glow had started rapidly to fade. There are many reasons to account for this disappointment, not all of them within Chamberlain's personal control. Yet the impression is strong that Chamberlain attached too great a significance to the intangible 'spirit' of Locarno, as if the ethereal *bonhomie* created in 1925 between Briand, Stresemann and himself could somehow permeate the conduct of diplomacy generally and create the sort of international society for which men of good will had sought in vain since the end of the Great War. 'It was the spirit of Locarno', he once wrote, 'to which I attached so much value and which I hoped would inform and guide the policy of the whole world'.[5]

Chamberlain, moreover, clearly believed that with the signing of the Locarno Pact Britain had contributed her major effort towards the pacification of Europe. Many had misunderstood Locarno to mark the start of active British participation in the affairs of Western Europe. In fact it represented the limit and extremity of British involvement in European affairs. In Chamberlain's own words, Britain occupied 'a semi-detached position' in relation to the European continent.[6] Now it would be for others to follow the example that had been set, but with only a minimum of prompting from Great Britain. As Chamberlain put it:

I see in certain quarters an idea springing up that it is the policy of His Majesty's

Government in some way to impose the policy of Locarno on other nations. This is not the case, nor do I believe that the polity of Locarno can be developed in that way. Any further pacts must be a natural growth among the nations interested, responding ... to the desires and hopes of the great mass of the peoples concerned.[7]

Chamberlain certainly hoped that 'with time and patience we might yet see some similar settlement as Locarno *mutatis mutandis* for the countries of Central Europe'. But 'the initiative must come from themselves'.[8] Without British leadership, however, such hopes were not to be fulfilled, and Europe could not escape the central meaning of Locarno as an act of British foreign policy. Chamberlain had given notice that there were areas of the continent where Britain was vitally concerned and areas where she was not. This was a fact with which the diplomats of Europe would have to reckon, yet, as Thomas Jones heard from a continental observer, 'Chamberlain's constant repetition of his indifference to all happenings east of the Rhine is most demoralising for Central and E. Europe'.[9]

Like his brother a decade later, Chamberlain also seemed to place too great a faith in the ability of reasonable men to work out their countries' differences in personal dialogue. The growing *rapport* between Chamberlain, Briand and Stresemann had indeed been an important factor in the realisation of Locarno, but thereafter Chamberlain put too much stress on what was in the nature of things a transient phenomenon, at the expense of the abiding force of national self-interest. He was too inclined to believe that every diplomatic difficulty could be cleared up by an afternoon's discussion between the three architects of Locarno.[10] As late as December 1928 he wrote, 'But the spirit was good and if Stresemann, Briand and I were left alone to find the solution, I think we should manage to secure the evacuation of the Rhineland within a reasonable time'.[11]

It was Chamberlain who took the initiative when he proposed that the 'Locarnites' should meet again at Geneva in the March following the signing of Locarno for a round table discussion. The precedent was thereby set for the Locarno 'tea parties', a pattern of diplomacy whereby for the next three and a half years the representatives of the Locarno powers gathered in private in one another's hotel rooms to discuss the outstanding international issues of the day. Despite the correctness and formality of his appearance and his stiffness of manner, such intimate gatherings were far more congenial to Chamberlain than the universality implied by the League. They appealed also to the other side of his character – his 'boyish enthusiasm, sincerity and optimism'.[12] He believed that the best way to relax tension, reduce suspicion, and develop communication was for the foreign ministers to meet face to face. This development meant, however, that the tea parties became far more important than the meetings of the League which generally occasioned them. Indeed the Locarno powers tended to arrogate to themselves questions which rightly were the concern of the League Council. If extended, this trend threatened to leave to the Council only 'such weighty matters as the appointment of the governing body of the International Cinematographic Institute at Rome'.[13] The very casualness and informality of Locarno diplomacy meant, moreover, that each man tended to interpret the decisions reached in a way that suited himself. The resulting misunderstanding and confusion could only cancel out the goodwill which the *tête-à-tête* meetings were supposed to engender.[14] The emphasis upon personal diplomacy naturally encouraged Chamberlain's conviction of his own indispensability to British foreign policy. This grew as the years went by. When an Assistant Secretary of the Foreign Office suggested that he alone could sort out the relations of Germany, Poland and Lithuania, Chamberlain noted: 'My bedside manner again! But there is a basis of truth for it and I may have to try. After all, it is the fact that personality counts for so much that makes this work so attractive'.[15]

Even allowing for Chamberlain's exaggerated faith in personal diplomacy, an even deeper myth underlay the Locarno settlement. Locarno was a positive achievement. It did make for a lessening of tension in the most sensitive European trouble-spot. But its long-term contribution to peace and security was less substantial. The spirit of Locarno was but a fragile base upon which to construct a lasting settlement. The idea which later gained credence that it represented a tragic missed opportunity is not altogether tenable. Between the rhetoric and the reality there always remained an unbridged divide. Nothing illustrates this better than the guarantee given by Great Britain to the Rhineland frontier. Having guaranteed both sides of the frontier, Britain was logically obliged to concert her military arrangements with all three countries concerned or with none. She chose the latter course. Yet the possibility that Britain could, without detailed military plans, react effectively to a flagrant violation of the frontier was highly improbable. In practical terms, therefore, the British guarantee might well prove to be without meaning.[16] Contemporaries and many later historians have contributed to the myth that in the years which followed Locarno Europe had its one real chance in the inter-war period of achieving lasting peace. Chamberlain played his part in the development of this illusion. With their signing, noted one historian, 'the treaties of Locarno gained an instant sanctity normally accorded only to motherhood and no politician in power dared speak against them'.[17] Chamberlain himself developed a fondness and affection for the men of Locarno, an attitude which led, for example, to an excessive indulgence towards the activities of Benito Mussolini.[18] He never tired of reminiscing about his achievement in 1925. He constantly looked back to Locarno as a watershed in the history of diplomacy. Its enduring impact was a source of intense satisfaction to him. When preparing a survey of foreign affairs for the Imperial Conference of 1926, Chamberlain professed to discern an 'amazing contrast' with the scenario which had confronted Lord Curzon only three years earlier.[19] In December 1927 he wrote: 'the recent meeting of the Council at Geneva gave fresh proof of the good work which we did at Locarno and of its vitality and influence.'[20]

But to suggest that after 1925 a new era was created which only came to an end with the death of Stresemann and the Wall Street Crash is a grotesque oversimplification. Strained relations between the major powers were evident long before 1929. Indeed in some senses Locarno changed nothing. The fellowship of that gathering could not disguise the fact that there remained next to each other a France fearful of her future security and a revisionist Germany, still potentially Europe's strongest power and voicing ever-increasing demands for changes to the *status quo* in her favour. Stresemann, Briand and Chamberlain had in no sense solved the German problem at Locarno. Though many lesser points were resolved, fundamental rivalries, antagonisms and national priorities remained unaltered throughout the Locarno era. As the foremost historian of these years concludes, 'The potential for a diplomatic revolution and the opportunity for transforming the armistice into a peace were more apparent than real.'[21]

As has been noted, Chamberlain made a conscious decision that it was no part of Britain's role to take the lead in the development and extension of the Locarno system. Even had his inclination been different, the pressures upon him in other directions might have been too strong to resist. 'The Foreign Secretary of the British Empire is a very busy man', noted Chamberlain's immediate successor, Arthur Henderson.[22] In the years after Locarno the multiplicity of problems in British diplomacy became far more apparent than it had been in the first twelve months of Chamberlain's Foreign Secretaryship. In May 1927 he wrote:

When I first came into this office I used to pray that there might be no crises in my time. I soon learned, however, that I was asking for something which was not within the limits of the attainable but I still pray though not with any very satisfactory result that I may only have to face one crisis at a time.[23]

This served to remind him that Britain was, as she always had been, a world rather than a European power and to divert his attention from the affairs of the continent. During the second part of his ministry Chamberlain was confronted by serious problems relating to Britain's position in Egypt and in China, and to the country's relations with the Soviet Union and the United States. These issues rather than questions such as German disarmament, troop reduction and evacuation of the Rhineland occupied Chamberlain's time and energy to the exclusion of almost everything else. At the beginning of 1927 he complained that China left him 'little freedom of time or mind for other problems'.[24] In May of that year he noted that 'the same twenty-four hours which witnessed the Debate in the House of Commons on [diplomatic relations with Russia] . . . have required decisions on the equally critical question of the evacuation of Peking and a crisis which, I fear, is unavoidable in Egypt'.[25] By that time German affairs were receding into the background of British foreign policy. Between December 1926 and September 1928 the Cabinet only had such matters on its agenda once.[26]

In addition to this diversification of the calls upon his time, Chamberlain's own energies and utimately his health began to fail. Never endowed with a robust constitution, Chamberlain constantly complained of the strain and tiredness brought on by his work at the Foreign Office and in 1928 he suffered a complete collapse of health, after which, according to many observers, he was never quite the same man again. After his illness Chamberlain himself noted:

I have had my lesson and am trying to confine myself to such work as I can do between breakfast and dinner. I have established the rule that I will not work as I used to do for two or three hours daily after dinner.[27]

In such circumstances there would not have been the opportunity, even had Chamberlain so wished it, for the sort of sustained diplomatic activity which had led to Locarno in 1925.

Had Chamberlain been inclined to build upon the achievement of Locarno, he would have been called upon to play a role for which he was not ideally equipped. The central problem of European diplomacy remained Franco-German relations and, if these were to be placed on an enduring basis, then Chamberlain would need to act as the honest broker between Paris and Berlin. This was in fact the role which Locarno theoretically defined for Britain. She had after all agreed not only to defend France against German attack, but also to defend Germany against the possibility of a French invasion. Germany, moreover, interpreted the British role as an assurance that there would be further and speedy concessions to the German point of view, particularly in relation to the question of occupying forces. But Chamberlain's respective views of France and Germany, formed very early on in his life, were only confirmed by his experience as Foreign Secretary. After some time he developed a genuine admiration for Stresemann, whom he saw as a political leader of exceptional courage. But he never regarded Stresemann as typical of his nation. Soon after coming to office he had concluded that Germans were blundering, thick-headed and politically inept.[28] He remembered them as the race which had provoked the outbreak of world war and, unlike so many of his generation, had not jumped on to the revisionist bandwagon of assuming that the Germans had been guiltless. His inner belief was that Germany nurtured a plan for the total reversal of the Versailles settlement, something which went far beyond his own policy of appeasing legitimate German grievances.

Chamberlain's irritation at German diplomacy in the weeks leading to the signing of the Locarno treaties has already been noted. In February 1926 he reviewed the course of events since Locarno and felt 'most strongly' that Germany had 'not done her share towards confirmation of the new relationship'.[29] By April, with growing problems in the Rhineland, his mood had hardened:

The moment that pressure upon them is relaxed they become intolerant and even insolent; they seem to understand nothing but a clenched fist; a concession provokes not gratitude but some new demand which, but for the concession, they would not have ventured to put forward. . . . They have . . . no gratitude or even appreciation of what, by great personal effort, has already been secured for them.[30]

In early 1927 he was ready to confide that the Germans were a 'very disagreeable people'.[31] Chamberlain usually excepted Stresemann from these strictures. But there was nothing in his attitude towards the German leader to match the esteem and affection which he reserved for Aristide Briand.[32] With the exception of his father, Chamberlain expressed profound admiration for very few figures during his long public life. With Briand, however, he tended to go to extremes, and there developed between the two men 'a close and affectionate intimacy'.[33] When Briand was absent from the international gatherings of the late 1920s, Chamberlain was never fully at ease.[34]

The result was that Chamberlain could never really approach Franco-German relations with a completely open mind. British policy might veer, but only between the limits of entente with France and détente with Germany.[35] In this attitude Chamberlain received little challenge from within Britain until the last months of his Foreign Secretaryship. The House of Commons posed few problems; Baldwin's interest in foreign affairs gave little sign of growing; and majority opinion inside the Foreign Office was deeply committed to the French entente, while the leading advocate of the German case, Lord D'Abernon, retired from the Berlin embassy in October 1926. Thus while Chamberlain developed an acute sensibility for the difficulties created by Briand's domestic political position, this was never matched by a corresponding appreciation of Stresemann's situation inside Germany. Though he often felt lurking misgivings about the direction of French foreign policy, he was always reluctant to use his own influence overtly to modify its course. Persuasion and not coercion had to be the extent of his effort. He would put 'steady gentle pressure on the French', but no more.[36] When in 1926 it was clear that France was not pursuing the question of troop reduction with the energy envisaged at Locarno, Chamberlain merely invited Lord Crewe to discuss the matter with Briand informally and at a moment of his own choosing.[37] When later in the year Chamberlain wrote personally to Briand about three outstanding questions which were causing concern – the number of troops occupying the Rhineland, the proposal to maintain troops in the Saar to safeguard the communications of the Rhineland armies, and the French desire for a permanent resident commission in the Rhineland – the message was almost lost amid Chamberlain's fulsome expression of affection and admiration for 'my dear friend'.[38]

The Foreign Secretary's hope was that the closer his *rapport* with Briand became the more confident would France be to appease German grievances. By 1927, however, the mood in Paris had changed and policy was being shaped by those who conceived French security in terms of occupation and fortification. In private conversation at Thoiry in September 1926 Briand and Stresemann seemed on the brink of a general settlement which might have transformed the whole future course of international relations. Between December 1926 and March 1927, however, Cabinet difficulties forced Briand to retreat to the stance of Poincaré and the French military hierarchy. Thus at the very time when, because of his other preoccupations, Chamberlain increasingly left the work of consolidating Locarno in Briand's hands, he was transferring responsibility to a man who could no longer deliver the goods.

In the last resort, therefore, though according to Lord Crewe Chamberlain always played on two chessboards, a German game and a French game,[39] there was little real doubt where his basic allegiance lay. The Inter-Allied Military Control Commission was withdrawn in January 1927 and in June Chamberlain agreed to make a statement implicitly criticising French policy over troop reduction, but this was to prove the limit of exclusive Anglo-German co-operation. By contrast, as the months passed, it became ever clearer that Chamberlain was prepared to keep British troops in the Rhineland until France secured the guarantees she was looking for from Germany – this despite mounting opinion in Great

Britain in favour of unilateral and unconditional withdrawal. Though he
wished to see an early end to allied occupation, he was not ready to 'press
the French government too hard upon this issue', and therefore did little to
aid Stresemann's campaign.[40] To the last he adhered to the view that
French requirements for security and reparation would have to be met
before Germany's demands for concessions.

At all events, Chamberlain remained almost totally immersed in the
affairs of the Foreign Office throughout Baldwin's second government.
The only exceptions came at the end of 1926 when Chamberlain acted
briefly as Home Secretary in the absence of Joynson-Hicks and in the
summer of 1927 when he deputised for Baldwin who was in Canada. At
the Home Office he found his most difficult task was deciding whether
convicted murderers were to be hanged or reprieved.[41] Some thought this
concentration on foreign policy a pity. Birkenhead noted in 1927 that
Chamberlain had 'very good judgement' and was 'generally right on
everything except Foreign Affairs'.[42]

With what seemed to be the supreme accomplishment of Locarno
behind him, Chamberlain became something of an elder statesman before
his time, removed from the day-to-day run of party politics. Locarno was
his achievement and he exulted in it. Even his Birmingham constituency
he tended to ignore, with almost disastrous results when it came to the
General Election in 1929. The Chamberlain family correspondence of
these years is littered with Neville's anxieties that his brother was not
being a good M.P. Less than a year after the signature of the Locarno
Pact, Neville remarked that his brother had 'been almost out of sight, but
remains a great figure, gradually becoming more hazy and legendary as he
is less familiar'.[43] In the House of Commons Chamberlain rarely
appeared except for foreign affairs debates. One young member of
parliament later recalled that he 'did not get to know him at all in these
years'.[44] To many he appeared already a relic from another age. He was
one of the last members to maintain the old tradition of wearing a top-hat
inside the chamber, and still used 'all the old parliamentary phrases of the
last century'.[45] Chamberlain gave the impression that he was 'not
interested in Home affairs', and took little part in the working out of the
great domestic issues of the day. At the time of the General Strike, for
example, he was absent with lumbago, even though Neville felt that 'at
such a time he ought to have been in London, where the cabinet, complete
but for himself, was meeting daily and sometimes twice a day'.[46]

* * *

Warning signs that Locarno might not, after all, herald the dawn of a
new age were not slow to arrive. It had been a pre-condition of the treaties

that Germany should enter the League, and though at Locarno there had been a clear understanding that she alone would be elevated to a permanent seat on the Council in recognition of her Great Power status, it was always likely that other countries would raise the whole question of the Council's membership. In fact, no sooner had Germany filed her application for membership than Brazil, Poland and Spain claimed permanent seats, while China and Persia lay in the wings with contingent claims. Chamberlain's handling of the ensuing crisis did much to tarnish his recently acquired laurels as one who intended to strengthen the League and its machinery. It also gave ammunition to those who felt that the Foreign Secretary too readily fell in with the policies of France. Critics in such bodies as the League of Nations Union looked on askance as he seemed to resurrect the worst features of the old diplomacy.

The major source of difficulty derived from the French intention to back the claims of Poland. This decision undoubtedly reflected misgivings about the failure of Locarno to afford to the countries of Eastern Europe the same sort of guarantee as that given to those in the West. When he visited Paris on 28 January 1926, however, Chamberlain seemed to accept the largely spurious argument that the elevation of Poland to a permanent seat on the Council would lead to a diminution of tension between herself and Germany. As he later explained, the presence of Poland at the Council on a basis of equality with Germany was the best means of promoting peace between the two countries.[47] But the Baldwin Cabinet had already agreed on 11 November to support the candidature of Spain. Chamberlain's reasoning was again somewhat unconvincing. He argued that in the event of a dispute involving the Great Powers going to the Council, because the interested parties would not be able to vote, the decision would rest with the non-permanent members of the Council. 'Does anyone think that a decision by a rump . . . so constituted would carry the weight which would be required to secure its acceptance?' Yet Spain, he believed, would add credibility to such a group, 'standing out by its present position and its past history from the ruck of little nations'.[48]

Chamberlain's policy was severely criticised by his Cabinet colleague, Lord Robert Cecil, now Lord Cecil of Chelwood; in the House of Commons, where the government's majority was cut by half; and by the League of Nations Union. 'Between ourselves', wrote the Foreign Secretary, 'I have the worst possible public opinion here'.[49] At the same time, Sweden, a non-permanent member of the Council, made it clear that she would veto all candidates apart from Germany. By mid-February Chamberlain sensed 'a deuce of a commotion' over the conflicting claims to permanent seats. He found the matter a complex problem with 'weighty reasons on both sides' and hoped to delay a final solution.[50] He recognised, however, that Poland's claim would meet with strong opposition and warned Briand that it might be in that country's best interests if she concentrated merely on securing a temporary seat.[51]

At the Special Assembly of the League in March Chamberlain made it clear that it was through private conversations and secret deals, particularly with Briand, that he intended to determine the future composition of the Council. Carried on behind the backs of the Assembly, these manoeuvres could not but damage the League's international reputation. His instructions from the Cabinet, which represented a substantial concession to Chamberlain's critics, emphasised that no change in the Council should be permitted which would have the effect of preventing or delaying the entry of Germany. The Foreign Secretary had now got himself into a difficult position in which whatever was decided was unlikely to meet with universal applause. As he put it to Tyrrell:

If Germany comes in without any means having been found to conciliate other opinion, her entry will be received with a shout of triumph by the German press and public and with a corresponding cry of anger in other quarters. In other words the moment which ought to be one of conciliation and to mark an advance in international relationship will be full of bitterness and contention.[52]

In the private discussions it was agreed that Poland should receive a non-permanent seat which Sweden obligingly made available for her. But Spain and Brazil, who had been excluded from these negotiations, were deeply offended. The former announced her intention to resign altogether from the League, while the latter threatened to block Germany's candidature. Though the possible withdrawal of Spain caused him some alarm, of Brazil Chamberlain was totally contemptuous. 'A flea can be excessively irritating', he scribbled to Tyrrell, but 'I suppose it remains true that it is better not to scratch'.[53] All that Chamberlain could do in these circumstances was to secure an adjournment of the Special Assembly until the autumn. There was an element of self-deception when he tried to take comfort in the fact that 'the Locarno reconciliation has been saved and indeed has shown its strength since it could withstand so great a strain'.[54]

There was something to be said for Chamberlain's logic. Should the crisis be resolved in such a way that either French or German opinion was dissatisfied, the work of reconciliation begun at Locarno might have been undone. But the question was whether such an eventuality had not been rendered more likely by Chamberlain's too ready acquiescence in French support for Poland, together with his handling of the Special Assembly. Even his brother felt obliged to comment critically:

Looking at it from the outside I think A. has been a little over-diplomatic. In his anxiety to say nothing that might arouse any foreign susceptibilities or encourage any hopes that might be disappointed or close any door that might conceivably remain unshut he managed to mystify the man in the street. . . .[55]

It was perhaps a sign that such misgivings were more widely held that the Cabinet chose Cecil to act as its sole representative on the Special League Committee which met to try to draw up a scheme to conciliate Poland, Brazil and Spain before the General Assembly meeting in September. Significantly, Cecil insisted that the meetings of the Committee be held in public – a marked contrast to Chamberlain's handling of the March negotiations. The Committee proposed the creation of three semi-permanent seats on the Council, the occupants of which would not be compelled to stand down after three years. Not even this compromise, however, could placate Spain and Brazil, who both submitted their resignations from the League. Thus, while Germany took her place in September without opposition, the League itself had been dealt a not inconsiderable blow and the feeling was widespread that Chamberlain was at least in part responsible for a less than satisfactory outcome. It was strange and yet not untypical that he seemed content with what had been achieved: 'So all goes well and I think that we are out of the wood.'[56]

The crisis of 1926 occasioned by Germany's entry raised the whole question of Chamberlain's attitude towards the League. If Locarno itself had given birth to unfounded optimism and *bonhomie*, the rather sordid squabble over Council membership served as a timely reminder that the diplomatic Utopia still lay some way off in the future. Most supporters of the League had welcomed Locarno because, at the very least, it would lead on to better things, and had awaited Germany's entry with enthusiasm. Yet it was not long before the recognition grew that German membership might transform the League, while the conduct of diplomacy inherent in the Locarno system could undermine it. One central paradox was that while most members looked to the League to maintain the *status quo*, Germany saw her admission as enhancing the possibilities of treaty revision. But above all else it was Chamberlain's own vision of the League which emerged in a new perspective.

Chamberlain's attitude towards the League of Nations and its potentialities remained throughout 'realistic', in other words limited and circumscribed. There would thus be occasions when there was no role for the League to play. When, for example, in the spring of 1927 trouble arose between Italy and Yugoslavia, Chamberlain looked for direct negotiations between the two countries. It was his earnest hope 'that there will be no cause to appeal to the League'.[57] Interestingly, unlike many of the League's well-wishers who regarded the absence of the United States as its major weakness, Chamberlain was not anxious for early American entry.[58] He argued in fact that 'if the League is killed it will be by the enthusiasts who will not recognise realities'.[59] He agreed that the League was an important factor in international affairs and indeed found it a more useful body than he had expected,[60] but he did not share the more extravagant hopes of, for example, the League of Nations Union. His policy was to let the League develop slowly and naturally, to avoid radical changes and ambitious attempts to recast its constitution and, significantly, to try 'to keep the four great Powers of Europe together, for if they are in agreement, no great trouble is to be expected'.[61] The impression given by his activities in the crisis of 1926 was only confirmed by subsequent statements. In 1927 he remarked that the League could expect less work, granted that the larger European problems had now been resolved, while a year later he reminded the Council that, although Britain would honour her existing obligations to the League, she would not incur new ones.[62] In a revealing comment Chamberlain noted after one particular set-back for the League:

If it teaches people that the League is not yet a gathering of angels wholly freed from human feelings and passions but a very human instrument, the best yet devised, but still singularly imperfect, it will have done good and perhaps have saved the League from undertaking, or having thrust upon it, tasks which it is not yet strong enough to perform.[63]

The League Council crisis also saw the first significant difficulties in Chamberlain's relations with Robert Cecil, who had been appointed Chancellor of the Duchy of Lancaster with special responsibility for League affairs at the formation of Baldwin's ministry. Cecil opposed the Polish claim and objected to the way in which Chamberlain resorted to private conversations instead of open diplomacy. To Baldwin he complained that he was continually having to accept responsibility for League policy to which he was opposed, and suggested that his relations with Chamberlain were as difficult as those of Lord Curzon with Lloyd George.[64] At one point Cecil pressed his resignation but, recognising that the issue was not sufficiently clear-cut and that his departure would be a great embarrassment to Chamberlain, agreed to stay on for the time being. At the back of his mind, however, lay the conviction that Chamberlain regarded the League 'merely as a convenient bit of machinery of the old diplomacy'.[65]

Partly because of the duality in British foreign policy which had so often existed since the war, and which Cecil's ministerial position was only likely to perpetuate, and partly because of the faith which he placed in his own abilities, Chamberlain resolved early in his Foreign Secretaryship whenever possible to represent his country in person at Geneva. In the long run this may have been a mistake. His manner when addressing the League often smacked of condescension and his speeches were punctuated by the occasional *faux-pas*, in which he would refer to 'your Council' and 'your Assembly' as if these were institutions in which he and his country had only an observer's interest.[66] One official remarked that Chamberlain's knowledge of French was 'a national disaster', while a fellow British delegate recalled that he spent most of his time in Geneva trying to prevent Chamberlain from making a speech in French.[67] The representatives of many other nations, who began by being impressed, later became irritated and annoyed by Chamberlain's performance at Geneva. He himself recognised that the British stance at the League was not always popular, but regarded this as the inevitable price of 'our preference for the real and the practical, and the cold douche of common sense which we administer'. These, he reminded Baldwin

are repugnant to the races who habitually express themselves in a much more rhetorical form, who love broad generalisations and noble sentiments, and are less careful about the precise meaning of the words they use and the undertakings they give than is compatible with our sense of what we owe to ourselves and others.[68]

From a purely practical point of view, though, the Foreign Secretary's frequent absences from London, besides adding to the burden and strain of which he so often complained, left him insufficient time to supervise the running of his department and none to initiate change and reform.[69]

1927 was the year in which Chamberlain became acutely aware that the problems confronting a British Foreign Secretary were not likely to be confined for long to the continent of Europe. The Britain which emerged from the Great War was, after all, still the world's leading power in the sense that she had interests and commitments across the globe unmatched by any other nation. The British Empire, so central a factor in the country's international status, stood now at its greatest ever territorial extent – larger even than the edifice over which Chamberlain's father had presided in the imperialist heyday at the turn of the century. The younger Chamberlain, however, was operating within a framework in which the central dilemma of over-extended commitments and inadequate resources was becoming ever more apparent.

As in the days of Joseph Chamberlain, a threat to the British position in China served as a timely but unlooked-for reminder of the world-wide scope of the nation's interests. As with the Boxer Rising of 1900, moreover, the breakdown of central authority in China manifested itself in nationalist reaction against the position of foreign powers, including

Great Britain. The Washington Nine Power Treaty of 1922 had envisaged international support for a stable Chinese government. Unfortunately it proved not to be within the capacity of the Chinese to create such a government. By the time that Chamberlain came to office China was in a state of civil war in which the main combatants were the Kuomintang to the South and various warlords in the North. In the course of his Foreign Secretaryship the situation became acute to the point where Britain massed 20,000 troops in Shanghai in 1927. By January of that year China had become his 'principal preoccupation'.[70] Chamberlain's problem was to protect British interests, while negotiating a revision in the status of foreigners in China which did not open the door to an extension of Soviet influence. His handling of the situation provoked considerable criticism and contributed to that steady waning of his reputation which characterised the post-Locarno years. His aim seemed to be to play down the problem and hope that the trouble would subside. As he explained to a Birmingham audience he was not acting for the present alone, but 'thinking of our relations with China for the next hundred years'.[71] He recognised also that in the post-war world the mood of the British people would not tolerate a reversal to a Palmerstonian response to Chinese events based on gunboat diplomacy. 'You can have no recognition', he told the British Minister in Peking, 'how profoundly pacific our people now are'.[72]

At the end of 1926 Chamberlain secured Cabinet support for the idea of revising in China's favour the international settlement which had been laid down in Washington in 1922 to secure the rights of interested powers.[73] Such a strategy, however, was rapidly overtaken by the course of events when early in January anti-foreign feeling culminated in the occupation of the British concession at Hankow. This development gave ample ammunition to those of Chamberlain's critics who thought his policy too passive. 'Austen', wrote Neville Chamberlain, 'must have been having an anxious time with those beastly Chinks in Hankow. . . . It is a very ticklish business and we shall be lucky if we get out of it safely'.[74] Chamberlain's position was certainly unenviable. No support was forthcoming from Japan or the United States and the British Minister in Peking, Sir Miles Lampson, was becoming increasingly impatient with his government's policy. Indeed the crisis seemed to confirm the misgivings of those who had opposed the abandonment under American pressure of the Anglo-Japanese alliance in 1922. Britain had evidently lost her ability to influence Japanese foreign policy, while at the same time America's attitude amounted 'to the avoidance of difficulties but never to the backing of a friend'. Chamberlain was unable to discover any 'policy behind the wavering and contradictory steps' of the State Department.[75] As Balfour put it:

[Chamberlain] is navigating unsounded waters in the worst possible weather with no charts to guide him in company with a fleet of nominally friendly Powers whose indecision, incompetence and selfishness add new terrors to the voyage.[76]

When it was clear that the much larger and more important British settlement in Shanghai was also under threat, the government was deeply divided as to what action to take,[77] and Chamberlain 'couldn't find one single member of the Cabinet to approve what he wanted to do'.[78] Eventually, though the Foreign Secretary wished to keep British troops at Hong Kong, hardliners such as Amery and Birkenhead ensured that a force of 20,000 men complete with tanks, aeroplanes and artillery was sent to Shanghai to prevent a repetition of what had happened at Hankow.[79] This stronger line was not without effect and the Chinese preoccupation faded in the second half of 1927, especially as the civil war began to recede to the North.

The difficulties which Chamberlain faced in China were typical reminders of the imperial legacy from which no British Foreign Secretary in the first half of the twentieth century could for long escape. The situation in Egypt was of the same order. There British troops had been in supposedly temporary occupation since 1882. A British Protectorate had been declared at the outbreak of war in 1914, but in February 1922 the British government unilaterally terminated the Protectorate, while reserving to its own control the security of British communications in Egypt, questions relating to the country's defence, the protection of foreign residents and minorities and the control of the supposedly jointly administered Sudan. Chamberlain's problem on coming into office was to negotiate a permanent settlement with the Egyptian government on the basis of the 1922 declaration. Yet any Egyptian administration which came to terms with the British on a basis which seemed detrimental to Egypt ran the serious danger of being overthrown by the strong Wafd party under Zaghlul.

The position was complicated at the outset for Chamberlain when on 19 November 1924 Sir Lee Stack, the Governor-General of the Sudan, was murdered in the streets of Cairo. This, indeed, was one of the first problems to confront the incoming Conservative Cabinet. Without consulting the government in London, the British High Commissioner, Lord Allenby, seized upon this incident as the pretext to present to the Egyptian government an ultimatum demanding not only an apology and the punishment of the murderers, but also the payment of £$\frac{1}{2}$ million indemnity, consent to further irrigation in the Sudan and the right of

Britain to appoint European officials. When the Egyptians produced an unsatisfactory reply, Allenby seized the customs and proposed to take hostages who would be shot in the event of further outrages against Europeans. At this point Chamberlain stepped in and sent out Nevile Henderson as Minister Plenipotentiary to Cairo in a move which Allenby understandably interpreted as a slight upon himself. It implied not only that Allenby's own position was being undermined but also that British policy as expressed in his ultimatum would be watered down. The Egyptian government capitulated in a way that apparently vindicated Allenby's action, but the High Commissioner announced his intention to resign. Although Chamberlain persuaded him to delay so as to prevent a political crisis in Britain, Allenby finally left Egypt in June 1925.[80]

His successor, Lord (George) Lloyd, was a personal friend of Chamberlain but, as with Allenby, the most striking characteristic of British policy towards Egypt over the next few years was friction between the Foreign Secretary and the British representative in Cairo. Chamberlain later expressed his policy in these terms:

If we want tolerable relations with the Egyptian Government, if we want to avoid a series of crises, any one of which might involve us in decisions and responsibilities of the gravest character, we must be content to work the 1922 declaration loyally and to give the Egyptians in the largest measure possible the independence which we promised them.[81]

Lloyd, however, seemed to doubt the capacity of the Egyptians to develop at the pace Chamberlain envisaged and in the face of hostility from the Foreign Office began to communicate directly with the Prime Minister.[82] Nonetheless, Chamberlain secured Cabinet approval for the idea of a formal Anglo-Egyptian Treaty, but internal Egyptian politics prevented any progress before 1927. In that year the situation became acute and in May Chamberlain, fearing that a crisis might not be avoidable, acceded to Lloyd's request for the despatch of battleships.[83] In the event the crisis was averted, but the conviction was gaining ground inside the Foreign Office that Lloyd was intent upon manufacturing a crisis in order to create the sort of situation in which Britain's will could be imposed.[84] Pressure upon Chamberlain to dismiss Lloyd was becoming strong,[85] but the latter took good advantage of a visit to London to put his point of view to members of the Cabinet. Even Neville Chamberlain admitted:

My sympathies are with Lloyd for it is tragic to hear of the decay of all the good work we have done there and of broken-hearted officials in despair over the future of the country.[86]

Neville feared that serious difficulties might arise and begged his brother to treat Lloyd with tact and sympathy. 'He declared he was exhausting himself in his efforts to do so, but I know what his manner is when he is being asked to do something he doesn't want to and I am anxious.'[87]

Chamberlain's response was to go over Lloyd's head and negotiate directly with the Egyptian Prime Minister, Sarwat, when he and King Faud visited Britain later in the year. By November Chamberlain felt that he had the basis of an acceptable treaty and secured Cabinet approval for it without too much difficulty, despite Lloyd's continuing efforts to thwart his policy.[88] The central elements of the proposed treaty were that Egypt was to become a member of the League, while British troops would remain in occupation for at least another ten years, and Britain's position in the Egyptian diplomatic corps, the Egyptian army and the administration of the Sudan would all be confirmed. When, however, the Egyptian leaders returned home it soon became apparent that no further progress would be made. An agreement in 1928 on the waters of the Nile proved to be the limit of Anglo-Egyptian co-operation. Chamberlain's relations with Lloyd continued along an uneasy path, especially when the Foreign Secretary heard that Lloyd was being openly critical of his government's policy in private conversation.[89] Indeed the very last despatch which Lloyd sent to Chamberlain before the latter left office contained a clear statement of the divergence which existed between the two men. Lloyd argued that he had always believed it would be most dangerous to make further concessions of substance to Egypt, no matter how reasonable in themselves, except in the context of a general settlement, which included Egypt's acceptance of Britain's minimum demands.[90] The intervention of the British General Election, however, meant that it would fall to Chamberlain's successor not only to continue the effort to settle Egyptian affairs, but also to resolve the problem of relations with the High Commissioner.

The year 1927 certainly represented a coincidence of crises in Chamberlain's tenure of the Foreign Office. To the problems of Egypt and China was added the question of terminating diplomatic relations with the Soviet Union. In the first months of the Baldwin government, Chamberlain, despite the furore over the Zinoviev letter, was firmly opposed to breaking off relations. 'It does no good and some harm'.[91] But the Intelligence Services had accumulated a great mass of information proving the continuous hostile activities of Soviet Agencies amounting to a provocation 'such as I suppose we have never tolerated from any government'.[92] At Chamberlain's suggestion a committee consisting of Balfour, Birkenhead, Cave, Cecil and himself was set up to consider the evidence. This body approved the maintenance of existing British policy and rejected the alternative of publishing the documents – which would have alerted the Soviets to the efficiency of the Intelligence Services – and breaking off relations.[93] After the General Strike of 1926, however, Anglo-Soviet relations deteriorated steadily and Chamberlain faced mounting pressure in the Cabinet led by Churchill, Joynson-Hicks and Birkenhead to change policy.[94] In February 1927 Chamberlain was still arguing in Cabinet for the preservation of diplomatic relations, but his position was becoming increasingly untenable.[95] For some time the Intelligence Services had been convinced that the Soviet Trade Delegation and the All Russian Co-operative Society (ARCOS) had been acting as a front for subversive activities and were anxious to search their premises in Moorgate. Eventually Chamberlain and Baldwin gave way to pressure from the Home Secretary and in May authorised the famous Arcos Raid, after which a diplomatic breach was inevitable. As the *Observer* commented, 'the strength of those members of the Cabinet who advocated a breach with Russia is the accomplished fact of the raid'.[96] The Arcos episode confirmed that the Soviet Trade Delegation was being used as a vehicle for Soviet subversion and with the evidence thus provided the government had little difficulty in breaking off relations and defeating a Labour censure motion in the House of Commons.[97] Chamberlain noted:

Our breach with the Soviet has been well received here and has created something like consternation in the ranks of the Soviet Government. I hear that there has been a first class row between Stalin and Litvinoff.[98]

Little, then, had gone right for Chamberlain since the end of 1925 and the heady days of his Locarno triumph. In the political atmosphere of the 1920s the issue of disarmament offered scope for a revival of his fortunes, but only if he could successfully tread a diplomatic minefield, which had defied many others before him and to which he had previously given little attention. In April 1927 he confessed that he was not well informed upon 'this subject of disarmament' and the cumulative pressure of Chinese, Egyptian and Russian developments gave him little opportunity to correct this state of affairs.[99] His lack of preparation was only too evident when representatives of Britain, the United States and Japan met in Geneva for a Three Power Naval Disarmament Conference that summer.[100] The British delegation was led by Bridgeman and Cecil, but Chamberlain, who during this time took over as acting Prime Minister while Baldwin was in Canada, exercised considerable influence over the course of proceedings from London. The conference was designed to extend the Washington agreements of 1922 on capital ships to other categories of fighting vessels. It began, however, with delegates hurling widely divergent schemes at one another. Chamberlain was appalled by what he regarded as the rigidity of the American attitude. The American delegates did nothing 'but repeat total tonnage, total tonnage; they have shown themselves deaf to argument and indeed unwilling to discuss our scheme on its merits'. The American claim was simply that whatever cruiser tonnage Britain had they must match it. In other words Chamberlain felt that the Americans were not thinking of limiting armaments to what was required for national security, but were making a claim to build for prestige. Nothing, he professed, since he had taken office, had given him more cause to worry.[101] Not surprisingly the conference 'collapsed disastrously amid mutual Anglo-American recrimination'.[102] While the Americans wanted to concentrate on constructing large cruisers armed with eight-inch guns, the British feared that this would soon render obsolete their own existing fleet of small cruisers mounting only six-inch guns.

The Naval Disarmament Conference proved also to be the occasion of Cecil's resignation from the government. In a letter to Baldwin he argued that arms limitation was the most important question of the day, reserved special condemnation for Churchill's attitude on this matter, and listed the past issues upon which he had been overruled.[103] Chamberlain, sensing that Cecil's resignation in the terms expressed might prove a considerable embarrassment to the government in general and himself in particular, tried to be conciliatory:

You and I, my dear Bob, have succeeded in working very well in all League matters. . . . Is this to be the end of it all? Are you going to throw up the sponge and do infinite damage to the cause because Winston said this or that in the course of one Cabinet . . .?[104]

His appeals were not without success. When Cecil's letter of resignation was finally published it had been watered down to the extent that its political impact was minimal. Indeed it almost appeared that Cecil did not really want to resign after all.[105] Chamberlain, though, was annoyed by the lack of support he had received from the Prime Minister. Baldwin, he wrote, 'left it to Hankey and me to settle what Cecil might publish and what his reply might be . . . I do not think it is fair of the Prime Minister to leave a matter of this personal character to be dealt with by others.'[106]

The Naval Conference of 1927 proved an unfortunate baptism for Chamberlain in the realm of Anglo-American relations, for by the following year this question had taken a central place among his concerns. At the height of his preoccupation with China he had noted:

Apparently nothing will cure the Americans of the view that they are a people apart morally as well as geographically and that our policy is dictated by selfish motives and an overbearing temper which have no counterpart in the United States . . . I find it a little hard to stomach their constant dislike of being seen walking down the street with us. . . .[107]

By the end of 1927 he confessed that it was 'a really heart-breaking task' to try to improve Anglo-American relations. Despite the alleviation of long-standing sores such as the Irish question and war debts, it still seemed 'to be as good business as ever to twist the lion's tail'.[108] 'The course which will be taken by the United States', he later confessed, 'is a riddle to which no-one . . . can give an answer in advance . . . the United States has no foreign policy. The ship drifts at the mercy of every gust of public opinion'.[109]

The combination of his experience of the previous year together with his inherent caution and realism ensured that Chamberlain viewed without great enthusiasm the far-reaching proposals enunciated by the American Secretary of State, Kellogg, at the beginning of 1928 to abolish war altogether as an instrument of policy. He suspected that the sweeping pretensions of Kellogg's initiative were largely explicable in terms of American electoral politics. Such, however, was the prevailing state of public opinion in Britain, that Chamberlain could not simply ignore the American proposals. The British ambassador in Washington urged, moreover, that there were positive advantages in any agreement which seemed to rule out war between Britain and the United States, and that British support for Kellogg's proposals might help allay American suspicion of everything relating to Europe and thus play a part in the reorientation of American foreign policy.[110] Chamberlain sought, therefore, to amend the proposals in such a way that Britain could, without prejudice to her own interests, accept the proposed pact. In May he reminded the American ambassador that there were certain regions of the globe where peace and safety were of vital concern to Great Britain. Interference in these regions could not be allowed, for their protection against attack was a matter of self-defence for the British Empire.[111] Chamberlain never found dealing with Kellogg an easy matter. The Secretary of State had convinced himself that 'anyone who does not at once say ditto to him is a chicaning, hair-splitting, pettifogger'.[112] Nonetheless agreement was reached in July and Britain signed the so-called Kellogg-Briand Pact on 27 August. It may have been little more than a moral gesture or a 'diplomatic kiss', but it would have been difficult for Chamberlain to have remained aloof.

Any good which might have been secured for Anglo-American relations by British adhesion to the Kellogg Pact could not compensate for the effects of an extraordinary gaffe which Chamberlain had committed earlier in the year. The so-called Anglo-French Compromise on Armaments, while bringing the country's relations with the United States to a post-war nadir, also called into question Chamberlain's judgment and emphasised again his too ready acquiescence in the will of France. As one historian has put it, 'from almost any view the

Anglo-French compromise must be judged an outstanding failure in British interwar diplomacy'.[113] The origin of the compromise lay in the deadlock which had existed at the League of Nations Preparatory Commission on Disarmament since the end of 1926. On the question of naval disarmament Britain had tried to limit fleets on the basis of specific categories, while France pushed for limitation by overall tonnage. In relation to land disarmament France insisted on maintaining conscript armies, while Britain pressed for their abolition. Visiting Geneva on 9 March 1928, Chamberlain gave Briand a clear indication that, if France would make concessions in naval matters, Britain would probably be able to give way over the military question. This proposal was bad enough because it was clearly likely to antagonise the Germans, for whom the French conscript army was a source of deep concern. It thus implied a clear departure from the principles which were supposed to underlie the Locarno agreements. But at least Chamberlain's initial proposals would have had the effect of bringing France into line with what had hitherto been a common Anglo-American stance on naval disarmament.

In the weeks which followed, however, Chamberlain allowed Briand to adjust the terms of the bargain in such a way that they became unacceptable not only to Germany but also to the United States. He showed, in fact, an astonishing disregard for American susceptibilities. Despite the opposition of many of his Cabinet colleagues, particularly Bridgeman, the First Lord of the Admiralty, and Cushenden, who had taken over responsibility for disarmament from Cecil, Chamberlain had secured agreement with France by the end of July. Britain conceded to the French view that trained reservists, small cruisers and small submarines should all be excluded from limitation agreements and that all the great naval powers should be accorded parity of tonnage in eight-inch gun cruisers and large submarines.[114] Such proposals not only represented a major departure from the disarmament policy which Britain had pursued at least since the Washington Conference of 1921–22, but seemed also calculated to antagonise Germany and the United States. It was difficult to avoid the conclusion that the agreement represented a private arrangement between the two countries, designed to exclude those categories of men and arms to which each was particularly committed.

Then, before informing any interested foreign government and without the prior consent of the Cabinet, Chamberlain announced the existence of an agreement between France and Britain on arms control to the House of Commons on 30 July. Though giving few details, he deceived the House by assuring a Labour backbencher that the compromise was restricted to purely naval proposals.[115] Not surprisingly the agreement soon caused widespread indignation, especially as the details gradually came to light.

Hailed in France as a quasi-military alliance, it caused grave disquiet in Germany and the United States, while antagonising left-of-centre opinion in Britain, which looked askance at this apparent return to the old diplomacy. Were Britain and France about totally to dominate Europe at Germany's expense? If the principle had been abandoned that trained reserves should be included in calculations relating to disarmament schemes, then, said the *Manchester Guardian*, 'it is more than a concession: it is a betrayal'.[116] A private arrangement between two countries on an issue of such universal importance could not but alienate the supporters of the League.

As Chamberlain was soon overtaken by illness it was left to others, and particularly Cushenden, to try to clear up the mess which he had largely been responsible for creating. The episode stands, however, as the least distinguished in his Foreign Secretaryship. The only tenable explanation for his actions seems to have been a misplaced belief that France and the United States were themselves on the verge of a bilateral disarmament agreement which would have isolated London.[117] But as David Carlton has concluded:

Chamberlain's motives must remain a matter for speculation, but consideration of the clumsiness of his premature statement to the House of Commons and the sheer ineptitude of much of his diplomacy in this affair does not add strength to the view that he was throughout working to a preconceived plan.[118]

When Chamberlain returned from his illness the whole question of Anglo-American relations and in particular the issue of belligerent rights still awaited resolution. Indeed Cushenden handed the matter back to Chamberlain in a state of some confusion.[119] It was 'a terrible tangle and puzzles me more than anything with which I have had to deal', confessed the Foreign Secretary. But he gradually came to the conclusion that the submission of any dispute arising out of the exercise of belligerent rights to arbitration – something which no British government had hitherto accepted – offered the best way forward.[120] With sustained opposition, however, in the Cabinet – especially from the Admiralty with which Chamberlain had had an uneasy relationship throughout his period as Foreign Secretary[121] – scant progress was made. Bridgeman, who wanted 'a little more of the Palmerston touch', felt that Foreign Office American policy was 'entirely lacking in length of view and based mainly on the alarmist reports of certain officials who have married American wives and are terribly apprehensive of strained relations'.[122] The improvement of relations with the United States thus became a major priority for MacDonald's new Labour government when it came into office in June 1929.

There seems little doubt that Chamberlain's less than stunning performance in the second half of his Foreign Secretaryship was in part the result of a deterioration in his health. 'After all', noted his brother, 'he hasn't got a lot of reserve vitality and I suppose the Foreign Office work is very hard because there is no let up'.[123] As crises seemed to confront him from all directions in the spring of 1927, he had confessed that he needed 'a rest physically even more than mentally', having taken only ten days away from work in the previous year and a half.[124] By August, after deputising for the Prime Minister while retaining his own departmental duties, he was 'more tired than I have ever felt in my life before',[125] while at the end of the year some erratic behaviour by Chamberlain on naval issues prompted Hankey to confess 'to having felt once or twice a shade of doubt as to whether his judgement is as good as it was'.[126] The crisis came in August 1928. Already under doctor's orders, Chamberlain caught a chill which developed into pneumonia. This in turn was followed by an attack of neuritis. 'It is really the result', commented Neville, 'of prolonged overwork by a man who hasn't got a great reserve of strength'.[127] A long holiday was now essential and between August and November the Foreign Office was left in the care of Lord Cushenden, the Chancellor of the Duchy of Lancaster, while Chamberlain went on a sea cruise which took him to the New World. Down to nine stone in weight, he was so weak that he had to be carried on board ship at Liverpool, while photographs published in the newspapers made it look as if he had had a stroke.[128] Neville doubted whether Chamberlain would be fit enough to resume his duties by the end of November, especially with the prospect of a General Election looming in 1929.[129]

When Chamberlain returned to London following his enforced absence through illness, he was given little opportunity for a gentle period of recuperation. Indeed for the first time there were signs that an effective political opposition was developing to the central tenet of his foreign policy, the entente with France. The Labour party had more or less gone along with Locarno in the belief that it represented the first step towards the conciliation of Europe. By the end of 1928 it was difficult to sustain that belief and criticism was mounting not only on the radical left, but also in the Liberal party and among Labour moderates such as Hugh Dalton. Even more alarming was the dissatisfaction among 'a large section of the best conservative opinion'.[130] Dalton believed that Chamberlain had thrown away a golden opportunity to build a lasting peace and referred scathingly to the policy of 'the fumbling fingers and the faltering feet'.[131] The new international order promised in the wake of Locarno had failed to materialise and Chamberlain stood condemned as the opponent of general disarmament and international arbitration, and the champion of the old diplomacy, balance of power politics and special alliances.[132] In particular he faced increasing unrest over the question of the evacuation of the Rhineland. Many Conservatives recognised that this might prove a vote-loser for the government in the forthcoming General Election and moves were afoot to get *The Times* to dissociate itself from Chamberlain's policy.[133]

On 3 December Chamberlain was asked in the House of Commons whether he supported German demands for immediate evacuation but replied evasively. His hope was that a forthcoming meeting with Briand and Stresemann at Lugano might offer the prospect of a satisfactory solution. Despite his mounting domestic difficulties Chamberlain maintained at Lugano the fundamentally pro-French stance that he had pursued throughout. Along with Briand he insisted that all discussions of evacuation would have to keep in step with progress in the negotiations for a revised reparations settlement. Only when satisfaction was secured on the latter question would complete evacuation begin. Chamberlain was reasonably happy with the Lugano meeting. The 'conversation à trois was unexpectedly favourable'.[134] Stresemann, though 'at first very sticky', became more reasonable when Briand was pinned down to a firm declaration on the conditions in which evacuation could take place. Chamberlain summed up:

The path is strewn with difficulties, but if we can avoid a continuation of public controversy, I should not be without hope of a satisfactory solution. For the first time I gathered the impression that Briand not only desired to end the occupation, but felt that public opinion in France had advanced to the point where on the conditions named, he would be able to carry it.[135]

Yet Chamberlain's domestic political position became no easier after Lugano with the Labour and Liberal parties pressing vigorously for immediate, unilateral and unconditional evacuation of the Rhineland. The time was ripe for a general critique of Chamberlain's conduct of his country's foreign policy, and to the attack over the Rhineland question were added renewed calls for improved relations with the United States and the re-establishment of diplomatic links with the Soviet Union. So worried was Chamberlain about his own and his government's position that, after returning from Lugano, he asked the British ambassador in Paris to draw the attention of the French leaders to his predicament. In other words Chamberlain was trying to play the card of domestic political difficulties which Briand had used to such effect throughout their association. He still, however, wanted only minimal pressure placed on France 'in the way that persuades instead of the manner which estranges'.[136] When, however, the French government failed to respond to these hints, Chamberlain had no alternative but to revert to his original strategy. Though 'the object of our policy is and must be to get the French out',[137] unilateral British evacuation would serve no purpose and complete evacuation would have to await French satisfaction on the question of reparations. He was not prepared to risk the entente with France, not only because of his profound Francophilia but also because he remained suspicious of German good faith. As he put it shortly before he left office:

Only the future would show whether Germany would really accept her present position or whether she would once again resort to arms and stake everything on the hazards of a new war. . . .[138]

With the opening of the New Year political attention had begun increasingly to focus on the prospects of a General Election, which would have to be held by the early autumn at the latest. Chamberlain's position at the age of sixty-five was inevitably a matter of some speculation. Back in 1927 Baldwin had discussed Chamberlain's future with him while the two men had been holidaying at Aix. Chamberlain was asked whether in the next parliament he would prefer to remain at the Foreign Office or go out with a peerage. His reply was that he would like to stay. This apparently pleased Baldwin who 'could see no successor to him now, though later on Edward Wood would make an admirable Foreign Secretary'.[139] Since then, of course, Chamberlain had experienced a serious illness from which many observers believed he had never fully recovered, and his capacity for sustained hard work had been permanently impaired. Bridgeman, for example, doubted whether Chamberlain was 'physically equal to his task and this makes him take an exaggerated view of the difficulties'.[140] The general stock of the government, moreover, had fallen and the great temptation for Baldwin was to try to give his Cabinet a brighter image by the inclusion of some new and younger faces. There was 'an air of staleness' about the Cabinet. It was as if Baldwin 'always produced the same cake at tea or the same pudding at dinner'.[141] In March Baldwin discussed with Neville Chamberlain and Tom Jones the possibility of making a clean sweep of all the over-sixties in the Cabinet – but with the exception of Chamberlain, 'whom I should have to keep at the Foreign Office as irreplaceable'.[142] Yet at the beginning of 1929 Baldwin had been giving thought to the possibility of a change at the Foreign Office – and one of a rather surprising character. In January he wrote to Lord Grey, who was then nearly blind, to sound out the former Liberal Foreign Secretary as to whether, in the event of a Conservative victory at the polls, he would be prepared to serve. This presumably represented an attempt by the Prime

Minister to win over League support for the government, but in the event Grey declined the invitation.[143] Even in March, despite his remarks to Neville and Tom Jones, Baldwin was toying with the idea of sending Churchill to the Foreign Office where 'he would have a rare chance of spreading himself and giving life and picturesqueness to what Austen has made a deadly dull business'.[144]

Yet despite many rumours Baldwin failed to carry out any Cabinet reshuffle before the election campaign began in May. In fact Chamberlain made a public announcement in Birmingham that Baldwin had asked him to go on at the Foreign Office if the Conservatives were to win, though Willie Bridgeman very much doubted whether the Prime Minister ever meant him to think this.[145] Chamberlain seems to have expected a Conservative victory – even if with a reduced majority from that of 1924.[146] But he had failed to appreciate the extent to which large numbers of voters had tired of the Tories. They appeared, as Lloyd George put it, 'torpid, sleepy, barren'.[147] In the moment of victory back in 1924 Neville Chamberlain had warned that 'unless we leave our mark as social reformers the country will take it out of us hereafter'.[148] Five years later his words seemed singularly prophetic. Despite a useful record of legislative achievement, the Conservative Cabinet now seemed to have little to offer. Most particularly its lack of remedies for the growing problem of unemployment seemed a major and perhaps fatal omission. Foreign policy is not often a decisive factor in the outcome of British General Elections, and it would be wrong to suggest that it was in 1929. Yet it was not without importance. Fifty-six per cent of Labour candidates criticised Chamberlain's foreign policy in their election addresses, and one historian has concluded that Chamberlain's policy may have 'cost the Tories many votes'.[149] To the average voter the hopes engendered by the Locarno Pact now resembled a fading sunset rather than a bright new dawn. By 1929 the achievement of four years before was not much of an asset on the hustings, and Chamberlain's more recent record at the Foreign Office commanded little credit. Chamberlain was widely seen to have been too friendly towards the French, especially at the expense of relations with Germany and the United States, while the apparent return of the trappings of secret diplomacy, together with Chamberlain's seeming lack of enthusiasm for general disarmament, had served to alienate many. Going around the country, Bridgeman was 'quite surprised at the universal dislike amongst our party of our foreign policy and of Austen',[150] while Tom Jones noted the 'wave of depression, not only through the ranks of Labour, but of moderate Liberals and many Conservatives', when Chamberlain announced that he would be remaining at the Foreign Office.[151]

As it was, Baldwin was spared the worries of Cabinet reconstruction when the election results showed that the Labour party, for the first time in its history, had emerged as the largest single force in the House of Commons. Chamberlain's own result in West Birmingham could not have been more dramatic. By the narrow margin of forty-three votes he was returned once more to Westminster. The problems of his own constituency encapsulated the limits of the achievement of the Baldwin government. It had become an area of decay. 'To pass over the border into Handsworth was like moving to another planet.' Before the campaign Chamberlain had not appreciated the magnitude of the problem. But after seeing the housing conditions he warned his family to expect defeat.[152] It all seemed a far cry from the municipal achievements of his father over half a century before. On further reflection Chamberlain was inclined to blame the whole style of Baldwin's leadership for the party's defeat. With some justification he concluded that the cry of 'safety first' had been appropriate in 1924 but had no compelling appeal five years on.[153] At all events, Neville found his brother contemplating the loss of office with equanimity, something which he himself found difficult to understand.[154]

* * *

The return to the ranks of opposition in the early summer of 1929 brought Chamberlain back into the mainstream of Conservative domestic party politics from which he had largely been removed since 1924. In particular, it brought him face to face again with the leadership of Stanley Baldwin and all its shortcomings. One immediate source of irritation was Baldwin's failure in the dissolution honours list to make any provision for Chamberlain's loyal acolyte, Oliver Locker-Lampson. The incident itself was of no intrinsic importance, but Chamberlain's reaction to it is characteristic of his tendency too readily to take offence, especially where Baldwin was concerned, and to make too big an issue of an essentially minor matter. Baldwin, in fact, had simply deferred to the opinion of the party whips, but for Chamberlain it was an occasion for a pompous riposte:

Your letter is a profound disappointment to me and it is useless to pretend that it does not hurt me. I have never before asked a personal favour of anyone and I shall not ask again. I thought that my services to the Party . . . entitled me to prefer such a request on behalf of one whose only fault was loyalty to his leader. . . . . In time I shall forget again the bitter memories which the refusal has called up from the oblivion to which I had consigned them. . . .[155]

The incident also served as a reminder that the split of 1922 had not been entirely healed. Chamberlain, too, now showed signs of his coalitionist past. Almost as soon as the Labour government was formed, talks were renewed between Lloyd George, Churchill and Chamberlain, with a view to upsetting the new administration and forming an anti-Socialist coalition. Neville Chamberlain heard that Churchill was ready to do a deal with Lloyd George over electoral reform and feared that his brother was also disposed in the same direction.[156] These echoes of the early twenties surfaced at a meeting of the shadow cabinet in July. There Chamberlain attempted to define the broad thrust of party policy. He asserted that this must be in the direction of some form of co-operation and ultimate fusion with the Liberal party and that this fact would have to be kept in mind in the formation of policy. Clearly this might mean the jettisoning of imperial preference. Not surprisingly, Chamberlain encountered bitter opposition from Leo Amery, for whom protection had always been far more of an ideological conviction than it ever was for himself.[157] By the New Year Chamberlain was ready to confide in private that he would not stand again for parliament if the party pressed the issue of Food Taxes.[158]

Chamberlain, though, could not really turn back the political clock. For one thing his own position within the Conservative ranks was much weaker than it had once been. Many Tories had been alienated by his pronouncement on the hustings about the Foreign Office, while Neville had been 'unpleasantly surprised to find how quickly his popularity in the party has been dissipated'. There was a growing feeling that he was now one of the 'old gang' who should make way for younger blood. Even as an international statesman it was widely thought that he was 'too continental to be a good representative of England'. Neville, in fact, hoped that Chamberlain would find congenial and remunerative business in the City, for the conviction was growing upon him that his brother was unlikely to hold office again.[159] Chamberlain indeed had already said that if a good offer were made to him outside politics on condition that he would have to give it up on returning to government, he would be ready to forsake further ministerial ambitions.[160]

For the time being, however, Chamberlain continued to take an interest in the government of the country and particularly the handling of the nation's foreign policy. He was disappointed to see Arthur Henderson rather than J. H. Thomas appointed to the Foreign Office as he had always regarded the former as 'very stupid and rather afraid of responsibility'.[161] Henderson, of course, had to assume responsibility for many of the problems which had by no means reached fruition when Chamberlain left office. That in Egypt soon became especially acute. In his last despatch to Lord Lloyd, written during the election campaign, Chamberlain had taken pains carefully to restate the governing principles of his policy. On the very day of the Conservative government's resignation Lloyd replied, saying that 'if he might be permitted a criticism', he thought that Chamberlain's policy was fundamentally wrong. Lloyd had always taken the view that extensive intervention in Egyptian internal affairs and even harshly repressive measures were called for if a satisfactory solution were to be reached. Henderson kept Chamberlain informed of Lloyd's attitude, but the former Foreign Secretary, 'in his present obscurity', declined to comment. In private, however, he made clear his doubts about extending Lloyd's appointment and pointedly absented himself from the House of Commons debate on 26 July, two days after Lloyd had resigned.[162]

It proved difficult to rouse Baldwin's interest on a range of issues, including the Egyptian question. As had been apparent before, the Conservative leader's qualities were not displayed at their best when the party was in opposition. As the autumn session of parliament approached, Chamberlain was concerned that the opposition had not declared its line on such matters within his own sphere of interest as Iraq, the Optional Clause, American negotiations and relations with the Soviet Union, and he urged Baldwin to summon meetings of the shadow cabinet before parliament met.[163] Chamberlain found Baldwin's lack of constructive leadership extremely depressing and, despite his many previous 'ups and downs ... pleasures and disappointments', had 'never felt so hopeless as now'.[164] In March 1930, however, he was instrumental in forcing Baldwin to set up a small Business Committee of senior ex-ministers, holding weekly meetings. Policy would now, he hoped, 'get proper consideration'.[165] In such inner councils Chamberlain could still play an important role, especially when 'Winston gets too intolerable' and Neville becomes 'speechless lest [he] should say too much'. 'A. then very often intervenes with those calm and measured utterances which bring the discussion back to earth and common sense'.[166] There was, however, little pleasure in working with a man such as Baldwin who seemed to be increasingly beleaguered within his own party and distrustful of his own supporters. Never had Chamberlain known 'so blunt a spearhead' or a man who 'left so large a gap between the recognition that he must act and action'.[167]

Nonetheless, despite Chamberlain's mounting hostility towards his leader, Baldwin chose him as his partner in the discussions with the government which began in the spring of 1930 on the future of India following the appearance of the Simon Report. The choice was not surprising, but was in many ways inappropriate. Chamberlain's contact with Indian affairs was now very distant and his views on Indian constitutional reform were notably less enlightened than Baldwin's own. He viewed, for example, with suspicion any over-hasty commitment to

Dominion status and was anxious that, in its own mind, the government should set a limit beyond which it would not go in the forthcoming Round Table Conference on India's future.[168] All the same, Baldwin characteristically allowed the Conservative side of the argument in the inter-party discussions to be dominated by Chamberlain. Yet while contributing little to the debate himself, Baldwin dropped hints that the two men were not in complete agreement on the Indian question.[169] By June Chamberlain's mind was 'beset with the Indian problem and all else seems trifling beside it'.[170] Once again, however, the episode served to show that Chamberlain's influence within the party was on the wane and that his past attitudes were still held against him.

It made Lord Irwin, the Viceroy, 'weep to think that ... S.B. should submit his judgement to Austen ... whose mind is always that of a log of wood'.[171] Yet when it came to choosing a delegation of four Conservatives for the forthcoming Round Table Conference, Lord Salisbury, who was by no means on the liberal wing of the party, opposed Baldwin's nomination of Chamberlain on the grounds that his role in the Irish negotiations almost a decade before suggested that he might make a similar capitulation over India. Sam Hoare remarked upon the irony that Chamberlain had been blocked despite adopting throughout the preliminary discussions a strong Conservative attitude against which not even the most extreme diehard could have taken any exception.[172] In the light of Salisbury's intervention Chamberlain withdrew from the Conservative delegation.[173]

The summer of 1930 also saw the beginnings of a concerted campaign by the press magnates, Beaverbrook and Rothermere, to replace Baldwin as Conservative party leader. As the whole party apparatus seemed on the verge of collapse, Neville, to Chamberlain's dismay, was induced to take on the role of Party Chairman. Chamberlain's attitude towards the press lords was bound to be equivocal. On the one hand he was himself no admirer of his party leader and doubted whether Baldwin could ever fully recover his position. 'A manifesto in his hands becomes "a wet blanket".' He was 'incapable of giving that active fighting lead which is so essential'.[174] Moreover the Beaverbrook-Rothermere campaign for Empire Free Trade still struck a chord in Joseph Chamberlain's son. Indeed in June Chamberlain was again beginning to wonder whether a united party, pursuing hard, continuous argument could not still manage to carry food taxes, while by November he had once more become convinced that the party would have to fight on the issue of food taxes or 'be for ever damned'.[175] On the other hand Chamberlain's sense of loyalty was still strong and, with Neville now clearly very much part of the Conservative leadership, nothing Chamberlain did should damage his prospects. The retirement of Baldwin at this point would be regarded as a triumph for the press magnates − 'in itself sufficiently revolting' − while Neville was adamant that any move to replace the party leader would have to come from the House of Commons.[176]

In fact the partnership of the two brothers seemed more fruitful than for many years past. For perhaps the first time Chamberlain began to drop his characteristic elder-brother manner and to treat Neville as an equal with the result that the latter felt 'much more sympathetic than at any time since we have been in the House together'.[177] Though 'driven nearly to despair by S.B.'s ways', the two Chamberlains were making progress with the party's affairs. 'N. does the heavy work and I do the trimmings.'[178] But it still annoyed Chamberlain that everywhere he went complaints about Baldwin were heaped upon him and he was obliged to put up a defence of the party leader in which he only half believed. 'The cart is always in a rut and my shoulder aches with continuous pushing at the wheel.'[179] Chamberlain therefore felt equally unhappy whether or not Baldwin was replaced, but came to the conclusion that, should it be decided that in the party's best interests Baldwin should go, he and Bridgeman, as senior ex-Cabinet ministers, should approach him jointly with this unpalatable message.[180] Baldwin, however, had qualities of political tenacity and survival to which Chamberlain never gave full credit, and by late October 1930 the latter was noting that the leader had 'got a new lease of life'.[181]

As far as his own future was concerned, Chamberlain regarded himself as still fitted to do good work in the sphere of foreign policy and did not think that there was anyone in sight on the Conservative benches to challenge him. He believed that Britain was losing influence in Europe generally and especially at the League. The international situation looked altogether more troubled than when he had left office. Mussolini's attitude had become more aggressive, Germany had lost the guiding hand of Stresemann, and France had moved violently away from the path of reconciliation with Germany. Thus while Chamberlain still nurtured hopes of returning to the Foreign Office, he recognised that the task of any incoming minister would not be easy. At the back of his mind, however, was the conviction that Henderson carried no weight in the councils of Europe and that only he could re-establish the sort of personal factor which he believed had so smoothed the paths of diplomacy in the later 1920s. To a large extent, of course, this was an illusion, for Chamberlain failed to understand the extent to which the whole pattern of international relations, under the impact of a worsening economic climate, was beginning to change irrespective of the force of personalities. Despite his clear belief in himself, Chamberlain was beginning to sense that younger members of the party were becoming not unnaturally impatient and would prefer 'my room to my company'.[182] Others viewed the situation more starkly. Bridgeman felt that the current press campaign against the so-called Old Guard was 'almost entirely directed against Austen and that he really has been the greatest factor in making S.B. and our party unpopular'.[183] By the beginning of the New Year, rumours were starting to grow that Chamberlain would be among those to be dropped from Baldwin's next Cabinet.[184] Yet in March Baldwin nominated Chamberlain, Eden and Hoare to represent the Conservatives in all-party discussions to prepare British policy for the forthcoming World Disarmament Conference in Geneva.[185]

The question of Chamberlain's future was by no means entirely academic since, by the beginning of 1931, opinion was widespread that the government could not survive for long. It was even felt by many that it might try to escape from its difficulties by resignation or dissolution, although Chamberlain could not see how a defeat which would force the government to resign could be engineered while the Liberal party, which held the balance of power, seemed determined not to force the issue.[186] As early as the resignation of Sir Oswald Mosley as Chancellor of the Duchy of Lancaster in the preceding May, Chamberlain had predicted that Labour would come to grief on the bankruptcy of its unemployment policy, though he recognised that the process would take time. He expected that Snowden's forthcoming budget would merely exacerbate the situation and lead to increased taxation and still further depression.[187] The problem was, however, that the Conservative party seemed in no fit state to take over the reins of government. Despite Chamberlain's efforts to smooth over the situation, Churchill finally broke with the leadership over the question of India in January 1931. Once again Chamberlain felt that Baldwin had mishandled the situation, giving Churchill 'a better exit than he had a right to expect'.[188] Within weeks the challenge to Baldwin's leadership had reached a peak with the decision of Sir Ernest Petter to stand on an anti-Baldwin platform against the official Conservative candidate in the by-election at St. George's, Westminster, and the subsequent withdrawal of the official candidate. Writing to his sister Ida, Chamberlain poured out his pent-up scorn for Baldwin in a way which revealed that he had never fully reconciled himself to serving under a man whom he had always regarded as his junior and inferior. Chamberlain clearly believed that, but for the unique circumstances of 1922–23, he might still be leading the party while Baldwin remained in comparative obscurity:

. . . we [are] unable to profit by all these favourable circumstances because S.B. is not a leader and nothing will ever make him one . . . S.B.'s leadership was always the 'accident of an accident'. Considering his total lack of many of the qualities which are ordinarily needed to bring a man even into the front rank, the largeness of his personal following in independent quarters and the considerable success which for a time he achieved were remarkable; but even more remarkable is the total slump which has followed. . . . Never has any party been more patient with incapacity; never has any man been given so many chances or pulled out of the water so many times; but I think that at last the end has come and that the party will be forced to get rid of its old man of the sea if it is not prepared to be drowned by him.[189]

Neville, on receipt of a memorandum from Sir Robert Topping, the Principal Agent, which presented a very gloomy picture of the state of feeling in the country, decided to consult Chamberlain, Cunliffe-Lister, Hoare, Eyres-Monsell, Hailsham and Bridgeman before taking any action. All were agreed about the strength of feeling against Baldwin and that the leader would have to be shown the memorandum. Over the timing of the operation, however, there was disagreement. As Baldwin was shortly due to make a major speech, both Neville and Hailsham inclined towards delay, while by contrast Austen telephoned his brother to the effect that the leader's forthcoming speech provided all the more reason for letting him know the reality of the situation rather than hiding it from him. But the developments in the St. George's constituency finally determined Neville to take action and Topping's memorandum was sent on 1 March.[190] Baldwin, though, was prepared to stand his ground and even toyed with the idea of resigning his seat in parliament in order to stand himself in St. George's.

As the by-election campaign proceeded, Chamberlain decided to force Baldwin's hand. With no warning to his brother he seized the opportunity of a meeting of the Business Committee on 11 March to demand that Neville should be released from the Central Office. The reason he gave was that Neville's presence was needed on the Conservative front bench in the Commons, where Churchill's withdrawal and the death of Worthington-Evans had left the party short of debating talent. But his real motive seems to have been his conviction that it was time for Baldwin to step down and his hope that Neville would be well placed to succeed him. Neville commented that 'it was pretty plain what he had in mind', and on reflection concluded that his brother was right and drew up a letter of resignation from the party chairmanship.[191] But at the same time Neville acted as a restraining hand in stopping Chamberlain from going directly to Baldwin to urge his resignation. As the heir apparent Neville's position was obviously more delicate than that of his elder brother. Once again, however, Chamberlain had under-estimated Baldwin's fighting qualities and a forceful speech in the Indian debate on 12 March, followed a week later by a blistering and celebrated attack on the press lords, did much to restore the leader's prestige.[192] Chamberlain, though, continued to think that Baldwin could not survive much longer and argued that the attacks of Beaverbrook and Rothermere were probably counter-productive in their effect and were only delaying Baldwin's departure. Yet when the new Conservative candidate, Alfred Duff Cooper, managed to hold St. George's with a five thousand majority, it was clear to most observers that the immediate crisis for Baldwin had passed.

Discussing the situation with Neville, Baldwin let it be known that he had been particularly annoyed with Chamberlain for his intervention over Neville's position as Party Chairman. Neville finally persuaded a reluctant Baldwin to call his senior colleagues together for 'a frank and open talk' to clear the air. When this took place on 25 March, Chamberlain again took the lead and showed the party leader 'little mercy'.[193] When Baldwin asked whether those present were now agreed that his leadership should continue, Chamberlain stressed that the dissatisfaction in the party went much deeper than the press attacks and derived from Baldwin's apparent inertia and lack of incisiveness. He would have to bestir himself and put a less negative message into his speeches if the situation were to be restored.[194]

But talk of Baldwin's resignation now faded. The political situation was clearly going to be determined by the fortunes of the Labour government rather than internal developments within the Conservative party. The signs were ominous. The total of registered unemployed was now over two and a half million; British exports had halved between 1929 and 1931; the crisis over the balance of payments had become acute; and the pressure upon sterling was intense. Yet few could have predicted the seismic upheaval which the political crisis of 1931 would entail, and which would materially affect the careers of all the nation's leading politicians. Certainly, Chamberlain showed no particular foresight, predicting in June that the Labour government would be in for another two years.[195] But for Chamberlain, too, the events of 1931 would prove a watershed, involving his removal from the highest councils of his party, where for three decades he had been entrenched, but at the same time opening up for him a last and not undistinguished phase in his political career.

Notes

1. A. Chamberlain to Ida Chamberlain 28 Nov. 1925, Chamberlain MSS, AC 5/1/370.
2. R. Cecil to Salisbury 8 Nov. 1925, Cecil MSS 51085.
3. House of Commons 18 Nov. 1925, cited M. Gilbert, *The Roots of Appeasement* p. 115.

4. A. Chamberlain to D'Abernon 4 Nov. 1925, Chamberlain MSS, AC 37/98.
5. A. Chamberlain to Sir J. Vaughan 10 Nov. 1925, ibid, AC 50/142.
6. 'Great Britain as a European Power', *International Affairs* 9 (1930) p. 188, cited Jacobson, *Locarno* p. 378.
7. As note 5.
8. A. Chamberlain to Kennard 9 Dec. 1925, Chamberlain MSS, AC 36/13/77.
9. T. Jones, *Whitehall Diary* ii, 129.
10. Jacobson, *Locarno* p. 69.
11. A. Chamberlain to H. Chamberlain 17 Dec. 1928, Chamberlain MSS, AC 5/1/463.
12. Jacobson, *Locarno* pp. 74–5.
13. F. Morley, *The Society of Nations* (Washington, 1932) p. 385; Craig and Gilbert, *The Diplomats* p. 44; Jacobson, *Locarno* p. 69; S. Marks, *The Illusion of Peace* (London, 1976) p. 82.
14. J. Jacobson, 'The Conduct of Locarno Diplomacy', *Review of Politics*, xxxiv (1972) p. 69.
15. A. Chamberlain to Ida Chamberlain 22 Jan. 1927, Chamberlain MSS, AC 5/1/406.
16. S. Marks, *Illusion* p. 72.
17. Ibid, p. 70.
18. Though Chamberlain certainly admired Mussolini – 'if I ever had to choose in my own country between anarchy and dictatorship, I expect I should be on the side of the dictator' [Petrie, *Life* ii, 290] – he recognised that at some time in the future the Duce might become a threat to European peace. 'I am disposed to say that Mussolini needs ten years of peace before he undertakes any adventure. In five years I should begin to watch him closely – which is not to say that I keep my eyes shut now.' A. Chamberlain to G. Clerk 29 Dec. 1926, F.O. 800/259. Chamberlain met Mussolini in complete privacy five times during his Foreign Secretaryship, but subsequent rumours of secret agreements and concessions are unfounded. P. Edwards, 'The Austen Chamberlain-Mussolini Meetings,' *Historical Journal* xiv, i (1971) pp. 153–64.
19. A. Chamberlain to M. Chamberlain 13 Oct. 1926, Chamberlain MSS, AC 4/1/1270.
20. A. Chamberlain to Miles Lampson 21 Dec. 1927, F.O. 800/261.
21. Jacobson, *Locarno* pp. 372–3.
22. Ibid, p. 365.
23. A. Chamberlain to G. Lloyd 8 May 1927, F.O. 800/260.
24. A. Chamberlain to Lord Balfour 22 Jan. 1927, Balfour MSS 49736.
25. A. Chamberlain to Lampson 27 May 1927, F.O. 800/261.
26. Jacobson, *Locarno* p. 127.
27. A. Chamberlain to Lloyd 20 Dec. 1928, Chamberlain MSS, AC 55/346.
28. A. Chamberlain to D'Abernon 11 Feb. 1925, ibid, AC 52/258.
29. Ibid, 2 Feb. 1926, AC 53/210.

30. Ibid, 23 April 1926, AC 53/222.
31. Minute by A. Chamberlain 25 Jan. 1927, cited Jacobson, *Locarno* p. 125.
32. For an appreciation of Briand by Chamberlain see *Down the Years* pp. 179–88.
33. Ibid, p. 180.
34. 'I miss Briand. I do not find Boncour easy to work with.' A. Chamberlain to Ivy Chamberlain 10 Dec. 1925, Chamberlain MSS, AC 6/1/627.
35. S. Marks, *Illusion* pp. 96–7.
36. Minute by A. Chamberlain 21 Dec. 1926, cited Jacobson, *Locarno* p. 124.
37. A. Chamberlain to Crewe 11 May 1926, Chamberlain MSS, AC 53/170.
38. A. Chamberlain to Briand 29 July 1926, ibid, AC 53/81.
39. Crewe to A. Chamberlain 17 Feb. 1925, ibid, AC 52/190.
40. A. Chamberlain to Howard 15 May 1928, ibid, AC 55/270.
41. A. Chamberlain to H. Chamberlain 20 Dec. 1926, ibid, AC 5/1/403.
42. Note by J. Davidson n.d., Baldwin MSS 161 f. 71.
43. N. Chamberlain to H. Chamberlain 10 Aug. 1926, Chamberlain MSS, NC 18/1/539.
44. H. Macmillan, *Winds of Change 1914–1939* (London, 1966) p. 174.
45. N. Chamberlain to Ida Chamberlain 27 March 1926, Chamberlain MSS, NC 18/1/520.
46. N. Chamberlain to Annie Chamberlain 7 May 1926, ibid, NC 1/26/364. Though he played no significant part in the government's handling of it, Chamberlain had firm views on the General Strike: 'But govt. and social order as well as liberty would go under if we did not beat it – and we shall.' A. Chamberlain to H. Chamberlain 8 May 1926, ibid, AC 5/1/382.
47. A. Chamberlain to R. Cecil 9 Feb. 1926, Cecil MSS 51078.
48. A. Chamberlain to D'Abernon 19 Feb. 1926, cited D. Carlton, 'Great Britain and the League Council Crisis of 1926,' *Historical Journal* xi, 2 (1968) p. 358.
49. Ibid, 26 Feb. 1926, cited Carlton p. 359.
50. A. Chamberlain to Ivy Chamberlain 13 Feb. 1926, Chamberlain MSS, AC 6/1/643.
51. A. Chamberlain to Drummond 16 Feb. 1926, ibid, AC 53/249.
52. A. Chamberlain to Tyrrell 9 March 1926, F.O. 800/259/224.
53. Note by A. Chamberlain for Tyrrell on AC 53/4, 27 April 1926; see also A. Chamberlain to R. Cecil 20 May 1926, Cecil MSS 51078.
54. A. Chamberlain to Buxton 20 March 1926, Chamberlain MSS, AC 53/89; A. Chamberlain to D'Abernon 29 March 1926, ibid, AC 53/218.
55. N. Chamberlain to H. Chamberlain 7 March 1926, ibid, NC 18/1/517.
56. A. Chamberlain to Ivy Chamberlain 8 Sept. 1926, ibid, AC 6/1/679. Spain returned to the League in 1928, but Brazil never did so.
57. A. Chamberlain to J. W. Hills 11 April 1927, ibid, AC 54/246.
58. A. Chamberlain to E. Howard 16 March 1927, ibid, AC 54/260.
59. A. Chamberlain to Buxton 20 March 1926, ibid, AC 53/89.
60. A. Chamberlain to F. S. Oliver 17 Jan. 1927, ibid, AC 54/408.
61. Ibid.

62. Birn, *League of Nations Union* p. 65.
63. A. Chamberlain to Lord Stonehaven 12 May 1926, F.O. 800/259/412.
64. S. Roskill, *Hankey* ii, 433.
65. Middlemas and Barnes, *Baldwin* p. 360.
66. S. Marks, *Illusion* p. 82.
67. T. Jones, *Whitehall Diary* ii, 161.
68. A. Chamberlain to S. Baldwin 16 Sept. 1927, Baldwin MSS 129 ff. 17–21.
69. Craig and Gilbert, *The Diplomats* pp. 43–4.
70. A. Chamberlain to G. Lloyd 11 Jan. 1927, F.O. 800/260.
71. *The Times*, 30 Jan. 1927.
72. A. Chamberlain to M. Lampson 11 April 1927, F.O. 800/260.
73. L. Amery, *Diaries* p. 488.
74. N. Chamberlain to H. Chamberlain 8 Jan. 1927, Chamberlain MSS, NC 18/1/556.
75. A. Chamberlain to Howard 25 April 1927, ibid, AC 54/264.
76. Balfour to Baldwin 10 Jan. 1927, Balfour MSS 49694.
77. C.f. Petrie, *Life* ii, 366–7; 'One great source of satisfaction to Austen ... was that there were no differences among his colleagues in the Cabinet with regard either to the despatch of the troops or to the conciliatory attitude to be adopted towards the Chinese if they refrained from violence.'
78. N. Chamberlain to H. Chamberlain 5 Feb. 1927, Chamberlain MSS, NC 18/1/561.
79. L. Amery, *Diaries* p. 502.
80. A. Chamberlain to Allenby 22 Dec. 1924, Chamberlain MSS, AC 51/5. For criticism of Chamberlain's handling of this situation see Churchill's draft letter to Birkenhead of 29 Nov. 1924. Gilbert, *Churchill* v, i, 275.
81. A. Chamberlain to Salisbury 1 Nov. 1927, ibid, AC 54/444.
82. Middlemas and Barnes, *Baldwin* p. 365.
83. A. Chamberlain to Lloyd 30 May 1927, Chamberlain MSS, AC 54/352.
84. Tyrrell to A. Chamberlain 15 June 1927, ibid, AC 54/476.
85. A. Chamberlain to H. Chamberlain 22 Oct. 1927, ibid, AC 5/1/435. Tyrrell warned: 'This led George [Lloyd] to observe that he did not consider himself to be a common or garden ambassador. ... He considers himself something between a Secretary of State and an ambassador or viceroy.' Tyrrell to A. Chamberlain 13 Sept. 1927, Baldwin MSS 129 ff. 22–3. See also Vansittart, *Mist Procession* p. 372.
86. N. Chamberlain to H. Chamberlain 16 July 1927, ibid, NC 18/1/582; see also N. Chamberlain Diary 15 July 1927, NC 2/22 and L. Amery, *Diaries* p. 516.
87. N. Chamberlain Diary 21 July 1927, Chamberlain MSS, NC 2/22.
88. Ibid, 4 Dec. 1927, NC 2/22; A. Chamberlain to Ida Chamberlain 12 Nov. 1927, AC 5/1/437.
89. A. Chamberlain to Lloyd 28 March 1928, AC 55/338.
90. Petrie, *Life* ii, 358.
91. A. Chamberlain to Ida and H. Chamberlain 11 July 1925, Chamberlain MSS, AC 5/1/358.

92. A. Chamberlain to S. Baldwin 24 July 1925, ibid, AC 52/81.
93. C. Andrew, 'British Intelligence and the Breach with Russia in 1927', *Historical Journal* 25, 4 (1982) p. 958.
94. Ibid, p. 959.
95. L. Amery, *Diaries* p. 496.
96. Middlemas and Barnes, *Baldwin* p. 458.
97. N. West, *MI5: British Security Service Operations 1909–1945* (Triad Paperback edn. 1983) pp. 65–70.
98. A. Chamberlain to Lloyd 30 May 1927, Chamberlain MSS, AC 54/352.
99. A. Chamberlain to R. Cecil 11 April 1927, Cecil MSS 51079. 'The whole subject has been left by me so entirely to Cecil that I am quite unable to make any precise propositions'. A. Chamberlain to Baldwin 12 Sept. 1927, Baldwin MSS 129 ff. 13–16.
100. D. Carlton, 'Great Britain and the Coolidge Naval Disarmament Conference of 1927', *Political Science Quarterly* LXXXIII (1968) pp. 573–98.
101. A. Chamberlain to Howard 10 Aug. 1927, F.O. 800/261; A. Chamberlain to M. Chamberlain 1 Aug. 1927, Chamberlain MSS, AC 4/1/1277.
102. D. Carlton, 'The Anglo-French Compromise on Arms Limitation, 1928', *Journal of British Studies* VIII (1969) p. 142.
103. R. Cecil to Baldwin 9 Aug. 1927, Chamberlain MSS, AC 54/28.
104. A. Chamberlain to Cecil 14 Aug. 1927, Cecil MSS 51079.
105. Birn, *League of Nations Union* pp. 67–8.
106. A. Chamberlain to N. Chamberlain 29 Aug. 1927, Chamberlain MSS, AC 35/1/39.
107. A. Chamberlain to Howard 8 May 1927, ibid, AC 54/266.
108. A. Chamberlain to H. Chamberlain 17 Dec. 1927, ibid, AC 5/1/441.
109. A. Chamberlain to Sir Malcolm Robertson 27 July 1928, F.O. 800/263.
110. Howard to A. Chamberlain 2 Feb. and 9 March 1928, Chamberlain MSS, AC 55/265, 267.
111. K. Robbins, *Munich 1938* (London, 1968) p. 39.
112. A. Chamberlain to Ivy Chamberlain 8 July 1928, Chamberlain MSS, AC 6/1/720.
113. D. Carlton, 'The Anglo-French Compromise' p. 162.
114. Ibid, p. 151.
115. House of Commons Debates, vol. 220, col. 1837.
116. *Manchester Guardian* 3 Aug. 1928, cited Craig and Gilbert, *The Diplomats* pp. 44–5.
117. Carlton, 'The Anglo-French Compromise' p. 151.
118. Ibid, p. 161.
119. Cushenden to A. Chamberlain 22 Nov. 1928, Chamberlain MSS, AC 55/127.
120. A. Chamberlain to Howard 6 Jan. and 5 Feb. 1929, ibid, AC 55/277, 282; A. Chamberlain to Tyrrell 8 Feb. 1929, F.O. 800/263.
121. 'Unhappily Chamberlain did not get along well with the Board of Admiralty.' S. Roskill, *Naval Policy between the Wars* i, (London, 1968)

p. 38; Bridgeman noted, 'For some odd reason anything which an Admiral said always irritated [Chamberlain] and the expression of any strong opinion by the Sea Lords was a red rag to him'. Diary, July 1929.

122. Bridgeman Diary Dec. 1928, July 1929.
123. N. Chamberlain to Ida Chamberlain 15 Aug. 1926, Chamberlain MSS, NC 18/1/540.
124. A. Chamberlain to Lloyd 30 May 1927, ibid, AC 54/352.
125. A. Chamberlain to N. Chamberlain 29 Aug. 1927, ibid, NC 1/27/95; A. Chamberlain to Wellesley 29 Aug. 1927, AC L. Add. 85. 'My own proper work has been doubled by the anxieties attendant on holding the fort for the P.M. in his absence.'
126. Roskill, *Hankey* ii, 454.
127. N. Chamberlain to H. Chamberlain 5 Aug. 1928, Chamberlain MSS, NC 18/1/622.
128. N. Chamberlain to Ida Chamberlain 3 Sept. 1928, ibid, NC 18/1/625; 'Austen I fear vy. serious – a stroke!' Churchill to Baldwin 2 Sept. 1928, Baldwin MSS 36 f. 76.
129. N. Chamberlain to Ida Chamberlain 20 Oct. 1928, Chamberlain MSS, NC 18/1/631.
130. A. Chamberlain to Tyrrell 18 Dec. 1928, ibid, AC 55/493.
131. Craig and Gilbert, *The Diplomats* p. 317.
132. Jacobson, *Locarno* p. 282.
133. Ibid, p. 243.
134. As note 130.
135. A. Chamberlain to Balfour 18 Dec. 1928, Chamberlain MSS, AC 55/22.
136. A. Chamberlain to Tyrrell 8 Feb. 1929, ibid, AC 55/503.
137. Note by A. Chamberlain, 1929, ibid, AC 55/432.
138. Chamberlain to R. Graham 8 April 1929, cited Jacobson, *Locarno* p. 246.
139. N. Chamberlain Diary, 7 Oct. 1927, Chamberlain MSS, NC 2/22.
140. Bridgeman Diary, July 1929.
141. A. Chamberlain to Ivy Chamberlain 11 April 1929, Chamberlain MSS, AC 6/1/752. Leo Amery believed that 'the public, especially our party, would be relieved by a change' at the Foreign Office, and regarded Chamberlain as 'the obvious successor to Balfour as principal Elder Statesman in a non-administrative office.' Amery to Baldwin 11 March 1929, Baldwin MSS 36 f. 90.
142. N. Chamberlain Diary, 11 March 1929, Chamberlain MSS, NC 2/22; T. Jones, *Whitehall Diary* ii, 174.
143. K. Robbins, *Sir Edward Grey* (London, 1971) p. 360; Birn, *League of Nations Union* p. 85.
144. M. Gilbert, *Churchill* v, 315.
145. Bridgeman Diary, July 1929.
146. A. Chamberlain to Lloyd 15 March 1929, F.O. 800/263.
147. H. Montgomery Hyde, *Baldwin* pp. 302–3.
148. N. Chamberlain to Ida Chamberlain 1 Nov. 1924, Chamberlain MSS, NC 18/1/458.

149. Jacobson, *Locarno* p. 280; W. McElwee, *Britain's Locust Years, 1918–1940* (London, 1962) p. 149. Asquith's widow wrote, 'You had an undistinguished lot and Austen Chamberlain was a serious handicap to you.' Lady Oxford to Baldwin 2 June 1929, Baldwin MSS 36 f. 221.
150. As note 145.
151. T. Jones, *Whitehall Diary* ii, 191–2.
152. A. Chamberlain to M. Chamberlain 13 May 1929, Chamberlain MSS, AC 4/1/1297.
153. A. Chamberlain to Ida Chamberlain 6 June 1929, ibid, AC 5/1/475.
154. N. Chamberlain to Ida Chamberlain 2 May 1929, ibid, NC 18/1/656.
155. A. Chamberlain to Baldwin 25 June 1929, ibid, AC 38/3/75.
156. N. Chamberlain to H. Chamberlain 21 July 1929, ibid, NC 18/1/662; L. Amery, *Life* ii, 507–8.
157. L. Amery, *Life* ii, 508.
158. Notes for Diary 11 March 1930, Hannon MSS 17/1.
159. N. Chamberlain to H. Chamberlain 13 Oct. 1929, Chamberlain MSS, NC 18/1/672. Times had now changed from the early days of Baldwin's government when Chamberlain and Churchill were 'engaged in a kind of wrestle for' the second place in the Cabinet. M. Gilbert, *Churchill* v, i, 358.
160. N. Chamberlain to Ida Chamberlain 29 June 1929, ibid, NC 18/1/660.
161. D. Carlton, *MacDonald versus Henderson* p. 16.
162. Ibid, p. 167; Roskill, *Hankey* ii, 478–9; A. Chamberlain to N. Chamberlain 9 Aug. 1929, Chamberlain MSS, NC 1/27/98.
163. A. Chamberlain to Baldwin 12 Oct. 1929, Baldwin MSS 116 f. 29.
164. A. Chamberlain to H. Chamberlain 19 Jan. 1930, Chamberlain MSS, AC 5/1/493.
165. A. Chamberlain to Ida Chamberlain 30 March 1930, ibid, AC 5/1/496.
166. N. Chamberlain to Ida Chamberlain 6 April 1930, ibid, NC 18/1/690.
167. A. Chamberlain to H. Chamberlain 14 June 1930, ibid, AC 5/1/504; A. Chamberlain to Ida Chamberlain 22 June 1930, AC 5/1/506.
168. Note by A. Chamberlain of meeting with Baldwin, MacDonald, Benn and Reading, 2 July 1930, ibid, AC 22/3/33.
169. A. Chamberlain to Ida Chamberlain 4 Aug. 1930, ibid, AC 5/1/510.
170. Petrie, *Life* ii, 377.
171. Lord Birkenhead, *Halifax* (London, 1965) pp. 287–8; see also M. Gilbert, *Churchill* v, ii, 180.
172. Salisbury to Baldwin 4 Aug. 1930, Baldwin MSS 104 ff. 23–6; Hoare to A. Chamberlain 14 Sept. 1930, Chamberlain MSS, AC 39/2/33; J. Cross, *Samuel Hoare* p. 131.
173. A. Chamberlain to Baldwin 11 Aug. 1930, Baldwin MSS 104 f. 30.
174. A. Chamberlain to N. Chamberlain 9 Oct. 1930, Chamberlain MSS, AC 39/2/40.
175. A. Chamberlain to H. Chamberlain 14 June 1930, ibid, AC 5/1/504; A. Chamberlain to Ida Chamberlain 2 Nov. 1930, AC 5/1/519.
176. A. Chamberlain to N. Chamberlain 9 Oct. 1930 and N. Chamberlain to A. Chamberlain 9 Oct. 1930, ibid, AC 39/2/39–40.

177. N. Chamberlain to H. Chamberlain 25 May 1931, ibid, NC 18/1/739.
178. A. Chamberlain to Ida Chamberlain 7 July 1930, ibid, AC 5/1/508.
179. Ibid, 19 July 1930, AC 5/1/508.
180. As note 174.
181. A. Chamberlain to H. Chamberlain 27 Oct. 1930, Chamberlain MSS, AC 5/1/518.
182. A. Chamberlain to Ida Chamberlain 2 Nov. 1930; A. Chamberlain to H. Chamberlain 9 Nov. 1930, ibid, AC 5/1/519–20.
183. R. James (ed), *Memoirs of a Conservative* p. 352; Bridgeman Diary, Dec. 1930.
184. M. Gilbert, *Churchill* v, ii, 249.
185. D. Carlton, *Anthony Eden* p. 27.
186. A. Chamberlain to Ivy Chamberlain 19 Jan. 1931, Chamberlain MSS, AC 6/1/778.
187. Ibid, 21 May 1930 and 3 Feb. 1931, AC 6/1/766, 786.
188. Ibid, 2 Feb. 1931, AC 6/1/785; A. Chamberlain to H. Chamberlain 27 Oct. 1930, AC 5/1/518; Gilbert, *Churchill* v, ii, 200–1.
189. A. Chamberlain to Ida Chamberlain 28 Feb. 1931, Chamberlain MSS, AC 5/1/532.
190. N. Chamberlain to H. Chamberlain 1 March 1931, ibid, NC 18/1/728; I. MacLeod, *Neville Chamberlain* p. 141.
191. N. Chamberlain Diary, 11 March 1931, Chamberlain MSS, NC 2/22; James (ed), *Memoirs of a Conservative* p. 360.
192. A. Chamberlain to M. Chamberlain 14 March 1931, Chamberlain MSS, AC 4/1/1307.
193. N. Chamberlain to H. Chamberlain 28 March 1931, ibid, NC 18/1/732.
194. N. Chamberlain Diary, 25 March 1931, ibid, NC 2/22; Bridgeman Diary, 28 March 1931; L. Amery, *Life* iii, 40.
195. A. Chamberlain to Ida Chamberlain 21 June 1931, Chamberlain MSS, AC 5/1/543.

CHAPTER NINE
ELDER STATESMAN

'Nature meant him for . . . an elder statesman.'
'I have pulled out the tooth and do not for a moment doubt that the operation was necessary, but the jaw still aches a little. Such is the way of nature.'[1]

The much vaunted role of elder statesman is not normally an easy one to fill in British political life. The dignity and respect which accompany seniority do not necessarily compensate for the absence of real power which the loss of office entails. Rather like old soldiers, semi-retired politicians tend to fade away and the process of withering can be both undignified and distressful. Austen Chamberlain was unusual, however, to the extent that his last years when he was out of office were among the most fruitful and distinguished of his career. Neville later wrote that

although only a private Member, in his last years his influence in the House of Commons was such as no other Member possessed and indeed was greater than when he himself had held high office.[2]

This was not simply a statement of fraternal respect. Lord Lee of Fareham confirmed that Chamberlain 'had become an accepted "Elder Statesman", with perhaps more influence in Parliament than he had ever enjoyed as a minister or party leader.'[3] The air of aloof superiority which in the 1920s had proved such a political handicap, especially to Chamberlain as party leader, became a decade later a point of magnetic attraction on the Tory backbenches. Neville noted that as his brother had grown older he had developed a sort of high, old-fashioned courtesy and consideration for others which, combined with his long experience of political affairs, gave him a unique position in the House of Commons.[4] One young M.P. recalled that 'in appearance, costume, method of speech, he seemed almost a survival. His top-hat, his eyeglass, his exquisite courtesy and his rotund oratory, marked him out from his colleagues.'[5] The result was that between 1931 and his death in 1937 Chamberlain was undoubtedly the most respected of Conservative back-benchers and it was to him that the young members, particularly those who came to find themselves at odds with the foreign policy of the National Government, looked for leadership and guidance. Thus 'the back-benches [gave] him what the Front Bench never did – disciples.'[6] The subsequent course of events has determined that another back-bencher, Winston Churchill, should occupy a unique role in the historiography of the 1930s. But by contemporaries Churchill was widely regarded as a failed politician and his attitude towards the problem of India served to isolate him almost completely from progressive opinion on the Conservative benches. Partly because his opinions on the Indian question were more in line with majority opinion in the Conservative party than were those of Churchill, Chamberlain tended to command more respect when he pronounced upon the deteriorating European situation than did his fellow ex-minister. As a former Foreign Secretary, Chamberlain's views inevitably carried considerable weight at a time when parliamentary attention was turning increasingly to international issues. Certainly, before 1937, Churchill did not begin to rival Chamberlain's position in the House of Commons. As Robert Cecil noted, 'I do not think Winston's queer manoeuvres matter one way or the other very much. He just lacks that bourgeois quality which makes Austen so formidable.'[7]

Chamberlain, though, did not assume his new role without difficulty or indeed discomfort. As he later reflected: 'For thirty years or more I have been at the very centre of events. After such an experience it is not easy to adjust oneself to the position of the fly on the wheel.'[8] As MacDonald's Labour government tottered towards collapse in the summer of 1931, to be replaced by a National Government formed under the same Prime Minister to deal with the country's financial crisis, Chamberlain played little part in those developments which were to determine the political climate of the next decade. When in late July Chamberlain walked across St. James's Park with his brother, discussing recent events, the whole idea of a National Government being formed came as news to him.[9] He was, though, clearly still hoping for high office. Realistically, his chances were slim. Not only was his age now against him, but with only four seats available for Conservatives in the new Cabinet, he was hardly likely to be favoured by Baldwin, especially as the claims of his brother could not be ignored. Moreover his own attitude towards Baldwin's party leadership over the previous year would not have been forgotten. When Chamberlain let it be known that he would not wish to join the government simply for a few weeks and then be dropped after a General Election, Baldwin indicated that he would prefer a younger man at the Foreign Office (Chamberlain presumed this would be Irwin), but raised the possibility for Chamberlain of the Lord Presidency of the Council, a peerage and leadership of the Upper House. Chamberlain ruled this out, but was prepared to consider the Lord Presidency in the Commons. He had not made up his mind whether to accept should he be asked to return to the office of Lord Privy Seal, but would certainly 'not go to one of the minor administrative offices which would be better bestowed on a younger man.'[10] When, however, a formal offer was made, it was that Chamberlain should become First Lord of the Admiralty outside the Cabinet. His official career was thus to close with an odd symmetrical precision since his first ministerial post had been as Civil Lord of the Admiralty thirty-six years earlier.

Chamberlain's first instinct was to decline the offer but, pressed by Neville who argued that 'he brought an element to the Cabinet discussions which no one else could contribute,'[11] he reluctantly accepted, deciding on reflection that the Admiralty 'with some duties was preferable to the Privy Seal with none.'[12] But though Neville noted that Chamberlain 'has come in very sweetly at the finish', the new First Lord felt bitterly resentful, not only about his own position but also about what he regarded as Baldwin's 'ugly self-centredness and lack of consideration for or appreciation of those who have helped him.' But, as he reflected, 'you can't make a silk purse out of a sow's ear.'[13]

But what must have rankled most with Chamberlain was the fact that, when the list of Cabinet appointments was announced, he learnt that the Foreign Office had been given not to a younger man such as Irwin but to an almost forgotten figure even older than himself. The Marquess of Reading, who was seventy-one years of age, had had a distinguished legal and imperial career, but had not held government office since resigning as Attorney General in 1913. Reading owed his inclusion in the Cabinet to little more than the fact that, in an all-party government, it was considered appropriate to include the Liberal leaders in both the Commons and the Lords, and he had succeeded Lord Beauchamp as leader in the Upper House as recently as the preceding winter. Though Neville had welcomed Reading's appointment to the Foreign Office as 'very suitable',[14] it was a bitter pill for his brother to swallow. With some reason, he must have considered himself a better qualified candidate for the post than the chosen incumbent. The situation was exacerbated when Chamberlain, on receipt of the Admiralty offer, sent a message to Ivy saying that he was returning to his first love, meaning the scene of his first ministerial appointment. She, however, interpreted this to mean the Foreign Office and wrote to congratulate him and to say that she knew Baldwin could not let him down. Neville believed that it was because Chamberlain felt himself lowered in his wife's eyes that he felt so miserable about the situation. The matter came to a head at an uncomfortable family dinner with Neville and Mary Carnegie:

It was rather painful as A had worked himself up into a very emotional condition and burst out that he was humiliated and treated as a back number. His lips trembled and tears came into his eyes and altogether he made us all very unhappy and uncomfortable.[15]

In the last resort it was probably Chamberlain's overriding sense of public duty which persuaded him to accept minor office, arguing, however, in private that any one of a dozen or twenty men could perform his duties equally well, while he alone could make 'the special contribution' in the office from which he had been excluded. Deep down he felt that he was now a mere cypher and was worried that the public image of him would not be of someone who had given all he could to help in a crisis, but of an old party hack who might be dangerous outside the government and must therefore 'have his mouth stopped with office.'[16]

Chamberlain's period as First Lord was both short and unhappy. His selection for this post was somewhat surprising in view of the strained relations that had existed between the Navy and himself for much of his Foreign Secretaryship in the twenties. As Bridgeman recalled, 'we were constantly fighting with his foreign policy, especially in regard to America.'[17] In public Chamberlain maintained a brave face over his disappointment. 'What a delightful office,' he remarked to Sam Hoare one morning in Hyde Park. 'Unlike the Foreign Office the Admiralty runs itself and the First Lord need not worry about it.'[18] His private correspondence, on the other hand, reveals a man who believed his talents were being wasted. On average he found less than an hour's work a day at the Admiralty:

So here I am: I linger over the morning papers, come down to the office, write my own letters . . .; spread the few scraps of work I get over as long as possible; lunch at the Club, come back here and somehow drag out the time; go back to the Club about 5.30 and read novels till 11 or 11.30 and then go to bed and sleep.[19]

Briefly, however, against the continuing background of the government's obsession with the economic situation, the Navy came into prominence with reports of a mutiny at the base at Invergordon. Though he had only become First Lord a little over a fortnight before the outbreak of indiscipline, Chamberlain must bear some of the responsibility for the insensitive imposition of pay cuts which brought the matter to a head. As Captain Roskill has pointed out, Petrie was a little too generous in relieving the First Lord of all criticism.[20] But at the time Chamberlain took over at the Admiralty his Labour predecessor, A. V. Alexander, had already assured the Cabinet that the Navy would accept cuts, provided they were in line with those being made elsewhere. A greater share of responsibility must be borne by the Sea Lords for their failure to brief the in-coming First Lord adequately.[21] Nonetheless, addressing the Cabinet on the last day of August, Chamberlain seemed unable to appreciate the extremely delicate point about a proposal to place men paid on the 1919 scale on to 1925 rates – a move which amounted effectively to a breach of contract. On 3 September he reported to the Admiralty Board that the Cabinet had been 'induced to overrule public pledges given to the Naval Service in the matter of pay and pensions.' In addition to the economies proposed by the May Committee, a further £2 million was to be lopped off the estimates for 1932–33 and the pay reduction would come into force as early as 1 October. Roskill soberly concludes that 'it would have been hard to conceive a scheme more calculated to unite the whole lower deck in opposition to the cuts.'[22]

A brief debate on the mutiny took place in the House of Commons on 17 September. It was marked by restraint on the part of the opposition and a tone of conciliation from the First Lord. Chamberlain said that 'The past is past. It is in the interest of everyone in the Navy or out of it to forget [the mutiny]. I am not going to look back. I am going to look forward.'[23] This stance ensured that there would be no courts martial in the aftermath of what had taken place. Chamberlain, in fact, seemed ready to accept on behalf of his ministry a measure of responsibility for what had happened. Even in his report to the monarch he admitted that 'the severity of the cuts . . . burst upon [the men] like a thunderclap,' while pleading in extenuation 'the rapidity with which events moved' and 'the very difficult conditions in which the Board had to act.' Then, writing on 4 October, he candidly admitted that 'we of the Board of Admiralty must accept some measure of blame. . . . We did not show all the foresight that might have been expected of us.'[24] His general instinct, however, was to play down the whole affair:

Happily it was confined to that one fleet and though it was rank insubordination there was nothing revolutionary or of what one ordinarily understands by mutiny about it. It was a 'down-tools' movement by men who were really frightened for their wives and homes and who were swept off their feet by the suddenness and severity of the cuts. No single act of disrespect to an officer or to the flag has been reported. On the whole good men gone wrong. All the ships quickly got back into apple pie order. . . .[25]

The Invergordon episode notwithstanding, Chamberlain generally had time on his hands during his brief stay at the Admiralty, although he did have some success in resisting cuts in the naval estimates. The temptation to be critical of the new government, at least in private, proved too strong to resist. He felt particularly sorry for his brother who, having suffered under a man as 'unhelpful and inert as S.B.', now complained that Ramsay MacDonald was 'infinitely worse.'[26] Chamberlain himself likened the Prime Minister to 'a bit of quaking jelly' and longed 'for a man' rather than a 'poor shivering mannikin.'[27] The lack of firm leadership was particularly worrying in the light of the discussions then proceeding at

Geneva on the question of disarmament. In view of his own disappointment it was not surprising that Chamberlain questioned Reading's capacity to handle these negotiations. 'He has no policy, I doubt if he has any ideas about or even knows of the problems arising at Geneva.' To the outside world Reading as Foreign Secretary was 'merely an interrogation mark.'[28]

By the end of September it was clear that if the National Government was to continue in existence it would need to seek a fresh mandate from the electorate, and in these circumstances Chamberlain welcomed Baldwin's determination to strive for an early election based upon a national appeal, but with a commitment to the introduction of tariffs to restore the balance of trade.[29] At this point and aware that there was no possibility that he, the hero of Locarno, would be offered the Foreign Office in a reorganised Cabinet, Chamberlain wrote to Baldwin publicly to waive his claim to future office in favour of younger men. Partly because of the expense which it involved and partly because it amounted to being little more than 'a glorified Under-Secretary,' the prospect of continuing at the Admiralty held no attraction for him. The next election, he therefore confided, would be his last and he could 'walk out with dignity and contentment.' 'Everything points,' he told his wife, 'to the time having come for me to ring down the curtain on my official life. It will not have been without fruit nor will the end be undignified.' His chief concern for the future would, as so often in the past, be 'the straitness and uncertainty of our means.'[30]

The King responded to the news of Chamberlain's pending retirement with a moving tribute to one whose public career exceeded even the monarch's own reign:

You may be assured that, after your devoted service during the last thirty-six years in Conservative and National Administrations, I feel that I am parting from, though not losing, an old and valued friend. Today, as you say, circumstances are wholly abnormal and I know that your present action in voluntarily with-drawing in order to make way for younger men, in order to further the best interests of your country and your colleagues, is in harmony with the public spirit and self-sacrifice which have always characterised your career. You have set a fine example and I trust that you may be given health and strength for many years to continue to help your Sovereign and your country.[31]

Despite such tokens of royal approval, however, it was not long before Chamberlain began to have misgivings about his own decision. When he got confirmation from Anthony Eden that Reading would not be continuing at the Foreign Office after the election and that Sir John Simon, the Liberal lawyer, was his most likely successor, the effect was electric:

He stopped in the middle of the Square and looked at me. 'I had not heard that,' he said. 'Had I known it was a possibility I would have tried to go back myself.'[32]

Still the feeling haunted Chamberlain that it was 'just at the F.O. that I think I could render service which no-one else can give' and his deeply, indeed overly, sensitive nature was offended by the conviction that, even if Baldwin and MacDonald had been in a position to offer him the post, they would not have wished to do so.[33] But at least there was some solace to be gained from the election result in West Birmingham where Chamberlain increased his personal majority from the precarious forty-three of 1929 to 11,900. Now he could confidently 'sing [his] Nunc Dimittis politically.'[34]

Over the next five and a half years, during which time the international situation steadily deteriorated and the mirage of lasting peace created at Locarno became ever less substantial, Chamberlain emerged as one of the leading back-bench critics of the National Government. Two qualifications need, however, to be noted – qualifications which served to temper the vehemence of his criticism. As in all his political activities, Chamberlain was first and foremost both loyal and moderate. On crucial occasions these qualities prevented him from coming out in outright opposition to the government. He was, he said, 'particularly anxious not to drift into that carping and critical attitude of the doings of my former colleagues which is the pit into which so many retired Ministers fall.'[35] The tendency, therefore, was for Chamberlain to emerge as the conscience of the MacDonald and Baldwin governments rather than their scourge. His attitude towards the League of Nations was of particular significance. Though Chamberlain viewed the international body as a strong moral force, he could not envisage it as an organisation with the power to coerce its members. He was, after all, the same man who, a decade earlier, had rejected the Geneva Protocol on the grounds that it aimed 'to preserve peace by organising war, and it may be, war on the largest scale.' There were, therefore, always strict limitations on Chamberlain's concept of collective security in these years.[36] In the second place Chamberlain was anxious to do nothing which might jeopardise the steady progression of his brother towards the premiership. Neville was obviously closely associated with the foreign policy of the National Government and, as the years went on, became one of its chief architects. This factor also was instrumental in setting Chamberlain upon a wary course. The sacrifice of giving up the seals of office in 1931 was relieved by the knowledge that Neville would 'carry on the good work and [that] it is safe in [his] hands.' Chamberlain was particularly gratified to see his brother elevated to the Exchequer where the latter was able through the signing of the Ottawa Agreements in 1932 to complete the 'great work' of their father in the attainment of Imperial Preference.[37]

During the first months of his semi-retirement from public life Chamberlain's mood fluctuated between mild optimism and near despair. In early November 1931 he assured Ivy that he had made the right decision, that he felt fit and relatively young and that he would 'find plenty of useful work to do and life [would] be full of interest.'[38] But to Neville just after Christmas he confessed that it was not easy to adapt to the role of an onlooker after being for so long in the very centre of events. He was 'genuinely anxious not to be a bore or an unhelpful critic' and asked for patience if his keen interest sometimes made him a little tiresome.[39] By the beginning of the following year Chamberlain admitted to being 'bored stiff'. The time he spent at the Commons hung very heavily on his hands and he was merely content to reflect that this would be his last parliament. Minor posts outside politics such as the chairmanship of the General Committee of the London School of Hygiene and Tropical Medicine and a Governorship at Rugby School did little to relieve his frustration, and by the autumn of 1932 Chamberlain confided that there was nothing in public affairs to console him. Though hiding his real feelings from Ivy, it was now his lot to 'eat my heart out in idleness and uselessness and see my work undone and feel myself unwanted and unregretted.'[40]

What finally rescued Chamberlain from this slough of despair was the growing conviction that he still had a role to play in alerting parliament and the country to the increasingly menacing international situation. He developed two platforms from which to operate. One was the backbenches of the House of Commons, where his seniority demanded that at the very least he be heard, while the other was the Executive of the League of Nations Union which he joined at the request of his party in February 1932. The significance of the latter position was that hitherto Lord Robert Cecil's national reputation had made it almost impossible for his views to be challenged on the Executive Committee. Chamberlain was able to change this and until 1936 acted as a brake on the prevailing tendencies of the Union, using the threat of his own resignation with all the skill that Cecil had employed in government in the twenties.[41] Chamberlain found on the Executive 'some of the worst cranks I have ever known . . . ready to dictate indifferently to H.M.G. or to the League how [every problem] should be handled'. He recognised, however, that the public standing of the League made it important for Conservative voices to be heard in the Union and to prevent left-wing views from gaining a monopoly, although he was anxious to remind Cecil that it was not the proper function of the Union to dictate policy to the League. This was the responsibility of the Council and Assembly.[42]

Ultimately it would be Germany upon which Chamberlain's thoughts and fears would focus, but in the first months of the National Government the threat to the peace seemed to come from further afield. Coming only days after Robert Cecil had asserted that 'there has scarcely been a period in the world's history when war seemed less likely than it does at present', the Japanese attack on Manchuria represented the first major challenge to the credibility of the League of Nations. Chamberlain's initial reaction was to support the Japanese action by recalling the profitable years of alliance between that country and Britain. He hoped that the government would do 'nothing to prevent the restoration to the full of the old Anglo-Japanese friendship.'[43] Even though his sympathies tended to shift towards the Chinese as the situation developed, Chamberlain remained opposed to unilateral British action and warned against attempting to thrust the country between the contending powers.[44] By this stage Chamberlain was more concerned with the European situation. That in Manchuria was probably beyond repair, whereas something useful in Europe could still be done. As a result, even moderate proposals such as the non-recognition of the Japanese puppet regime of Manchukuo, a general embargo on arms shipments to Japan and acceptance of the League Assembly's plans for a settlement were seen by Chamberlain as futile and possibly dangerous gestures, threatening to throw Britain 'into the forefront of a conflict on behalf of the League'.[45] Not surprisingly Cecil was angered by Chamberlain's determination not to act. 'His power of doing nothing amounts to genius.'[46]

As the cold wind of economic recession in Europe hastened the growth of political extremism on the continent, Chamberlain was increasingly concerned at the collapse of the Locarno spirit. He saw a 'Germany which has forgotten Stresemann and a France which rejects Briand.' He was sad to think that 'the spirit of those sunny days' had 'faded so quickly' and could not help thinking that the situation might have been very different but for subsequent mistakes in British policy. He held out little hope for the World Economic Conference and was concerned for Neville upon whom this burden had been placed.[47] He had heard that the post-war generation in Germany was anxious, after dealing with the Jews, Socialists and Communists within the state, to strike out at the Poles. The international situation looked 'worse . . . than at any time since 1914' and Chamberlain's fear was that 'the powder magazines may blow up at any moment.'[48] As France grew anxious in the face of an increasingly menacing German neighbour, it no longer seemed clear whether the British guarantee of 1925 still held good.[49] In the disarmament negotiations at Geneva everyone was 'at sixes and sevens', 'hesitating and floundering, lacking any sure aim or certain guidance.' A visit to Geneva in the autumn of 1932 left Chamberlain profoundly anxious and convinced that neither MacDonald nor Simon had a policy, both merely 'content with patchwork.'[50] As the Prime Minister's pronouncements on foreign affairs became increasingly woolly and vague, Chamberlain was driven to comment: 'Does he know what he wants or what he means? If he does, no one else does ... I have not a ghost of an idea what he is at.'[51]

Chamberlain was one of the first British observers to recognise the menace posed by Adolf Hitler, who became German Chancellor on 30 January 1933. Never one of those ready to join in the popular critique of the Versailles settlement as an iniquitous *diktat* – he once asked 'what kind of life we should be living in this country [and] what ransom we should have to pay if Germany had won'[52] – Chamberlain was adamant that the new German regime was not one to which concessions could be made. 'To a Germany much, to *this* Germany nothing'. MacDonald's loose use of the phrase 'equality of status' in relation to Germany naturally filled him with alarm.[53] He recognised also the probable links between the domestic brutality of the Nazi regime and its likely external concomitants:

The temper of the new German Government repels me in its domestic aspects and fills me with anxiety for its possible consequences in foreign affairs.[54]

To this extent Chamberlain could claim to have seen through two of the central fallacies which undermined the conduct of British foreign policy in the 1930s. Six months of Hitlerian rule would suffice to 'see the death of effective parliamentaryism' [sic] and, if the right wing secured a majority in the German elections, then 'God help us all'.[55] In Chamberlain's mind everything would ultimately turn on British policy, and if Hitlerism could not be defeated by showing that it did not pay, then he was ready to despair of peace.[56] Would Germany be allowed to rearm while Britain continued to press others to disarm? 'Have we in fact a policy and is the Cabinet behind it and do our representatives abroad know what it is if it indeed exists?'[57]

Chamberlain's first major parliamentary pronouncement on the German question came in a debate on 13 April 1933. Coming so soon after Hitler's assumption of power, and because it encapsulates the essence of what was to be Chamberlain's consistent line on this issue, the speech merits quotation:

What is this new spirit of German nationalism? The worst of all-Prussian Imperialism, with an added savagery, a racial pride, an exclusiveness which cannot allow to any fellow-subject not of 'pure Nordic birth' equality of rights and citizenship within the nation to which he belongs. Are you going to discuss revision with a Government like that? . . . Germany is afflicted by this narrow, exclusive, aggressive spirit, by which it is a crime to be in favour of peace and a crime to be a Jew. This is not a Germany to which we can afford to make concessions.[58]

In the following month Chamberlain reiterated his concern that there was a direct connection between the internal activities of the Nazi regime and its conduct in the wider world: 'I still feel that the spirit which manifests itself in the proscription of a whole race within the boundaries of Germany is a spirit which if allowed to prevail in foreign affairs will be a menace to the whole world'. He drew attention also to the belligerent outbursts of leading German politicians, including Von Papen's pronouncement that warfare was to a man what child-bearing was to a woman, something without which his life was not complete.[59] Again on 5 July Chamberlain uttered a further warning:

Whether you read the story of the twenty or thirty years which preceded the war, or whether you read the story of the post-war years, you will find the same thing. While something is refused to Germany it is vital. If you say 'Well, we will give it to you and now our relations will, of course, be on a satisfactory footing', it loses all value from the moment that she obtains it and it is used by her merely as a stepping-off place for a further demand.[60]

These speeches were among the most impressive performances of Chamberlain's parliamentary career; yet like Churchill, though for somewhat different reasons, he gained few converts in the House of Commons. He was listened to with the respect due to an elder statesman but little more. As a result no effective challenge to the foreign policy of the National Government emerged. Yet in Chamberlain's mind Simon was 'a very bad Foreign Secretary. He has no policy, is very pleased with himself and wholly unconscious of the effect he produces on others'. It was 'the wrong place to put him'. Anthony Eden would have been a much better choice, and might have been less intent on 'running after Germany', and giving the impression that she was 'getting away with it'.[61] Neither the Foreign Office staff nor Britain's representatives abroad knew what Simon was doing nor what they should be aiming for. He had allowed the Germans to think that they had got Britain on the run.[62] Though stressing that he was not himself a candidate for the succession, Chamberlain pleaded with Neville to try to remove Simon from office.[63] He was also among those who hoped in 1935 to see Lloyd George included in the administration. The East Wavertree by-election, in which the intervention of Randolph Churchill served to lose the seat for the government, convinced him that a wide-ranging reconstruction of the government was needed. The opposition of Neville to the return of Lloyd George was, however, an insurmountable obstacle.[64] Recognising that Ramsay MacDonald was now an 'incubus' and would soon have to retire from the premiership, Chamberlain saw in Baldwin a 'bad though inevitable successor'. Yet the prospect that a General Election might see the return of a pacifist-inclined Labour government filled him with even greater alarm.[65]

Nor did Chamberlain find consolation in the activities of the League of Nations Union, where his 'sleeping partnership . . . [had] become a shirt of Nessus'. 'I find all that body of public opinion with which I am associated more and more estranged from the Union', he told Gilbert Murray. The one-sided way in which the Peace Ballot of 1934 was organised annoyed him considerably. Chamberlain and some of his associates had drawn up a blue paper to point out the shortcomings of the ballot and to counter a green paper which was being distributed on behalf of the Union of Democratic Control. In the end neither paper was circulated. By the end of the year Chamberlain's resignation from the Union seemed imminent.[66]

Chamberlain's other major parliamentary interest of this time − the future government of India − seemed more capable of solution and to offer scope for fruitful action. As a former Secretary of State for India and one-time unwitting contender for the Viceroyalty, Chamberlain was a natural choice to serve on the government's joint select committee on India. His support, and that of Lord Derby in the Upper House, was vital to the successful passage of the Government of India Bill through parliament. If the government could show that it had the backing of such men, it could afford to override the opposition of right-wing critics such as Churchill. As a result, the Secretary of State, Sir Samuel Hoare, was ready to make concessions to Chamberlain, such as promising additional powers to Indian governors in relation to terrorism, in return for his support. Hoare recognised the crucial importance of Chamberlain's consent: 'Unless . . . independent leaders like Eddie [Derby] and Austen back us, neither the Government nor the Bill will survive'.[67] Chamberlain too appreciated the significance of his own role. 'Certainly the Govt. ought to be grateful to me, for if I had gone against them, there isn't a doubt but that they would have been beaten and indeed, unless I had exerted myself, I don't think they could have obtained a working majority'. As so often in the past it was Chamberlain's sense of loyalty and rectitude which dictated his course of action. 'If I had been a little differently made, it was a glorious opportunity to follow Palmerston's example and "give Johnny Russell a tit for his tat"'.[68] But Chamberlain was disturbed that on this matter he should find himself at odds with Churchill, with whom on questions of foreign policy he was increasingly speaking with a common voice and for

whom he felt a growing regard.[69] Indeed, while the two men went their
separate ways on India, they combined successfully at the beginning of
1935 to persuade the government to set up an enquiry, in the form of a
sub-committee of the C.I.D., into the question of defence against
bombing, on lines recommended by Professor Lindemann.[70]

By this stage Chamberlain had decided to reverse his earlier decision
and to stand yet again for parliament at the next election.[71] Despite the
repeated suggestions throughout his career that he was not in the truest
sense a genuinely political animal, Chamberlain could not bring himself to
make the final break from public life. He was in any case far more certain
than in 1931 that he could still perform a useful function. His financial
situation remained however a cause of great concern. Almost all his
capital had gone and he had little left apart from his current income. As
soon as his daughter Diane was married, he planned to change his whole
way of life and move into a much smaller house. The expense involved was
a compelling factor in his decision in October 1933 to refuse the offer of
the sinecure post of Lord Warden of the Cinque Ports.[72] A proposed
lecture tour of the United States in 1933, designed almost entirely to make
money, failed to materialise, but Chamberlain did manage to complete a
volume of autobiographical essays, published as *Down the Years,* though
experiencing some difficulty in spinning out the book to the required
length.[73]

The publication of the government's Defence White Paper in March
1935 gave Chamberlain a renewed opportunity to warn of the German
menace. The policy of making concessions to the Nazis had served only to
step up the latter's demands. 'I warned [Simon] that if he took the first slap
in the face quietly, he would invite another.'[74] Asked by the Chief Whip to
move an amendment drafted by the Foreign Secretary to the opposition's
vote of censure, Chamberlain took exception to 'a piece of Simonian
smugness' and drew up an amendment of his own.[75] His speech proved to
be the most telling of the debate. Neville noted that 'he made all the points
I wanted made and made them most effectively. He had quite an ovation,
when he sat down'.[76] Particularly telling was the response which he made
to Clement Attlee, deputy leader of the Labour party, who had suggested
that national salvation lay in the renunciation of armaments:

If war breaks out, if we become involved in a struggle . . . do you think he will
hold the language he held today? If he does, he will be one of the first victims of
the war, for he will be strung up by an angry, and justifiably angry, populace to
the nearest lamp post.

Yet while Chamberlain seemed to recognise that some overwhelming
force would be needed to restrain Hitler, as the architect of Locarno he

still envisaged collective security in terms of regional pacts, of 'agreements among nations in a particular region, whose fates are so knit with one another that they cannot be indifferent to what happens in that area and who on any aggression in that area will be found ready to help in the repression of the aggressor'. He took the occasion to restate the guiding principles which had motivated his conduct of the nation's diplomacy back in 1924–25:

Obligations which are universal are, in the nature of things, obligations which people are not very ready to fulfil. . . . You would not get this country, you would not get our people – it is not our governors, but our people – to consent to sending their sons out to die for all those glorious phrases which the right honourable gentlemen opposite so used and so abused, in order to destroy Manchuquo or in order to enforce peace in South America.

But perhaps of greater pertinence to the present situation was Chamberlain's apparent realisation, not it seems shared by the government, that in the last resort Nazi Germany did not necessarily share the devotion of all reasonable men to the maintenance of peace. The real danger of war might arise 'not by accident but of set purpose . . . to achieve some object of national ambition, national aggrandisement or national revenge which it cannot satisfy by peaceful means'.[77]

Chamberlain picked up the same point on 2 May when questioning the Foreign Secretary about his recent visit to Berlin. What sort of impression had Simon gathered from his conversations with German leaders? 'Is it a Germany that is really willing and anxious to come to an agreement? Or is it a Germany that is pushing here, seizing there, drilling her own people daily, building up this immense fleet, building a new navy?'[78] In private he complained that the visit had been mishandled since it had only served to divide Britain from France at a time when unity between the two countries was absolutely vital. In the course of two days Simon had given Chamberlain three different reasons for his actions, at least one of which was untrue since it contradicted the other two. 'I should not like to go tiger shooting with him myself.'[79] By May Chamberlain was describing Simon as 'a positive danger', who could be ousted by backbench pressure if Chamberlain himself were to take the lead. Characteristically, however, he refused to do so, and Simon survived until a government reshuffle, to coincide with MacDonald's retirement from the premiership, saw him transferred to the Home Office where he had also served during the Great War.[80] There is some evidence that Chamberlain was Baldwin's first choice to succeed Simon at the Foreign Office,[81] but in the event the position went to Sir Samuel Hoare, while Anthony Eden assumed responsibility for League of Nations affairs – a division of work of which

Chamberlain, perhaps recalling his own troubled partnership with Robert Cecil a decade earlier, was highly critical.[82]

Hoare's brief tenure of the Foreign Office was dominated by the question of Italian designs in Abyssinia. When in the spring of 1935 it had become clear that Mussolini was preparing for an African campaign, the Foreign Office asked Chamberlain to write to his friend Grandi, the Italian ambassador in London, to make informal representations of Britain's concern. Chamberlain stressed the importance of Anglo-Italian friendship, but warned that if Italy sought an armed solution of the Abyssinian question the effect on British opinion would be deplorable. Italian aggression would also weaken public law in Europe and encourage Germany to fresh provocation:

the friends of Italy cannot view without grave anxiety the prospect of a considerable part of the Italian forces being locked up for an indefinite term in Africa whilst the European situation is so critical and whilst no assurance has been received from Germany that she will respect Austrian independence and refrain from further interference in the internal affairs of that country.[83]

This passage illustrates the dilemma in which Chamberlain now found himself. For Chamberlain the Abyssinian affair was somewhat similar to the earlier Manchurian crisis to the extent that it tended to divert attention from graver problems within Europe. Never an out and out champion of the League, Chamberlain was unsure in his own mind whether the most effective restraint upon German aggression would be the League itself or a friendly Italy. This uncertainty prevented Chamberlain from giving a strong lead to backbench opinion in the course of the crisis, such as might have forced the government into a whole-hearted policy of collective security. In public Chamberlain seemed ready to back the League. In the Commons on 11 July he asserted that

We are coming very near to what may be a test case for the League as to whether it does mean collective security; whether it does mean anything for any one or nothing for any one. It is not to be supposed that the League can be flouted under the eyes of Europe, that League methods can be repudiated, a policy of force and conflict engaged in and that the League can pass all that by, because it happens to occur in Africa and not in Europe, without thereby destroying the value of collective security not for Africa only but for Europe . . . .[84]

In private, however, he confessed that whatever action was taken would damage the government at home and increase danger in Europe. 'I see not a ray of light through these dark clouds.' He was clear that Britain should not take action alone, but doubted whether French support would be forthcoming. 'But if Abyssinia is swallowed up under the eyes of [the]

XVII (*top left*) Ida Chamberlain (Birmingham University)

(*top right*) Hilda Chamberlain (Birmingham University)

(*bottom*) With Ivy, Diane and Joseph Jnr. (Birmingham University)

XVIII (*top and bottom*) Campaigning in West Birmingham (Birmingham University)

missed a golden opportunity to bring discontented Conservatives into the opposition lobbies, Chamberlain had in fact simply seized upon the Labour leader's remarks as a pretext for a course of action upon which he had already determined. He did after all now expect to succeed the unfortunate Hoare. Indeed, Chamberlain made it clear in another part of his speech that, while he rejected the Hoare-Laval proposals, he was still looking for a compromise solution to the Abyssinian crisis – a compromise of which he presumably expected to be the architect in the coming months.[96]

With the enforced sacrifice of Samuel Hoare there was widespread speculation that he would now be replaced by Chamberlain. Neville, surprised that his brother seemed ready to assume office again, heard that Hoare himself favoured Chamberlain as his successor.[97] Even an unfriendly observer such as 'Chips' Channon admitted that Chamberlain would make an 'excellent stop-gap for a few months until the Government regains its prestige'.[98] Eden believed that this was the moment for a respected statesman to go to the Foreign Office and regarded Chamberlain as the best choice. He carried more weight in foreign affairs than any other candidate and his integrity was nowhere questioned. Though his age might make it difficult for Chamberlain to hold office for long, the short-term situation was compelling. Eden conveyed this opinion to the Prime Minister, but Baldwin had other ideas.[99] On the day following the Commons debate Baldwin asked Chamberlain to call on him to discuss the situation. The Prime Minister promised the 'same frankness that has always prevailed between us', but the interview turned into one of the most embarrassing in the long political association of the two men. Baldwin professed that he would have loved to reappoint Chamberlain to the Foreign Office, but feared that the latter would not be able to stand the strain. No one would believe that the appointment could be more than temporary or that Chamberlain could possibly last out the Parliament. Chamberlain found this part of the interview 'very characteristic. "We were not amused" '. Worse, though, was to follow, as Baldwin, drawing upon the parallel of Ramsay MacDonald, spoke of the dangers of a politician becoming unfit for his work without himself being aware of the fact. It soon became clear that Baldwin intended to offer the post to Anthony Eden, who thus became Foreign Secretary at the age of 38. Chamberlain narrowly kept his temper in the course of the interview, but was clearly galled at being told he was too old for office by a Prime Minister only four years his junior. He later summed up the conversation most succinctly: 'He told me I was ga-ga'.[100] Churchill reflected, 'Poor man, he always plays the game and never wins it'.[101]

Baldwin's behaviour is open to a variety of interpretations. It is possible that Chamberlain had been over sanguine about the Prime Minister's original 'offer'. Alternatively Baldwin may have been upset by Chamberlain's failure to give whole-hearted support to the government at the meeting of the Foreign Affairs Committee. Perhaps it was the final dismissal of a man who had exhausted his usefulness and could now be safely ignored. Certainly the general impression was that Baldwin had 'allowed Austen to pilot the Government barque through stormy water in the House in the belief that he was about to take office'.[102] From Chamberlain's point of view the incident represented the last straw in his long, but often chequered, relationship with the 'worst Prime Minister since that other great and good man, Aberdeen'.[103] He was convinced that, had he thought it compatible with the public interest, he could have so reduced Baldwin's majority in the Commons as to force his resignation. Chamberlain reflected upon the contrast between Baldwin's public image and the real man whom he, Chamberlain, had come to despise:

They think him a simple, hardworking, unambitious man, not a 'politician' in the abusive sense in which they so often use the word, whom nothing but a stern sense of duty keeps at his ungrateful task, a man too of wide and liberal mind who has educated his party. And we know him as self-centred, selfish and idle, yet one of the shrewdest not to say slyest of politicians, but without a constructive idea in his head and with an amazing ignorance of Indian and foreign affairs and of the real values of political life.[104]

At all events Baldwin, possibly on the prompting of Oliver Locker-Lampson,[105] sought to make amends in a way that served only to rub salt into Chamberlain's wounds. Seeing Chamberlain again on 21 December, Baldwin offered him a non-departmental post in the Cabinet to advise on foreign affairs and defence. Chamberlain concluded, however, that after Baldwin had taken such pains to emphasise that he thought him unfit for hard work, he was looking not for Chamberlain's experience and advice, but merely for his name to patch up the government's damaged reputation.[106] The similarly hurtful offer a decade earlier of the Washington embassy must have passed through his mind as Chamberlain politely but firmly declined Baldwin's invitation.[107]

Though he later worked closely with him, Winston Churchill had little confidence in Eden at this date. 'I expect the greatness of his office will find him out. Austen would have been far better.'[108] In fact the New Year saw Churchill and Chamberlain co-operating as vigilant critics of the National Government's foreign policy, though Chamberlain continued to have misgivings about the appearance of any anti-government cabal. Churchill later recalled that in the last year of Chamberlain's life they had worked more closely together than at any time in a political association of nearly forty years.[109] A pro-rearmament group began to meet regularly to discuss strategy. Chamberlain noted that although the group expressed a wide range of options, all were agreed that the German menace was a potentially fatal one and that dealing with this danger had been too long delayed.[110] One of these meetings at Lord Winterton's Sussex home in May provoked comments in the press about a meeting of the 'Anti-Baldwin Shadow Cabinet'. The premier was evidently rattled and uncharacteristically declared that it was 'a time of the year when midges came out of dirty ditches'.[111] Channon suspected 'dark schemes to torpedo the government', but this would not have been in Chamberlain's nature, particularly in view of Neville's presence in the Cabinet.[112] Nonetheless, Chamberlain did cause his brother considerable embarrassment early in April when joining with Churchill to ask for an explicit denial that the government contemplated handing over Tanganyika to Germany in an exercise of colonial appeasement.[113] Neville felt it impossible to state that in no circumstances would the government consider the surrender of its mandate.[114]

Chamberlain was also among those who began pressing in February 1936 for the formation of a Ministry of Defence to unify the work of the three service ministries. He was in no doubt that Churchill should be recalled to the Cabinet to head it, and was alarmed that Baldwin was rumoured to be considering Ramsay MacDonald for the post. 'In my view there is only one man who by his studies and his special abilities and aptitudes is marked out for it and that man is Winston Churchill.'[115] He doubted, however, whether such an appointment would meet with Neville's approval, let alone the Prime Minister's. Neville had suggested to Baldwin that his brother should head a new defence enquiry committee and, somewhat surprisingly, the premier 'rather liked the idea', though agreeing that the approach would be more likely to succeed if it came from Neville and not himself.[116]

Chamberlain, however, declined to be considered and seemed to be moving towards a stance of outright opposition to the government when he delivered an uncharacteristically sharp attack in the Commons debate on 14 February. A personal assault on Baldwin and his mistakes caused 'a mild sensation'[117] and reflected the fact that relations between the two men were now at their nadir. The speech amounted to a stiff lecture on Baldwin's complete failure to have a policy. Chamberlain showed how the Prime Minister had been wrong in his estimate of German air strength, and expressed his own view in favour of a Minister of Defence to preside over the C.I.D. and to guide the Chiefs of Staff.[118] The speech crystallised the thoughts of a growing number of M.P.s about the premier's mental inertia. Chamberlain later explained: 'I thought that Baldwin had become too complacent and needed convincing that the situation was regarded by his friends as serious, and I chose the occasion of Friday's debate because it was conducted entirely on non-party lines and could not be perverted in any way to the purpose of a Vote of Censure'. He was anxious, Chamberlain added, 'lest Baldwin's selection for the post should not be adequate'.[119]

Two days later Neville went to see the Prime Minister who had concluded that the best thing would be for Neville himself to take the new defence portfolio, while Chamberlain took over at the Exchequer at least until Neville succeeded Baldwin as premier.[120] The plan always seemed an unlikely one and Baldwin may have made the suggestion in the knowledge that it would not attract Neville. At all events the latter made no mention of the offer of the Exchequer when speaking with his brother, while Chamberlain made it clear that he would refuse the Defence Ministry were it offered to him. Neville noted: 'As for me, he recognised that I had changed (developed) a good deal since we sat in Cabinet together . . . but he did not think it would be a good thing that I should take the job'.[121] Ultimately Baldwin opted for Inskip, the Attorney General, as the man to whom the fewest objections could be made. Chamberlain, however, was alarmed that this was a 'man with no experience in administration who has never given a thought to problems of defence . . . . You will see that I am being driven into opposition or nearly so'.[122]

Consideration of governmental appointments took a back seat as Europe witnessed the latest step in the unfolding of Hitler's grand design when, in March 1936, German forces reoccupied the Rhineland. Though recognising the situation to be grave, Chamberlain's initial response to this new development was cautious. Within a week, however, he was writing ominously of the 'complete triumph' of Germany and the 'ultimate ruin' of Great Britain.[123] To the House of Commons he stressed that what was at stake was not a parochial squabble between France and Germany, but whether in future the rule of law or the law of force should prevail.[124] The same theme characterised a speech to the Birmingham Jewellers' Association. 'Was there any international morality or law or had we returned to the rule of force in which the strongest did what he liked and the weakest went to the wall?'[125] Chamberlain now foresaw the future pattern of Nazi aggression. 'What attitude', he asked the Commons on 1 April, 'shall we take if Austrian independence is threatened or destroyed whether by an attack from outside or by a revolution fostered and supported from outside?' The independence of Austria was the key to the situation, for 'if Austria perishes, Czechoslovakia becomes indefensible'. Thereafter a German dominated Central European Empire would become a reality with incalculable consequences for the whole of the British

Empire.[126] Britain needed to do some hard thinking about the concept of 'collective security' to decide whether it was anything more than 'a pretty phrase to adorn a meaningless speech'.[127]

His own preference, however, remained for a Locarno-type policy – a definite guarantee of peace in the area where Britain was vitally interested and the restriction of obligations elsewhere.[128] Consequently Chamberlain regarded the continuation of sanctions against Italy, now that Abyssinia had been conquered, as foolish and dangerous:

The Italo-Abyssinian dispute is a side-issue, and most of us, whether sanctionist or not, are thinking more of the danger threatening from Germany.[129]

Chamberlain was still in touch with Grandi and the latter played upon his susceptibility to flattery to encourage him to think that Anglo-Italian friendship and co-operation was still a realisable goal and that he, Chamberlain, could be one of its major architects.[130] The situation in Europe was, Chamberlain believed, so dangerous that a struggle in the Mediterranean could not be risked.[131] Yet Chamberlain saw that the state of public opinion would make it very difficult to pursue 'the only wise policy' – to call off sanctions and restore the Stresa Front of Britain, France and Italy.[132] This issue finally prompted his resignation from the executive of the League of Nations Union in June. Lord Milner's widow wrote to express her relief that Chamberlain's name would no longer be used 'for the purposes of the Angells and Noel Bakers'.[133]

By the summer of 1936 Chamberlain was canvassing a proposal for a secret session of the Commons to discuss defence and foreign policy. Both Neville and Baldwin were hostile to the idea, but as a sop suggested a deputation of senior back-benchers to whom things could be said which were impossible on the floor of the House. The meeting duly took place on 28 and 29 July, with Chamberlain leading for the Commons and Salisbury for the Lords. Churchill and Horne were also among the delegation while Baldwin and Inskip represented the government.[134] The meeting produced little evident result. Amery noted after a similar deputation to Inskip in November, 'We all went out with long faces'.[135] The government knew that it still had the backing of the vast majority of the House of Commons. Though Chamberlain noted that Baldwin's stock was falling rapidly, 'yet the Party still rallies to him when attacked'.[136] Neville sensed that Chamberlain, 'getting more and more tied up with Winston's crowd', had lost some of his influence with the Commons, who suspected him of anti-Baldwinism.[137] Many remained totally unmoved by Chamberlain's warnings. Channon noted after one 'really stupid speech in which [Chamberlain] attacked Germany with unreasoning violence', 'he is ossified, tedious and hopelessly out of date'.[138]

By the autumn, moreover, the country's attention had been diverted from the international situation to the crisis in the monarchy at home. Chamberlain found the whole episode a tiresome distraction. He hoped against hope that the new King's sense of public duty would force him to subordinate his personal feelings to the needs of the state, but eventually concluded that Edward VIII did not know how to be King. Of Mrs. Simpson he was totally contemptuous. 'I am told that I have met her, but she left no impression upon me', while Baldwin's handling of the crisis he found excessively generous to the King.[139] But it was irritating that one consequence of the abdication was the postponement of Baldwin's long predicted retirement and therefore of Neville's accession to the premiership. Though the relationship of the two brothers had never been entirely easy since the early 1920s, Chamberlain sincerely wanted to see Neville reach the ultimate pinnacle of political life. Yet his attitude towards his younger brother remained to the end somewhat condescending. Eden recalled a dinner party at which Neville ventured to express an opinion on the European situation, whereupon Chamberlain interjected, 'Neville, you must remember you don't know anything about foreign affairs'. Many subsequent commentators would have regarded this view as prophetic.[140]

The autumn saw Chamberlain still vigorously pursuing his chosen course. Eden invited him to assume an unofficial mission to make contact with Mussolini,[141] while Chamberlain also took the lead in warning against approaches from von Ribbentrop for British friendship on the basis of a common opposition to communism. 'If our friendship is to be sought, let it be for its own sake. ... The verbal contests of Nazi and Bolshevik are not worth the bones of a British Grenadier.'[142] There was time too for some sentimental journeys. In November 1936 he received an honorary degree at Lyons at the invitation of Edouard Herriot and the following January paid a final visit to Paris. There he spoke with Blum, the Prime Minister, and visited the École des Sciences Politiques where he had studied half a century earlier. The last letter of his long correspondence with his sisters was written in March 1937. Appropriately its subject matter was not politics, but his enduring interest in his garden:

When I went to bed last night, it was raining; when I woke up this morning it was snowing and now it is all slush! When will my garden be ready and shall I be able to plant the flowering trees and bushes that I want to see there? I had hoped to be planting this weekend but the work takes longer than I had expected.[143]

The end came with some suddenness. Chamberlain suffered a mild heart attack on 12 March and was confined to his home. Four days later he seemed to be on the mend and got up for lunch. In the evening he decided to take a bath. Neville recorded what happened next:

A moment later he called Ivy; she ran upstairs and found that he had dried himself and put on his vest and drawers and sat down in a chair. He had then fallen over striking his head against the basin. She got some brandy as he was still breathing and he just gulped it down but died immediately. The doctor who was called in said he had not suffered at all. It was a merciful end far preferable to Father's 8 years of martyrdom. But it is a great shock and I feel stunned.[144]

To the Archbishop of Canterbury Neville later wrote:

from my earliest days I have looked up to Austen with perhaps much more deference, as well as affection, than is usually the case where the difference of years is so small. He was a rare good brother to me, and the only one I had.[145]

On the following day tributes were paid in the House of Commons. Lloyd George recalled their partnership in the days of coalition and spoke of 'a man who strained the point of honour always against himself. . . . No public man of our time . . . sacrificed more to integrity, to honour and to loyalty to friends, to his party and to his country.'[146] But it was Baldwin who produced the most moving tribute. 'Whatever S.B. cannot do', noted Tom Jones, 'he can speak a funeral oration.'[147] Less eloquently, but perhaps with more prescience, 'Chips' Channon noted that 'there must be rejoicing in Germany tonight that this desiccated patriarch . . . is no more'.[148] With the funeral over, Neville, now only weeks away from the premiership, recorded in the privacy of his diary:

This afternoon we have been to St. Marylebone Cemetery beyond Hampstead to see the urn deposited in the grave. The flowers were marvellously beautiful and the spot chosen looks over a wide view. The birds were singing in the trees and I felt it was a good place.[149]

Notes

1. L. Amery, *Life* iii, 71; A. Chamberlain to N. Chamberlain 5 Nov. 1931, Chamberlain MSS, NC 1/27/100.
2. C. Petrie, *Chamberlain Tradition* pp. 280–1; N. Chamberlain to H. Chamberlain 6 Dec. 1931, Chamberlain MSS, NC 18/1/764.
3. A. Clark, *Innings* p. 339. Vansittart noted: 'From a joke after Locarno he became an oracle in Westminster. "Let us hear what Austen has to say" became a refrain for younger men.' *Mist Procession* p. 549.
4. C. Petrie, *Chamberlain Tradition* p. 280.
5. H. Macmillan, *Winds of Change* pp. 174–5. Macmillan remembered Chamberlain as 'the last man whom I have seen to sit in the Speaker's chair

as a convenient place from which to listen to a debate . . . I have never seen anyone try to do so, except Austen. Nor do I think anyone else could have got away with it.'

6. B. Cartland, *Ronald Cartland* (London, 1941) p. 70.
7. R. Cecil to G. Murray 16 June 1936, cited K. Robbins, *Munich* p. 125; A. Chamberlain to H. Chamberlain 3 Oct. 1931, Chamberlain MSS, AC 5/1/556.
9. N. Chamberlain diary 24 July 1931, ibid, NC 2/22.
10. A. Chamberlain to Ivy Chamberlain 24 Aug. 1931, ibid, AC 6/1/801.
11. Ibid; Neville pointed out 'that his name wd. carry great weight abroad.' N. Chamberlain diary 25 Aug. 1931, NC 2/22.
12. A. Chamberlain to Ivy Chamberlain 26 Aug. 1931, ibid, AC 6/1/803.
13. Ibid; N. Chamberlain to Annie Chamberlain 25 Aug. 1931, NC 1/26/449.
14. N. Chamberlain diary 24 Aug. 1931, ibid, NC 2/22.
15. N. Chamberlain to Annie Chamberlain 27 and 29 Aug. 1931, ibid, NC 1/26/451, 452; N. Chamberlain to H. Chamberlain 27 Aug. 1931, ibid, NC 18/1/754.
16. A. Chamberlain to Ida Chamberlain 31 Aug. 1931, ibid, AC 5/1/551.
17. Bridgeman diary, Aug. 1931.
18. Lord Templewood, *Nine Troubled Years* (London, 1954) p. 23.
19. A. Chamberlain to Ivy Chamberlain 4 and 27 Sept. 1931, Chamberlain MSS, AC 6/1/810, 813.
20. S. Roskill, *Naval Policy,* i, 38; Petrie, *Life* ii, 382.
21. S. Roskill, *Naval Policy between the Wars* vol. ii (London, 1976) p. 119; Bridgeman diary, Aug. 1931.
22. S. Roskill, *Naval Policy* ii, 92–3.
23. House of Commons Debates vol. 256, col. 1120.
24. S. Roskill, *Naval Policy* ii, 118; S. Roskill, *Hankey* ii, 557. 'If at any future time it should become necessary to ask a similar sacrifice of men actually serving, explanation, enquiry and consultation must take place before, and not after, the decision is taken.' A. Chamberlain to George V 25 Sept. 1931, Chamberlain MSS, AC 39/3/38.
25. A. Chamberlain to M. Chamberlain 27 Sept. 1931, Chamberlain MSS, AC 4/1/1312.
26. K. Young, *Stanley Baldwin* p. 97.
27. A. Chamberlain to Ivy Chamberlain 5 Oct. 1931, Chamberlain MSS, AC 6/1/824.
28. Ibid, 3 and 4 Sept. 1931, AC 6/1/809, 810.
29. A. Chamberlain to Ida Chamberlain 26 Sept. 1931, ibid, AC 5/1/555.
30. A. Chamberlain to Baldwin 28 Oct. 1931, Baldwin MSS 45 f. 188; A. Chamberlain to Ivy Chamberlain 2 and 3 Oct. 1931, Chamberlain MSS, AC 6/1/820–1.
31. H. Nicolson, *George V* p. 495.
32. Lord Avon, *Facing the Dictators* (London, 1962) p. 22.
33. A. Chamberlain to Ivy Chamberlain 10 Oct. 1931, Chamberlain MSS,

AC 6/1/828; A. Chamberlain to Ida Chamberlain 11 Oct. 1931, ibid, AC 5/1/560.

34. A. Chamberlain to Ivy Chamberlain 28 Oct. 1931, ibid, AC 6/1/847.
35. A. Chamberlain to F. S. Oliver 26 Jan. 1932, ibid, AC 39/5/12.
36. N. Thompson, *The Anti-Appeasers* (Oxford, 1971) p. 61; D. Birn, 'The League of Nations Union and Collective Security', *Journal of Contemporary History* 9, 3, (1974) p. 142. In 1933 Chamberlain opposed the concept of a League Air Force because 'it would change the whole character of the League, perverting it from an instrument for preserving peace into an engine for waging war.' A. Chamberlain to R. Cecil 3 April 1933, Chamberlain MSS, AC 40/5/26.
37. A. Chamberlain to N. Chamberlain 5 Nov. 1931, ibid, NC 1/27/99, 100. Compare the rather strange statement of Harold Nicolson that, in rising to the premiership, Neville would 'have triumphed over . . . the subtle hostility of his brother Austen.' H. Nicolson, *Diaries and Letters 1930–1939* (London, 1966) p. 246. Though there was always, after the fall of the Lloyd George Coalition, a certain feeling of reserve between the two brothers, Chamberlain greatly admired Neville's abilities and welcomed his political advancement.
38. A. Chamberlain to Ivy Chamberlain 4 Nov. 1931, Chamberlain MSS, AC 6/1/856.
39. A. Chamberlain to N. Chamberlain 27 Dec. 1931, ibid, NC 1/27/103. Neville assured his brother: 'I do want your help and advice in political matters in which I recognise that I am still but a child in comparison with your vast experience of responsibility.' N. Chamberlain to A. Chamberlain 28 Dec. 1931, ibid, AC 39/3/53.
40. A. Chamberlain to Ida Chamberlain 28 Feb. 1932, ibid, AC 5/1/576; A. Chamberlain to H. Chamberlain 11 Sept. 1932, ibid, AC 5/1/596.
41. D. Birn, *League of Nations Union* p. 128.
42. A. Chamberlain to W. Tyrrell 13 Feb. 1933, Chamberlain MSS, AC 40/5/12; A. Chamberlain to F. S. Oliver 3 Aug. 1933, ibid, AC 40/5/84; A. Chamberlain to R. Cecil 11 Jan. 1932, Cecil MSS 51079 f. 194.
43. House of Commons Debates 22 March 1932, vol. 263, col. 912. 'At the beginning of these troubles, having regard to all the provocations sustained by Japan, my sympathy was almost wholly on her side.' A. Chamberlain to Marquis Tokugaura 1 March 1933, Chamberlain MSS, AC 40/5/3.
44. House of Commons Debates 27 Feb. 1933, vol. 275, col. 69.
45. D. Birn, *League of Nations Union* pp. 105–6.
46. Ibid, p. 105.
47. A. Chamberlain to Ida Chamberlain 14 Feb. 1932 and 12 June 1933, Chamberlain MSS, AC 5/1/574, 620; A. Chamberlain to Ivy Chamberlain 24 May 1933, ibid, AC 6/1/1018.
48. A. Chamberlain to Ivy Chamberlain 17 March 1933, ibid, AC 6/1/981.
49. Ibid, 13 March 1933, AC 6/1/978.
50. Ibid, 5 Oct. 1932, AC 6/1/898; A. Chamberlain to Ida Chamberlain 9 Oct. 1932, ibid, AC 5/1/597.

51. A. Chamberlain to H. Chamberlain 26 March 1933, ibid, AC 5/1/612.
52. D. Elletson, *Chamberlains* p. 263.
53. A. Chamberlain to Ida Chamberlain 14 May 1933, Chamberlain MSS, AC 5/1/616; A. Chamberlain to Ivy Chamberlain 20 May 1933, ibid, AC 6/1/1015. 'The only hope of peace is to make it plain to the Germans that whilst we would do our best to meet the legitimate claims of a peaceful Germany, we will do nothing for a Germany which outrages humanity at home and menaces her neighbour's peace.' A. Chamberlain to H. Armstrong 17 July 1933, ibid, AC 40/5/72.
54. A. Chamberlain to Wickham Stead 15 May 1933, ibid, AC 40/5/64. 'The spirit which inspires this campaign against the Jews inside Germany is the spirit which inspired the attempt of Germany to dominate the world before the Great War.' A. Chamberlain to E. Canning 25 April 1933, ibid, AC 40/4/14.
55. A. Chamberlain to Ivy Chamberlain 14 Feb. 1933, ibid, AC 6/1/949.
56. Ibid, 15 May 1933, AC 6/1/1007.
57. A. Chamberlain to H. Chamberlain 13 Aug. 1933, ibid, AC 5/1/629.
58. M. Gilbert, *Roots of Appeasement* p. 139; N. Thompson, *Anti-Appeasers* p. 58.
59. D. Elletson, *Chamberlains* pp. 253–4.
60. Ibid, p. 254.
61. A. Chamberlain to H. Chamberlain 3 July 1933, Chamberlain MSS, AC 5/1/624; A. Chamberlain to Ida Chamberlain 22 Oct. 1933 and 3 Feb. 1934, ibid, AC 5/1/636, 650.
62. A. Chamberlain to H. Chamberlain 10 Feb. 1934, ibid, AC 5/1/651.
63. A. Chamberlain to N. Chamberlain 11 Nov. 1934, ibid, NC 1/27/119.
64. A. Chamberlain to Ida Chamberlain 9 Feb. 1935, ibid, AC 5/1/689; Petrie, *Life* ii, 399. Neville commented: 'I fear [Austen] doesn't realise all the wiles of that most artful little mischief maker.' N. Chamberlain to Ida Chamberlain 2 Feb. 1935, Chamberlain MSS, NC 18/1/904.
65. A. Chamberlain to H. Chamberlain 16 Feb. 1935, ibid, AC 5/1/690.
66. A. Chamberlain to R. Cecil 18 July 1934, Cecil MSS 51079 ff. 227–8; A. Chamberlain to G. Murray 19 Nov. 1934, Chamberlain MSS, AC 40/6/55; N. Chamberlain to H. Chamberlain 28 July and 15 Dec. 1934, ibid, NC 18/1/881, 899; L. Amery, *Life* iii, 159; D. Birn, *League of Nations Union* p. 148; N. Thompson, *Anti-Appeasers* pp. 71–2.
67. S. Hoare to Stanley 22 May 1934, cited M. Gilbert, *Churchill* v, 536; J. Cross, *Hoare* p. 168. Derby later told Beaverbrook: 'I have taken your advice and throughout have religiously followed Austen.' Derby to Beaverbrook 3 Nov. 1934, Beaverbrook MSS C/114.
68. A. Chamberlain to Ida Chamberlain 15 Dec. 1934, Chamberlain MSS, AC 5/1/680.
69. A. Chamberlain to Churchill 25 Oct. 1934, M. Gilbert, *Churchill* v, 2, 893.
70. M. Gilbert, *Churchill* v, 624; R. James, *Churchill* p. 244; S. Roskill, *Hankey* iii, 145–6.

71. A. Chamberlain to Ivy Chamberlain 21 Feb. 1934, Chamberlain MSS, AC 6/1/1027.
72. A. Chamberlain to N. Chamberlain 15 Jan. 1935, ibid, NC 1/27/120. Vansittart described Chamberlain's last years, spent 'in straits and a small flat' from which he emerged 'immaculate in frayed white shirt and shiny tail coat.' *Mist Procession* p. 549.
73. *Politics from Inside,* based on letters to Mary Chamberlain during the period of Joseph Chamberlain's illness, appeared in 1936.
74. A. Chamberlain to Ivy Chamberlain 6 March 1935, Chamberlain MSS, AC 6/1/1036C.
75. A. Chamberlain to H. Chamberlain 9 March 1935, ibid, AC 5/1/692.
76. N. Chamberlain to Annie Chamberlain 12 March 1935, ibid, NC 1/26/506.
77. House of Commons Debates, 11 March 1935, vol. 299, cols. 71–78; L. Amery, *Life* iii, 161–2; H. Macmillan, *Winds* p. 402.
78. M. Gilbert, *Churchill* v, 2, 1166.
79. A. Chamberlain to Ida Chamberlain 24 March 1935, Chamberlain MSS, AC 5/1/693.
80. A. Chamberlain to H. Chamberlain 5 May 1935, ibid, AC 5/1/698.
81. S. Roskill, *Hankey* iii, 173.
82. Templewood, *Nine Troubled Years* p. 136.
83. N. Thompson, *Anti-Appeasers* p. 79.
84. Avon, *Dictators* p. 245.
85. A. Chamberlain to Ivy Chamberlain 7 July 1935, Chamberlain MSS, AC 6/1/1048. In relation to Manchuria Chamberlain had commented: 'The strength of the League is not in its sanctions . . . but in ascertaining facts, focussing the moral opinion of the world on the issue and thus bringing to bear a world opinion which renders conciliation effective.' A. Chamberlain to G. Murray 11 Feb. 1932, ibid, AC 39/5/18.
86. Record of conversation 20 Aug. 1935, Templewood MSS VIII: 1; J. Cross, *Hoare* p. 209; Templewood, *Nine Troubled Years* p. 160. By November Chamberlain accepted the need for an embargo on oil. D. Birn, *League of Nations Union* p. 161.
87. *The Times* 1 Nov. 1935; N. Thompson, *Anti-Appeasers* p. 79; A. Chamberlain to H. Chamberlain 20 Oct. 1935, Chamberlain MSS, AC 5/1/710.
88. House of Commons Debates 5 Dec. 1935, vol. 307, cols. 347–353; N. Thompson, *Anti-Appeasers* p. 66; J. Cross, *Hoare* p. 242.
89. A. Chamberlain to Ida Chamberlain 15 Dec. 1935, Chamberlain MSS, AC 5/1/717.
90. I. Colvin, *Vansittart in Office* (London, 1965) p. 83.
91. L. Amery, *Life* iii, 185; H. Macmillan, *Winds* pp. 446–7; T. Jones, *Diary with Letters* p. 161; J. Robertson, 'The Hoare-Laval Plan', *Journal of Contemporary History* 10, 3 (1975) p. 453.
92. J. Cross, *Hoare* p. 252; Templewood, *Nine Troubled Years* pp. 186–7.
93. R. James, *Chips* p. 49.

94. House of Commons Debates, vol. 307, col. 2040; N. Thompson, *Anti-Appeasers* p. 92.

95. R. Horne to Beaverbrook 19 Dec. 1935, Beaverbrook MSS, BBK C/178.

96. N. Chamberlain diary 21 Dec. 1935, Chamberlain MSS, NC 2/23a; H. Macmillan, *Winds* p. 451; J. Cross, *Hoare* p. 259; N. Thompson, *Anti-Appeasers* pp. 92–3; J. Robertson, 'Hoare-Laval' p. 454.

97. N. Chamberlain to S. Baldwin 22 Dec. 1935, Baldwin MSS 47 ff. 181–2.

98. R. James, *Chips* p. 49.

99. Avon, *Dictators* pp. 315–16.

100. A. Chamberlain to N. Chamberlain 20 Dec. 1935, Chamberlain MSS, NC 1/27/124; Memorandum by A. Chamberlain, 'Invitation to join Mr. Baldwin's Government, December 1935', ibid, AC 41/1/68; N. Thompson, *Anti-Appeasers* pp. 94–5; Avon, *Dictators* p. 316.

101. Churchill to Clementine Churchill 26 Dec. 1935, M. Gilbert, *Churchill* v, 2, 1363.

102. Beaverbrook to Derby 21 Feb. 1936, cited A. Taylor, *Beaverbrook* p. 360.

103. A. Chamberlain to H. Chamberlain 15 March 1936, Chamberlain MSS, AC 5/1/729.

104. A. Chamberlain to Ida Chamberlain 28 Dec. 1935, ibid, AC 5/1/719.

105. N. Chamberlain diary 10 Feb. 1936, ibid, NC 2/23a.

106. A. Chamberlain to H. Chamberlain 23 Dec. 1935, ibid, AC 5/1/718.

107. Middlemas and Barnes, *Baldwin* p. 894; H. Montgomery Hyde, *Baldwin* p. 411; M. Cowling, *The Impact of Hitler* (Cambridge, 1975) p. 102.

108. M. Gilbert, *Churchill* v, 2, 1363.

109. Churchill to Ivy Chamberlain 18 March 1937, Chamberlain MSS, AC 59/83.

110. D. Elletson, *Chamberlains* p. 264.

111. Winterton, *Orders* pp. 216–7; R. James, *Churchill* pp. 264–5; H. Croft, *My Life of Strife* (London, 1949) p. 285.

112. R. James, *Chips* p. 61.

113. L. Amery, *Life* iii, 248.

114. N. Chamberlain to Ida Chamberlain 13 April 1936, Chamberlain MSS, NC 18/1/956.

115. A. Chamberlain to H. Chamberlain 15 Feb. 1936, ibid, AC 5/1/725.

116. N. Chamberlain diary 10 Feb. 1936, ibid, NC 2/23a.

117. T. Jones, *Diary with Letters* p. 174; Winterton, *Orders* p. 214. Neville recorded: 'While A. was speaking [Baldwin] murmured sotto voce "This is an unexpected attack" and though I see various papers say it was not intended to be that, I know how I should regard it if I were in S.B.'s place.' N. Chamberlain to Ida Chamberlain 16 Feb. 1936, Chamberlain MSS, NC 18/1/949.

118. N. Chamberlain diary 16 Feb. 1936, Chamberlain MSS, NC 2/23a.

119. M. Gilbert, *Churchill* v, 706; A. Chamberlain to Midleton 18 Feb. 1936, Chamberlain MSS, AC 41/3/18.
120. Middlemas and Barnes, *Baldwin* p. 909; N. Chamberlain diary 19 Feb. 1936, Chamberlain MSS, NC 2/23a.
121. N. Chamberlain diary 19 Feb. 1936, ibid, NC 2/23a.
122. A. Chamberlain to H. Chamberlain 15 March 1936, ibid, AC 5/1/729.
123. Ibid; A. Chamberlain to Ida Chamberlain 7 March 1936, AC 5/1/728.
124. House of Commons Debates 26 March 1936, vol. 310, cols. 1482–7.
125. D. Elletson, *Chamberlains* pp. 263–4.
126. Ibid, p. 264.
127. House of Commons Debates 26 March 1936, vol. 310, cols. 1482–7.
128. A. Chamberlain to H. Chamberlain 28 March 1936, Chamberlain MSS, AC 5/1/730; A. Chamberlain to G. Murray 25 June 1936, ibid, AC 41/3/52.
129. A. Chamberlain to E. Wadsworth 24 June 1936, ibid, AC 41/4/43.
130. N. Thompson, *Anti-Appeasers* pp. 97–8; K. Robbins, *Munich* p. 123.
131. N. Thompson, *Anti-Appeasers* p. 72; D. Birn, *League of Nations Union* pp. 164–5.
132. A. Chamberlain to H. Chamberlain 10 May 1936, Chamberlain MSS, AC 5/1/733; N. Chamberlain to Ida Chamberlain 10 May 1936, ibid, NC 18/1/960.
133. Lady Milner to A. Chamberlain 28 June 1936, ibid, AC 41/3/56.
134. N. Chamberlain diary 5 July 1936, ibid, NC 2/23a; Middlemas and Barnes, *Baldwin* p. 946.
135. L. Amery, *Life* iii, 197.
136. A. Chamberlain to Ida Chamberlain 20 June 1936, Chamberlain MSS, AC 5/1/738.
137. N. Chamberlain to Ida Chamberlain 4 July 1936, ibid, NC 18/1/968.
138. R. James, *Chips* p. 73.
139. H. Montgomery Hyde, *Baldwin* p. 495; L. Amery, *Life* iii, 215; Clark, *Innings* p. 332.
140. Avon, *Dictators* p. 445.
141. A. Chamberlain to Ida Chamberlain 14 Nov. 1936, Chamberlain MSS, AC 5/1/749.
142. M. Gilbert and R. Gott, *The Appeasers* (London, 1963) pp. 28–9. To Gilbert Murray Chamberlain wrote on 11 Jan. 1936: 'I would not trust [the Soviet Union] round the corner with my life any more than my purse.' AC 41/3/7.
143. A. Chamberlain to H. Chamberlain 7 March 1937, Chamberlain MSS, AC 5/1/762.
144. N. Chamberlain diary 16 March 1937, ibid, NC 2/24a.
145. K. Feiling, *Neville Chamberlain* p. 293.
146. R. James, *Chips* p. 117; H. Nicolson, *Diaries and Letters* p. 296.
147. T. Jones, *Diary with Letters* p. 325.
148. R. James, *Chips* p. 117.
149. N. Chamberlain diary 19 March 1937, Chamberlain MSS, NC 2/24a.

CONCLUSION

'I dreamed like others of being some day head of a ministry that should make some history, domestic and imperial.'[1]

'... you will be remembered also as the statesman who was also the verray parfait gentil knight.'[2]

'Sir Austen Chamberlain ... slow thinking, slow moving, commonplace, uninspired and uninspiring.'[3]

In 1915 the waspish Margot Asquith commented, 'Austen is more of a shopkeeper than a merchant – he has no greatness.'[4] Chamberlain himself once said that great men are like high mountains. One has to be away from them to appreciate them.[5] But not even the passage of almost seventy years has served to endow Austen Chamberlain with greatness. 'Excellence of character rather than capacity,' was the most that Lloyd George was prepared to concede in a judgment from which it is hard to dissent.[6] Yet his career remains one of considerable distinction. For forty-five years he was a member of the House of Commons. In his public tribute after Chamberlain's death, Stanley Baldwin stressed Chamberlain's position as an outstanding parliamentarian, ending with a play on the phrase, well known to all members of the Commons, 'Who Goes Home.' Within this long career Chamberlain was for three decades at the very centre of the British political scene. He was elevated to major office as early as 1903, yet Winston Churchill could still write of the possibility of his heading a government as late as December 1935.[7] In a sense, then, Chamberlain's career was the fulfilment of the political vision created by his ambitous father, determined that the family name should continue to shine into a second generation of national statesmen. Yet that same career provides an interesting contrast between the way in which a man's life may be mapped out for him and the extent to which it is determined by chance and fate.

For the very reason that Chamberlain so often came near to seizing the most glittering prizes in public life, his career invites, indeed compels, the historian to speculate for a moment in the dangerous but tantalising realm of 'counter-history.' Had Chamberlain pressed his candidature for the party leadership in 1911, when still under fifty years of age, it is just possible that he could have remained at the helm of his party for up to twenty years. Had he accepted Lloyd George's offer to stand down in 1922, the premiership would surely have been his, even allowing for the exercise of the royal prerogative. Had he been rehabilitated into the Conservative ranks in 1923 rather than a year later, his claims to succeed the ailing Bonar Law as Prime Minister might have been irresistible, while Stanley Baldwin remained a politician of the second rank.[8] Yet contrary thoughts force themselves forward. Chamberlain, as party leader in the last years before the Great War, would not have been able to give the party the sort of unequivocal lead on the Irish issue for which its members craved. It seems, moreover, unlikely that he could have survived the tariff crisis of 1912–13, especially while his father watched menacingly from the political sidelines. Yet if political leadership in these years was a daunting task, it had become even more so by the time that Chamberlain did inherit the position in 1921. As he himself said, 'I would sooner have been leader ten years ago than now.'[9] The brief and unhappy experience of Chamberlain's party leadership instils no confidence that a Chamberlain premiership would have been more successful or that it could have lasted long.

Despite the warm tributes of those who knew him well – 'Austen's is a beautiful nature, as straight as a die,' noted Lord Selborne[10] – the conclusion is inescapable that with many others he created a poor impression and that often he did not handle men well. Subtlety and political dexterity were never his strong points. His friend F. S. Oliver once remarked:

Theoretically I wish you had more of the Italian spirit, more suppleness, more sense of currents and gusts and other invisible but potent influences.... You are one of those that must always be breaking their heads if stone walls happen to be on the line of their charge.[11]

Above all Chamberlain lacked the ability to inspire those whom he led. As the crisis of 1922 approached, William Ormsby-Gore wrote in terms that could be applied to the whole of Chamberlain's career:

As for Mr. Chamberlain's position, it was put to me best by a bookey, who said, 'you can't get any backers if you won't declare to win and tell everybody you are only going to ride for a place.'[12]

Many found Chamberlain a poor listener. Even Neville noted that 'A. does not readily take suggestions either on gardens or politics.'[13] When hearing views with which he did not agree, Chamberlain's tendency was to 'put on that air of patient and pained resignation.'[14] The adjective 'stiff' is employed too frequently in descriptions of him for it not to reflect some reality. F. S. Oliver was once moved to remark that Chamberlain must have included someone at Madame Tussaud's among his maternal ancestors.[15] But if political leaders do not find listening easy, they must at least be able to convey their own ideas and views with conviction and

clarity. Here too Chamberlain was found wanting. If one feature stands
out above all others from his party leadership it is a breakdown in
communications. The dignity of high office increased his natural tendency
towards aloofness. It may be that not all criticism of him in this respect is
justified. Chamberlain was so shortsighted that, without his monocle,[16] he
often failed to recognise acquaintances even at close range. But again the
complaint was voiced too frequently for it not to have had some
substance. Then, after he had ceased to be leader, Chamberlain could
never forget that he had once held the top post himself and, in his opinion,
might still be holding it, but for the principles which he had refused to give
up. Baldwin's leadership was, he once exclaimed, the 'accident of an
accident.'[17] There is no need for a deep and searching analysis of
Chamberlain's character to explain why he never became Prime Minister
– the premiership would almost certainly have been his had the lottery of
events worked out only slightly differently. But Chamberlain's personality
does contain the flaws which would have militated against a long or
successful stay in 10 Downing Street.

'Of course,' noted Chamberlain, 'I should have liked to be Prime
Minister and to have tried whether I could not do some good work in that
capacity.'[18] With this opportunity denied him, such historical attention as
has been accorded to Chamberlain has largely concentrated on his
Foreign Secretaryship and, in particular, the achievement of the Treaty of
Locarno. But Locarno became invested with a moral significance which
transcended the practical importance of anything it achieved.[19] With
some perception Neville remarked at the moment the treaty was
concluded that only if its results were

such as to ensure peace as everyone believes today then Locarno will be famous
in history and A. will have established on a sure basis his reputation as among the
greatest of Foreign Secretaries.[20]

Chamberlain hoped that by Locarno another Armageddon could be
averted and Europe move towards a new concert in which a contented
Germany would be restored to the family of nations. Yet the Foreign
Secretary lacked the resource, the stamina and perhaps the will to see this
vision to a successful conclusion. He put to one side too many of the
difficulties that Locarno left unresolved. As Lloyd George remarked:

It is no use standing on the shores of Maggiore Lake like a stork on one leg,
looking preternaturally wise and feeling very satisfied because he has swallowed
one trout.[21]

Ready always to take the part of France, Chamberlain never really
tackled the central problem that Briand, unlike Stresemann, saw Locarno

not as a first step towards revision of the Versailles settlement but as a first step on the road to German compliance. Nor did he fully think through the implications of a treaty which, by sanctifying the frontiers in one part of Europe, inevitably served to place a question mark over those in another.

Rather than his Foreign Secretaryship, therefore, it is Chamberlain's last years, when out of office but still concentrating his attention on the foreign arena, which do him most credit. Like Churchill, but unlike so many other contemporaries, Chamberlain made a successful transition in his understanding of the European situation over the fundamental dividing line posed by Hitler's assumption of power in January 1933. His appreciation of the nature of the Nazi regime and the reawakening of his own inherent Germanophobia, only partially suppressed in the 1920s, combined to make him one of the most perceptive back-bench critics of the National Government's foreign policy. In July 1928, when supporting the continuation of the Ten Year Rule in British Defence Planning, Chamberlain had suggested that war with France was 'inconceivable', while he could not imagine either Germany or Italy contemplating war with Britain 'at any rate for many years to come.'[22] Yet by 1933 he was aware that an entirely new situation existed in which British foreign policy was in need of complete revision. From his corner-seat below the gangway under the gallery of the House of Commons, he proceeded to warn the government of the folly of its myopic attitude towards the German menace. Paradoxically, such a stance set him increasingly at odds with his younger brother, and yet he remained determined that nothing should impede Neville's path towards 10 Downing Street. Had he lived beyond 1937, Chamberlain would not have emerged, as did Churchill, as a great war leader, but his record in the 1930s – a decade which destroyed so many reputations – will stand comparison with those of most contemporaries.

'A man who enters politics young', noted Chamberlain in one of his more reflective moments, 'must be either extraordinarily gifted with foresight or singularly incapable of profiting by experience, if he does not find it necessary to modify and largely to recast his views in the course of his life.'[23] In the case of Chamberlain himself, this dictum rings only partially true. Certainly he was born a Liberal and died a Conservative, but the first was a factor over which he had no control, the second a matter of conviction. Increasingly, after his father's death, his radical pedigree seemed to have lost its significance in the determination of his own political outlook. He could still write in 1927, 'Scratch me and you will find the Nonconformist', but this was a label of little more than nominal importance for him.[24] Throughout his life Chamberlain was an inherent conservative, cautious, circumspect and conventional in all he did, the 'mirror of good form and tradition.'[25] 'If ever I have a wild idea', said Robert Cecil, 'I always take it to Austen in order to hear everything that can be said against it.'[26] Even so, Chamberlain's long political career divides naturally around the First World War. The death of his father, the seismic impact of the first total war in the country's history and the increasing realisation that the post-war political landscape would be significantly different from anything that had existed before 1914 all combined to reorientate Chamberlain's political outlook and priorities. The typical Chamberlain of the pre-war era is a somewhat reluctant and hesitant radical, pursuing the goals and ideals of his father though lacking something of the older man's conviction, intensity and passion. The post-war Chamberlain is a man determined to preserve the existing fabric of ordered society against the threat of Socialism, ready to envisage the abandonment of earlier beliefs to ensure this greater end. By the early 1920s he had come to see that the logic of electoral politics might compel a party political realignment unthinkable in the pre-war era. Yet consistent features run through the whole of Chamberlain's public life, none more than his unshakable loyalty, even where this damaged his own political standing and future prospects. Just as his advocacy of his father's cause lost him much support among Conservative Unionists before the War, so too his commitment to Lloyd George and Birkenhead lost him first the party leadership and second the prospect of the premiership in the early 1920s. He held 'the old-fashioned belief that it was necessary to conduct one's self in politics like a man of honour.'[27] Principles for Chamberlain were 'immutable and fixed laws' not 'expedients suitable to the moment.'[28]

Chamberlain was in no sense a political intellectual. 'I have never been good', he once confessed, 'at a philosophy of politics.'[29] His views were often extremely perceptive as in the cases of the changed political realities after 1918 and the threat posed in the thirties by Nazi Germany, but such insights owed more to gut feeling than to intellectual analysis. Born into a tradition of Nonconformity, religion did not play a large part in his life. Not usually given to metaphysical speculations he tried occasionally to rationalise his own beliefs and philosophy. As an undergraduate he wrote:

Do I feel a yearning for a something divine, a life hereafter and a God? Yes indeed; it is in me; it may be sentiment, yet I cannot root it out. . . . But this I do know, that no good action here is without result. . . . We still may toil and do our little best until in some long distant age there comes a Paradise on Earth if not in Heaven.[30]

Nearly forty years later he still found it difficult to conceptualise his own feelings:

So it is with my thoughts of the Beyond. I can imagine nothing which satisfies me and so I think I hope for oblivion, to be forgetting but not all forgot.'[31]

Chamberlain's family life is central to an understanding of his political career. To have lived for the first forty years of his life in the same house as the magisterial figure who was his father left an incalculable impression upon him. 'My choice of a political career', he noted, 'combined with my late marriage has given me an intimacy and friendship with my Father which I think are rare in such a relationship and certainly make it very beautiful and precious in our case.'[32] From his earliest steps into the political arena Chamberlain must have known that he would always be judged in comparison with the great Joe. He once recalled his first intervention in the House of Commons – a question to Asquith, then Home Secretary, which failed to elicit a satisfactory answer. As he left the House, an old door-keeper stopped him and said:

That won't do, Sir. You'll never get on if you submit like that. Mr. Chamberlain wouldn't have put up with it.[33]

But Chamberlain could not have foreseen that by the end of his career he would be overshadowed once again by a member of his own family. His relationship with Neville was never one of total intimacy. It was not altogether easy for Chamberlain to watch his brother move towards the fulfilment of their father's ambition – a path that had been mapped out for himself. As late as 1936 Neville noted that Austen 'always finds it difficult to realise that I am no longer his little brother.'[34] Chamberlain's relations with the women in his family were altogether more important to him. To his wife, Ivy, he was devoted. He regarded his step-mother, Mary, as a sister, although their relations cooled after her re-marriage. His sisters, Ida and Hilda, were his closest confidantes. Whatever problems Chamberlain's family background may have caused him in his political career, his private life was always a source of great joy, allowing him to put the cares of the political world into perspective:

I do not think that there was ever anything in this world more beautiful than the family life of Highbury . . . I would sooner have gone without to my dying day than rest content with anything less beautiful than the example I had before me.[35]

His own marriage reproduced the happy family atmosphere of earlier years:

What are politics to a man who is happily, most happily married and has two delightful children and a very united, very loveable family circle?[36]

As with his father and brother, Austen Chamberlain's power base lay in the Midlands. But despite his long career as an M.P. Chamberlain was not a particularly good constituency member. Unlike Joseph and Neville he did not have the early grounding in local politics which might have given him a stronger interest in and commitment to the day-to-day concerns of his electorate. Despite his often expressed attachment to Birmingham his whole career was geared towards the national and not the local political canvas. In the privacy of his family correspondence Neville repeatedly drew attention to the way in which his brother was neglecting his constituency duties. At the beginning of 1917 he wrote: 'he goes so seldom to his constituency that he is getting to be more and more a stranger.'[37] Even at election times Chamberlain seemed to take the loyalty of his constituents for granted:

I daresay it will be all right on the day but I confess I wish A. were going to spend a bit of his holiday down here.[38]

When Neville suggested that a little more effort was required,

he very testily replied that he *might* go down for a month, and he *might* take a house in the division, but he wasn't prepared to hold the seat on such terms and if his people thought he wasn't doing enough he was quite ready to place his resignation in their hands.[39]

When in 1924 there was a possibility of one of the brothers transferring to the rock-safe Edgbaston constituency, preliminary soundings revealed that while Neville would be readily accepted, there was no enthusiasm for Austen.[40]

In one respect Chamberlain's neglect of grass-roots politics was surprising, since his own constituency of West Birmingham displayed in graphic terms the problem confronting the twentieth-century Conservative party in the face of Labour's challenge. His constituency was one where 'apart from the clergy there is hardly a resident who is not dependent on manual labour or on the keeping of some little shop in the back street.'[41] Birmingham would not remain indefinitely loyal to the Unionist cause simply because of the past civic services of the Chamberlain family. Chamberlain once admitted that he could not understand 'why anyone who lives in [West Birmingham] slums should not be a Socialist, a Communist or a Red Revolutionary.'[42] Yet only towards the end of his career did he become conscious of the social problems which remained to be tackled in his home city.[43] It came as a surprise to him that West Birmingham had become 'one vast slum.' 'I did not know *how* bad it was.'

The housing conditions are inexpressible – over crowding, floors rotted into holes, paper falling off damp walls, plaster falling from the ceilings, stopped up drains, stenches and death.[44]

But Chamberlain's neglect of his constituency was only part of a larger problem. Though he certainly enjoyed politics – his readiness to return to office when over seventy years of age surely confirms this – political life was never all-consuming for him. 'There are moments', he once noted, 'when I ask myself whether the game is worth the candle and whether any public duty calls upon me to slave and endure at so thankless a task.'[45] All politicians no doubt express weariness of public life and exasperation at the perverse course of events, but such expressions of feeling are too often repeated in the course of Chamberlain's career to be ignored. 'Changes and losses', he noted in 1915, had already 'killed any joy in politics and my ambition if I ever had any.'[46] This, though written during the War, was a constant refrain of his whole political life, not particularly surprising in one who derived 'greater enjoyment of doing nothing than any other member of the family.'[47] What kept him in the political world for so long was above all a sense of duty. The concepts of public service and civic duty were inevitable in a man born into a Victorian political family and were merely confirmed by Chamberlain's conventional training at Rugby and Cambridge. Leo Amery's words, written thirty years ago, may sound somewhat dated to a modern ear, but they are not without significance:

He was one of those men – the very backbone of England – who, born and bred in the tradition of public service, have given their lives to the faithful fulfilment of their duty as it came to them and to the maintenance of the standards which they set before themselves.[48]

Towards the end of his life Chamberlain himself wrote:

I think I know what is my duty from day to day and, though I may not always do it, that knowledge suffices for my daily guidance and I am content to await the greater knowledge which will come to me when my course is ended. . . . Do you know Cecil Spring Rice's hymn? It is the perfect expression of the faith in which I have lived.[49]

Appropriately enough, Spring Rice's 'I vow to thee my country' was sung at Chamberlain's funeral eight months after these words were written.

Notes

1. A. Chamberlain to Ida Chamberlain 4 Nov. 1917, Chamberlain MSS, AC 5/1/45.
2. N. Chamberlain to A. Chamberlain 4 Nov. 1931, ibid, AC 39/4/17.
3. Note on Austen Chamberlain, Thomas Williams MSS.
4. M. Gilbert, *Winston Churchill* iii, 2, 898–9.
5. R. James (ed.), *Chips* p. 27.
6. Lord Beaverbrook, *Decline and Fall of Lloyd George* p. 223.
7. W. S. Churchill, *The Gathering Storm* (London, 1950 reprint edn.) p. 160.

8. C.f. R. Blake, *The Conservative Party from Peel to Churchill* (London, 1972 edn.) pp. 214–5.
9. A. Chamberlain to M. Chamberlain 25 Aug. 1921, Chamberlain MSS, AC 4/1/1207.
10. Notes on Cabinet colleagues, Selborne MSS 80 ff 285–9.
11. F. S. Oliver to A. Chamberlain 19 Jan. 1913, Chamberlain MSS, AC 60/97.
12. W. Ormsby-Gore to A. Bonar Law 17 Oct. 1922, Bonar Law MSS 111/19/92.
13. N. Chamberlain to H. Chamberlain 20 July 1918, Chamberlain MSS, NC 18/1/177.
14. Ibid, 7 July 1918, NC 18/1/175.
15. L. Amery, *Diaries* p. 208.
16. Chamberlain suffered considerable damage to his left eye when playing rackets at Rugby School. When he became short-sighted in his right eye, he chose to use a monocle. Information provided by Chamberlain's daughter, Mrs. T. Maxwell.
17. A. Chamberlain to Ida Chamberlain 28 Feb. 1931, Chamberlain MSS, AC 5/1/532.
18. Ibid, 16 March 1923, AC 5/1/268.
19. G. A. Grun, 'Locarno: Idea and Reality', *International Affairs* xxxi, 4 (Oct. 1955) p. 480.
20. N. Chamberlain Diary 22 Oct. 1925, Chamberlain MSS, NC 2/21.
21. J. Campbell, *The Goat in the Wilderness* p. 171.
22. M. Gilbert, *Winston Churchill* v, 290.
23. A. Chamberlain to Lord Farrer 9 Nov. 1926, Chamberlain MSS, AC 24/8/22.
24. Petrie, *Life* ii, 321.
25. As note 3.
26. C. P. Scott, *Diaries* p. 133.
27. F. Williams, *A Pattern of Rulers* (London, 1965) p. 20.
28. A. Chamberlain to Ivy Chamberlain 2 Aug. 1924, Chamberlain MSS, AC 6/1/549.
29. A. Chamberlain to N. Chamberlain 24 Sept. 1917, ibid, NC 1/27/12.
30. A. Chamberlain to Sayle 27 Oct. 188?, ibid, AC L. Add 68. Chamberlain grew up with an attitude of some animosity towards organised religion. J. Ramsden (ed.), *Sanders* p. 99.
31. A. Chamberlain to H. Chamberlain 30 March 1919, ibid, AC 5/1/123.
32. A. Chamberlain to M. Chamberlain 30 March 1913, ibid, AC 4/1/968.
33. Ibid, 21 July 1908, AC 4/1/316.
34. N. Chamberlain diary 19 Feb. 1936, NC 2/23a.
35. A. Chamberlain to M. Chamberlain 3 Jan. 1908, AC 4/1/203.
36. Ibid, 20 April 1913, AC 4/1/996.
37. N. Chamberlain to H. Chamberlain 27 Jan. 1917, NC 18/1/99.
38. Ibid, 20 Sept. 1924, NC 18/1/452.
39. N. Chamberlain to Ida Chamberlain 27 Sept. 1924, NC 18/1/453.
40. Ibid, 11 Oct. 1924, NC 18/1/455.

41. A. Chamberlain to H. Armstrong 6 Nov. 1931, AC 39/3/41.
42. A. Chamberlain to Ida Chamberlain 18 Nov. 1922, AC 5/1/250.
43. Hilda Chamberlain Memoir, 1956, BC 5/10/1.
44. A. Chamberlain to M. Chamberlain 31 May 1929, AC 4/1/1297.
45. A. Chamberlain to G. Lloyd 1 July 1920, AC 18/1/10.
46. A. Chamberlain to Balfour 27 June 1915, Balfour MSS 49736.
47. A. Chamberlain to H. Chamberlain 22 Oct. 1892, Chamberlain MSS, NC 1/19/81.
48. L. Amery, *Life* ii, 304.
49. A. Chamberlain to Ellen, Lady Askwith 15 July 1936, Chamberlain MSS, AC 58/123.

THE LIBERAL UNIONISTS

Gladstone's first Home Rule Bill of 1886 was opposed not only by the Conservatives under Lord Salisbury but also by ninety-three Liberals, led by Joseph Chamberlain and the Marquess of Hartington, who were determined to maintain the Union between England and Ireland. In the years which followed there were abortive attempts to negotiate terms of reunion among the Liberal factions, but with their breakdown the Liberal Unionists moved increasingly closer to the Conservatives and finally accepted office under Lord Salisbury in 1895. Then Chamberlain became Colonial Secretary and Hartington (now Duke of Devonshire) Lord President of the Council. Though united on the Irish issue the Liberal Unionists spanned the whole spectrum of Liberal politics ranging from old-style Whigs to progressive radicals. This made the complete assimilation of the Chamberlainite group into the Conservative fold a difficult task, particularly after the Colonial Secretary's démarche on the question of tariff reform in 1903. Despite their partnership with the Conservatives the Liberal Unionists maintained a separate organisation with separate funds. In 1900 they claimed the allegiance of sixty-eight M.P.s; after the General Election of December 1910 the figure stood at thirty-five. A formal merger took place in 1912 by which time the question of Ireland was beginning to re-emerge into political prominence. Hartington was President of the Liberal Unionists from 1886 to 1904, when he was succeeded by Joseph Chamberlain who held the position until 1912.

TARIFF REFORM

Following the Conservative party's catastrophic split in the 1840s over the Repeal of the Corn Laws, free trade became the economic orthodoxy of both parties by the 1860s. Indeed with the country's growing prosperity it became for most an article of faith. Nonetheless there always remained an under-current of opposition inside the Conservative ranks. The agricultural depression of the 1870s brought fresh calls for fair trade and retaliatory tariffs, but these found little support among industrialists. By the beginning of the new century, however, the situation was changing. Many industrialists were now ready to attribute Britain's relative industrial decline to the way in which rival states had developed their own industry behind the protective wall of tariff barriers. The imperial crisis at the turn of the century explains why the renewed call for tariffs took the form that it did. Chamberlain's dramatic démarche of 1903 needs to be set in the total context of his tenure of the Colonial Office from 1895. The Colonial Secretary was convinced that Britain was in danger of squandering her imperial inheritance and that only a consolidated empire would enable Britain to survive in the new century of Super Powers. The lesson of the Boer War and Chamberlain's determination to restore British supremacy in Southern Africa brought matters to a head. The introduction of tariffs would enable them to be remitted in favour of the countries of the Empire, thereby creating an Imperial Zollverein. At the same time the revenue from tariffs would solve some of the problems confronting the Exchequer and enable Chamberlain to introduce the sort of social reforms on a national scale to which his earlier municipal career in Birmingham had already been dedicated. In this way a strand of consistency links Chamberlain, the radical mayor, and Chamberlain, the imperialist Colonial Secretary. Much hard-headed thinking thus underlay the campaign for tariff reform. But there was also a strong element of visionary sentimentalism. It remains uncertain whether a united Empire was ever a viable proposition or indeed whether it was really in Britain's interests to pursue such a goal. It was a striking fact, with which Joseph Chamberlain never grappled with any success, that Britain's trade with foreign states, which might be endangered by a system of Imperial Preference, had always been more important to her than her imperial trade.

THE MESOPOTAMIAN CAMPAIGN

Though it began with a squalid murder in Bosnia, the Great War soon developed world-wide proportions. Though historical attention has concentrated upon the Western Front, the War saw British soldiers fighting in Syria, at Archangel, in East Africa, on the Caspian and in the Caucasus. The campaign in Mesopotamia began with a suggestion from the India Office that a reinforced brigade might be sent to encourage Arab support for the Allies and to confirm the sheiks of Mohammerah and Kuwait in their existing allegiance. In addition there existed the more tangible aim to protect Anglo-Persian oil installations on Abadan Island. With the agreement of the Government of India a force arrived on 23 October 1914, shortly before Turkey entered the War on the side of the Central Powers.

The campaign represented a typical example of the lack of clear-sighted planning which characterised the whole of the British war effort. There developed an irresistible drift towards pushing a little further, step by step, with no clear appreciation of why this was being done or of where ultimate objectives might lie. Particularly when it came to the decision to advance on Baghdad, the British government thought less of strategic advantage than of the chance to refurbish its own prestige, damaged by the continuing stalemate on the Western Front and the set-backs of the ill-fated Gallipoli adventure. In short the Mesopotamian Expedition contributed less to the winning of the War than to its exhausting prolongation.

THE VERSAILLES SETTLEMENT

The collapse at the end of the Great War of four great empires in Europe and the Near East presented the statesmen who arrived in Paris to negotiate the peace settlement with problems on a scale which no previous international congress had confronted. What resulted was an honest attempt to cope with intractable problems. Probably no settlement could have satisfied the idealistic hopes of those who now clamoured for a treaty which would banish war for ever from the canvas of international politics. The old balance of power had gone for ever and the failure of the United States to ratify the treaty and take her part in the maintenance of the settlement deprived Europe of the only force capable of sustaining a new balance. The peacemakers had to carry on their negotiations against a background of revolution, economic disruption and famine which Europe had not known since the upheavals of 1848.

The settlement which emerged was a strange concoction reflecting the conflicting aims, ambitions and aspirations of the three leading nations in the negotiations, France, Britain and the United States, and of their leaders, Clemenceau, Lloyd George and Wilson. Divided from one another on crucial issues, the three men also struggled with themselves to reconcile understandable motives of revenge with idealistic hopes of reconciliation. The treaty therefore combined elements of the old diplomacy with aspects of the new. The lofty idealism of the League was matched by the damning indictment of the War Guilt Clause, which held Germany responsible for bringing the War about and for all the destruction which it had occasioned. The attempt to give self-determination to the peoples of the old empires has to be matched against the unacceptable restrictions placed upon the German nation, in whose negotiation Germany was allowed no part and which were designed to prevent her re-emergence as a Great Power.

Those who suggest that Versailles was foredoomed to disaster and that it contained within it the seeds of an inevitable future conflict argue with the benefit of too much hindsight. Nevertheless two major criticisms remain. In talking the language of idealism and vision, the treaty set itself too high a standard against which, when measured, it was bound to be found wanting. In addition there was always a glaring gap between the provisions of the treaty and the machinery available to enforce it. In the long-term Versailles depended on consent and that consent was never achieved.

THE LEAGUE OF NATIONS

The League of Nations was the most tangible expression of the belief which grew up during the course of the Great War that war itself was the product of a corrupt form of secret diplomacy and power politics, and that its future prevention could be assured if the states of the world had a forum in which to sort out their differences in open discussion. Though outstandingly the creation of the American President, Woodrow Wilson, the idea of a League had powerful support inside Great Britain, particularly on the political left, but also among such Conservatives as Lord Robert Cecil, Under-Secretary of State for Foreign Affairs, 1916–19.

Yet from its creation the League suffered from serious shortcomings. Russia was absent while Germany was excluded. The United States, upon whose strength so much depended, refused to ratify the peace treaty and thereby rejected the League's Covenant. By linking the treaty with the League the Allies ensured that Germany would regard the new international organisation as a club of the victors designed merely to preserve the territorial *status quo* created at Versailles. As a result Germany was bound to feel alienated from the outset. The League had no peace-keeping force and, though members were required to co-operate in a collective effort to keep the peace, policy decisions by the Council and the Assembly had to have the unanimous consent of all states represented. From Great Britain's point of view the defection of the United States opened up the frightening vista that she might, despite her diminished resources, be forced into the role of international policeman. As a result Conservative politicians in particular viewed the League with supicion and guarded against the extension of its activities.

The League enjoyed some success in the 1920s in settling minor disputes, but its reliance on moral pressure made it relatively helpless when dealing with larger powers. By the end of the 1930s it had ceased to carry much weight in international relations, even though popular support for it remained strong.

BIOGRAPHICAL NOTES

Acland-Hood, Alexander; 1st Baron St. Audries (1853–1917)
A Conservative M.P. between 1892–1911, he became Vice-Chamberlain of H.M. Household (1900–02) and was Government Chief Whip (1902–05). He stayed on as Chief Whip when the party went into opposition, but as party organisation came under closer scrutiny his position became increasingly vulnerable. As Chief Whip he had the almost impossible task of managing the party both inside parliament and in the country. The two General Election defeats of 1910 sealed his fate and he retired from his position following the restructuring of party organisation which took place in 1911.

Amery, Leopold C.M.S. (1873–1955)
First elected to parliament in 1911, he was a casualty of the Labour landslide in 1945. He was a correspondent for *The Times* during the Boer War and saw active service in Flanders and the Balkans (1917–18). He was Parliamentary Under-Secretary for the Colonies (1919–21), Parliamentary and Financial Secretary to the Admiralty (1921–22), First Lord of the Admiralty (1922–24), Colonial Secretary (1924–29), Secretary of State for the Dominions (1925–29) and Secretary of State for India (1940–45). A life-long advocate of Imperial Preference, he was a loyal follower of Joseph Chamberlain. During the 1930s he emerged as a backbench critic of the foreign policy of the National Government.

Balcarres, 10th Earl of; David A. E. Lindsay, 27th Earl of Crawford (1871–1940)
A Conservative M.P. between 1895 and 1913, he was appointed Chief Whip following the enquiry into party organisation in 1911, but had to give up the post following his succession to the Earldom of Crawford in 1913. Subsequently he became President of the Board of Agriculture and Fisheries (1916), Lord Privy Seal (1916–19), Chancellor of the Duchy of Lancaster (1919–21) and First Commissioner of Works (1921–22).

Birrell, Augustine (1850–1933)
A Liberal M.P. between 1889 and 1900, and 1906 and 1918. He was President of the Board of Education (1905–07) and Chief Secretary for Ireland (1907–16). Though he was in charge of the Liberal government's Irish policy for nine years, he never became a leading member of the

Cabinet. He was universally blamed for his failure to foresee the Easter Rising of 1916 and this event led to the effective end of his political career.

Briand, Aristide (1862–1932)
An ubiquitous figure in the political history of the French Third Republic for three decades, he first became Prime Minister of France in 1909. He headed the French government during some of the most difficult months of the First World War, although his ministry collapsed in some disarray in 1917. After the war he emerged as a champion of reconciliation with Germany and became a stable element at the Quai d'Orsay through the changing ministries of the later 1920s.

Bridgeman, William C; 1st Viscount Bridgeman (1864–1935)
Bridgeman was Conservative M.P. for Oswestry between 1906 and 1929. After service in the Whips' Office he was successively Parliamentary Secretary to the Ministry of Labour (1916–19), Parliamentary Secretary to the Board of Trade (1919–20), Parliamentary Secretary to the Mines Department (1920–22), Home Secretary (1922–24) and First Lord of the Admiralty (1924–29). In his last post he found himself increasingly at odds with Austen Chamberlain at the Foreign Office.

Cecil, Lord Hugh; 1st Baron Quickswood (1869–1956)
A son of the former Prime Minister, The Third Marquess of Salisbury, he was Conservative M.P. for Greenwich (1895–1906) and for Oxford University (1910–37). He gave his name to the 'Hughligans', a group of young and talented backbench critics of Balfour's government. A fine orator, he never fulfilled his early promise and never held government office.

Cecil, Lord Robert; Viscount Cecil of Chelwood (1864–1958)
Elder brother of Lord Hugh, Cecil was a Conservative M.P. from 1906 to 1910 and from 1911 to 1923. He was Parliamentary Under-Secretary for Foreign Affairs (1916–19), Minister of Blockade (1916–18), Lord Privy Seal (1923–24) and Chancellor of the Duchy of Lancaster (1924–27). His long career is associated with the causes of Free Trade, the Established Church and the League of Nations.

Chaplin, Henry; 1st Viscount Chaplin (1840–1923)
A Conservative M.P. between 1868 and 1906, and 1907 and 1916, Chaplin's primary interests were racing and hunting rather than politics. 'No one', said Lord Willoughby de Broke, 'was half such a country gentleman as Henry Chaplin looked'. He was Chancellor of the Duchy of

Lancaster (1885–86), President of the Board of Agriculture (1889–1892) and President of the Local Government Board (1895–1900). One of his last political acts was to go to the Carlton Club in October 1922 to protest against the continuation of the Coalition.

Crewe, Marquess of; Robert O. A. Crewe-Milnes (1858–1945)
Crewe's long political career in Liberal politics encompassed the offices of Viceroy of Ireland (1892–95), Lord President of the Council (1905–08 and 1915–16), Colonial Secretary (1908–10), Lord Privy Seal (1908–11 and 1912–15), Secretary of State for India (1910–15), President of the Board of Education (1916), Ambassador to Paris (1922–28) and Secretary of State for War (1931). During the First World War he often deputised for Grey at the Foreign Office while the latter rested his failing eyesight.

Curzon of Kedleston, Marquess; George N. Curzon (1859–1925)
Curzon was Under-Secretary of State for India (1891–92), Under-Secretary of State for Foreign Affairs (1895–98), Viceroy of India (1898–1905), Lord Privy Seal (1915–16), Lord President of the Council (1916–19 and 1924–25), Leader of the House of Lords (1916–24) and Foreign Secretary (1919–24). Viceroy at the age of thirty-nine, he was perhaps ill-suited to subordinate roles. On securing a second-class degree he is said to have announced: 'Now I shall devote the rest of my life to showing the examiners that they have made a mistake.' After failing to become Prime Minister in 1923 he is said to have remained in a state of collapse for several hours.

D'Abernon, 1st Viscount (1857–1941)
A Conservative M.P. from 1899 to 1906, he later turned to diplomacy and was Ambassador to Berlin from 1920–26. There he played a prominent part in the origins of the Locarno agreements.

Derby, 17th Earl of; Edward G. V. Stanley (1865–1948)
Conservative M.P. for Westhoughton (1892–1906), he succeeded to his father's title in 1908 and became a local Conservative party boss – 'King of Lancashire'. He was Financial Secretary to the War Office (1900–03), Postmaster General (1903–05), Under-Secretary of State for War (1916), Secretary of State for War (1916–18 and 1922–24) and Ambassador to Paris (1918–20). Haig said of him: 'Like the feather pillow he bears the mark of the last person who sat on him.'

Garvin, James L. (1868–1947)
Garvin was editor of *The Outlook* (1905–06), *Pall Mall Gazette* (1912–15) and *The Observer* (1908–42). This biographer of Joseph Chamberlain turned *The Observer* from a languishing newspaper into a profitable concern in two years. He was finally dismissed from *The Observer* by Lord Astor, (for advocating the return of Beaverbrook to Churchill's wartime government), after more than a generation of independently-minded journalism.

Goulding, Edward A; 1st Baron Wargrave (1862–1936)
Conservative M.P. for Devizes (1895–1906) and for Worcester (1908–22). His defection from Austen Chamberlain to Bonar Law was influential in determining the outcome of the 1911 leadership contest.

Grandi, Count Dino (1895–   )
An Italian politician and diplomat who was Ambassador in London from 1932 to 1939. He then became Minister of Justice. Implicated in the overthrow of Mussolini, he escaped to Portugal and was condemned to death, in his absence, at the Ciano Trial in January 1944.

Haldane, Richard B.; Viscount Haldane (1856–1928)
A Liberal M.P. from 1885–1911, he was Secretary of State for War (1905–12) and Lord Chancellor (1912–15). His career appeared to have been ended by his supposed Germanophile sympathies, but he re-emerged as Lord Chancellor in Ramsay MacDonald's first Labour government.

Hankey, Maurice P.A.; 1st Baron Hankey (1877–1963)
Hankey was Secretary to the Committee of Imperial Defence (1912–38), to the War Cabinet (1916–19) and to the Cabinet (1919–38). He was also Clerk of the Privy Council from 1923 to 1938. With the coming of the Second World War he became Minister without Portfolio (1939–40), Chancellor of the Duchy of Lancaster (1940–41) and Paymaster General (1941–42). Balfour once expressed the opinion that 'without Hankey we should have lost the [First World] War.'

Hardinge of Penshurst, 1st Baron (1858–1944)
This influential diplomat played an important part in setting the anti-German orientation of the Foreign Office before 1914. He was Assistant Under-Secretary of State for Foreign Affairs (1903–04), Ambassador in St. Petersburg (1904–06), Permanent Under-Secretary at the Foreign Office (1906–10 and 1916–20), Viceroy of India (1910–16) and Ambassador to Paris (1920–22). The fact that his career was not

350 Gentleman in Politics

destroyed by the Mesopotamian fiasco in 1917 owed much to Austen Chamberlain's loyalty.

Herriot, Edouard (1872–1957)
A French Radical politician whose career spanned several decades. His electoral victory at the head of the Cartel des Gauches in 1924 was the crucial factor in making possible the agreement with Ramsay MacDonald known as the Geneva Protocol.

Horne, Robert S.; Viscount Horne of Slamannan (1871–1940)
Horne was Conservative M.P. for Glasgow, Hillhead, from 1918 to 1937. He was Minister of Labour (1919–20), President of the Board of Trade (1920–21) and Chancellor of the Exchequer (1921–22). After the fall of the Coalition Horne made his career in the City his first priority.

Jones, Dr. Thomas (1870–1955)
Professor of Economics at the Queen's University, Belfast (1909–10), Jones joined the Cabinet Secretariat at its formation in 1916 and remained as Deputy Secretary until 1930. In this position he was close to several Prime Ministers, especially Baldwin, many of whose speeches he wrote. On joining the Secretariat he was urged by Sir Maurice Powicke to keep a diary to help the historians of the future. This he did.

Joynson-Hicks, William, 1st Viscount Brentford (1865–1932)
Known as 'Jix', he was a Conservative M.P. from 1908 to 1910 and from 1911 to 1929. He was Parliamentary Secretary to the Overseas Trade Department (1922–23), Postmaster and Paymaster General (1923), Financial Secretary to the Treasury (1923), Minister of Health (1923–24) and Home Secretary (1924–29). In his last post he had responsibility for handling the General Strike.

Lane-Fox, George R.; 1st Baron Bingley (1870–1947)
A Conservative M.P. between 1906 and 1931, his only government appointment was as Parliamentary Secretary for the Mines Department (1922–24 and 1924–28). He was a member of the West Riding County Council.

Lansdowne, 5th Marquess of; Henry Charles K. Petty-Fitzmaurice (1845–1927)
During a long career in public service Lansdowne was Under-Secretary of State for War (1872–74), Under-Secretary of State for India (1880), Governor-General of Canada (1883–88), Viceroy of India (1888–94),

Secretary of State for War (1895–1900), Foreign Secretary (1900–05) and Minister without Portfolio (1915–16). As Foreign Secretary he presided over the Anglo-Japanese Alliance and the Anglo-French Entente. For many years Unionist leader in the House of Lords, Lansdowne's famous letter to the *Daily Telegraph* in 1917, calling for a compromise peace to preserve civilisation, cost him much support.

Lee, Arthur H.; Viscount Lee of Fareham (1868–1947)
A Conservative M.P. from 1900 to 1918, Lee was then raised to the peerage. He was Civil Lord of the Admiralty (1903–05), Parliamentary Secretary to the Ministry of Munitions (1915–16), Minister of Agriculture and Fisheries (1919–21) and First Lord of the Admiralty (1921–22). Lee is best remembered for his gift of the Chequers estate to the nation.

Lloyd, Sir George A.; 1st Baron Lloyd (1879–1941)
Lloyd combined careers in politics and diplomacy. A Conservative M.P. (1910–18 and 1924–25), he was Governor of Bombay (1918–23), High Commissioner for Egypt (1925–29) and Colonial Secretary and Leader of the House of Lords (1940–41).

Locker-Lampson, Oliver S. (1875–1946)
A Conservative M.P. for 35 years (1910–45), he never held government office. He was Hon. Secretary of the Unionist Working Men's Candidate Society.

Long, Walter H.; Viscount Long of Wraxall (1854–1924)
Long entered parliament as a Conservative in 1880 and remained there with only brief interludes until he was raised to the peerage in 1921. He was successively Parliamentary Secretary to the Local Government Board (1886–92), President of the Board of Agriculture (1895–1900), President of the Local Government Board (1900–05 and 1915–16), Chief Secretary for Ireland (1905), Colonial Secretary (1916–19) and First Lord of the Admiralty (1919–21). An unsuccessful candidate for the party leadership in 1911, Long represented the traditional landowning influence in Conservative politics, and exercised a powerful sway within the party over several decades.

McKenna, Reginald (1863–1943)
A Liberal M.P. from 1895 to 1918, McKenna was Financial Secretary to the Treasury (1905–07), President of the Board of Education (1907–08), First Lord of the Admiralty (1908–11), Home Secretary (1911–15) and Chancellor of the Exchequer (1915–16). He first attracted attention

through attacks on Austen Chamberlain during the latter's first period at the Exchequer. Offered the Exchequer by Baldwin in 1923, McKenna failed to find a parliamentary seat and decided to continue his career in banking.

Milner, Sir Alfred; Viscount Milner (1854–1925)
Milner was High Commissioner for South Africa (1897–1905), a member of the War Cabinet (1916–19), Secretary of State for War (1918–19) and Colonial Secretary (1919–21). This leading Imperialist was the focal point of the so-called Kindergarten of admiring young followers who had gathered round him in South Africa. But for much of his career Milner seemed reluctant to enter the mundane world of party politics.

Montagu, Edwin S. (1879–1924)
Montagu was Liberal M.P. for Cambridgeshire from 1906 to 1922. He was Parliamentary Under-Secretary of State for India (1910–14), Financial Secretary to the Treasury (1914–16), Chancellor of the Duchy of Lancaster (1915 and 1916), Minister of Munitions (1916) and Secretary of State for India (1917–22). Though a Jew Montagu opposed the Balfour Declaration of 1917. He was closely tied to Asquith, and resigned in 1922 over the publication of the Government of India's protest at the Treaty of Sèvres.

Oliver, Frederick S. (1864–1934)
A man of business and publicist, Oliver entered the firm of Debenham and Freebody in 1892 and made it into a major business. An advocate of Home Rule All Round, he was a long-time friend and correspondent of Austen Chamberlain.

Pretyman, Ernest G. (1860–1931)
A Conservative M.P. (1895–1906 and 1908–23), Pretyman was Civil Lord of the Admiralty (1900–03 and 1916–19), Parliamentary and Financial Secretary to the Admiralty (1903–05) and Parliamentary Under-Secretary for Trade (1915–16). A specialist in agricultural questions, Pretyman proposed Austen Chamberlain for the leadership of the party in 1921.

Salisbury, 4th Marquess of; James E. H. Gascoyne-Cecil (1861–1947)
Cecil was a Conservative M.P. from 1885 to 1892 and from 1893 to 1903, when he succeeded his father, the former Prime Minister. He was Under-Secretary of State for Foreign Affairs (1900–03), Lord Privy Seal (1903–05 and 1924–29), President of the Board of Trade (1905),

Chancellor of the Duchy of Lancaster (1922–23) and Lord President of the Council (1922–24). Representing the traditional Tory strain in Conservative politics, Salisbury found himself increasingly out of sympathy with Baldwin's leadership, but he remained influential within the party into the years of the Second World War.

Salvidge, Sir Archibald T. J. (1863–1928)
A brewer by profession, Salvidge developed the political management of Liverpool in the Unionist interest into a fine art in the years before 1914. He became chairman of the Conservative National Union in 1913 and enjoyed a long and sometimes difficult relationship with Lord Derby in their efforts to determine the political complexion of Lancashire.

Sandars, John S. (1853–1934)
Sandars was Private Secretary to Arthur Balfour (1892–1915). In this position he exercised considerable influence for which he was much resented by many leading Unionists. Especially after 1905 Balfour delegated much business to him and leading colleagues found it necessary to use Sandars as a means of indirect approach to their leader and as a way of discovering the views of Balfour himself.

Sanders, Robert A.; 1st Baron Bayford (1867–1940)
A Conservative M.P. from 1910 to 1923 and from 1924 to 1929, Sanders served in the Whips' Office before becoming Parliamentary Under-Secretary to the War Office (1921–22) and Minister of Agriculture and Fisheries (1922–24). A typical country Tory, Sanders was Deputy Chairman of the Conservative party (1917–22).

Scott, Sir Leslie F. (1869–1950)
Scott was Conservative M.P. for Liverpool Exchange (1910–29) and briefly held the office of Solicitor General in 1922.

Selborne, 2nd Earl of; William W. Palmer (1859–1942)
Palmer was an M.P. (first Liberal, then Liberal Unionist) from 1885 to 1895. He was Under-Secretary of State for the Colonies (1895–1900), First Lord of the Admiralty (1900–05), High Commissioner for South Africa (1905–10) and President of the Board of Agriculture and Fisheries (1915–16). Though not a Chamberlainite in the years before the First World War, Selborne became a close colleague of Austen Chamberlain during Asquith's coalition government. He was married to Lord Salisbury's sister.

Steel-Maitland, Sir Arthur H.D.R. (1876–1935)
Austen Chamberlain's private secretary from 1903 to 1905, Steel-Maitland became a Conservative M.P. in 1910. A year later he became the first Chairman of the Party, in which position he had responsibility for the organisation of Conservative politics outside Westminster. He was Parliamentary Under-Secretary of State for the Colonies (1915–17), Joint Parliamentary Under-Secretary of State for Foreign Affairs and Parliamentary Secretary to the Board of Trade (1917–19) and Minister of Labour (1924–29).

Stresemann, Gustav (1878–1929)
A German statesman of the ill-fated Weimar Republic, Stresemann was dedicated to revising the Treaty of Versailles in Germany's favour. Served briefly as Chancellor in 1923 and thereafter dominated the German Foreign Ministry until his premature death in 1929.

Wilson, Field-Marshal Sir Henry H. (1864–1922)
A distinguished military career saw Wilson as Director of Military Operations (1910–14), Assistant Chief of the General Staff (1914), British Military Representative at the Supreme War Council (1917) and Chief of the Imperial General Staff (1918–22). He served in France from 1914 to 1916. His brief career as a Conservative M.P. in 1922 came to an end when he was assassinated by I.R.A. terrorists.

Younger, Sir George; 1st Viscount Younger of Leckie (1851–1929)
Younger was Conservative M.P. for Ayr (1906–22). After serving as President of the National Union of Conservative Associations in Scotland, he became Chairman of the whole party organisation in 1916, which post he held until 1923. He was later Party Treasurer (1923–29).

SOURCES

Manuscript

Akers-Douglas Papers	Kent County Record Office.
L. S. Amery Papers	In the possession of the Rt. Hon. Julian Amery, M.P.
Baldwin Papers	Cambridge University Library.
A. J. Balfour Papers	British Library.
Gerald Balfour Papers	In the possession of Lord Balfour.
Balfour of Burleigh Papers	In the possession of Lord Balfour of Burleigh.
Beaverbrook Papers	House of Lords Record Office.
Blumenfeld Papers	House of Lords Record Office.
Bonar Law Papers	House of Lords Record Office.
Bridgeman Papers	In the possession of Lord Bridgeman.
Cecil of Chelwood Papers	British Library.
Austen, Joseph, Neville and Beatrice Chamberlain Papers	Birmingham University Library.
Austen Chamberlain (Private Foreign Office) Papers	Public Record Office.
Curzon Papers	India Office Library.
Derby Papers	Liverpool Central Library.
Griffith-Boscawen Papers	Bodleian Library.
H. A. Gwynne Papers	Bodleian Library.
Hannon Papers	House of Lords Record Office.
Hewins Papers	Sheffield University Library.
Lloyd George Papers	House of Lords Record Office.
Long Papers	Wiltshire County Record Office.
Montagu Papers	Trinity College Library, Cambridge.
Northcote Papers	Public Record Office.
Pollock Papers	Bodleian Library.
St. Aldwyn (Hicks Beach) Papers	Gloucestershire County Record Office.
Salisbury (4th Marquess) Papers	In the possession of the Marquess of Salisbury.
Sandars Papers	Bodleian Library.
Sanders Papers	Conservative Party Research Department.

Selborne Papers   Bodleian Library.
Steel-Maitland Papers   Scottish Record Office.
J. St. Loe Strachey Papers   House of Lords Record Office.
Templewood (Hoare) Papers   Cambridge University Library.
Wargrave (Goulding) Papers   House of Lords Record Office.
Thomas Williams Papers   In the possession of the Hon.
                                     H. Williams.
Willoughby de Broke Papers   House of Lords Record Office.
Worthington-Evans Papers   Bodleian Library.

Newspapers etc.
Daily Mail
The Observer
The Outlook
Sunday Times
The Times

Gleanings and Memoranda

Hansard

Books
[place of publication is London unless otherwise stated]

L. S. Amery,   *My Political Life* (3 vols., 1953–55).
H. H. Asquith,   *Memories and Reflections* (2 vols, 1928).
S. Aster,   *Anthony Eden* (1976).
Lord Avon,   *Facing the Dictators* (1962).
A. W. Baldwin,   *My Father: The True Story* (1955).
A. J. Barker,   *The Neglected War* (1967).
J. Barnes and
D. Nicholson (eds.),   *The Leo Amery Diaries* (vol. 1, 1980).
C. Barnett,   *The Collapse of British Power* (New
                             York, 1972).
R. Bassett,   *1931: Political Crisis* (1958).
Lord Beaverbrook,   *Decline and Fall of Lloyd George*
                             (1963).
Lord Beaverbrook,   *Men and Power 1917–18* (1956).
Lord Beaverbrook,   *Politicians and the War 1914–1916* (vol.
                             2, 1932).
H. Béraud,   *Men of the Aftermath* (1929).
1st Earl of Birkenhead,   *Contemporary Personalities* (1924).

2nd Earl of Birkenhead,	*F.E.: the Life of F. E. Smith, First Earl of Birkenhead* (1959).
2nd Earl of Birkenhead,	*Halifax* (1965).
D. S. Birn,	*The League of Nations Union 1918–1945* (Oxford, 1981).
R. Blake,	*The Conservative Party from Peel to Churchill* (1972 edn.).
R. Blake,	*The Unknown Prime Minister: the Life and Times of Andrew Bonar Law 1858–1923* (1955).
N. Blewett,	*The Peers, the Parties and the People: the General Elections of 1910* (1972).
P. Brendon,	*Eminent Edwardians* (Boston, 1980).
B. C. Busch,	*Hardinge of Penshurst* (Connecticut, 1980).
J. Campbell,	*Lloyd George: the Goat in the Wilderness 1922–1931* (1977).
J. Campbell,	*F. E. Smith: First Earl of Birkenhead* (1983).
D. Carlton,	*Anthony Eden* (1981).
D. Carlton,	*Macdonald versus Henderson* (1970).
B. Cartland,	*Ronald Cartland* (1941).
Lord Cecil of Chelwood,	*All the Way* (1949).
Lord Cecil of Chelwood,	*A Great Experiment* (1941).
A. Chamberlain,	*Down the Years* (1935).
A. Chamberlain,	*Politics from Inside: An Epistolary Chronicle 1906–1914* (1936).
Lord Chilston,	*Chief Whip: the Political Life and Times of Aretas Akers-Douglas* (1961).
R. S. Churchill and M. Gilbert,	*Winston S. Churchill* (5 vols, 1966–76; and companion volumes.)
R. S. Churchill,	*Lord Derby: King of Lancashire* (1959).
W. S. Churchill,	*The Gathering Storm* (1950 edn.).
A. Clark (ed.),	*A Good Innings: the Private Papers of Viscount Lee of Fareham* (1974).
I. Colvin,	*The Life of Lord Carson* (vol. 2, 1934).
I. Colvin,	*Vansittart in Office* (1965).
C. Cook,	*The Age of Alignment* (1975).
C. Cooke and D. Batchelor, (eds.),	*Winston S. Churchill's Maxims and Reflections* (Boston, 1947).
M. Cowling,	*The Impact of Hitler* (Cambridge, 1975).
M. Cowling,	*The Impact of Labour* (Cambridge,

1971).

G. A. Craig and   *The Diplomats 1919–1939* (Princeton,
F. Gilbert (eds.),   1953).
D. M. Cregier,   *Bounder from Wales* (Missouri, 1976).
Lord Croft,   *My Life of Strife* (1949).
J. A. Cross,   *Lord Swinton* (Oxford, 1982).
J. A. Cross,   *Sir Samuel Hoare: a Political
                          Biography* (1977).

Lord D'Abernon,   *An Ambassador of Peace: Lord D'
                          Abernon's Diary* (vol. 3, 1930).

G. Dangerfield,   *The Damnable Question* (1979 p.b.
                          edn.).

G. Dangerfield,   *The Strange Death of Liberal England*
                          (1936).

E. David (ed.),   *Inside Asquith's Cabinet* (1977).
D. Dilks, (ed.),   *Retreat from Power* (vol. 1, 1981).
B. Dugdale,   *Arthur James Balfour* (vol. 2, 1936).
M. Egremont,   *Balfour: the Life of Arthur James
                          Balfour* (1980).

D. H. Elletson,   *The Chamberlains* (1966).
R. C. K. Ensor,   *England 1870–1914* (Oxford, 1936).
K. Feiling,   *The Life of Neville Chamberlain* (1946).
N. Fisher,   *The Tory Leaders: Their Struggle for
                          Power* (1977).

A. Fitzroy,   *Memoirs* (n.d.).
Lord Francis-Williams,   *A Pattern of Rulers* (1965).
P. Fraser,   *Lord Esher* (1973).
J. L. Garvin and   *The Life of Joseph Chamberlain* (6 vols.,
J. Amery,   1932–1969).
M. Gilbert,   *The Roots of Appeasement* (1966).
M. Gilbert and R. Gott,   *The Appeasers* (1963).
I. Gilmour,   *Inside Right: A Study of Conservatism*
                          (1977).

A. Gollin,   *Balfour's Burden* (1965).
A. Gollin,   *The Observer and J. L. Garvin* (1960).
A. Gollin,   *Proconsul in Politics* (1964).
J. Grigg,   *The Young Lloyd George* (1973).
J. Grigg,   *Lloyd George: The People's Champion
                          1902–1911* (1978).

H. J. Hanham,   *Elections and Party Management*
                          (1959).

C. Hazlehurst,   *Politicians at War* (1971).

Lord Hemingford,	*Backbencher and Chairman* (1946).
R. F. V. Heuston,	*Lives of the Lord Chancellors 1885–1940* (Oxford, 1964).
Lady V. Hicks Beach,	*Life of Sir Michael Hicks Beach* (2 vols., 1932).
B. Holland,	*The Life of Spencer Compton, Eighth Duke of Devonshire* (2 vols., 1911).
C. H. D. Howard (ed.),	*Joseph Chamberlain: A Political Memoir 1880–1892* (1953).
H. M. Hyde,	*Baldwin: the Unexpected Prime Minister* (1973).
H. M. Hyde,	*Carson: the Life of Sir Edward Carson, Lord Carson of Duncain* (1953).
H. M. Hyde,	*Lord Reading* (1967).
J. Jacobson,	*Locarno Diplomacy: Germany and the West 1925–1929* (Princeton, 1972).
P. Jalland,	*The Liberals and Ireland* (Brighton, 1980).
R. R. James (ed.),	*Chips: the Diaries of Sir Henry Channon* (1967).
R. R. James,	*Churchill: A Study in Failure 1900–1939* (1970).
R. R. James (ed.),	*Memoirs of a Conservative* (1969).
R. Jenkins,	*Asquith* (1964).
R. Jenkins,	*Mr. Balfour's Poodle* (1954).
T. Jones,	*A Diary with Letters 1931–1950* (1954).
T. Jones,	*Whitehall Diary* (ed. K. Middlemas, 3 vols., 1969–1971).
D. Judd,	*Balfour and the British Empire* (1968).
D. Judd,	*Lord Reading* (1982).
D. Judd,	*Radical Joe* (1977).
M. Kinnear,	*The Fall of Lloyd George* (1973).
S. Koss,	*Asquith* (1976).
T. F. Lindsay and M. Harrington,	*The Conservative Party 1918–1979* (1979).
D. Lloyd George,	*War Memoirs* (2 vol.edn., 1938).
I. Macleod,	*Neville Chamberlain* (1961).
H. Macmillan,	*The Past Masters* (1975).
H. Macmillan,	*Winds of Change 1914–1939* (1966).
S. Marks,	*The Illusion of Peace: International Relations in Europe 1918–1933* (1976).
V. Massey,	*What's Past is Prologue* (Toronto,

1963).

L. Masterman, *C. F. G. Masterman: a Biography* (1939).

W. McElwee, *Britain's Locust Years* (1962).
W. N. Medlicott, *British Foreign Policy since Versailles 1919–1963* (1968).

K. Middlemas and J. Barnes, *Baldwin* (1969).

Earl of Midleton, *Records and Reactions 1856–1939* (1939).

R. Millar, *Kut: The Death of an Army* (1969).
K. O. Morgan, *Consensus and Disunity: The Lloyd George Coalition Government 1918–1922* (Oxford, 1979).

F. Morley, *The Society of Nations* (Washington, 1932).

B. K. Murray, *The People's Budget 1909–1910: Lloyd George and Liberal Politics* (Oxford, 1980).

Lord Newton, *Retrospection* (1941).
H. Nicolson, *Diaries and Letters 1930–1939* (1966).
H. Nicolson, *King George V* (1952).
F. S. Northedge, *Troubled Giant* (1966).
F. Owen, *Tempestuous Journey* (1954).
H. Pelling, *Winston Churchill* (1974).
H. Pelling, *Social Geography of British Elections 1885–1910* (1967).

C. Petrie, *The Chamberlain Tradition* (1938).
C. Petrie, *The Life of George Canning* (1930).
C. Petrie, *The Life and Letters of the Right Hon. Sir Austen Chamberlain* (2 vols., 1939–1940).

C. Petrie, *Walter Long and his Times* (1936)
A. N. Porter, *The Origins of the South African War* (Manchester, 1980).

R. Pound and G. Harmsworth, *Northcliffe* (1959).

R. M. Punnett, *Front Bench Opposition* (New York, 1973).

J. Ramsden, *The Age of Balfour and Baldwin 1902–1940* (1978).

J. Ramsden (ed.), *Real Old Tory Politics: The Political*

	Diaries of Robert Sanders 1910–1935 (1984).
E. T. Raymond,	*Uncensored Celebrities* (1918).
R. Rempel,	*Unionists Divided* (Newton Abbot, 1972).
C. à C. Repington,	*The First World War* (vol. I, 1920).
Lord Riddell,	*More Pages from My Diary 1908–1914* (1934).
Lord Riddell,	*Lord Riddell's Intimate Diary of the Peace Conference and After, 1918–1923* (1933).
K. Robbins,	*Sir Edward Grey* (1971).
K. Robbins,	*Munich 1938* (1968).
S. Roskill,	*Hankey: Man of Secrets* (3 vols., 1970–1974).
S. Roskill,	*Naval Policy Between the Wars* (2 vols., 1968–1976).
P. Rowland,	*The Last Liberal Governments* (2 vols., 1968–1971).
P. Rowland,	*Lloyd George* (1975).
A. K. Russell,	*Liberal Landslide: The General Election of 1906* (Newton Abbot, 1973).
S. Salvidge,	*Salvidge of Liverpool* (1934).
J. R. Seeley,	*The Expansion of England* (ed. J. Gross, Chicago, 1971).
F. Stevenson,	*The Years that are Past* (1967).
E. Sutton (ed.),	*Stresemann: His Diaries, Letters and Papers* (1940).
A. Sykes,	*Tariff Reform in British Politics 1903–1913* (Oxford, 1979).
A. J. P. Taylor,	*Beaverbrook* (1972).
A. J. P. Taylor (ed.),	*Lloyd George: A Diary by Frances Stevenson* (1971).
A. J. P. Taylor (ed.),	*My Darling Pussy* (1975).
Lord Templewood,	*The Empire of the Air* (1957).
Lord Templewood,	*Nine Troubled Years* (1954).
N. Thompson,	*The Anti-Appeasers* (Oxford, 1971).
R. D. Thorpe,	*The Uncrowned Prime Ministers* (1980).
Lord Vansittart,	*The Mist Procession* (1958).
N. Waites (ed.),	*Troubled Neighbours* (1971).
D. Walder,	*The Chanak Affair* (1969).
B. Webb,	*Our Partnership* (1948).

N. West,   *M15: British Security Service*
                             Operations, 1909–1945 (p.b. edn.,
                             1983).
W. Wilkinson,   *Tory Democracy* (New York, 1925).
T. Wilson (ed.),   *The Political Diaries of C. P. Scott*
                             1911–1928 (1970).
Lord Winterton,   *Orders of the Day* (1953).
Lord Winterton,   *Pre-War* (1932).
G. M. Young,   *Stanley Baldwin* (1952).
K. Young,   *Arthur James Balfour* (1963).
K. Young,   *Churchill and Beaverbrook* (1966).
K. Young,   *Stanley Baldwin* (1976).

Articles

C. Andrew,   'British Intelligence and the Breach with
                             Russia in 1927', *Historical Journal* 25, 4
                             (1982).
D. Birn,   'The League of Nations Union and
                             Collective Security', *Journal of*
                             Contemporary History 9, 3 (1974).
D. Carlton,   'The Anglo-French Compromise on
                             Arms Limitation, 1928', *Journal of*
                             British Studies VIII (1969).
D. Carlton,   'Great Britain and the Coolidge Naval
                             Disarmament Conference of 1927',
                             Political Science Quarterly LXXXIII
                             (1968).
D. Carlton,   'Great Britain and the League Council
                             Crisis of 1926', *Historical Journal* xi, 2
                             (1968).
D. J. Dutton,   'Unionist Politics and the Aftermath of
                             the General Election of 1906: a
                             Reassessment', *Historical Journal* 22, 4
                             (1979).
P. Edwards,   'The Austen Chamberlain-Mussolini
                             Meetings', *Historical Journal* XIV, 1
                             (1971).
P. Fraser,   'Unionism and Tariff Reform: the Crisis
                             of 1906', *Historical Journal* V, 2 (1962).
D. Goold,   'Lord Hardinge and the Mesopotamia
                             Expedition and Inquiry 1914–1917',

	Historical Journal 19, 4 (1976).
G. A. Grun,	'Locarno: Idea and Reality', *International Affairs* xxxi, 4 (1955).
J. Jacobson,	'The Conduct of Locarno Diplomacy', *Review of Politics* xxxiv (1972).
P. Jalland,	'United Kingdom Devolution 1910–1914: political panacea or tactical diversion', *English Historical Review* XCIV, 373 (1979).
D. Lammers,	'Arno Mayer and the British Decision for War: 1914', *Journal of British Studies* xii, 2 (1973).
B. K. Murray,	'The Politics of the People's Budget', *Historical Journal* xvi, 3 (1973).
G. D. Phillips,	'Lord Willoughby de Broke and the Politics of Radical Toryism, 1909–1914', *Journal of British Studies* xx, i (1980).
M. D. Pugh,	'Asquith, Bonar Law and the First Coalition', *Historical Journal* xvii, 4 (1974).
J. Robertson,	'The Hoare-Laval Plan', *Journal of Contemporary History* 10, 3 (1975).
F. G. Stambrook,	' "Das Kind" – Lord D'Abernon and the Origins of the Locarno Pact', *Central European History* i, 3 (1968).
A. Sykes,	'The Confederacy and the Purge of the Unionist Free Traders, 1906–1910', *Historical Journal* xviii, 2 (1975).
R. C. Trebilcock,	'A "Special Relationship" – Government, Rearmament and the Cordite Firms', *Economic History Review* xix, 2 (1966).
C. C. Weston,	'The Liberal Leadership and the Lords' Veto, 1907–1910', *Historical Journal* xi, 3 (1968).

INDEX

League of Nations Union, the, 239–40,
252, 270, 307–8, 311, 321.
Lee, Arthur (Lord Lee of Fareham), 57–8,
126, 232, 300, **biographical note 351.**
Liberal Unionists, the, 22, **340.**
Liberal Unionist Council, the, 52.
Lindemann, Professor Frederick, 312.
Lloyd, Lord, 113–14, 274–5, 286–7,
biographical note 351.
Lloyd George, David, attacks the
Chamberlains over munitions, 25; 1909
Finance Bill, 64–51; 1910,
memorandum on coalition government,
71–2; scheme for sickness and
unemployment benefit, 85; Parliament
Bill, 85; works with Chamberlain at
Treasury, 114–15; misgivings over
direction of War, 118; War Office, 127;
Ireland, 129–30, 141; fall of Asquith,
131–4; Chamberlain's resignation,
137–8; relations with Law and
Chamberlain, 138, 163–4, 174;
recruitment of press lords, 139–40;
invites Chamberlain to join War
Cabinet, 141; offers Chamberlain the
Admiralty, 142; appoints Chamberlain
to the Exchequer, 155–6; gives
generous support to Chamberlain,
160–1; treatment of Curzon, 161;
absences abroad, 162, 166; Irish
settlement, 167–71; proposes election in
1922, 172–3; offer to step down, 176;
honours scandal, 179, 188; Genoa
Conference, 179–80; unpopularity of,
with Conservatives, 189–90, 197, 214;
Chanak incident, 191–2; resignation,
199; Chamberlain's commitment to,
201, 222; and proposals for new
coalition, 286; Chamberlain hopes for
return of, in 1935, 310–11; tribute on
Chamberlain's death, 1; comments on
Chamberlain, 36, 164, 323, 330, 332.
Local option, 28.
Locarno, Treaties of, proposal for Anglo-
French Pact, 241–3; German proposal
of mutual security pact, 242; Cabinet
discussions, 244–6; Chamberlain
prepares the ground for the Conference,
246–8; the Conference and initialling of
the Pact, 248; assessment of, 250–3,
261–2, 332–3.
Locarno tea parties, 260–1.

Locker-Lampson, Oliver, 204, 211, 285,
318, **biographical note 351.**
London School of Hygiene and Tropical
Medicine, 307.
Londonderry, Marquess of, 42, 78.
Long, Walter, 35, 52, 59–62, 87, 92–5, 97,
117, 130, 133–4; 177–8, 193–4, 202,
biographical note 351.
Lugano, Meeting at, 282.
Luther, 248.

Macmillan, Harold, 5.
MacDonald, James Ramsay, 213–15,
221, 234, 238, 240, 245, 280, 301, 304,
306, 309, 311, 313, 317, 319.
MacNeese, Surgeon-General, 122.
Mahan, Alfred T., 23.
Malcolm, Ian, 136.
Manchuria, non-intervention in, 250, 308.
Manpower Board, the, 129.
Martineau, Fanny, 14.
Massey, Vincent, 246.
May Committee, the, 304.
Maxse, Leo, 3, 55, 57, 170.
McKenna, Reginald, 129, 133, 208,
biographical note 351.
Mesopotamian Campaign, the, 120–6,
135, **342.**
Mesopotamian Commission, the, 124,
126, 136.
Midleton, Earl of, see Brodrick, William
St. John.
Milner, Viscount, 24, 56, 116–17, 119,
126, 134, 140, 159, **biographical note
352.**
Milner, Viscountess, 321.
Montagu, Edwin, 136–8, 142, 155–6, 162,
biographical note 352.
Morley, Viscount, 104, 114, 127.
Mosley, Sir Oswald, 290.
Mowatt, Sir Francis, 29.
Murray, Gilbert, 311.
Mussolini, Benito, 248, 262, 289, 314,
322.

Naval Disarmament Conference, 276–7.
Newport by-Election, 193, 196–7.
Newton, Lord, 86.
Nixon, General Sir J. E., 121, 124–5, 136.
Nobel Prize, 230.
Northcliffe, Viscount, 56, 139–40, 156.